Praise for

THE AMAZING "TRUE" STORY OF A TEENAGE SINGLE MOM

Top Ten Book of the Year, *Entertainment Weekly*
Winner New York Foundation of the Arts Award in Drawing
Will Eisner Comic Industry Award in the Graphic Novel, nominee
Top Ten Quick Pick for Young Adults, ALA
Notable Books, ALA

"A superheroine for our times. Poignant. Redemptive.
Purest testimony to the strength of motherly love. A book that actually makes
you think about the world instead of just escaping it—this is the year's best bet."
—*Entertainment Weekly*

"You can read this comic book in less than an hour—and never forget it.
—*Redbook*

"Not only will this book speak to teens in similar situations or those with friends like the author,
but it also serves to inform the adults who work to help all teens realize their potentials."
—*American Library Association*

"It's a refreshingly nonlecturey picture of what it's really like to be a teen mom."
—*Seventeen*

"A book teens will like, whether they're steady fans of graphic novels or not."
—*Booklist*

Dedicated to
Stacie,
Gordon

GRAYMALKIN
MEDIA

Published by Graymalkin Media

www.graymalkin.com

Portions of this book originally appeared in the *Welfare Mother's Voice*. Grateful acknowledgement is made to the *Welfare Mother's Voic*e for permission to reprint.

The entomological drawings were originally conceived at the University of Arkansas and are the property of that institution. Grateful acknowledgement is made to the University of Arkansas for permission to reprint.

This edition published in 2015 by Graymalkin Media

ISBN: 978-1-63168-034-2

1 3 5 7 9 10 8 6 4 2

AUTHOR'S NOTE: I made this book to copy myself and take to GED (high school equivalency) programs. My purpose was to help single moms feel worthy to pursue their rights to an equal access to education and provide them with the information to do so, since young moms often miss out on high school guidance counseling.

That, for me, is the sole purpose of this book. While the people and events are true, many facts and events are generalized and details altered in order to better achieve this goal, and to also protect the privacy of particular individuals.

KATHERINE ARNOLDI, PhD, was a Fulbright Fellow (2008–2009) and has been awarded two New York Foundation of the Arts awards (Fiction and Drawing), a Newhouse Award, The Henfield Transatlantic Fiction Award and the Dejur Award. A Pro-Choice advocate for equal rights to education for single moms, she lives in New York City and teaches at City University of New York.

Visit www.KatherineArnoldi.com

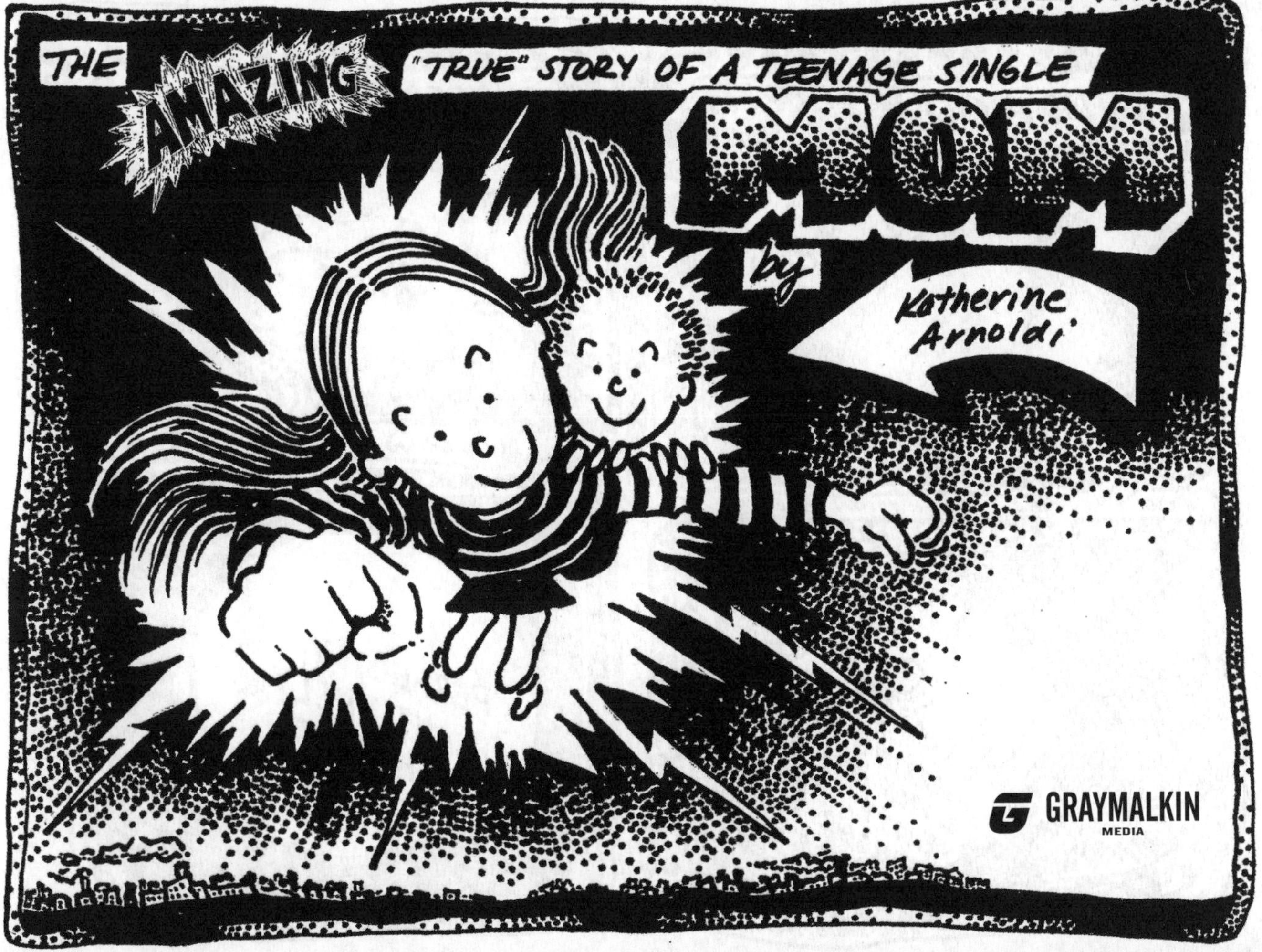
THE
AMAZING
"TRUE" STORY OF A TEENAGE SINGLE
MOM
by
Katherine Arnoldi
GRAYMALKIN
MEDIA

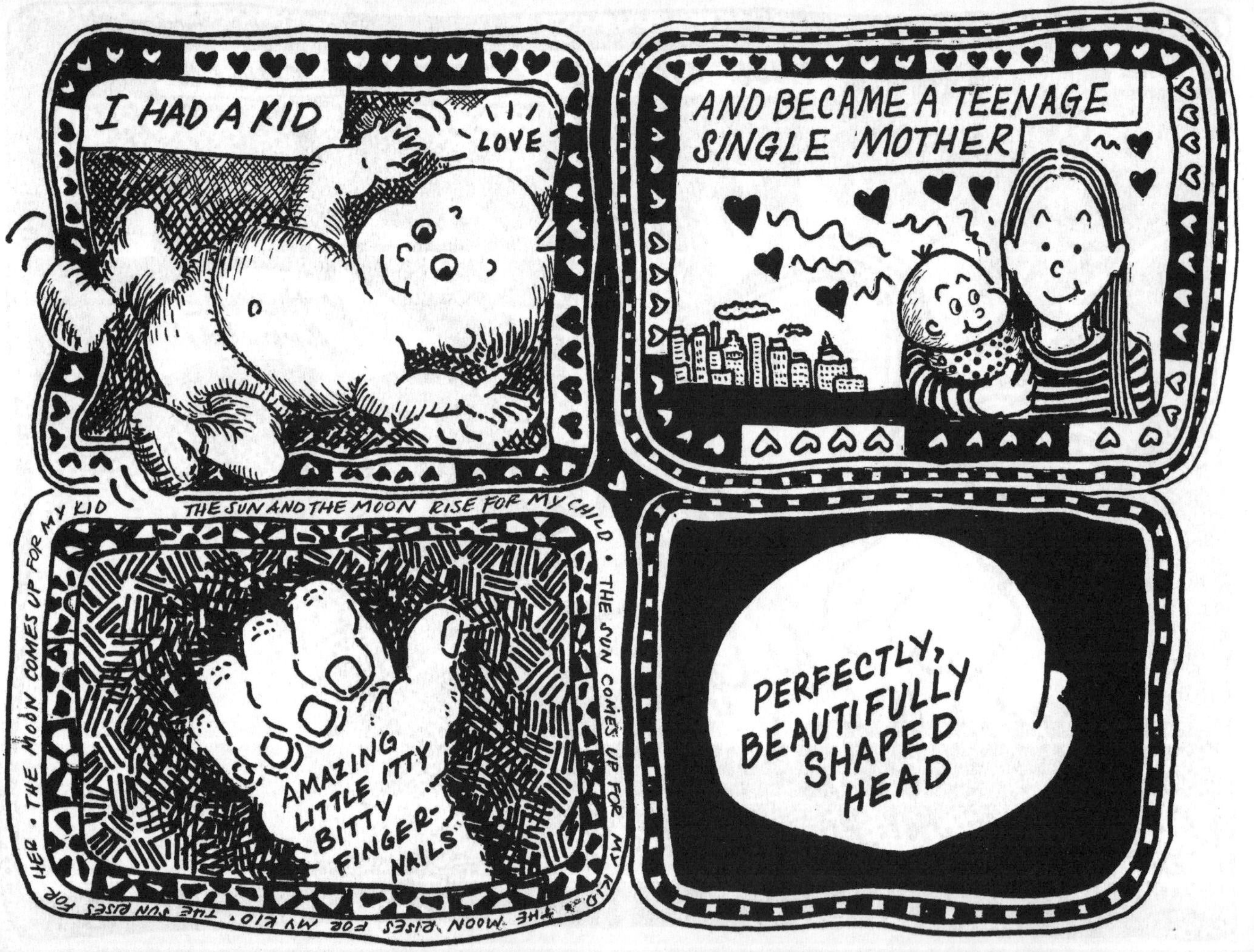
I HAD A KID
LOVE
AND BECAME A TEENAGE SINGLE MOTHER
THE SUN AND THE MOON RISE FOR MY CHILD • THE SUN COMES UP FOR MY KID. THE MOON RISES FOR MY KID. THE SUN RISES FOR HER • THE MOON COMES UP FOR MY KID
AMAZING LITTLE ITTY BITTY FINGER-NAILS
PERFECTLY, BEAUTIFULLY SHAPED HEAD

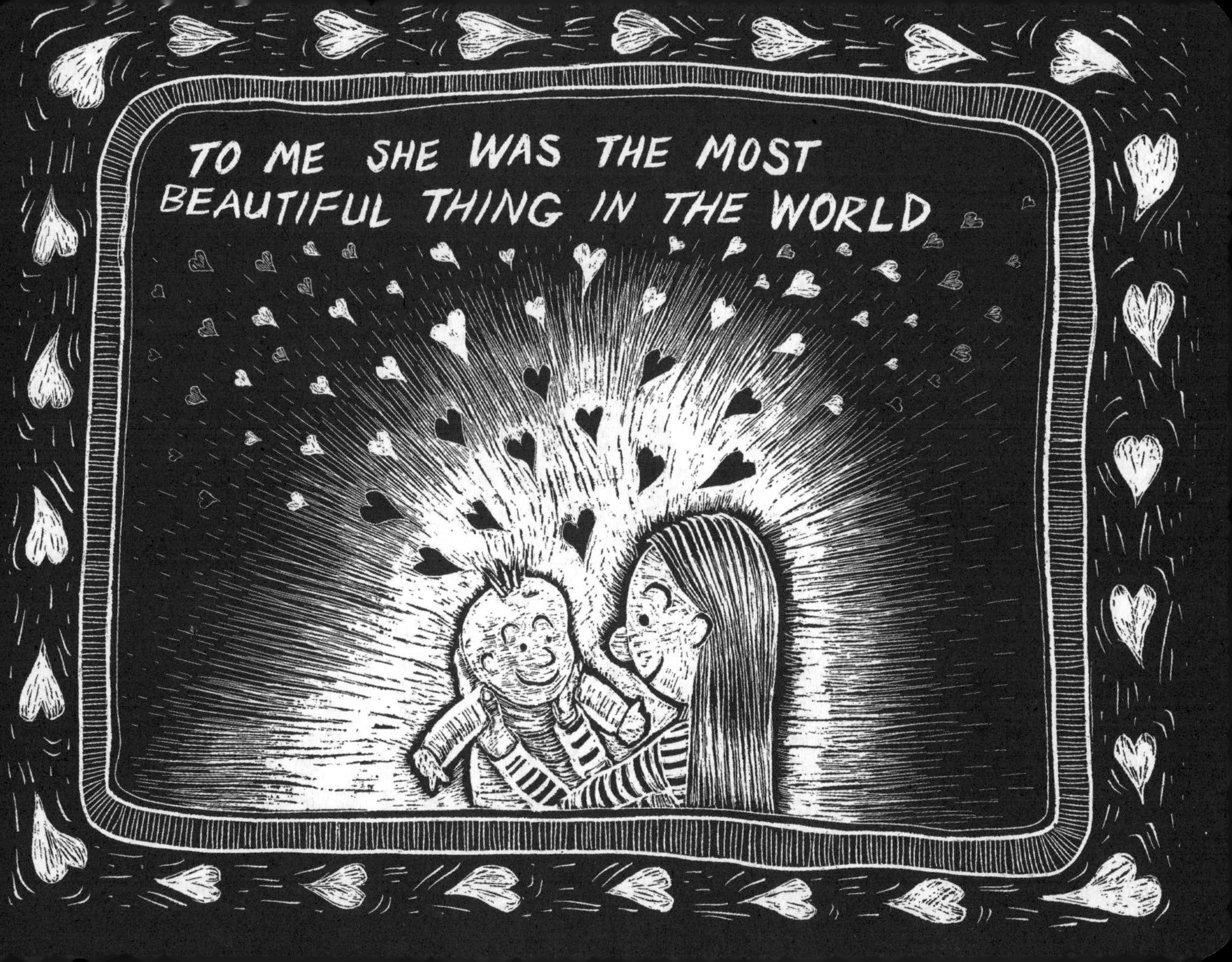
TO ME SHE WAS THE MOST BEAUTIFUL THING IN THE WORLD

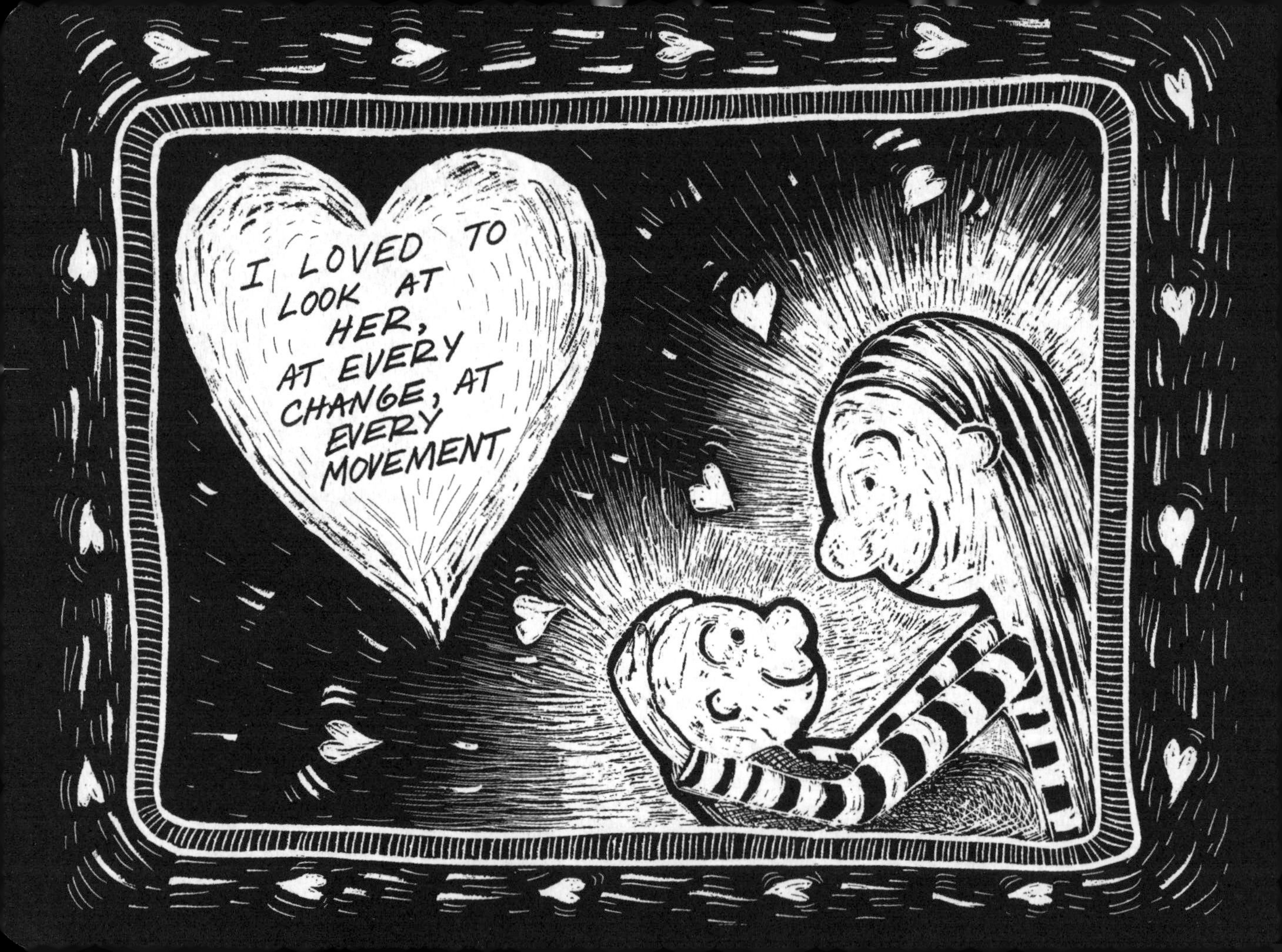
I LOVED TO LOOK AT HER, AT EVERY CHANGE, AT EVERY MOVEMENT

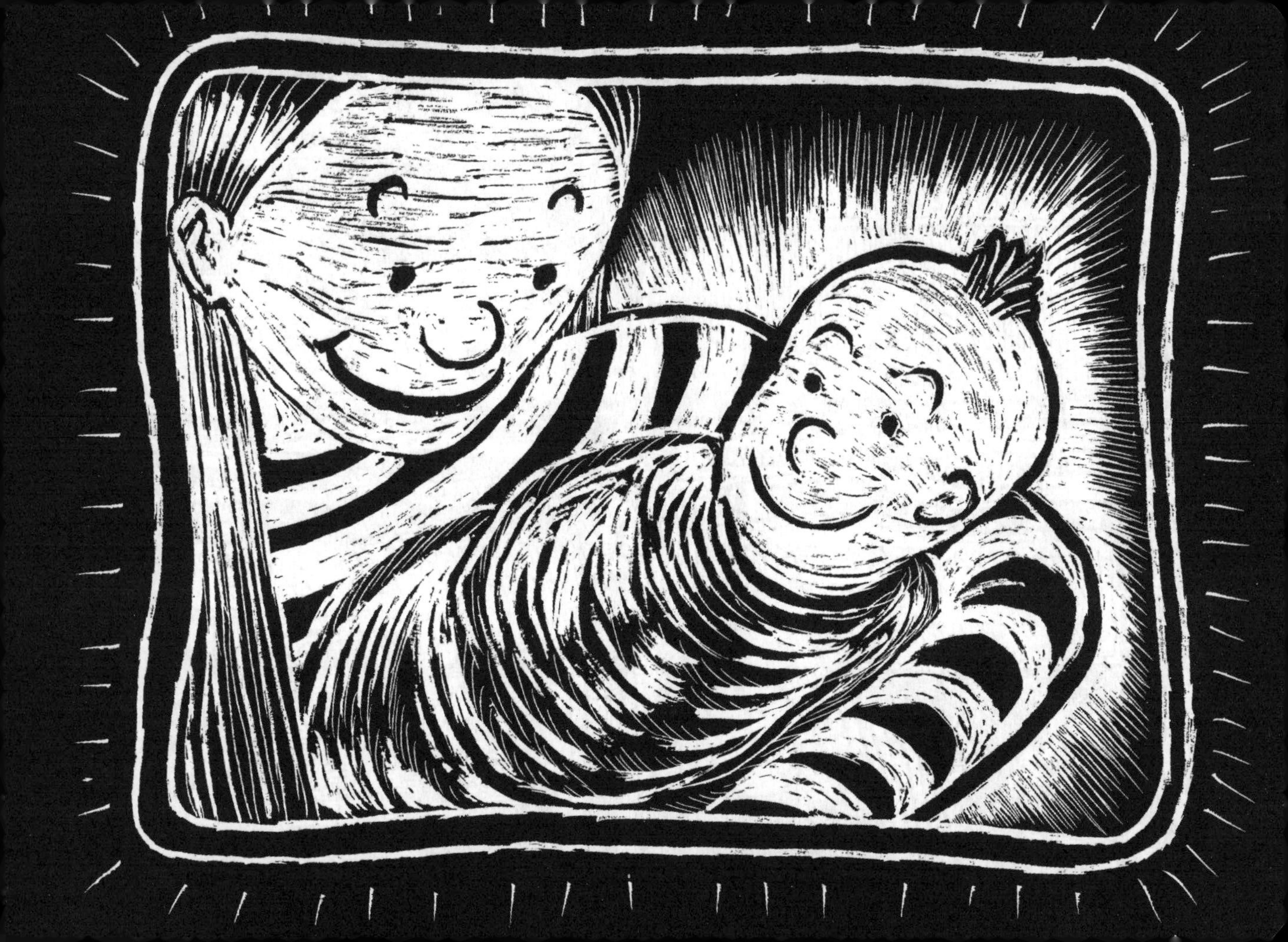

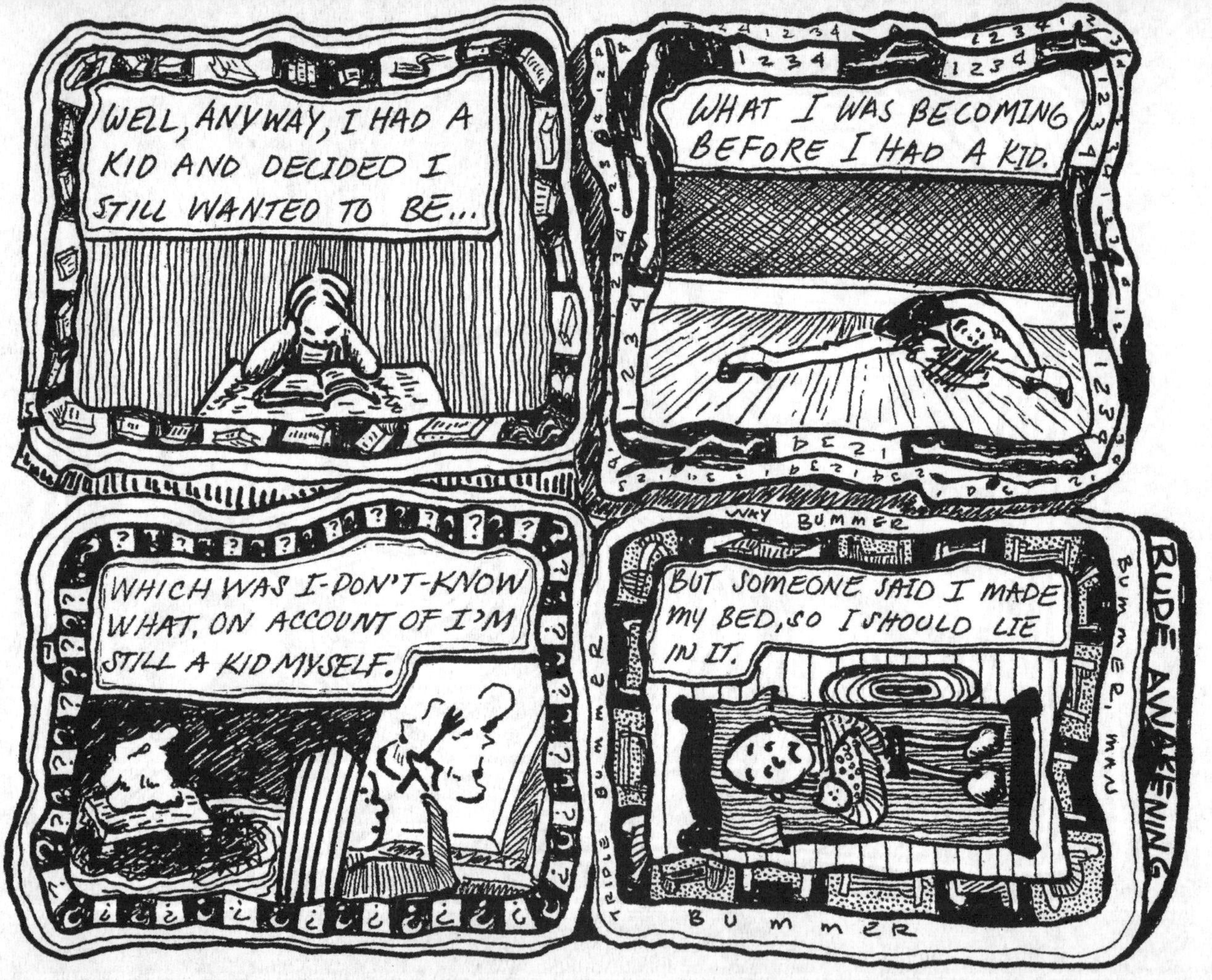

WELL, ANYWAY, I HAD A KID AND DECIDED I STILL WANTED TO BE...
WHAT I WAS BECOMING BEFORE I HAD A KID.
WHICH WAS I-DON'T-KNOW WHAT, ON ACCOUNT OF I'M STILL A KID MYSELF.
BUT SOMEONE SAID I MADE MY BED, SO I SHOULD LIE IN IT.
BUMMER
TRIPLE BUMMER
BUMMER, MAN
BUMMER
RUDE AWAKENING

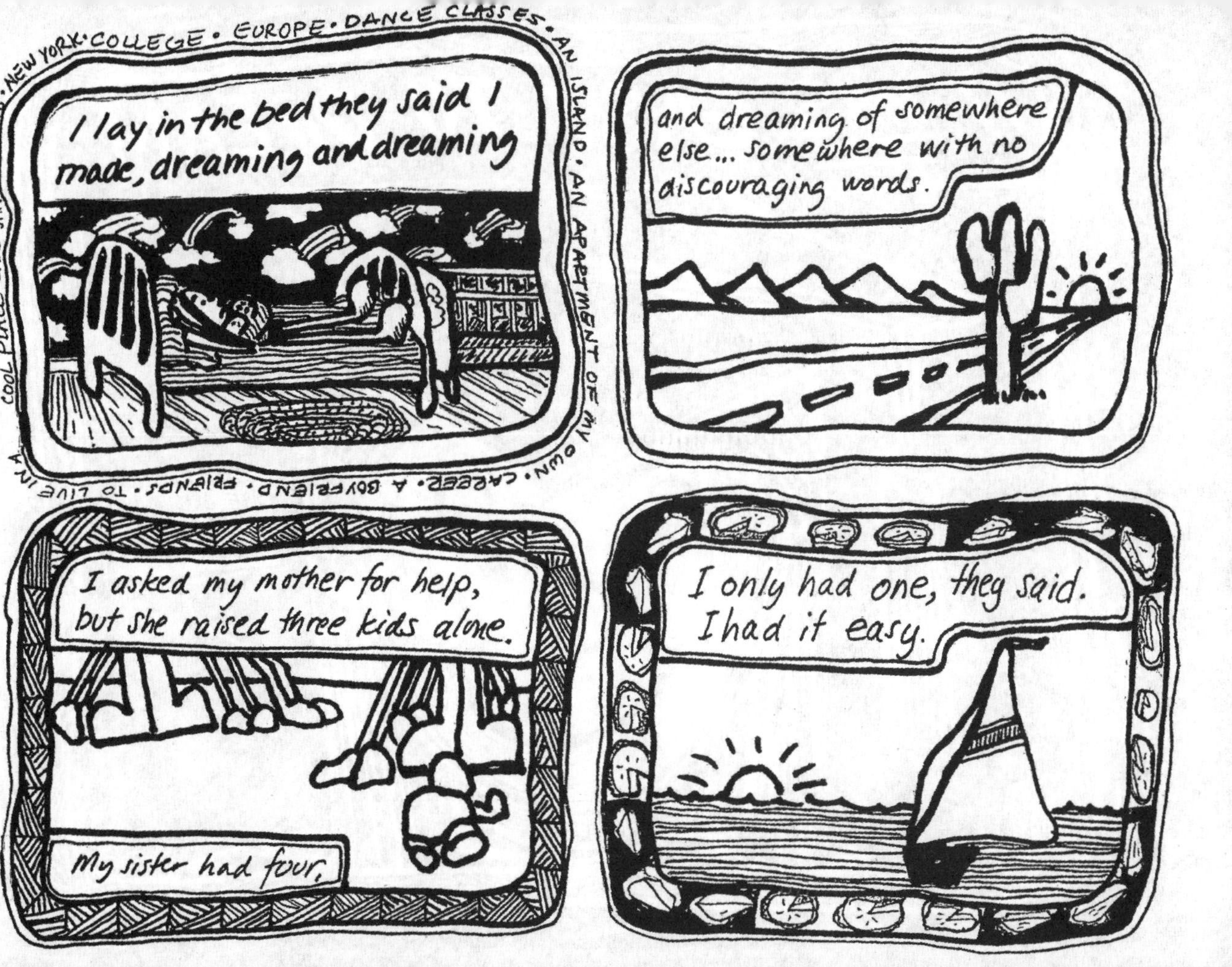

NEW YORK · COLLEGE · EUROPE · DANCE CLASSES · AN ISLAND · AN APARTMENT OF MY OWN · CAREER · A BOYFRIEND · FRIENDS · TO LIVE IN A COOL PLACE LIKE SAN FRANCISCO ·
I lay in the bed they said I made, dreaming and dreaming
and dreaming of somewhere else... somewhere with no discouraging words.
I asked my mother for help, but she raised three kids alone.
My sister had four.
I only had one, they said. I had it easy.

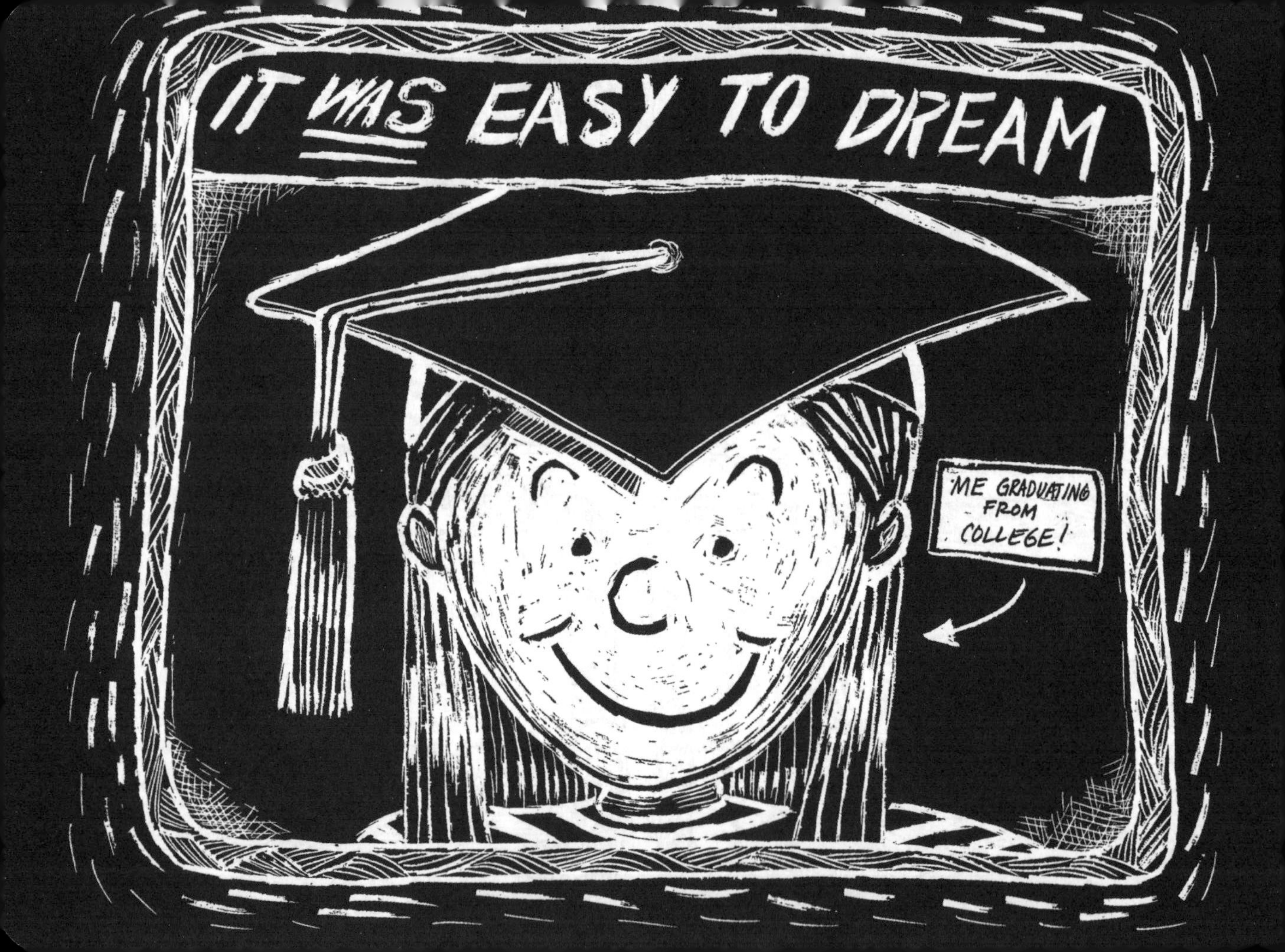
IT WAS EASY TO DREAM
ME GRADUATING FROM COLLEGE!

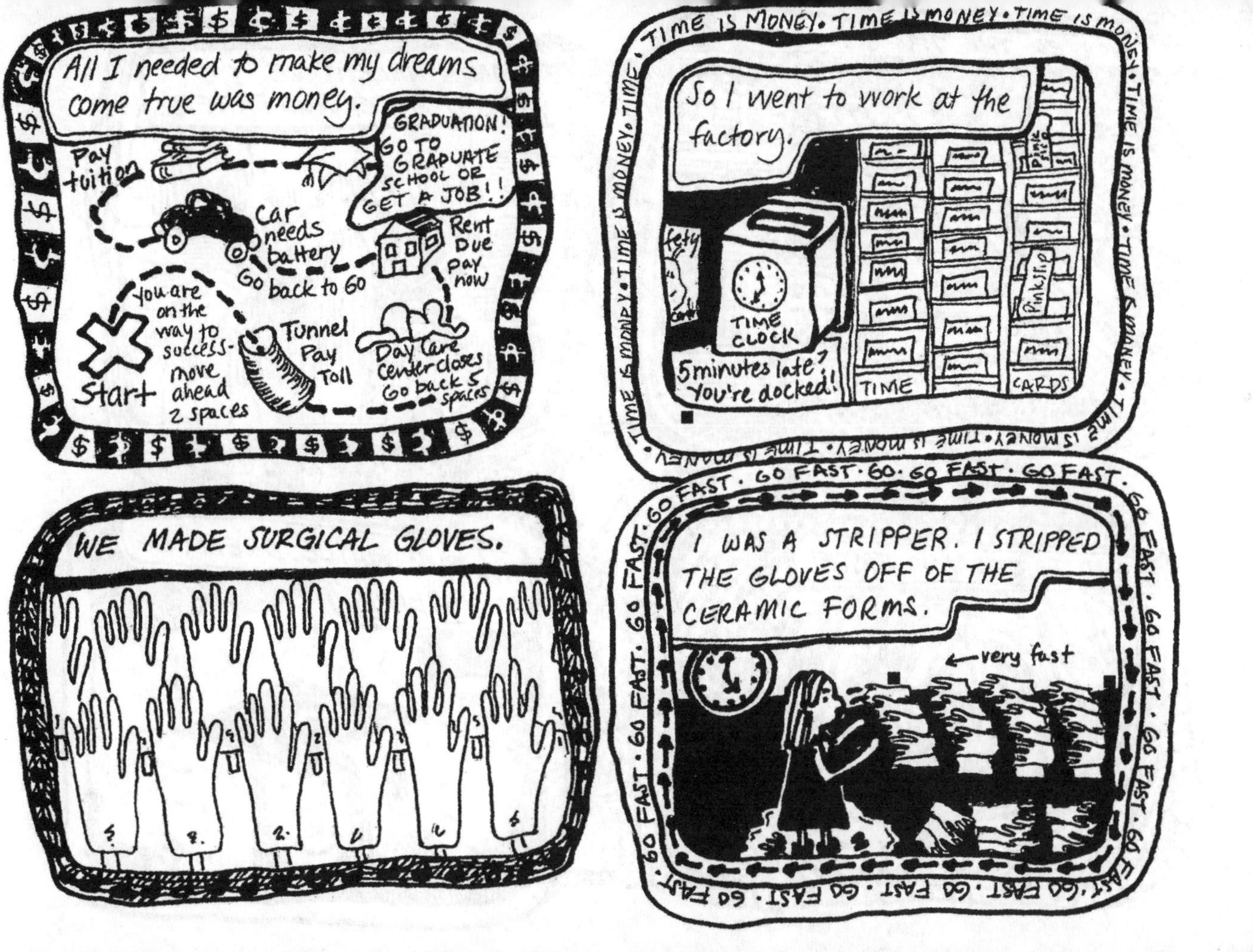
All I needed to make my dreams come true was money.
Pay tuition
GRADUATION! GO TO GRADUATE SCHOOL OR GET A JOB!!
Car needs battery
Go back to GO
Rent Due pay now
you are on the way to success - move ahead 2 spaces
Start
Tunnel Pay Toll
Day Care center closes Go back 5 spaces
TIME IS MONEY • TIME IS MONEY • TIME IS MONEY • TIME IS MONEY • TIME IS MONEY • TIME IS MONEY • TIME IS MONEY • TIME IS MONEY • TIME IS MONEY • TIME IS MONEY
So I went to work at the factory.
TIME CLOCK
5 minutes late? You're docked!
TIME CARDS
Pink slip
WE MADE SURGICAL GLOVES.
GO FAST • GO FAST • GO • GO FAST • GO FAST • GO FAST • GO FAST • GO FAST • GO FAST • GO FAST • GO FAST • GO FAST • GO FAST • GO FAST • GO FAST
I WAS A STRIPPER. I STRIPPED THE GLOVES OFF OF THE CERAMIC FORMS.
←very fast

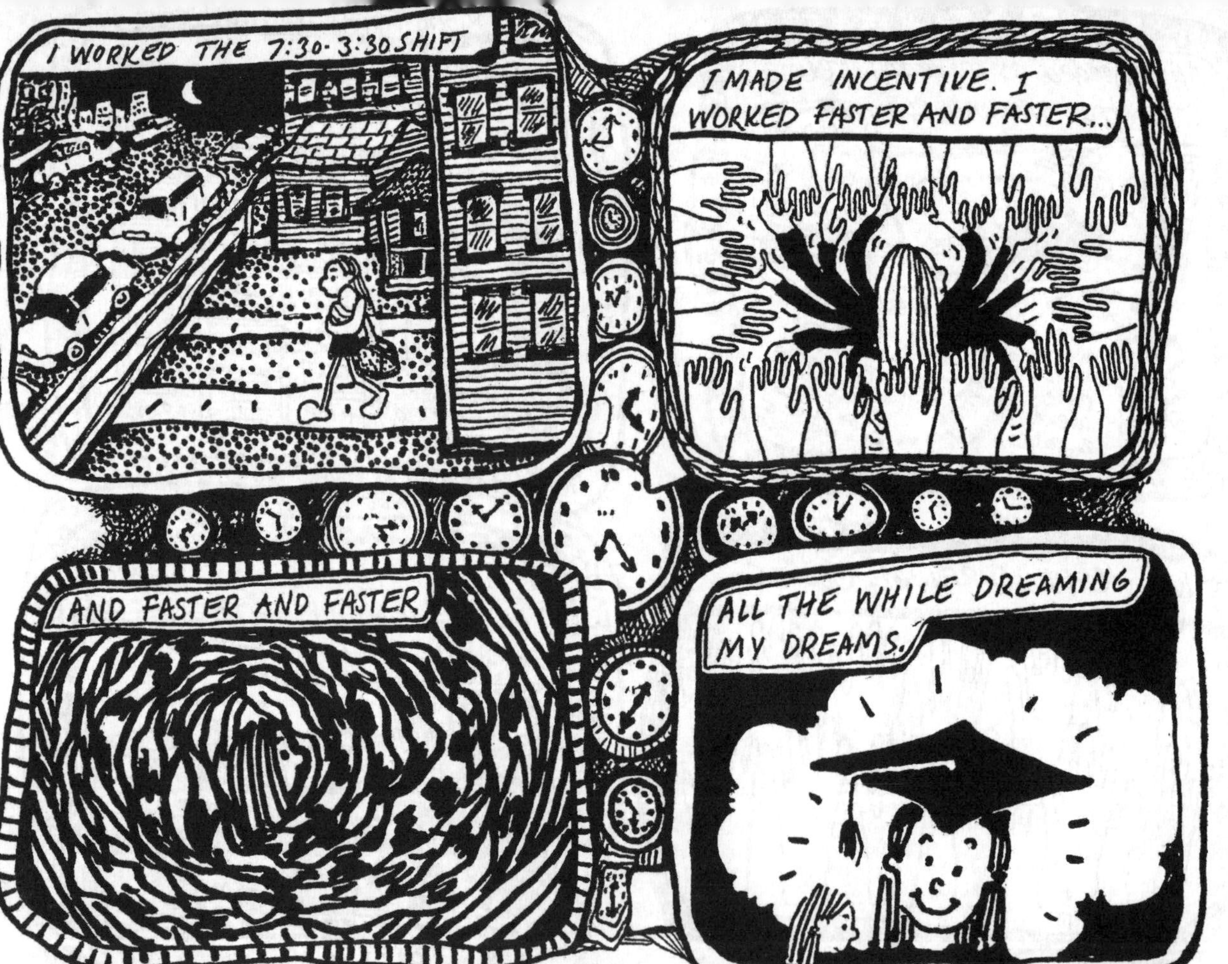
I WORKED THE 7:30-3:30 SHIFT
I MADE INCENTIVE. I WORKED FASTER AND FASTER...
AND FASTER AND FASTER
ALL THE WHILE DREAMING MY DREAMS.

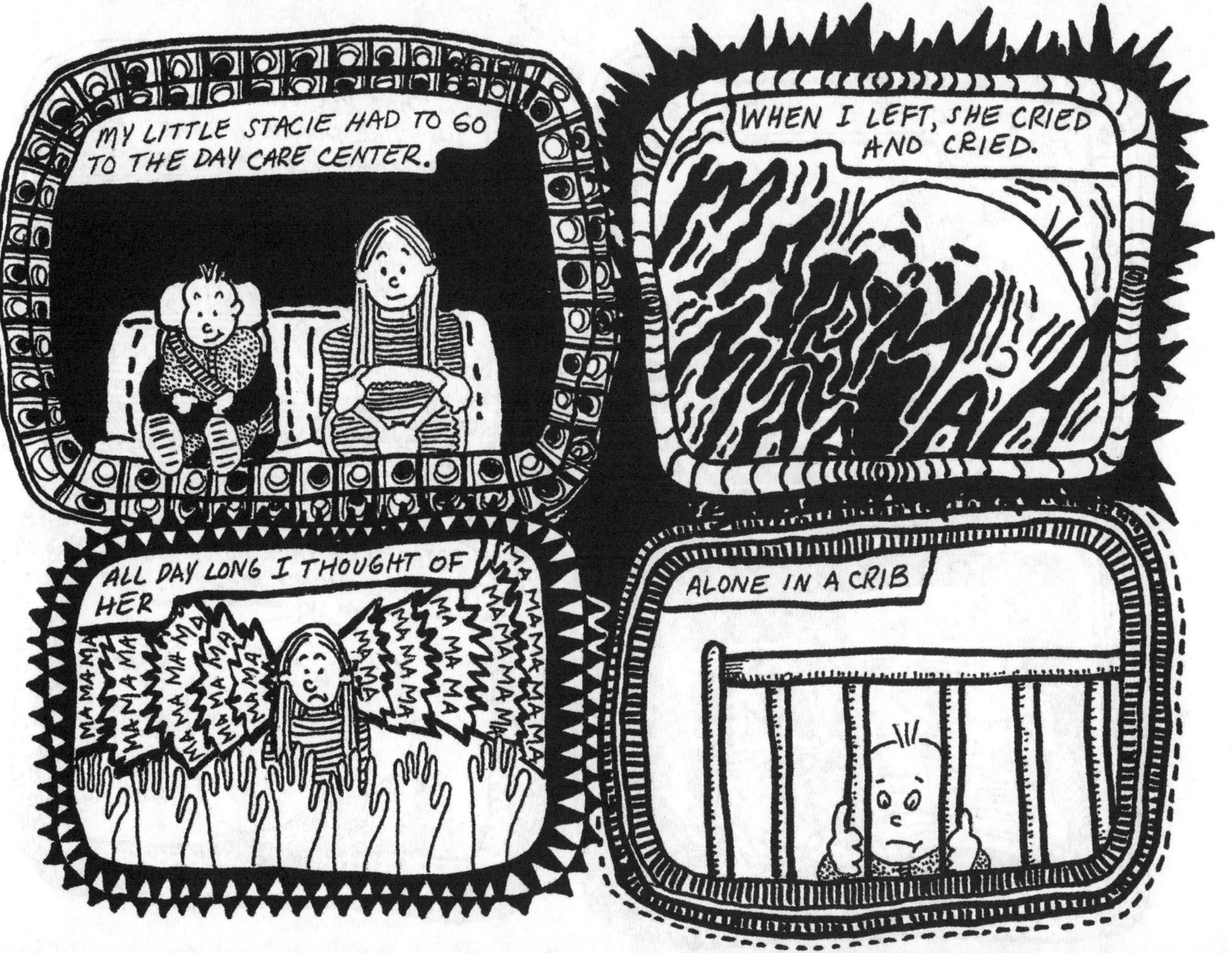
MY LITTLE STACIE HAD TO GO TO THE DAY CARE CENTER.
WHEN I LEFT, SHE CRIED AND CRIED.
ALL DAY LONG I THOUGHT OF HER
ALONE IN A CRIB

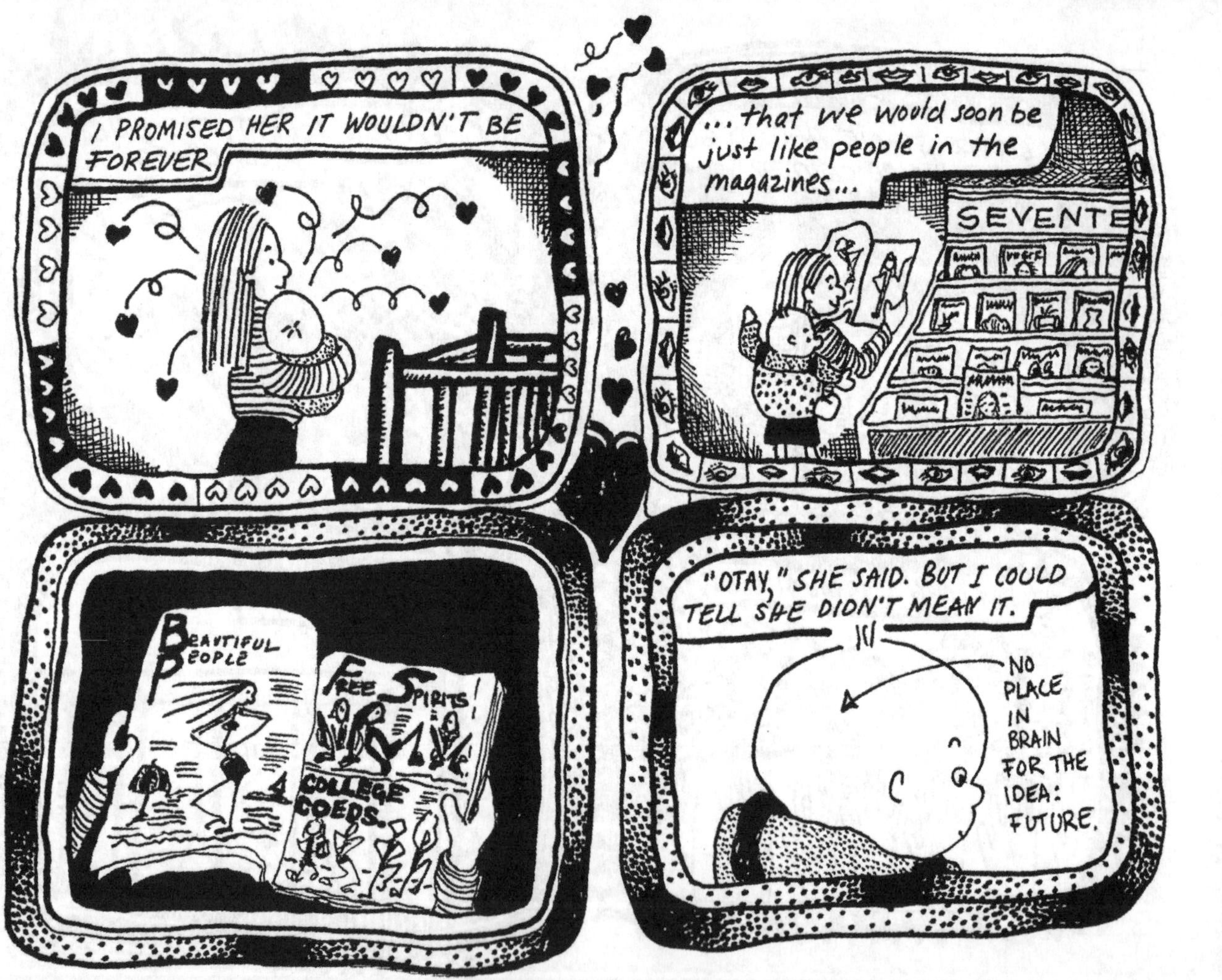
I PROMISED HER IT WOULDN'T BE FOREVER
...that we would soon be just like people in the magazines...
SEVENTE
BEAUTIFUL PEOPLE
FREE SPIRITS!
COLLEGE COEDS..
"OTAY," SHE SAID. BUT I COULD TELL SHE DIDN'T MEAN IT.
NO PLACE IN BRAIN FOR THE IDEA: FUTURE.

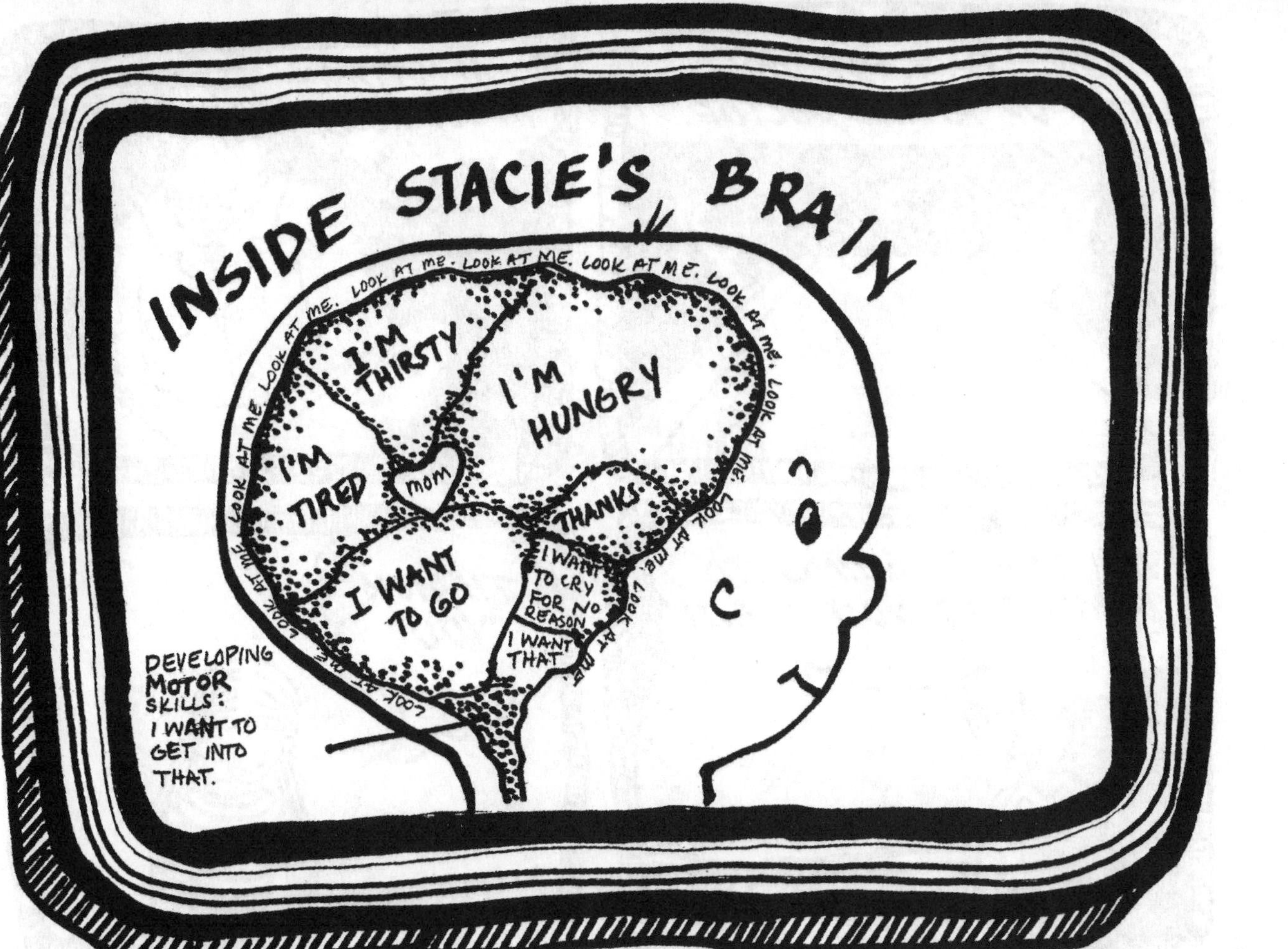
INSIDE STACIE'S BRAIN
LOOK AT ME. LOOK AT ME. LOOK AT ME. LOOK AT ME. LOOK AT ME. LOOK AT ME. LOOK AT ME. LOOK AT ME. LOOK AT ME. LOOK AT ME. LOOK AT ME. LOOK AT ME. LOOK AT ME. LOOK AT ME.
I'M THIRSTY
I'M HUNGRY
I'M TIRED
MOM
THANKS
I WANT TO GO
I WANT TO CRY FOR NO REASON
I WANT THAT
DEVELOPING MOTOR SKILLS: I WANT TO GET INTO THAT.

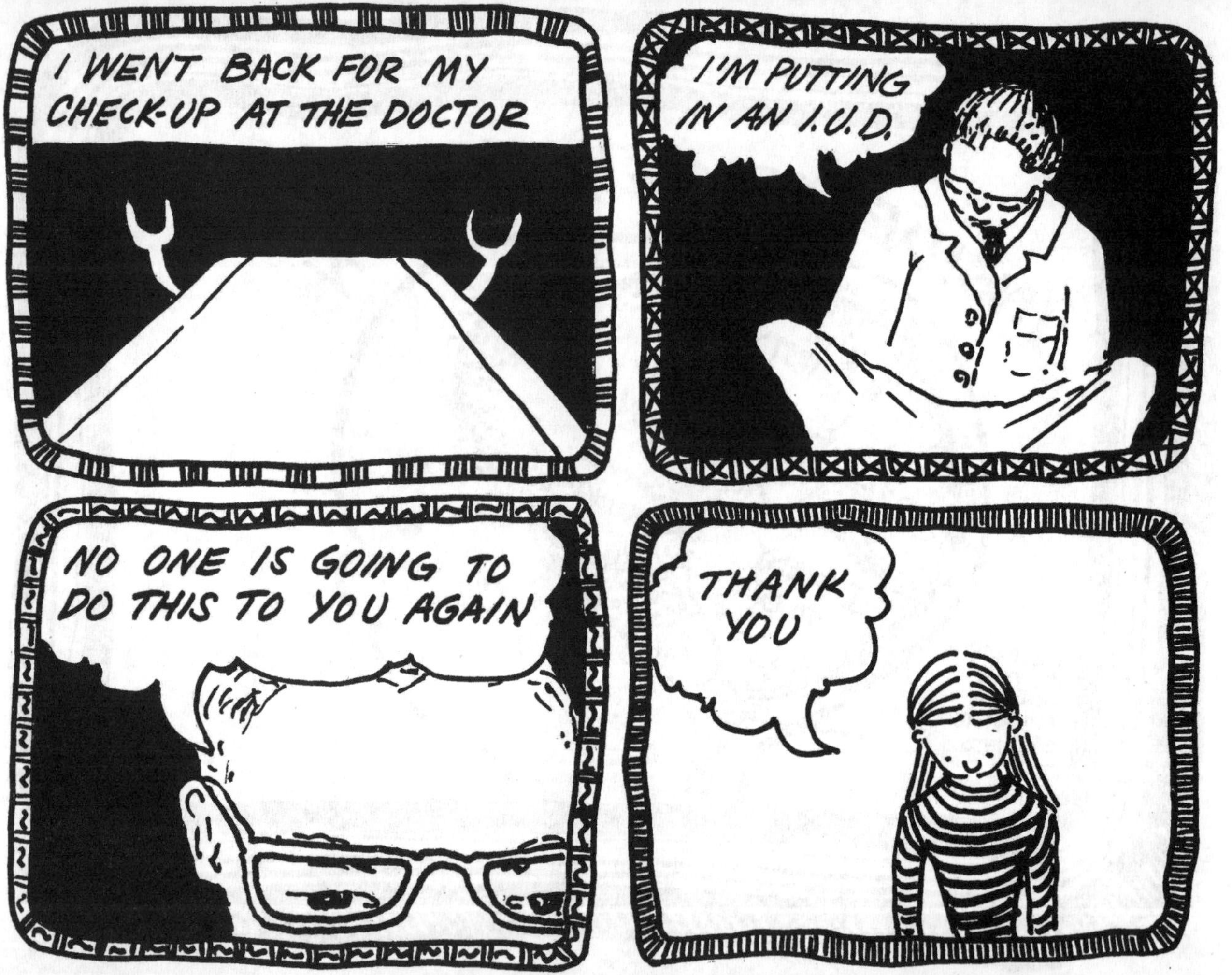
I WENT BACK FOR MY CHECK-UP AT THE DOCTOR
I'M PUTTING IN AN I.U.D.
NO ONE IS GOING TO DO THIS TO YOU AGAIN
THANK YOU

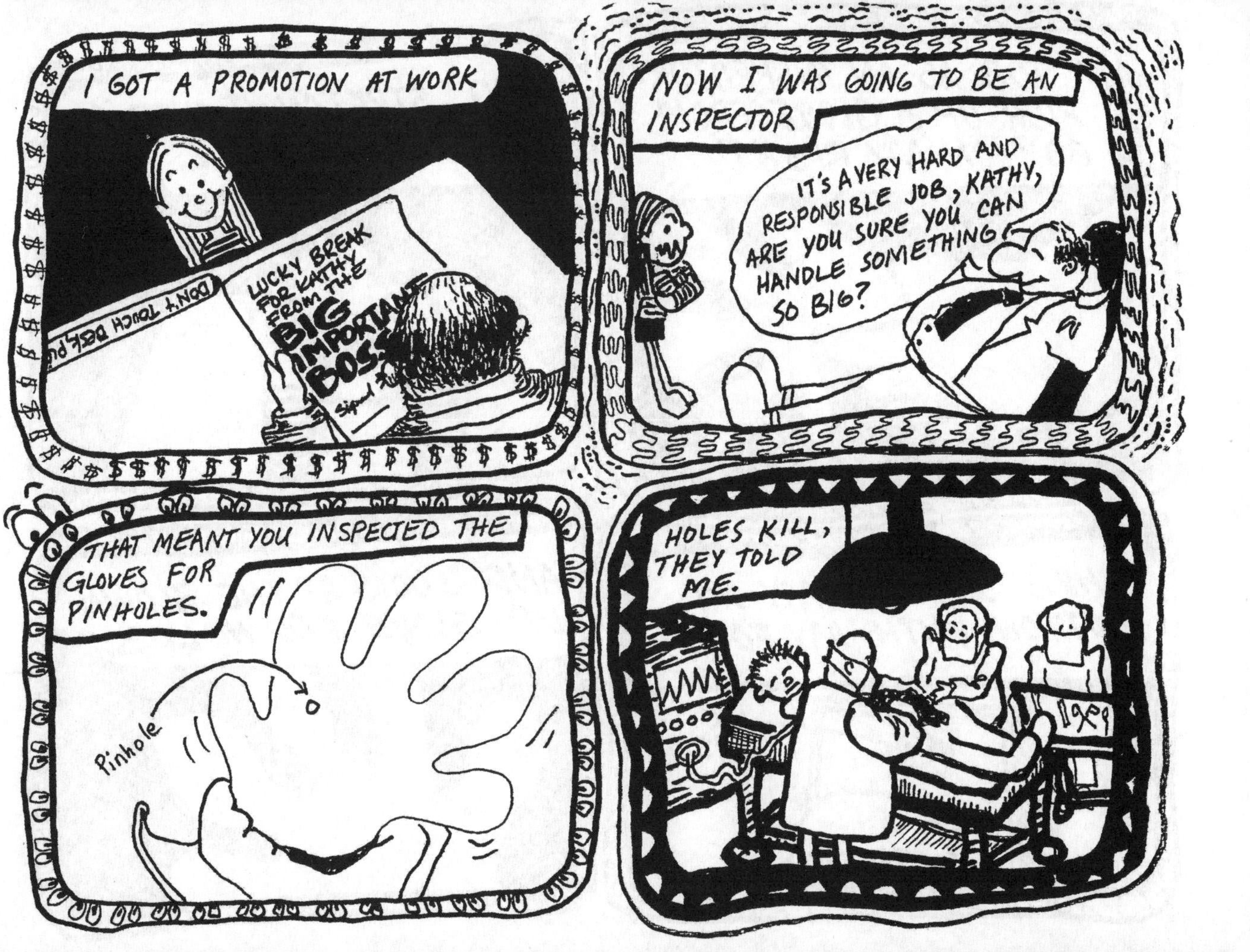
I GOT A PROMOTION AT WORK
LUCKY BREAK FOR KATHY FROM THE BIG IMPORTANT BOSS
NOW I WAS GOING TO BE AN INSPECTOR
IT'S A VERY HARD AND RESPONSIBLE JOB, KATHY, ARE YOU SURE YOU CAN HANDLE SOMETHING SO BIG?
THAT MEANT YOU INSPECTED THE GLOVES FOR PINHOLES.
Pinhole
HOLES KILL, THEY TOLD ME.

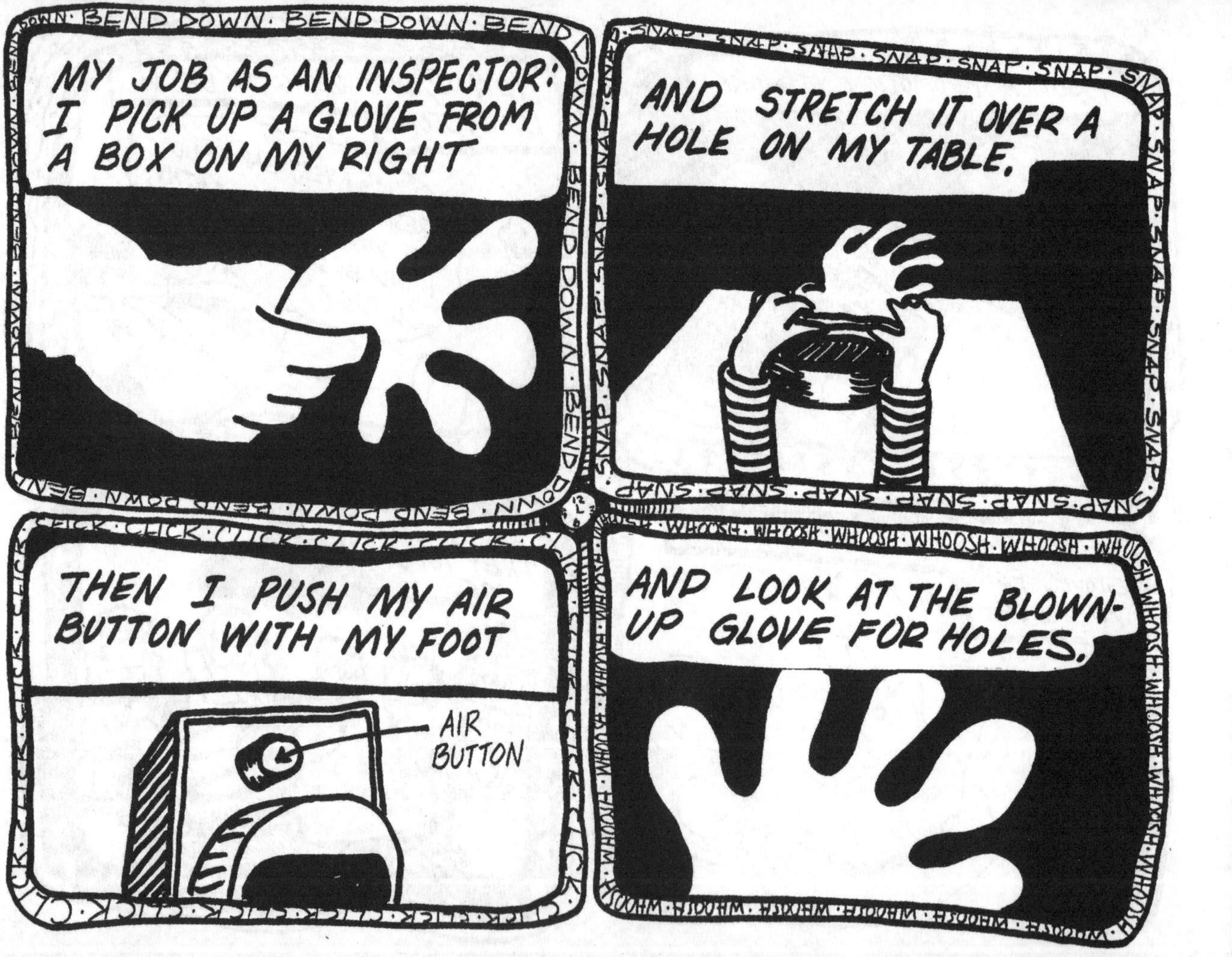
BEND DOWN
MY JOB AS AN INSPECTOR: I PICK UP A GLOVE FROM A BOX ON MY RIGHT
SNAP
AND STRETCH IT OVER A HOLE ON MY TABLE.
CLICK
THEN I PUSH MY AIR BUTTON WITH MY FOOT
AIR BUTTON
WHOOSH
AND LOOK AT THE BLOWN-UP GLOVE FOR HOLES.

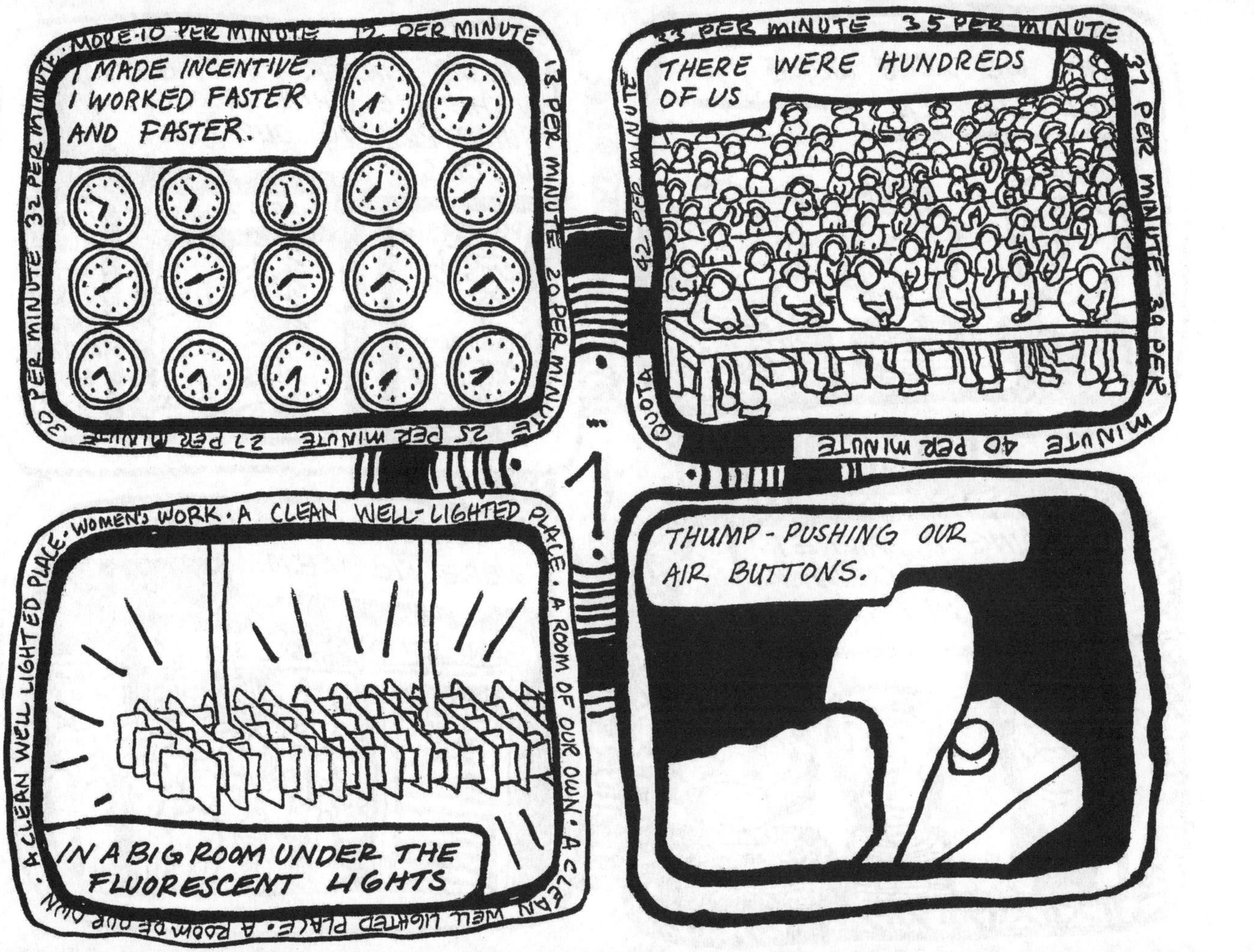

MORE·10 PER MINUTE 12 PER MINUTE 13 PER MINUTE 20 PER MINUTE 25 PER MINUTE 27 PER MINUTE 30 PER MINUTE 32 PER MINUTE
I MADE INCENTIVE. I WORKED FASTER AND FASTER.
33 PER MINUTE 35 PER MINUTE 37 PER MINUTE 39 PER MINUTE 40 PER MINUTE QUOTA 42 PER MINUTE
THERE WERE HUNDREDS OF US
WOMEN'S WORK · A CLEAN WELL-LIGHTED PLACE · A ROOM OF OUR OWN · A CLEAN WELL LIGHTED PLACE · A ROOM OF OUR OWN · A CLEAN WELL LIGHTED PLACE ·
IN A BIG ROOM UNDER THE FLUORESCENT LIGHTS
THUMP-PUSHING OUR AIR BUTTONS.

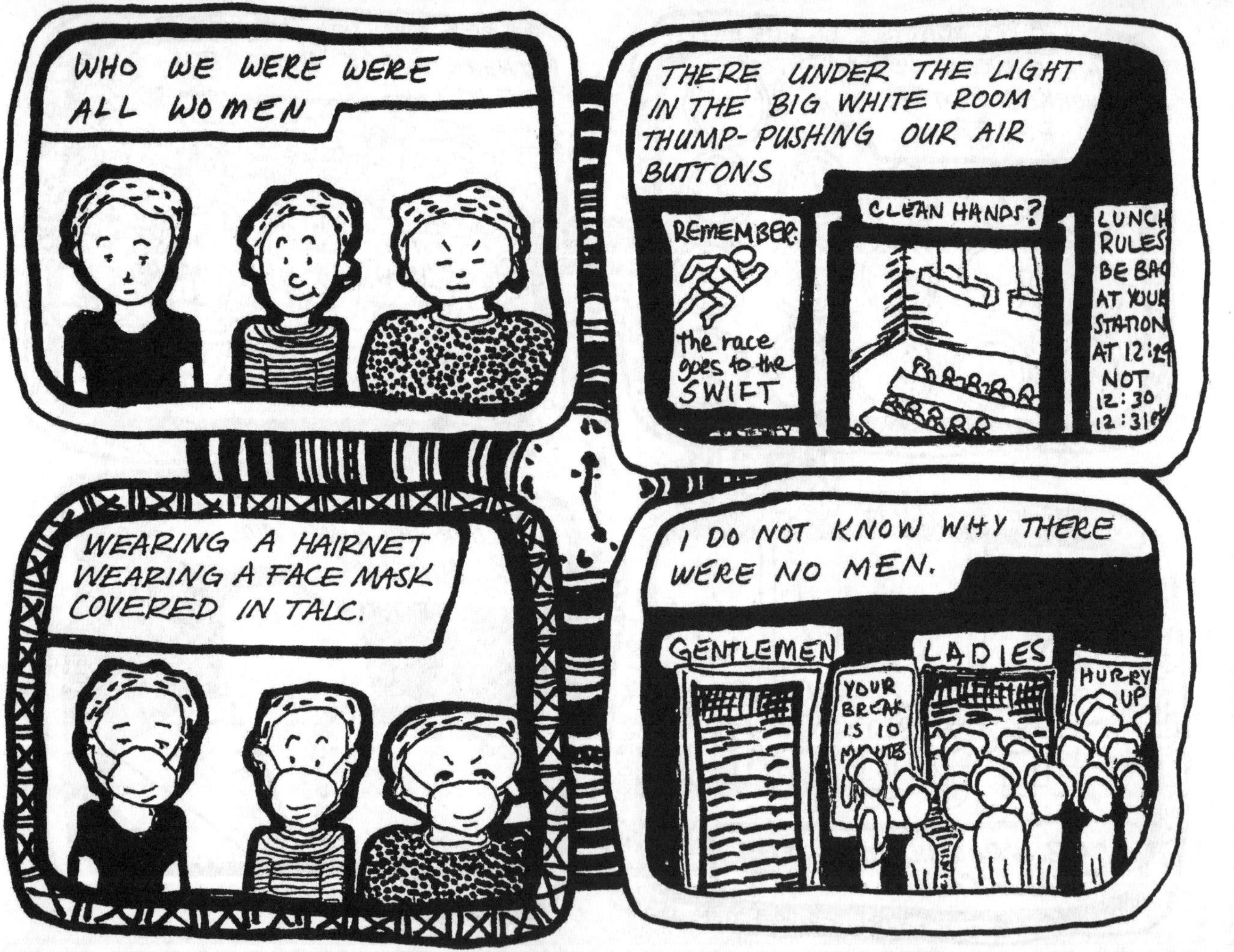
WHO WE WERE WERE ALL WOMEN
THERE UNDER THE LIGHT IN THE BIG WHITE ROOM THUMP-PUSHING OUR AIR BUTTONS
REMEMBER: the race goes to the SWIFT
CLEAN HANDS?
LUNCH RULES BE BAC AT YOU STATION AT 12:29 NOT 12:30 12:31
WEARING A HAIRNET WEARING A FACE MASK COVERED IN TALC.
I DO NOT KNOW WHY THERE WERE NO MEN.
GENTLEMEN
LADIES
YOUR BREAK IS 10 MINUTES
HURRY UP

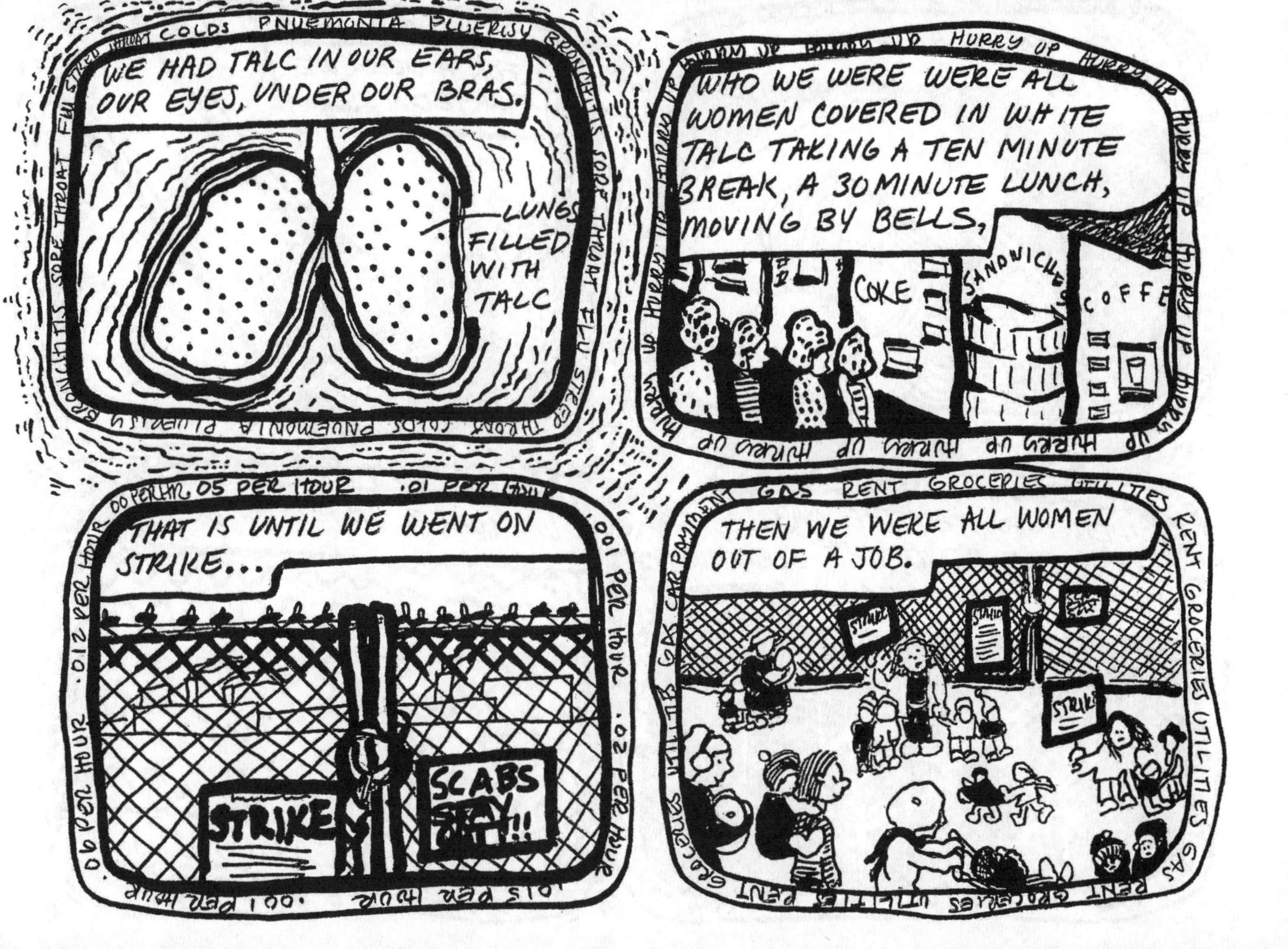
WE HAD TALC IN OUR EARS, OUR EYES, UNDER OUR BRAS.
LUNGS FILLED WITH TALC
COLDS PNUEMONIA PLUERISY BRONCHITIS SORE THROAT FLU STREP THROAT
WHO WE WERE WERE ALL WOMEN COVERED IN WHITE TALC TAKING A TEN MINUTE BREAK, A 30 MINUTE LUNCH, MOVING BY BELLS,
COKE
COFFE
HURRY UP HURRY UP HURRY UP
THAT IS UNTIL WE WENT ON STRIKE...
.05 PER HOUR .01 PER HOUR .001 PER HOUR .02 PER HOUR .015 PER HOUR .06 PER HOUR .012 PER HOUR
STRIKE
SCABS STAY OUT!!
THEN WE WERE ALL WOMEN OUT OF A JOB.
GAS RENT GROCERIES UTILITIES CAR PAYMENT
STRIKE

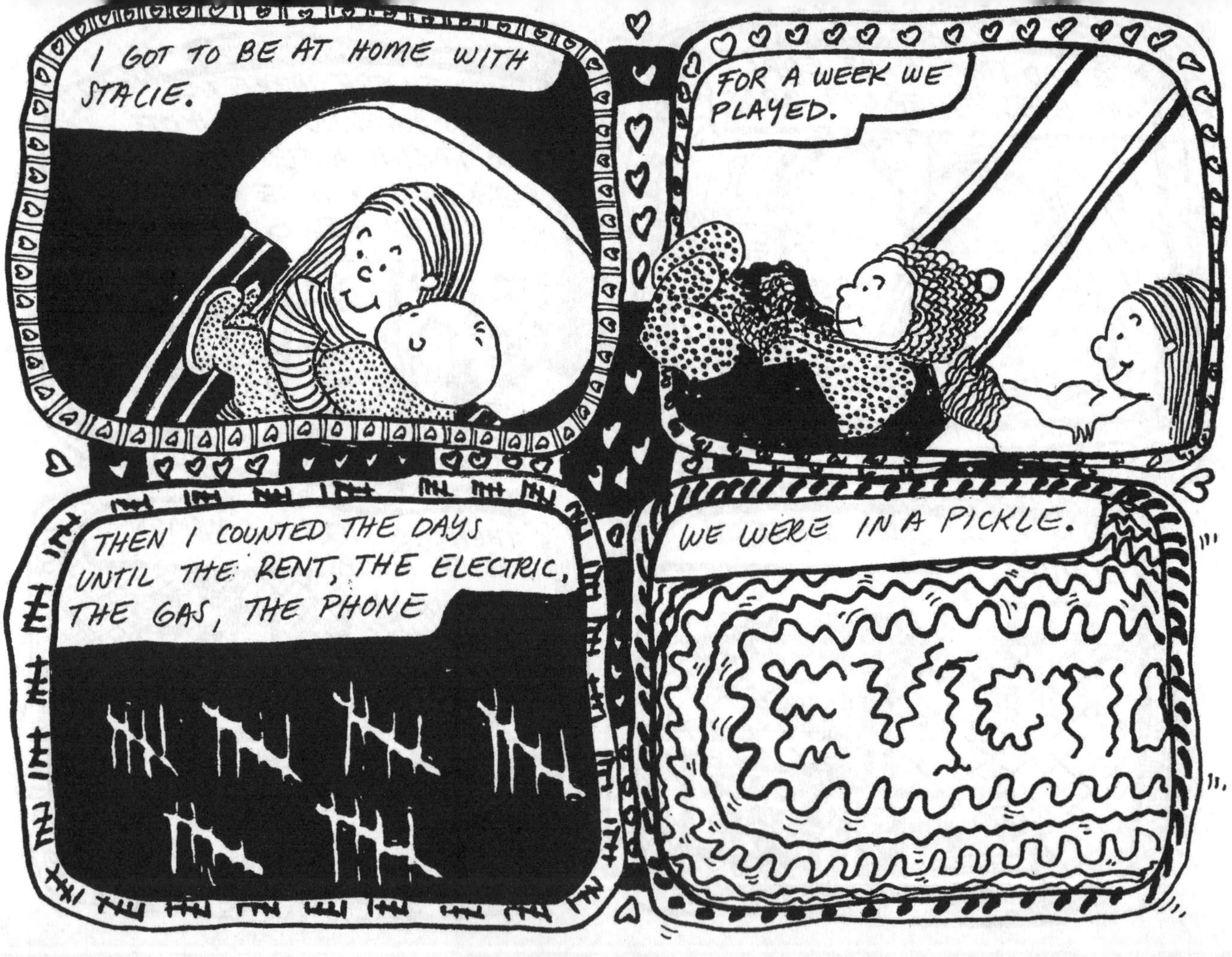
I GOT TO BE AT HOME WITH STACIE.
FOR A WEEK WE PLAYED.
THEN I COUNTED THE DAYS UNTIL THE RENT, THE ELECTRIC, THE GAS, THE PHONE
WE WERE IN A PICKLE.

ALL THE FACTORIES IN MY TOWN WERE NOT HIRING OR ELSE THEY WERE CLOSED.

CLOSED

THEY ALL MOVED SOUTH.

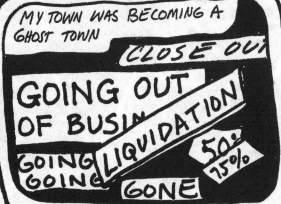

MY TOWN WAS BECOMING A GHOST TOWN

CLOSE OUT

GOING OUT OF BUSIN

LIQUIDATION

GOING GOING

50% 75%

GONE

WITHOUT A JOB IN SIGHT.

WANT ADS

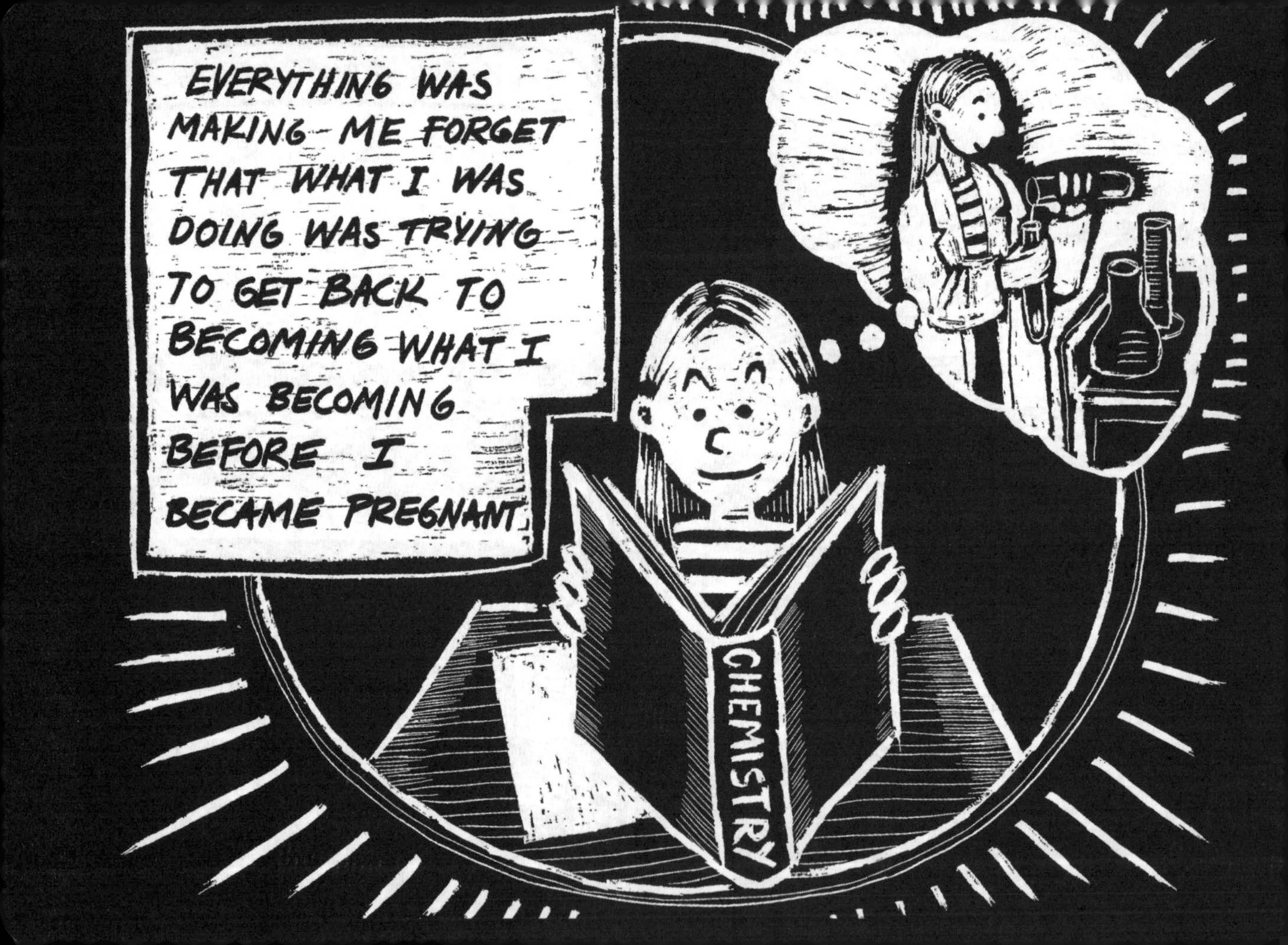
EVERYTHING WAS MAKING ME FORGET THAT WHAT I WAS DOING WAS TRYING TO GET BACK TO BECOMING WHAT I WAS BECOMING BEFORE I BECAME PREGNANT
CHEMISTRY

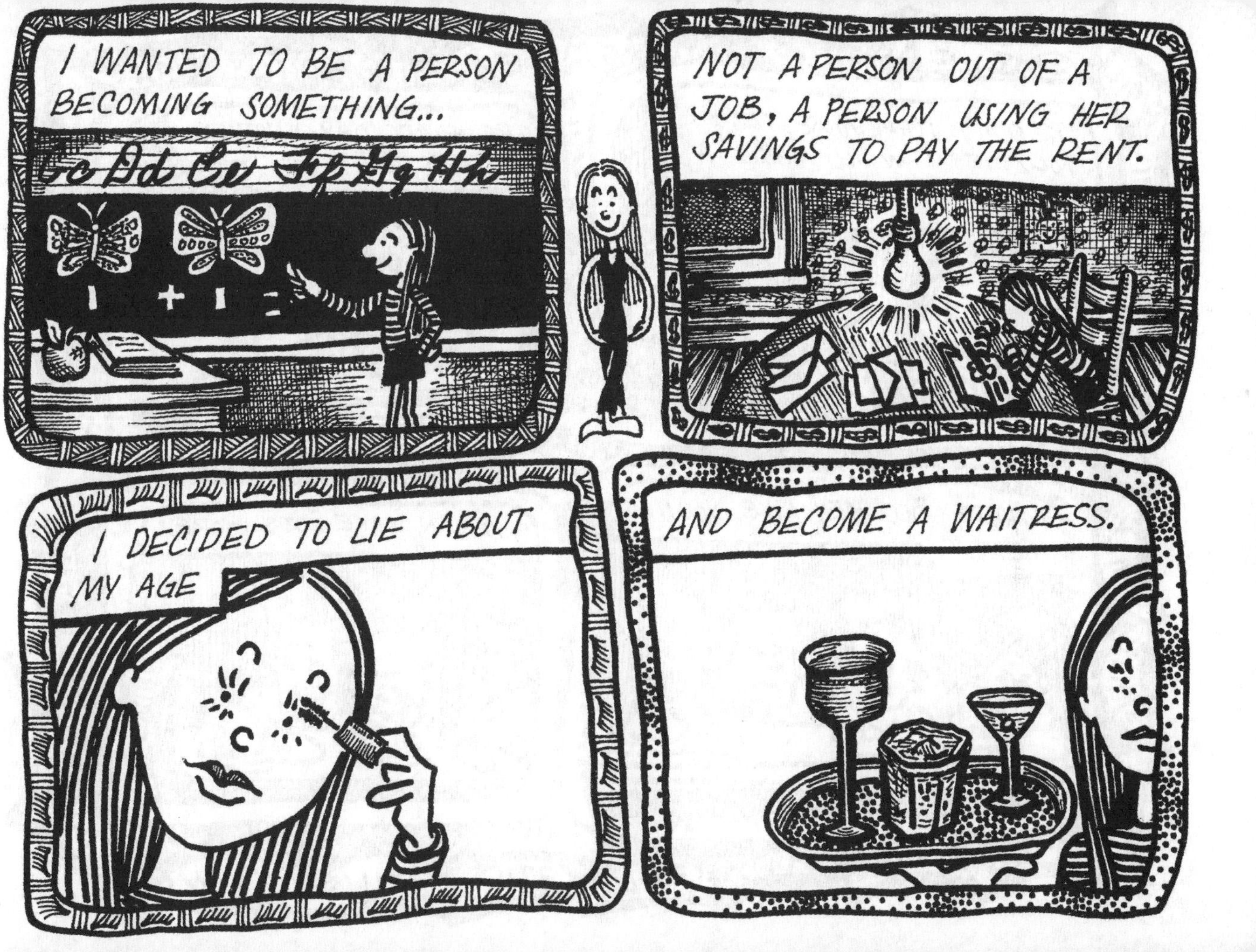
I WANTED TO BE A PERSON BECOMING SOMETHING...
NOT A PERSON OUT OF A JOB, A PERSON USING HER SAVINGS TO PAY THE RENT.
I DECIDED TO LIE ABOUT MY AGE
AND BECOME A WAITRESS.

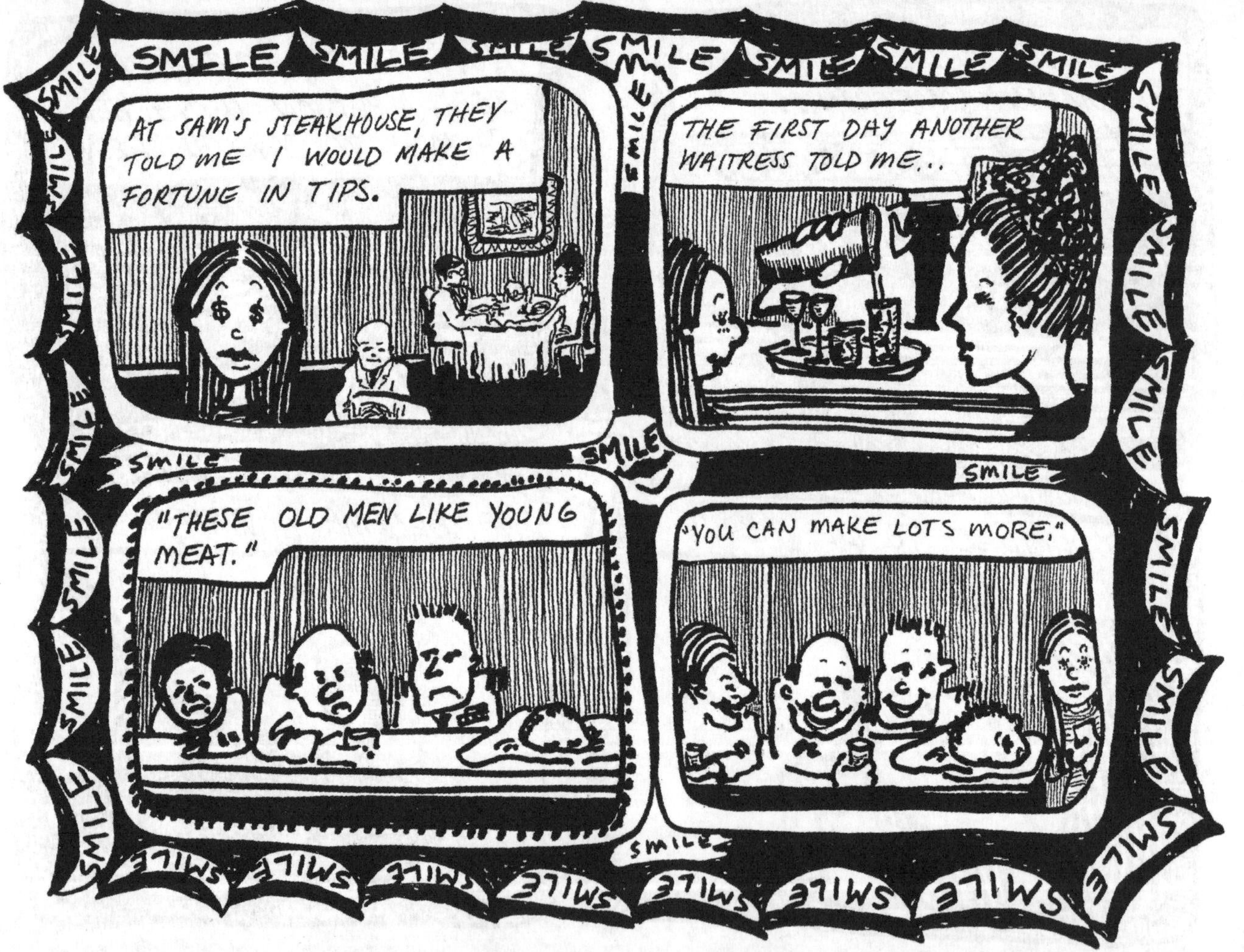
AT SAM'S STEAKHOUSE, THEY TOLD ME I WOULD MAKE A FORTUNE IN TIPS.
THE FIRST DAY ANOTHER WAITRESS TOLD ME...
"THESE OLD MEN LIKE YOUNG MEAT."
"YOU CAN MAKE LOTS MORE."
SMILE SMILE SMILE SMILE SMILE SMILE SMILE

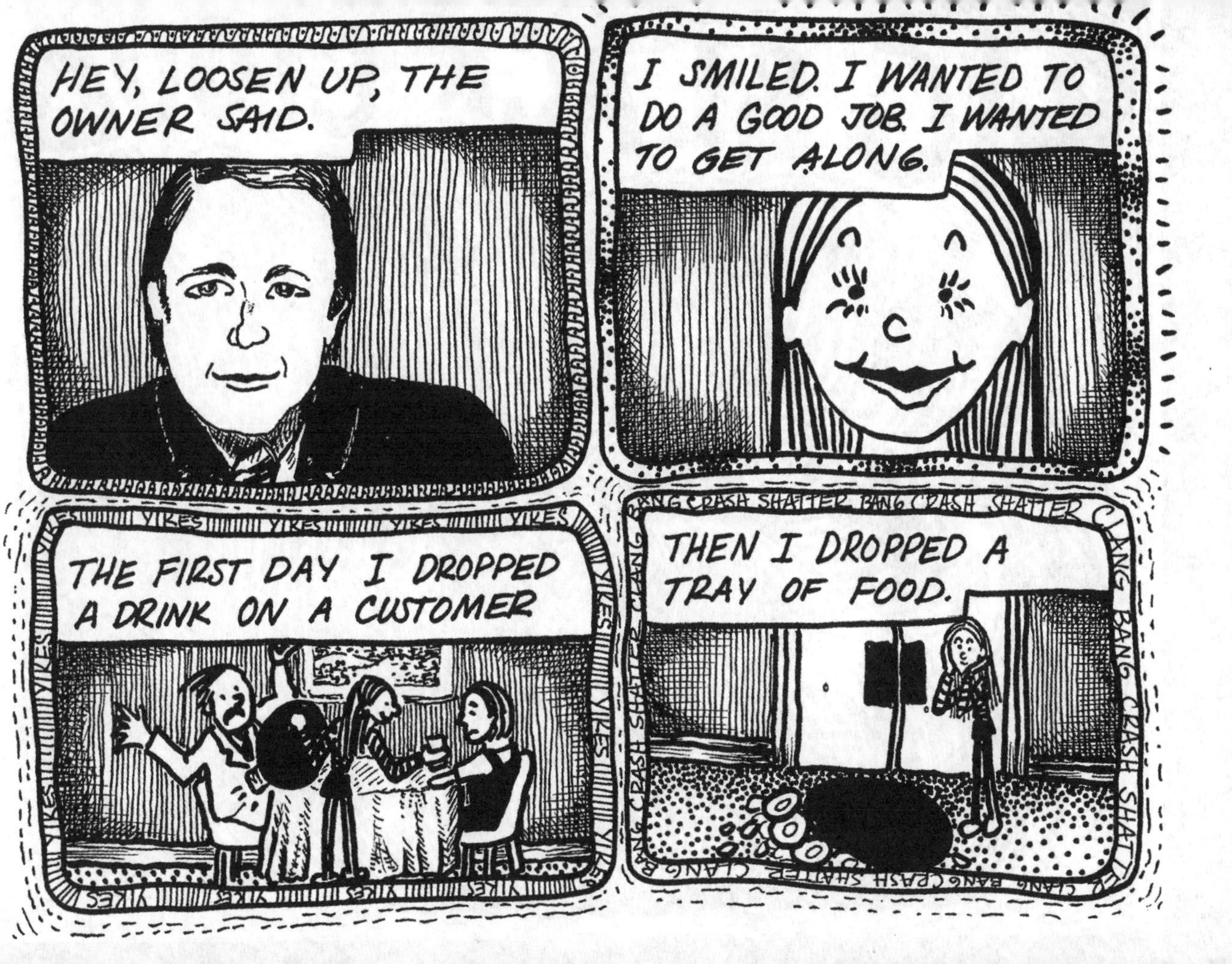
HEY, LOOSEN UP, THE OWNER SAID.
I SMILED. I WANTED TO DO A GOOD JOB. I WANTED TO GET ALONG.
YIKES YIKES YIKES YIKES
THE FIRST DAY I DROPPED A DRINK ON A CUSTOMER
BANG CRASH SHATTER BANG CRASH SHATTER CLANG
THEN I DROPPED A TRAY OF FOOD.

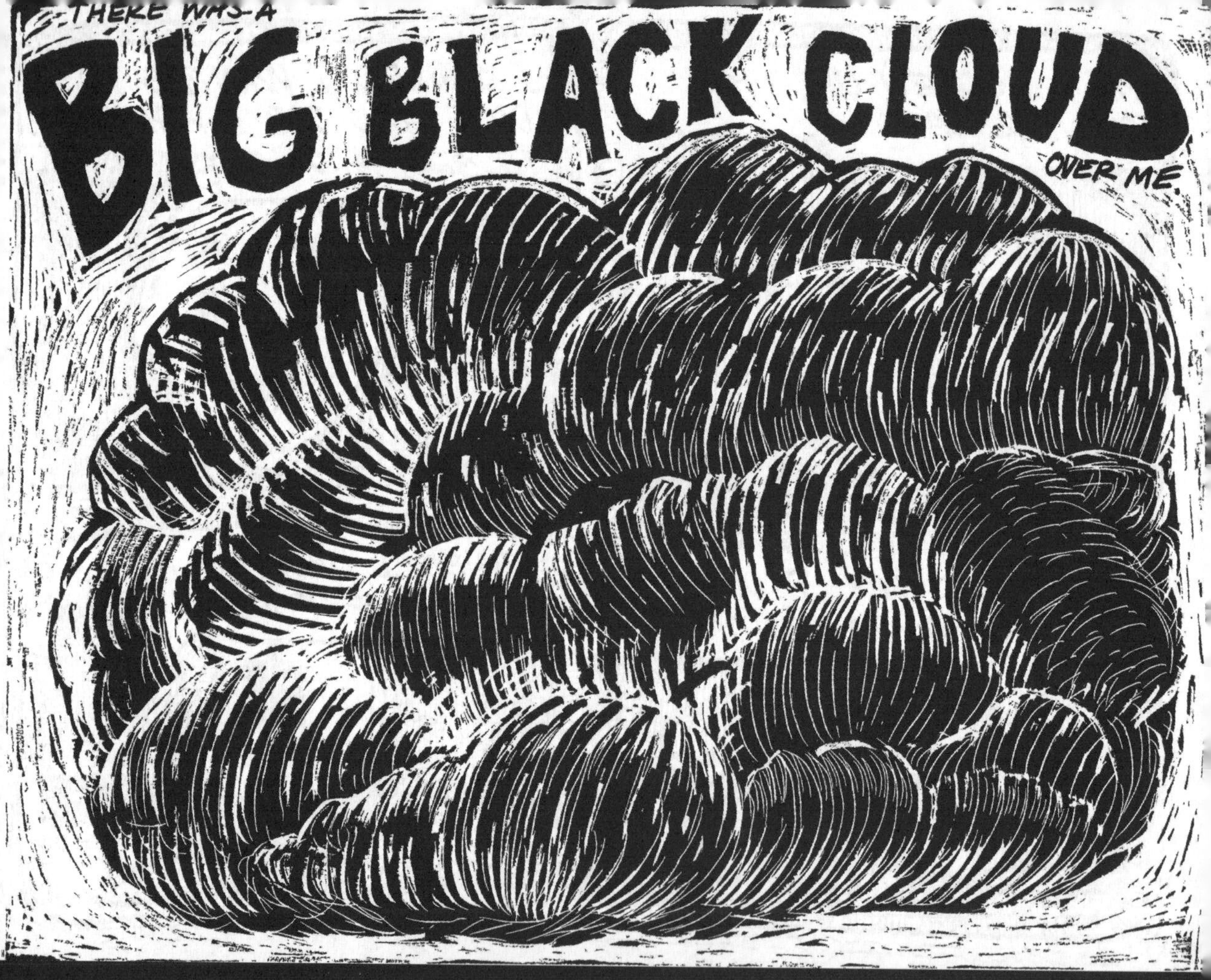
THERE WAS A
BIG BLACK CLOUD
OVER ME.

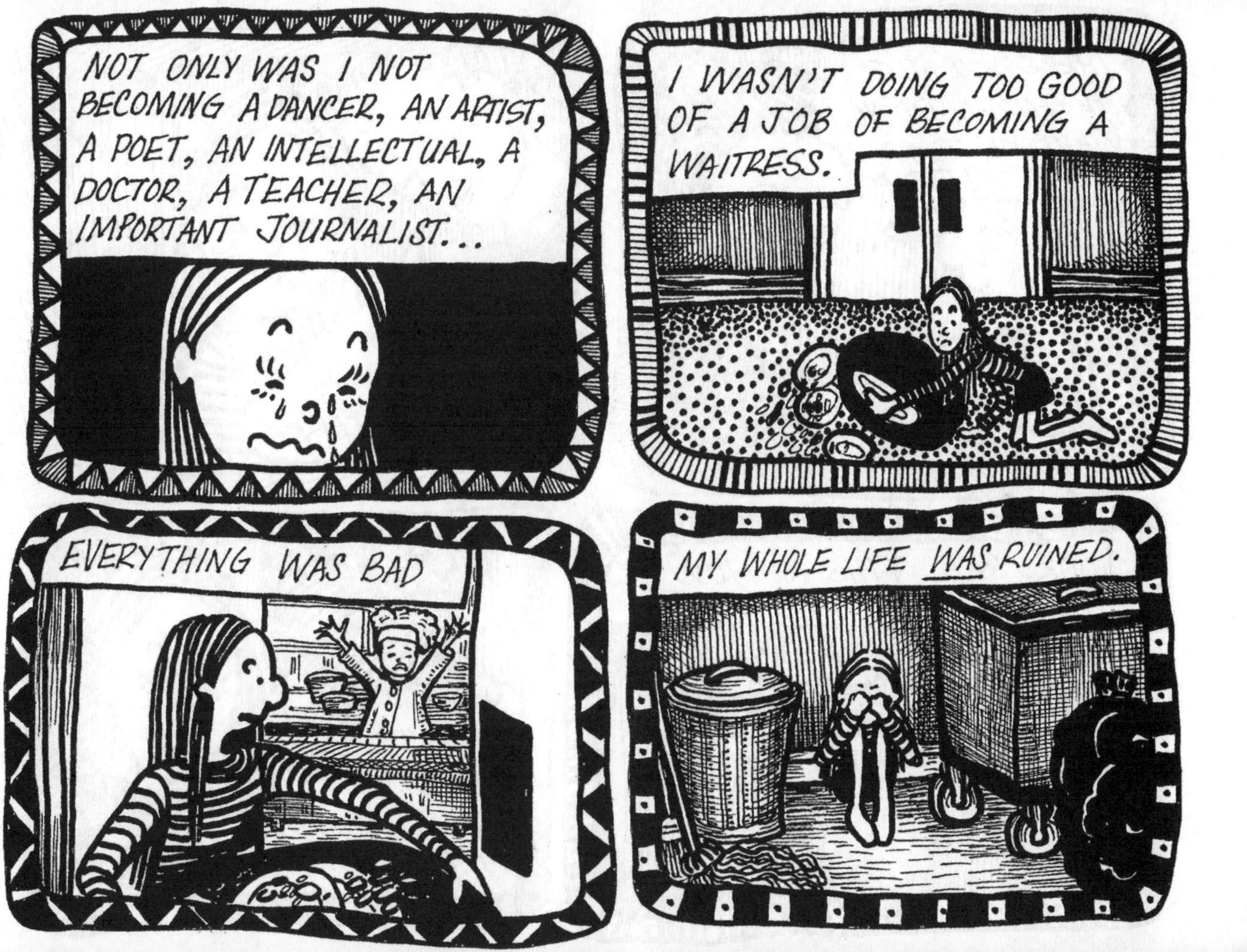
NOT ONLY WAS I NOT BECOMING A DANCER, AN ARTIST, A POET, AN INTELLECTUAL, A DOCTOR, A TEACHER, AN IMPORTANT JOURNALIST...
I WASN'T DOING TOO GOOD OF A JOB OF BECOMING A WAITRESS.
EVERYTHING WAS BAD
MY WHOLE LIFE WAS RUINED.

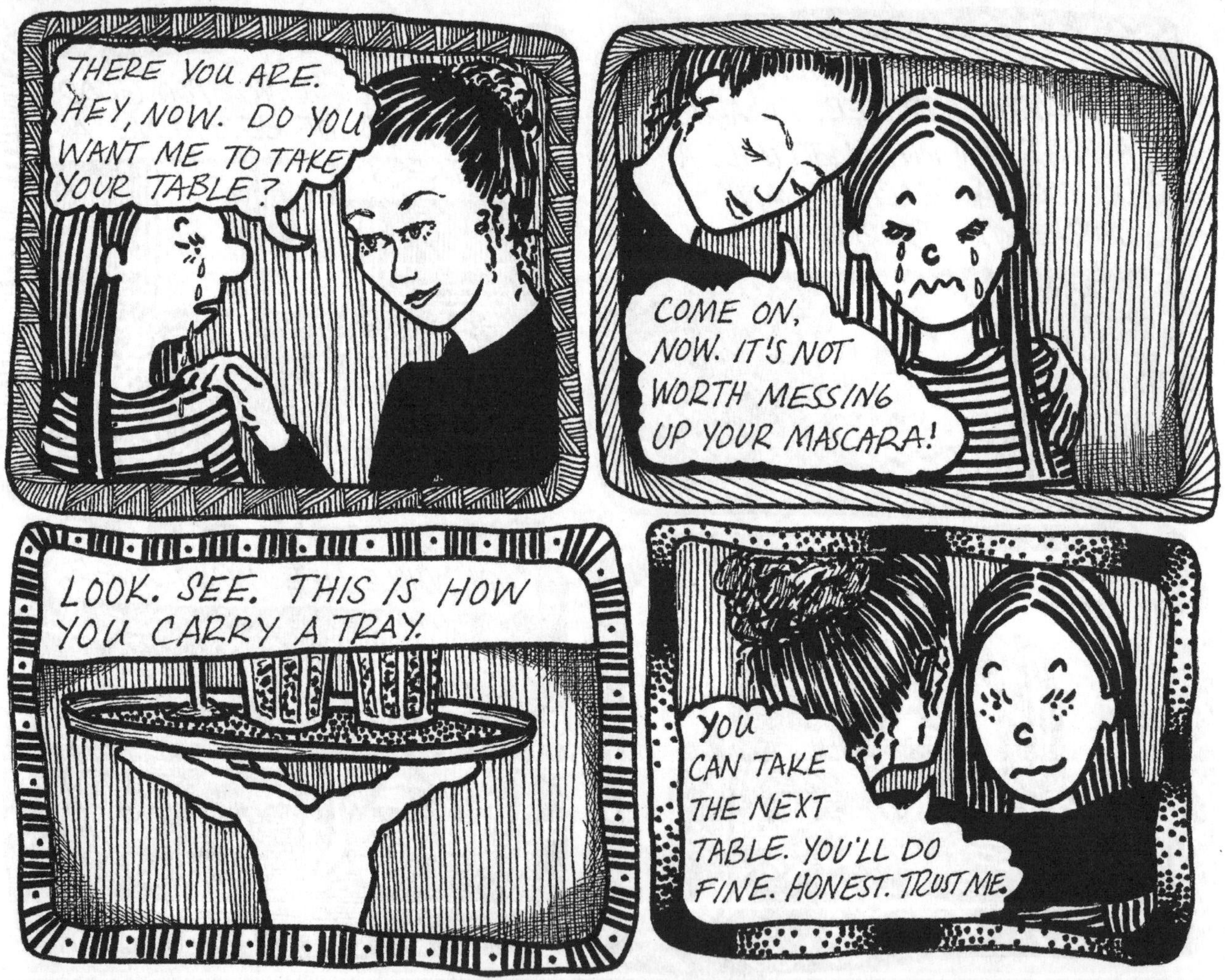
THERE YOU ARE. HEY, NOW. DO YOU WANT ME TO TAKE YOUR TABLE?
COME ON, NOW. IT'S NOT WORTH MESSING UP YOUR MASCARA!
LOOK. SEE. THIS IS HOW YOU CARRY A TRAY.
YOU CAN TAKE THE NEXT TABLE. YOU'LL DO FINE. HONEST. TRUST ME.

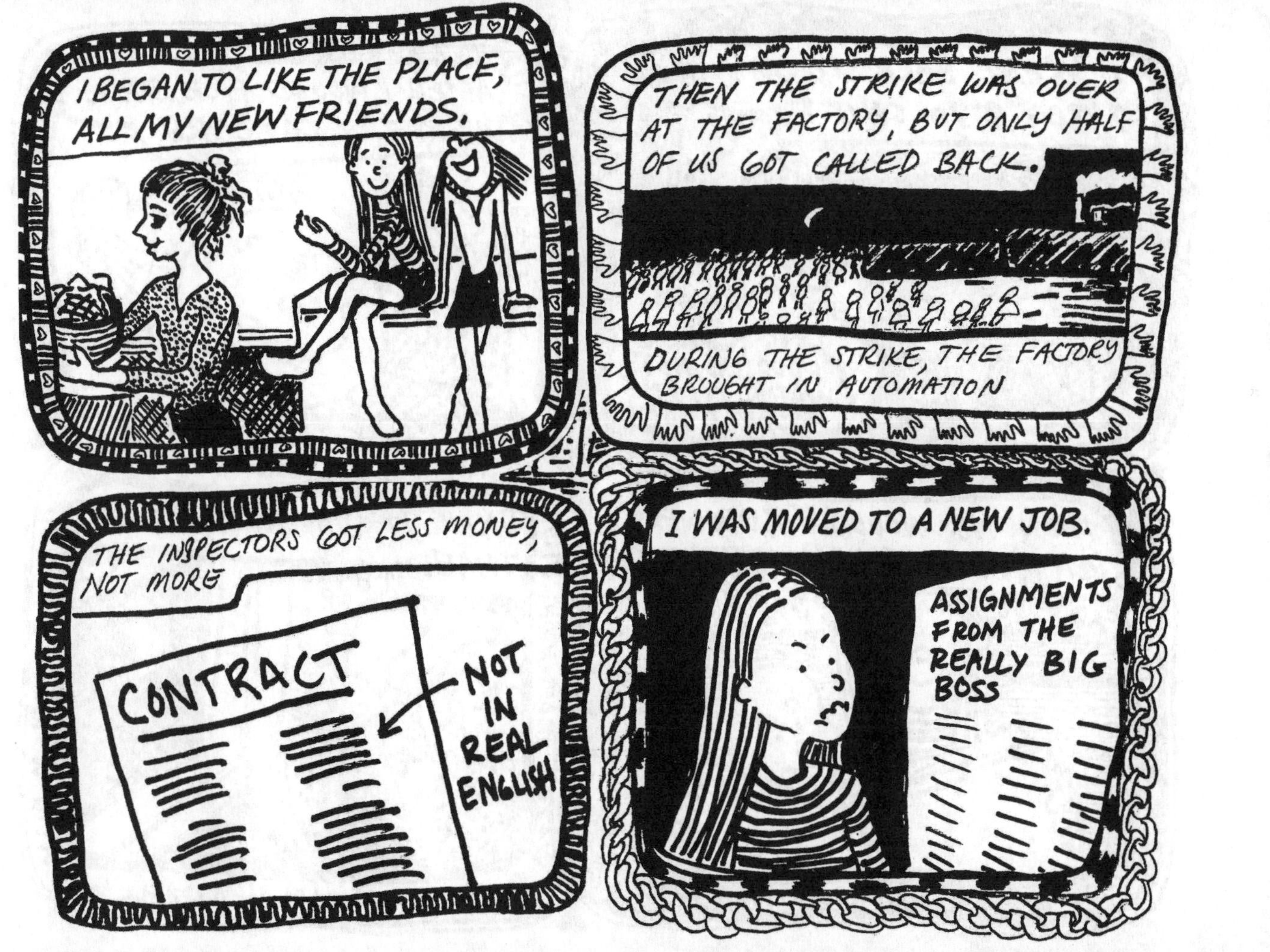
I BEGAN TO LIKE THE PLACE, ALL MY NEW FRIENDS.
THEN THE STRIKE WAS OVER AT THE FACTORY, BUT ONLY HALF OF US GOT CALLED BACK.
DURING THE STRIKE, THE FACTORY BROUGHT IN AUTOMATION
THE INSPECTORS GOT LESS MONEY, NOT MORE
CONTRACT
NOT IN REAL ENGLISH
I WAS MOVED TO A NEW JOB.
ASSIGNMENTS FROM THE REALLY BIG BOSS

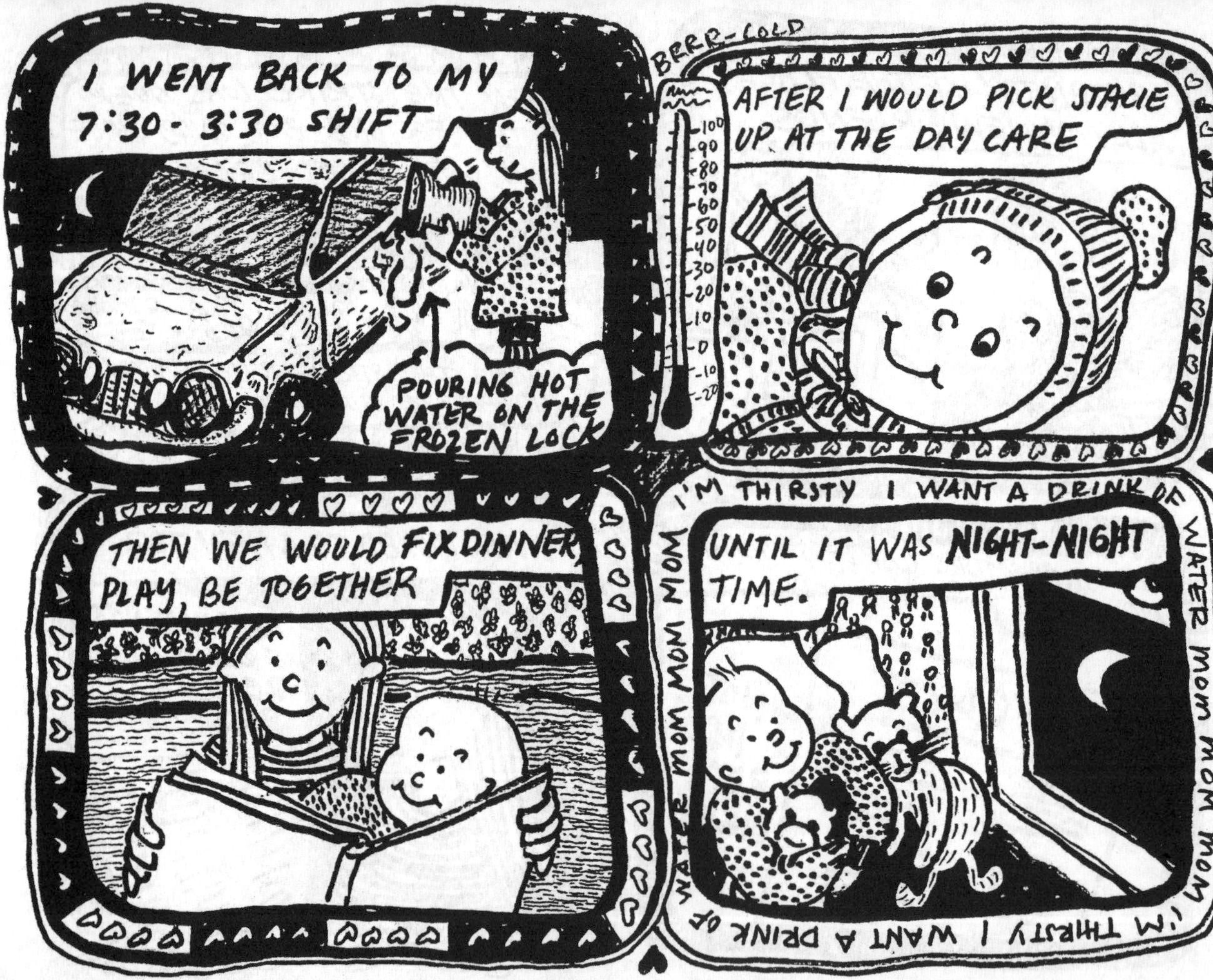
I WENT BACK TO MY 7:30 - 3:30 SHIFT
POURING HOT WATER ON THE FROZEN LOCK
BRRR-COLD
100
90
80
70
60
50
40
30
20
10
0
-10
-20
AFTER I WOULD PICK STACIE UP AT THE DAY CARE
THEN WE WOULD FIX DINNER, PLAY, BE TOGETHER
UNTIL IT WAS NIGHT-NIGHT TIME.
I'M THIRSTY I WANT A DRINK OF WATER MOM MOM MOM MOM
I'M THIRSTY I WANT A DRINK OF WATER MOM MOM MOM

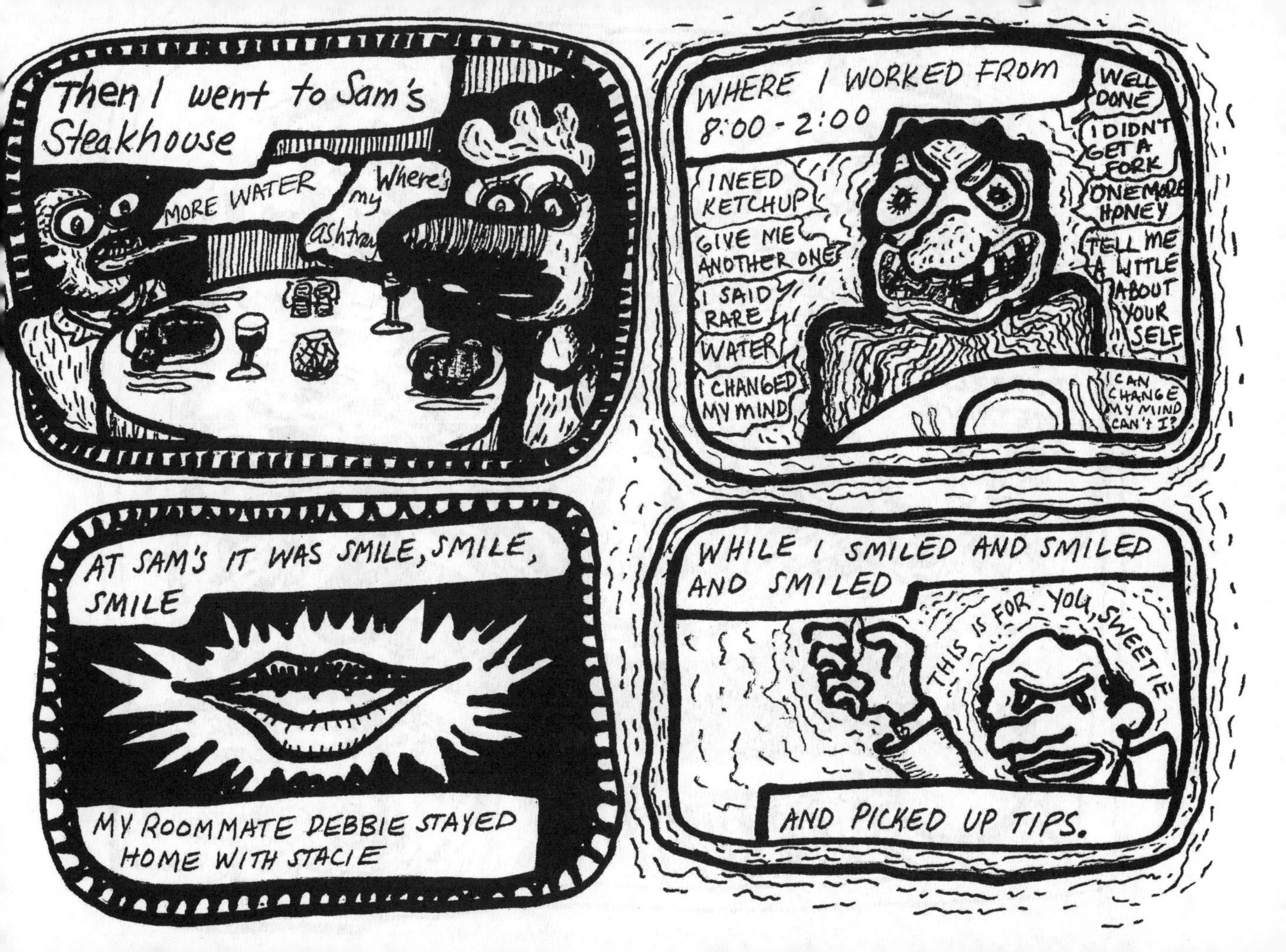
Then I went to Sam's Steakhouse
MORE WATER
Where's my ashtray
WHERE I WORKED FROM 8:00 - 2:00
WELL DONE
I DIDN'T GET A FORK
ONE MORE HONEY
TELL ME A LITTLE ABOUT YOUR SELF
I NEED KETCHUP
GIVE ME ANOTHER ONE
I SAID RARE
WATER
I CHANGED MY MIND
I CAN CHANGE MY MIND CAN'T I?
AT SAM'S IT WAS SMILE, SMILE, SMILE
MY ROOMMATE DEBBIE STAYED HOME WITH STACIE
WHILE I SMILED AND SMILED AND SMILED
THIS IS FOR YOU, SWEETIE
AND PICKED UP TIPS.

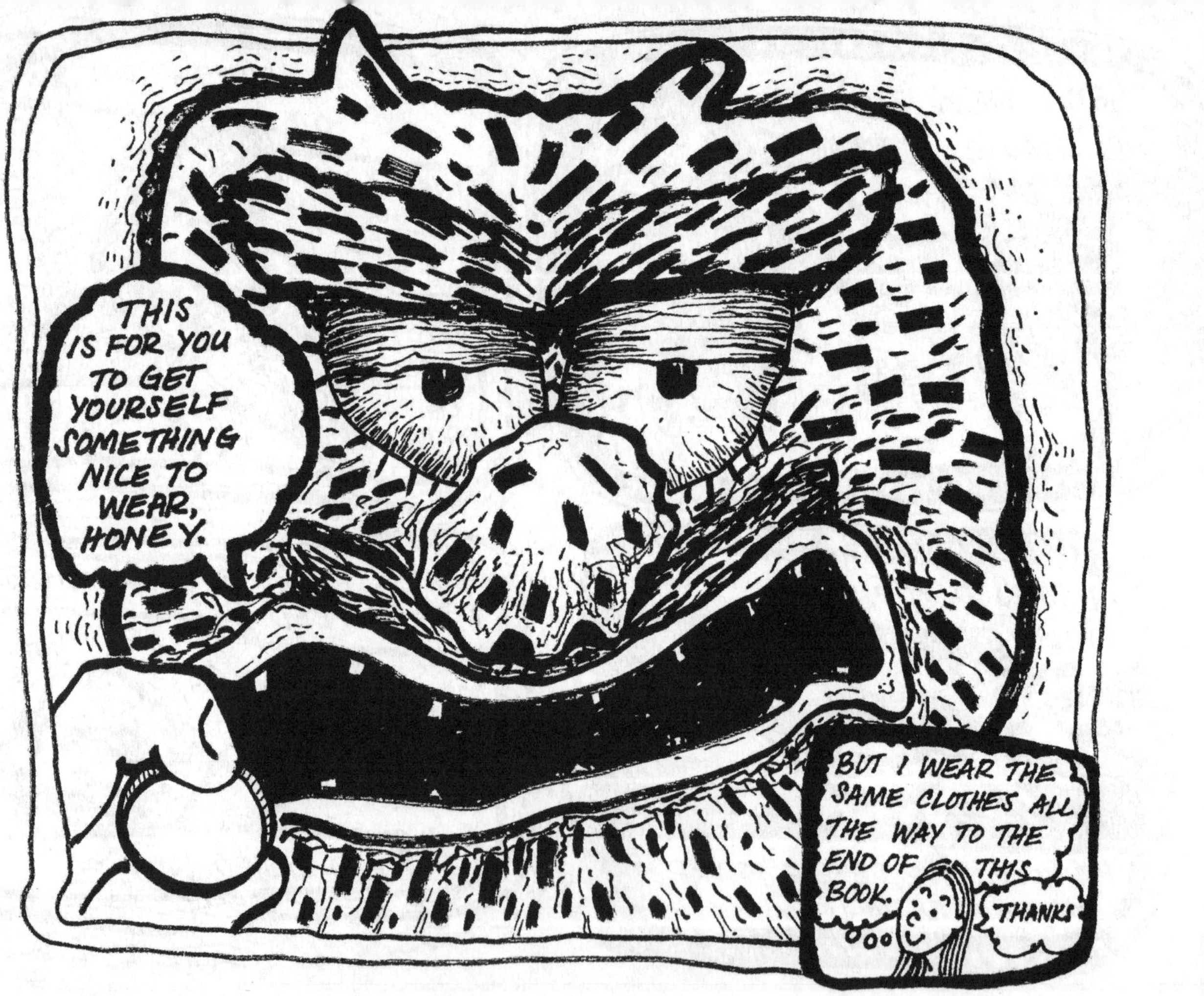
THIS IS FOR YOU TO GET YOURSELF SOMETHING NICE TO WEAR, HONEY.
BUT I WEAR THE SAME CLOTHES ALL THE WAY TO THE END OF THIS BOOK.
THANKS

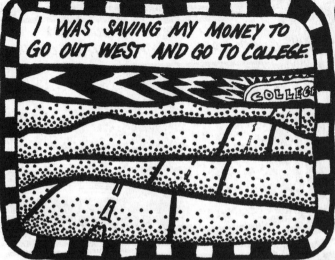
I WAS SAVING MY MONEY TO GO OUT WEST AND GO TO COLLEGE.

I ALMOST HAD ENOUGH.

THEN I GOT SICK I HAD A PAIN IN MY SIDE, MY BACK. IT WAS PNUEMONIA.

I HAD TO QUIT MY WAITRESS JOB

BUT I KEPT WORKING AT THE FACTORY. I DIDN'T WANT A PINK SLIP.

DON'T BE LATE OR ELSE!!! NO SICK KIDS ALLOWED 2 PINK SLIPS = WARNING 4 PINK SLIPS = YOU'RE FIRED 1 PINK SLIP = NO PROMOTION

TIME CLOCK

PINK SLIP

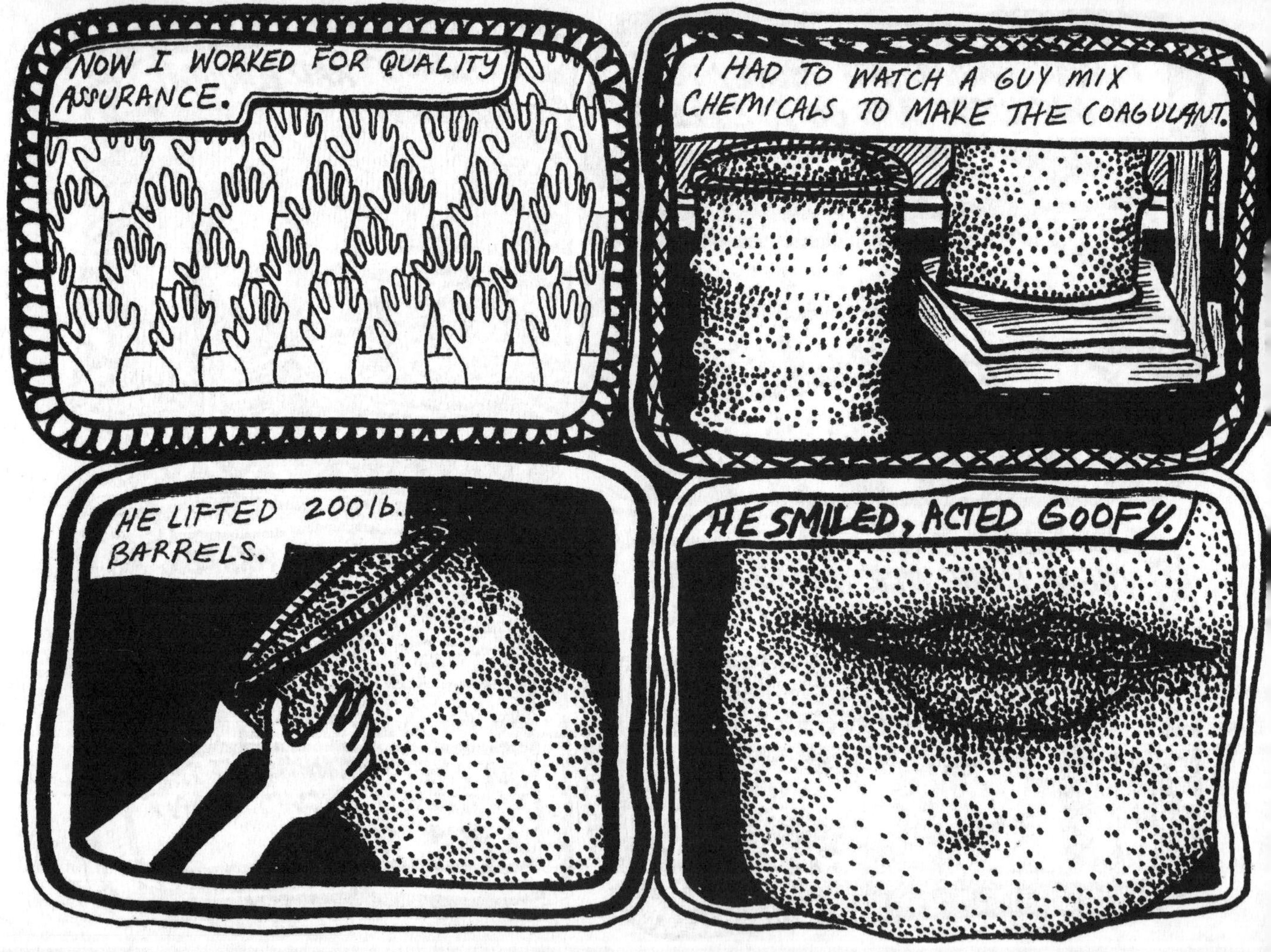
NOW I WORKED FOR QUALITY ASSURANCE.
I HAD TO WATCH A GUY MIX CHEMICALS TO MAKE THE COAGULANT.
HE LIFTED 200lb. BARRELS.
HE SMILED, ACTED GOOFY.

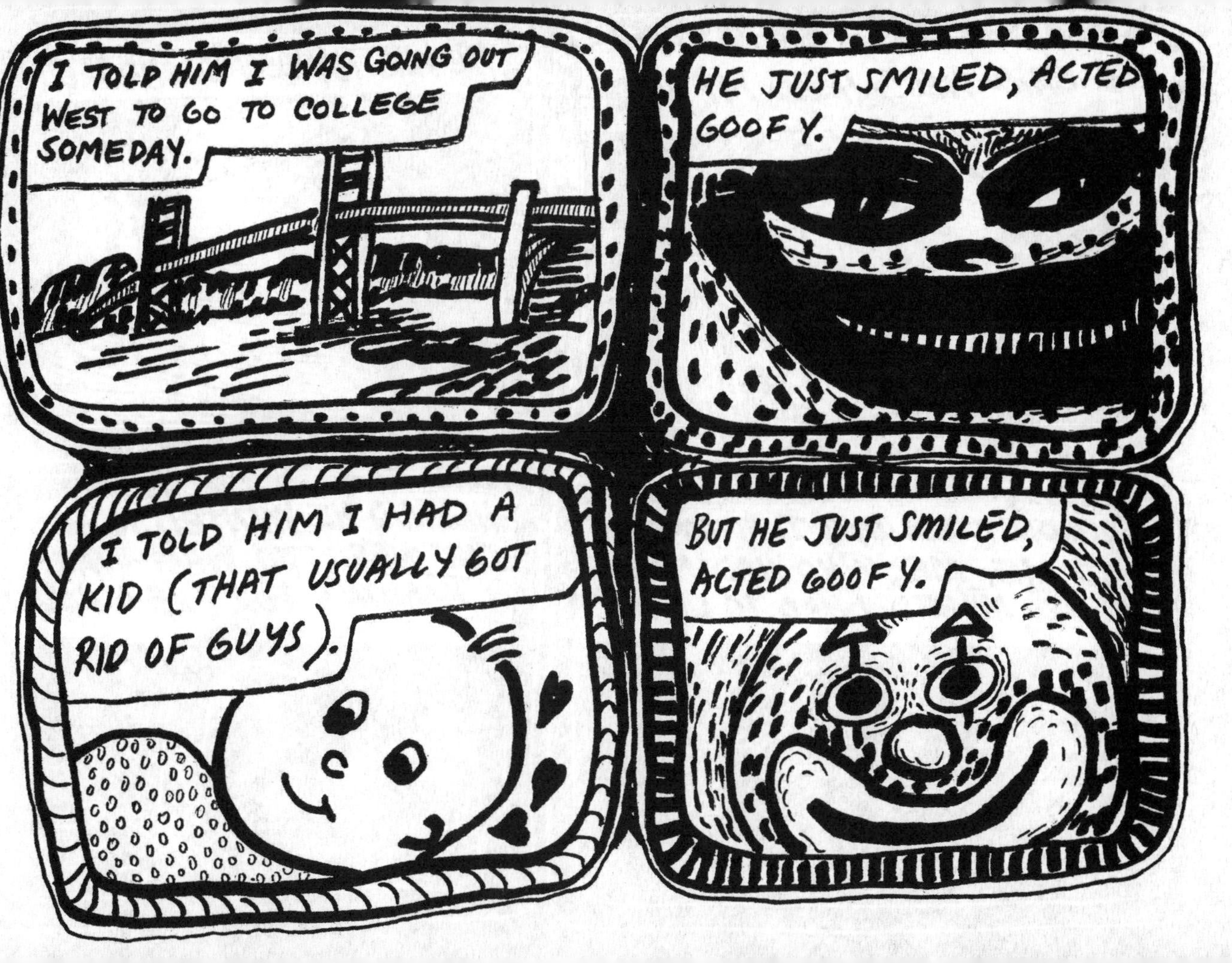
I TOLD HIM I WAS GOING OUT WEST TO GO TO COLLEGE SOMEDAY.
HE JUST SMILED, ACTED GOOFY.
I TOLD HIM I HAD A KID (THAT USUALLY GOT RID OF GUYS).
BUT HE JUST SMILED, ACTED GOOFY.

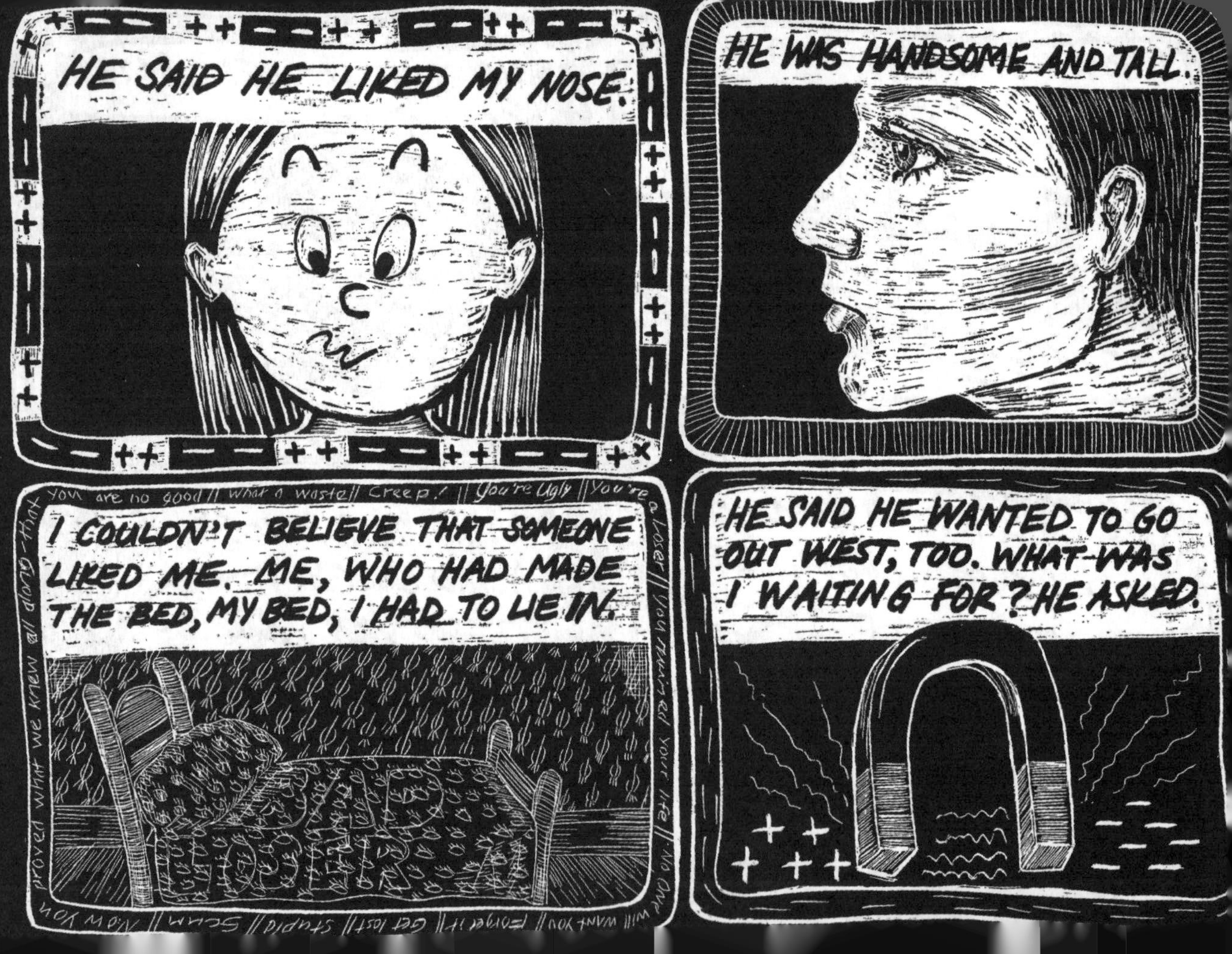
HE SAID HE LIKED MY NOSE.
HE WAS HANDSOME AND TALL.
I COULDN'T BELIEVE THAT SOMEONE LIKED ME. ME, WHO HAD MADE THE BED, MY BED, I HAD TO LIE IN.
You are no good // What a waste // Creep! // You're Ugly // You're a Loser // You ruined your life // No one will want you // Forget it // Get lost! // Stupid // Scum // Now you proved what we knew all along - that
HE SAID HE WANTED TO GO OUT WEST, TOO. WHAT WAS I WAITING FOR? HE ASKED.

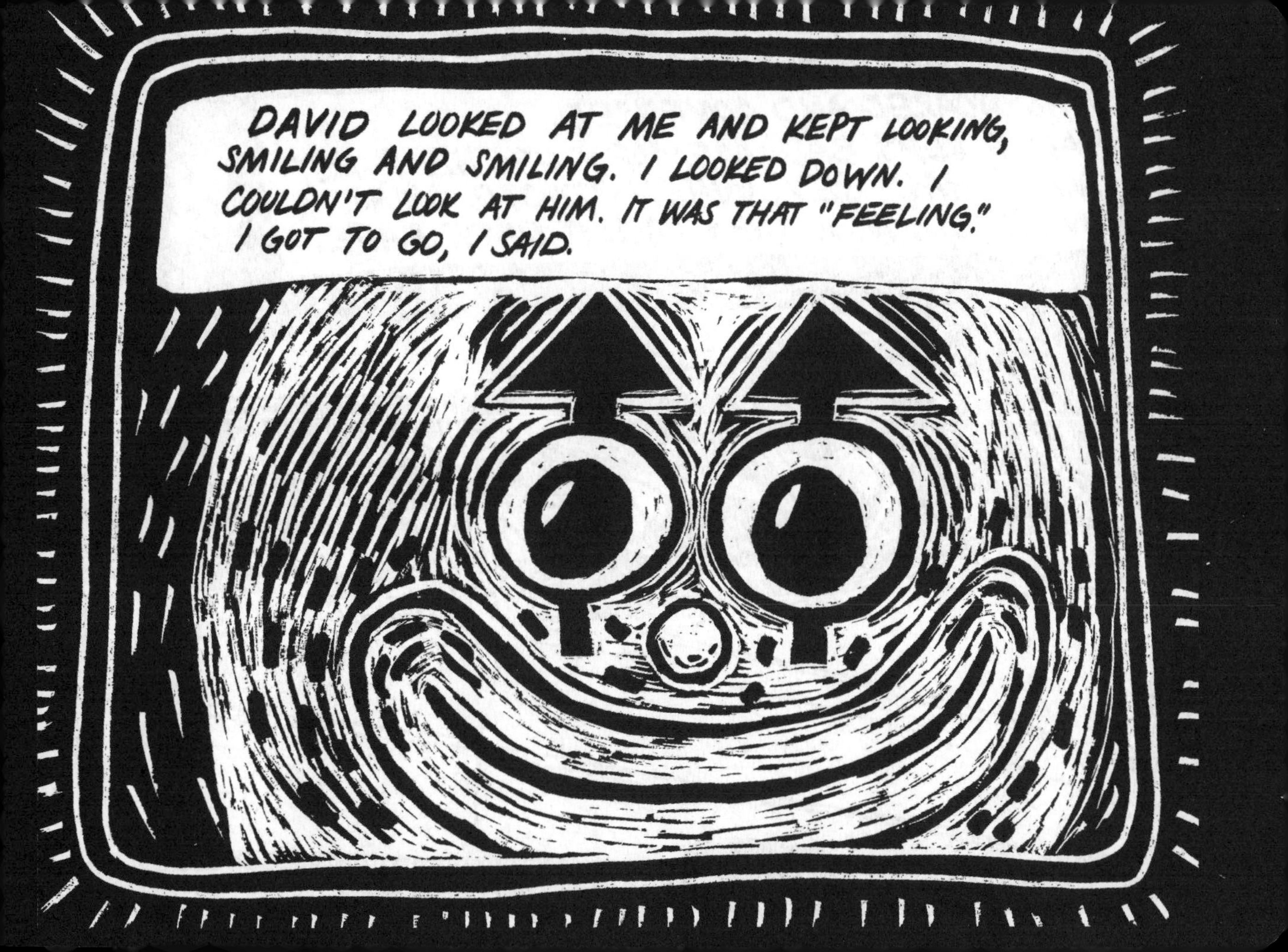
DAVID LOOKED AT ME AND KEPT LOOKING, SMILING AND SMILING. I LOOKED DOWN. I COULDN'T LOOK AT HIM. IT WAS THAT "FEELING." I GOT TO GO, I SAID.

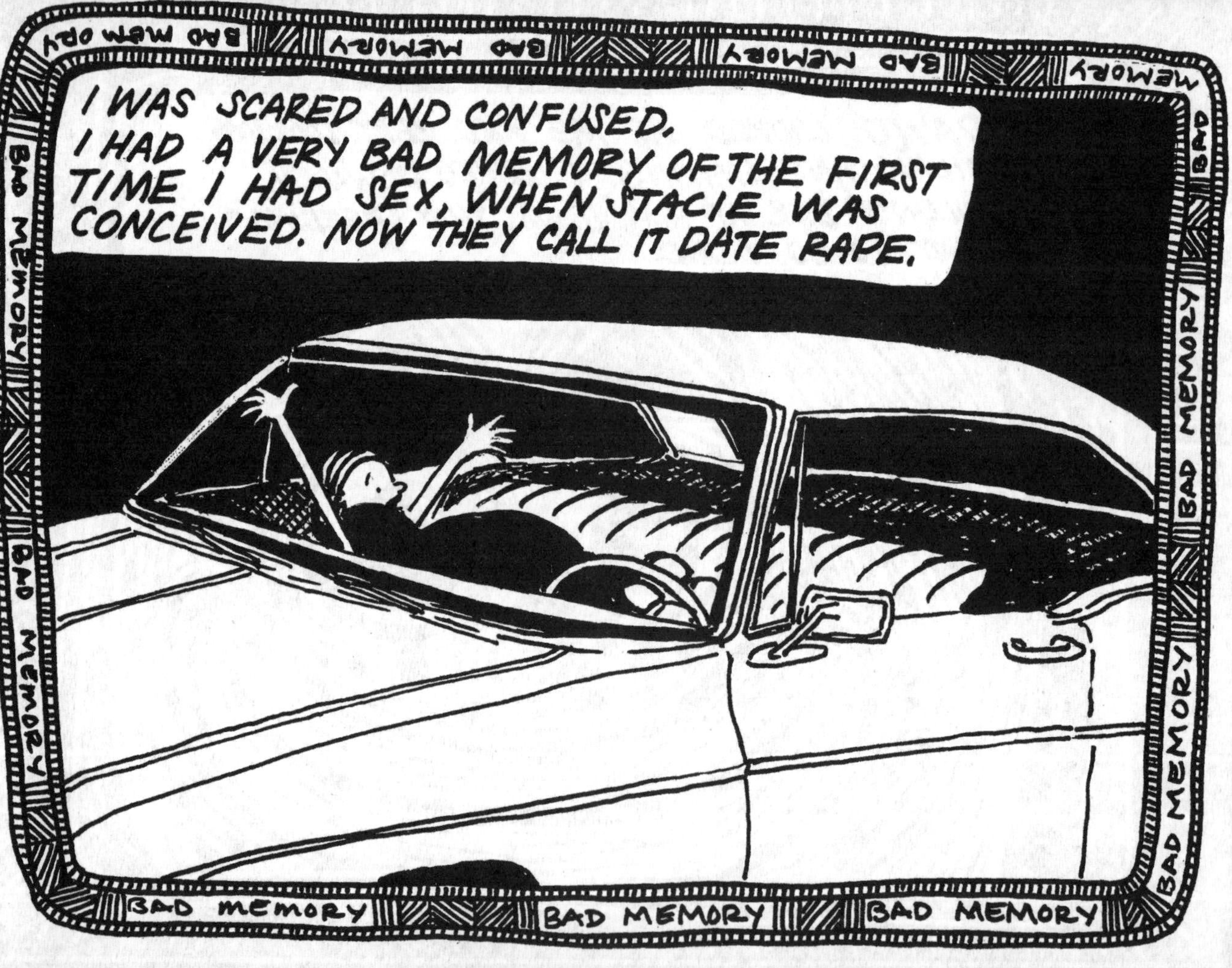
I WAS SCARED AND CONFUSED.
I HAD A VERY BAD MEMORY OF THE FIRST TIME I HAD SEX, WHEN STACIE WAS CONCEIVED. NOW THEY CALL IT DATE RAPE.
BAD MEMORY
BAD MEMORY
BAD MEMORY

MEAN WHILE...

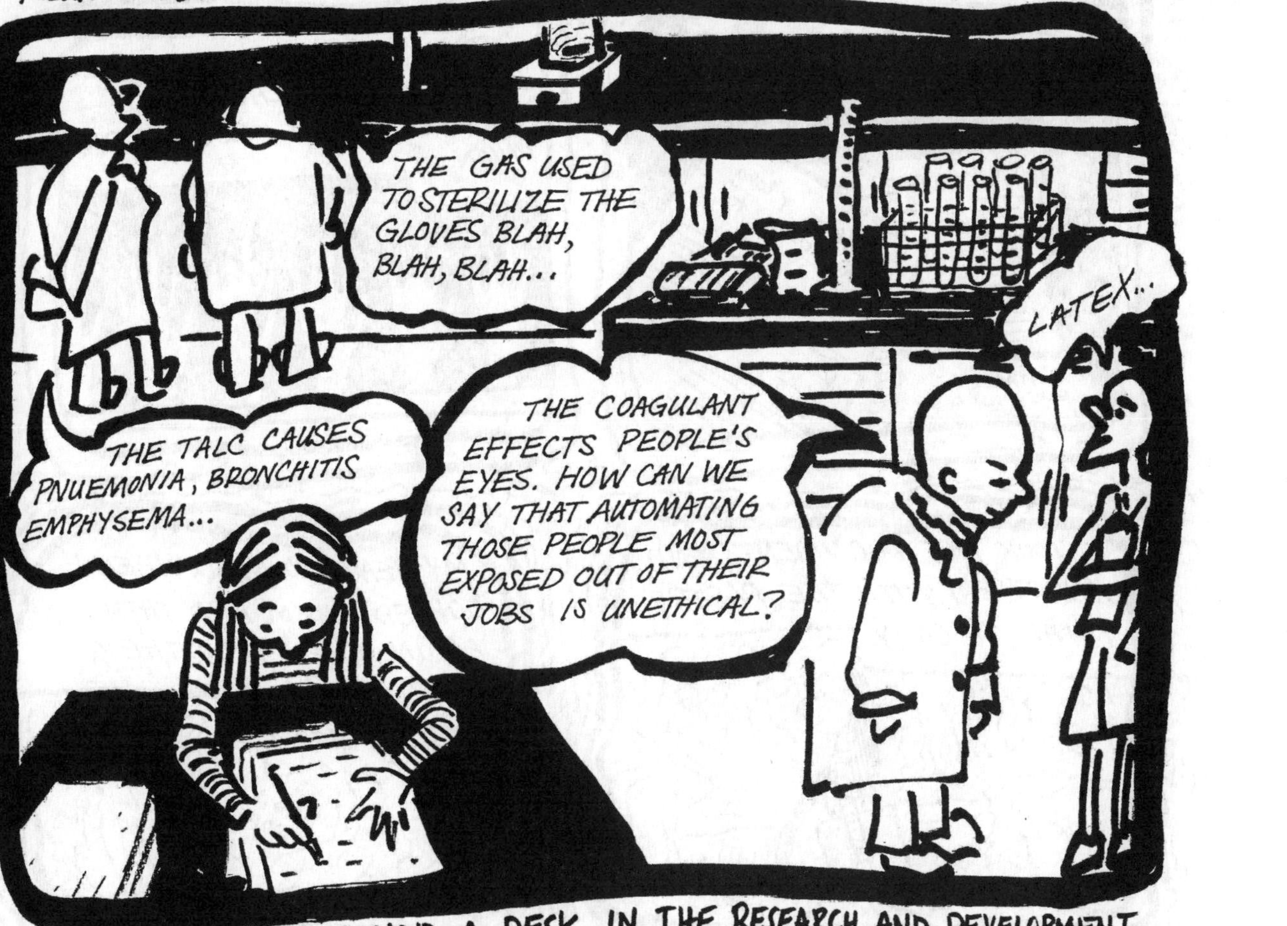
THE GAS USED TO STERILIZE THE GLOVES BLAH, BLAH, BLAH...
LATEX...
THE TALC CAUSES PNUEMONIA, BRONCHITIS EMPHYSEMA...
THE COAGULANT EFFECTS PEOPLE'S EYES. HOW CAN WE SAY THAT AUTOMATING THOSE PEOPLE MOST EXPOSED OUT OF THEIR JOBS IS UNETHICAL?

AT MY NEW JOB I HAD A DESK IN THE RESEARCH AND DEVELOPMENT LABORATORY.

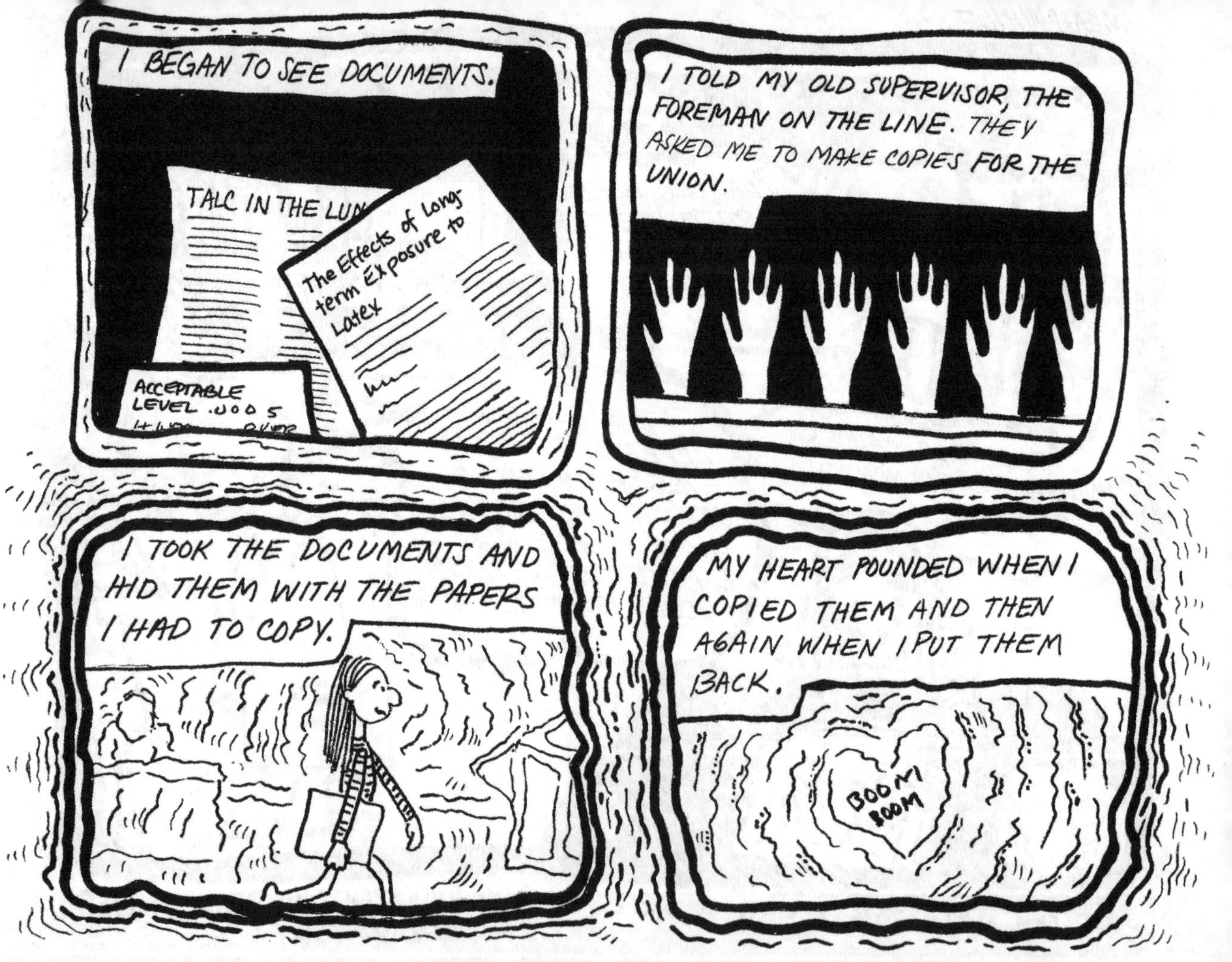
I BEGAN TO SEE DOCUMENTS.
TALC IN THE LUN
The Effects of Long-term Exposure to Latex
ACCEPTABLE LEVEL .0005
I TOLD MY OLD SUPERVISOR, THE FOREMAN ON THE LINE. THEY ASKED ME TO MAKE COPIES FOR THE UNION.
I TOOK THE DOCUMENTS AND HID THEM WITH THE PAPERS I HAD TO COPY.
MY HEART POUNDED WHEN I COPIED THEM AND THEN AGAIN WHEN I PUT THEM BACK.
BOOM BOOM

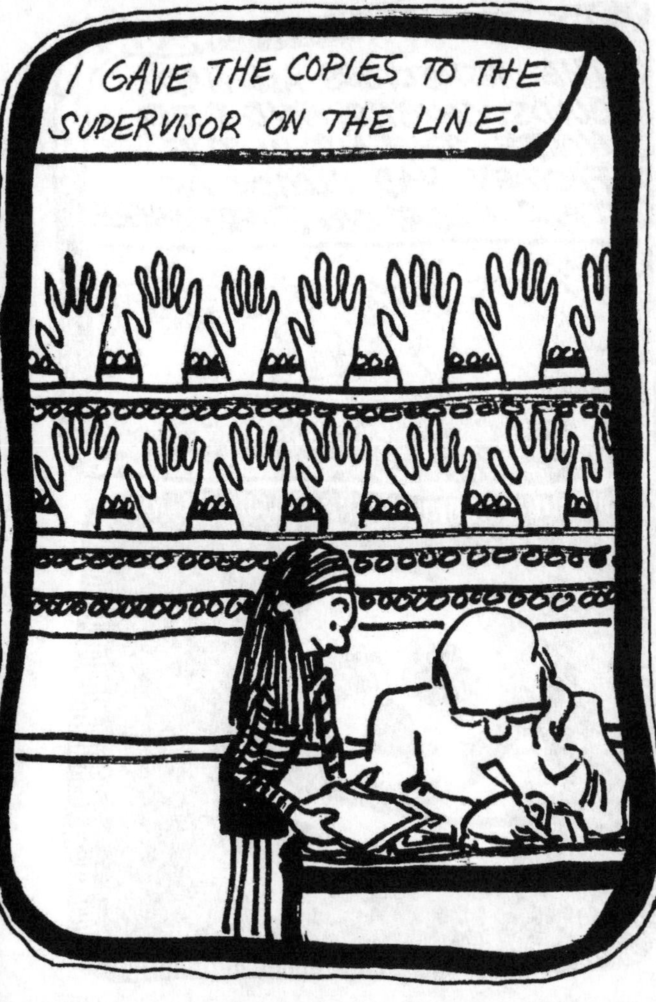
I GAVE THE COPIES TO THE SUPERVISOR ON THE LINE.

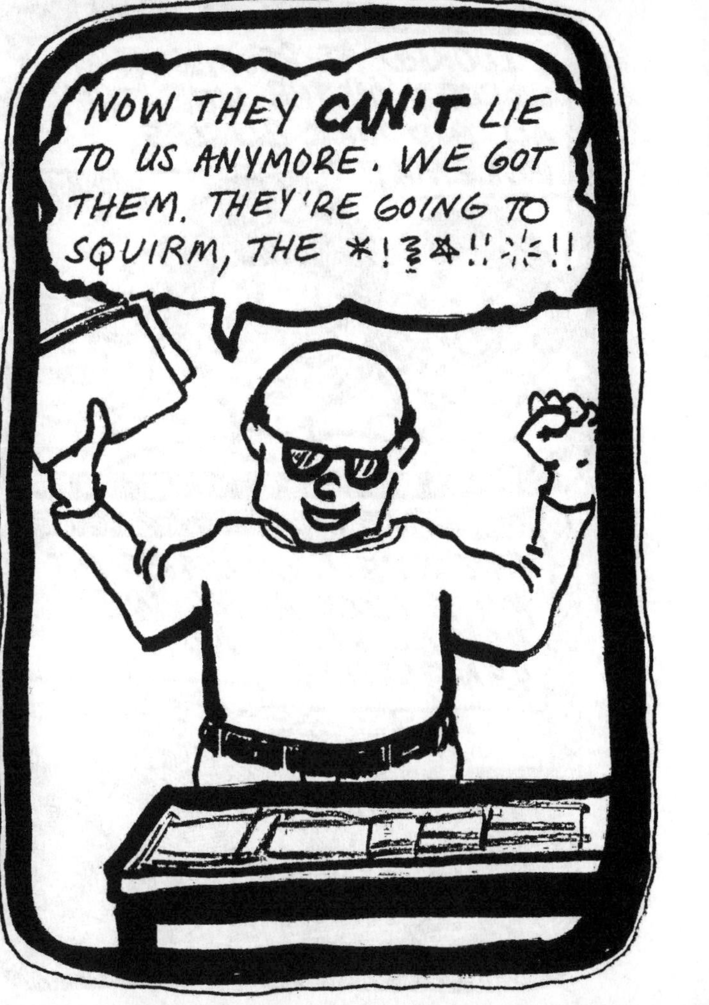
NOW THEY CAN'T LIE TO US ANYMORE. WE GOT THEM. THEY'RE GOING TO SQUIRM, THE *!?☆!!☆!!

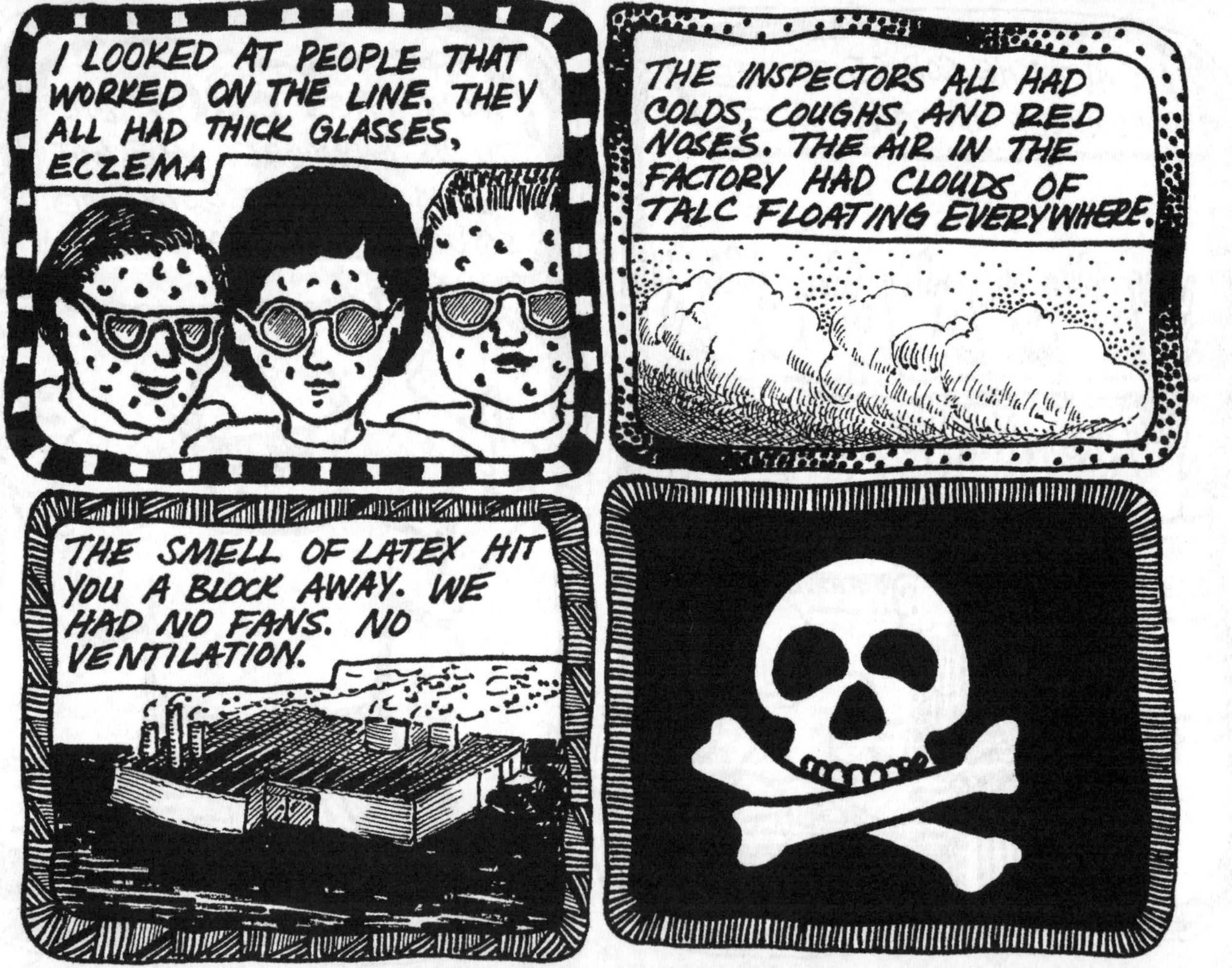
I LOOKED AT PEOPLE THAT WORKED ON THE LINE. THEY ALL HAD THICK GLASSES, ECZEMA
THE INSPECTORS ALL HAD COLDS, COUGHS, AND RED NOSES. THE AIR IN THE FACTORY HAD CLOUDS OF TALC FLOATING EVERYWHERE.
THE SMELL OF LATEX HIT YOU A BLOCK AWAY. WE HAD NO FANS. NO VENTILATION.

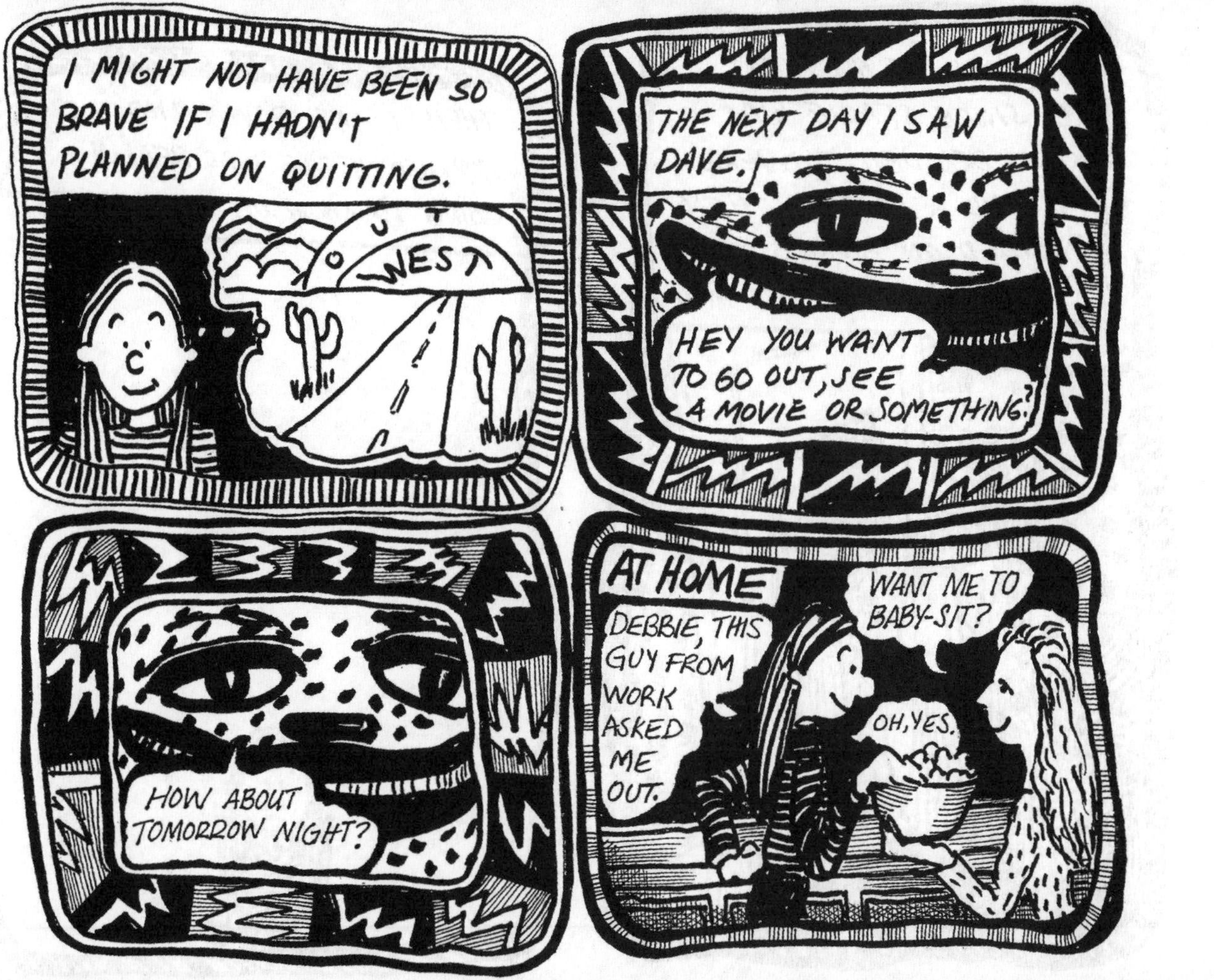
I MIGHT NOT HAVE BEEN SO BRAVE IF I HADN'T PLANNED ON QUITTING.
OUT WEST
THE NEXT DAY I SAW DAVE.
HEY YOU WANT TO GO OUT, SEE A MOVIE OR SOMETHING?
HOW ABOUT TOMORROW NIGHT?
AT HOME
DEBBIE, THIS GUY FROM WORK ASKED ME OUT.
WANT ME TO BABY-SIT?
OH, YES.

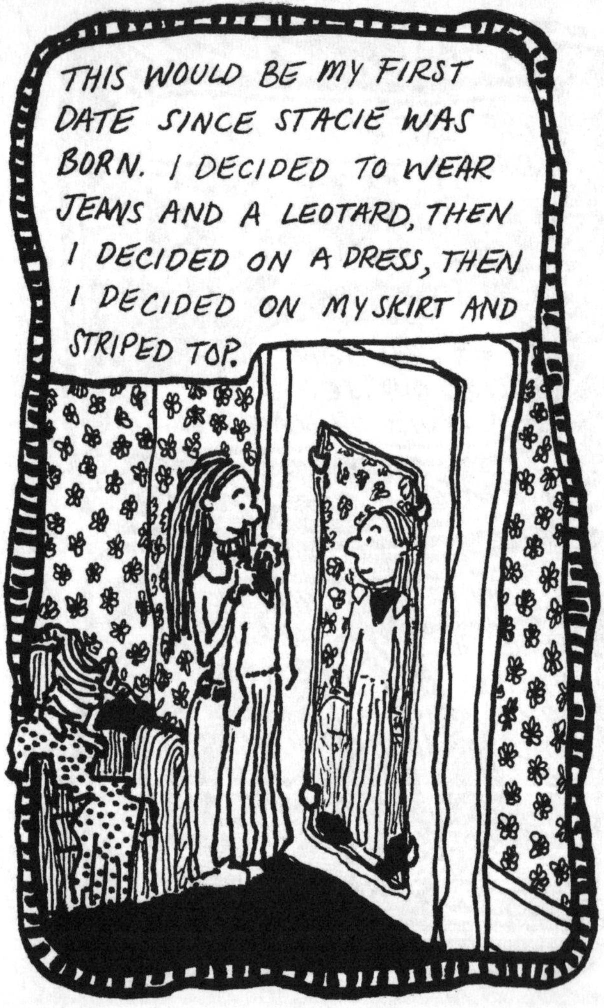
THIS WOULD BE MY FIRST DATE SINCE STACIE WAS BORN. I DECIDED TO WEAR JEANS AND A LEOTARD, THEN I DECIDED ON A DRESS, THEN I DECIDED ON MY SKIRT AND STRIPED TOP.
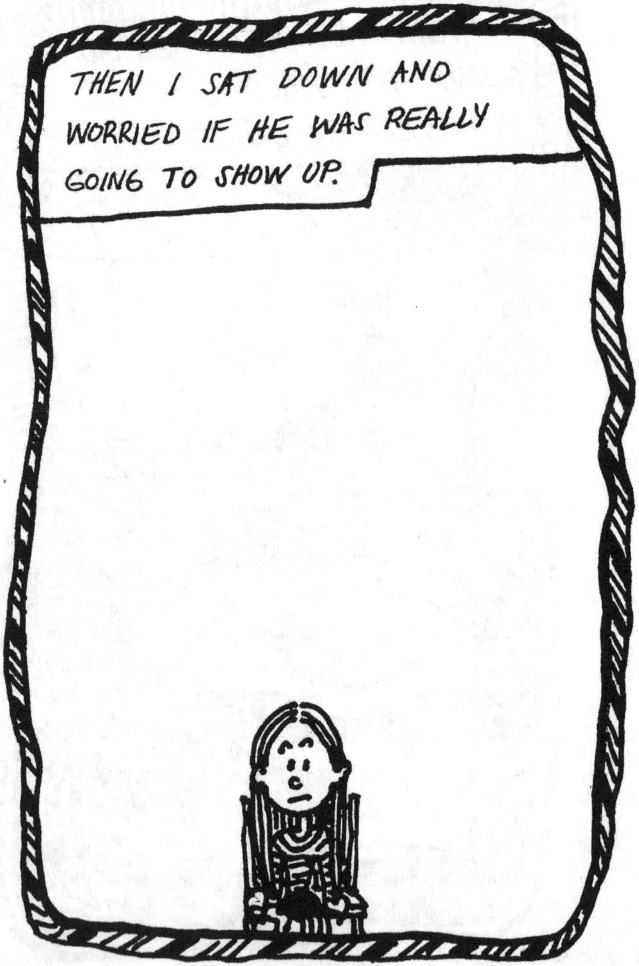
THEN I SAT DOWN AND WORRIED IF HE WAS REALLY GOING TO SHOW UP.

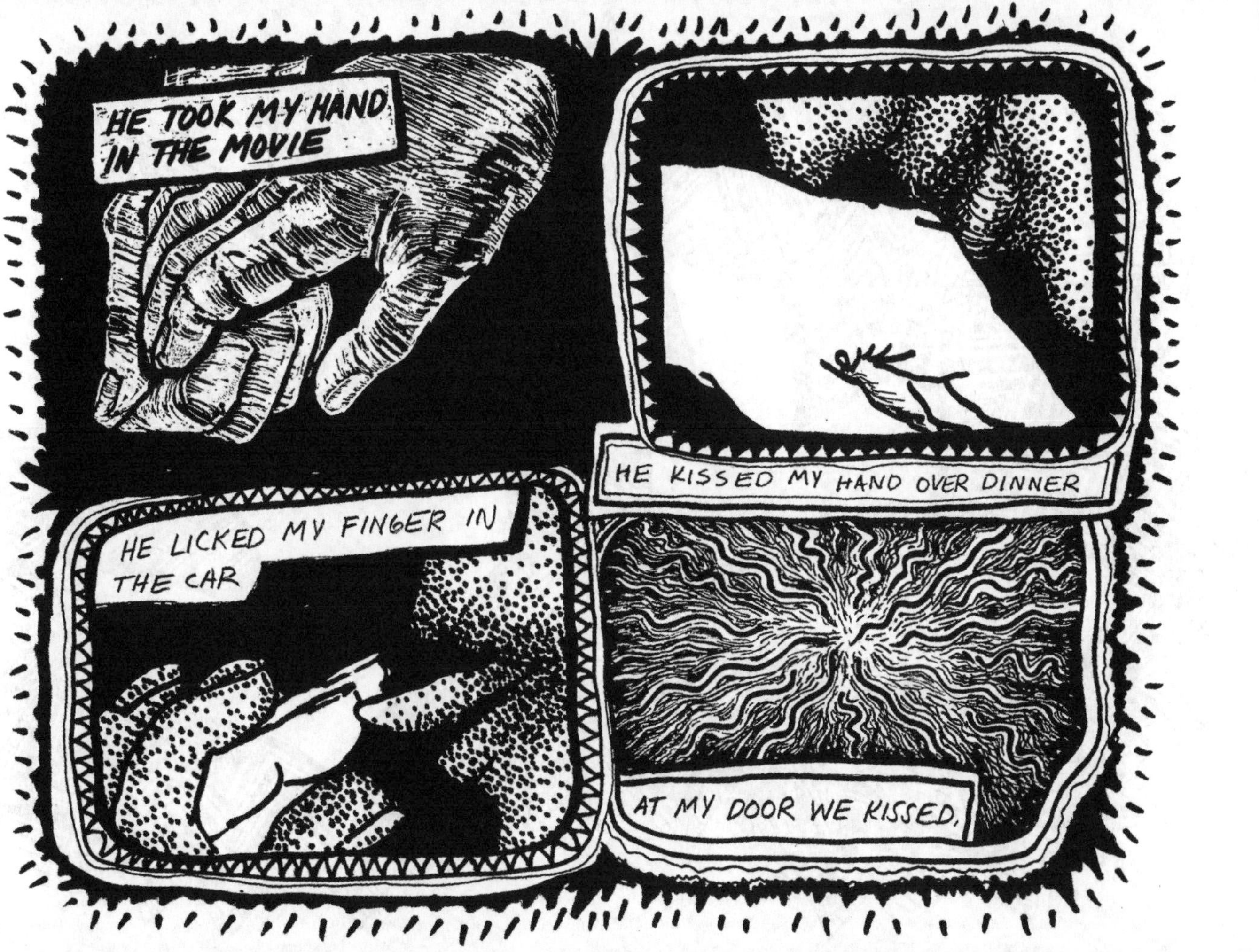
HE TOOK MY HAND IN THE MOVIE
HE KISSED MY HAND OVER DINNER
HE LICKED MY FINGER IN THE CAR
AT MY DOOR WE KISSED.

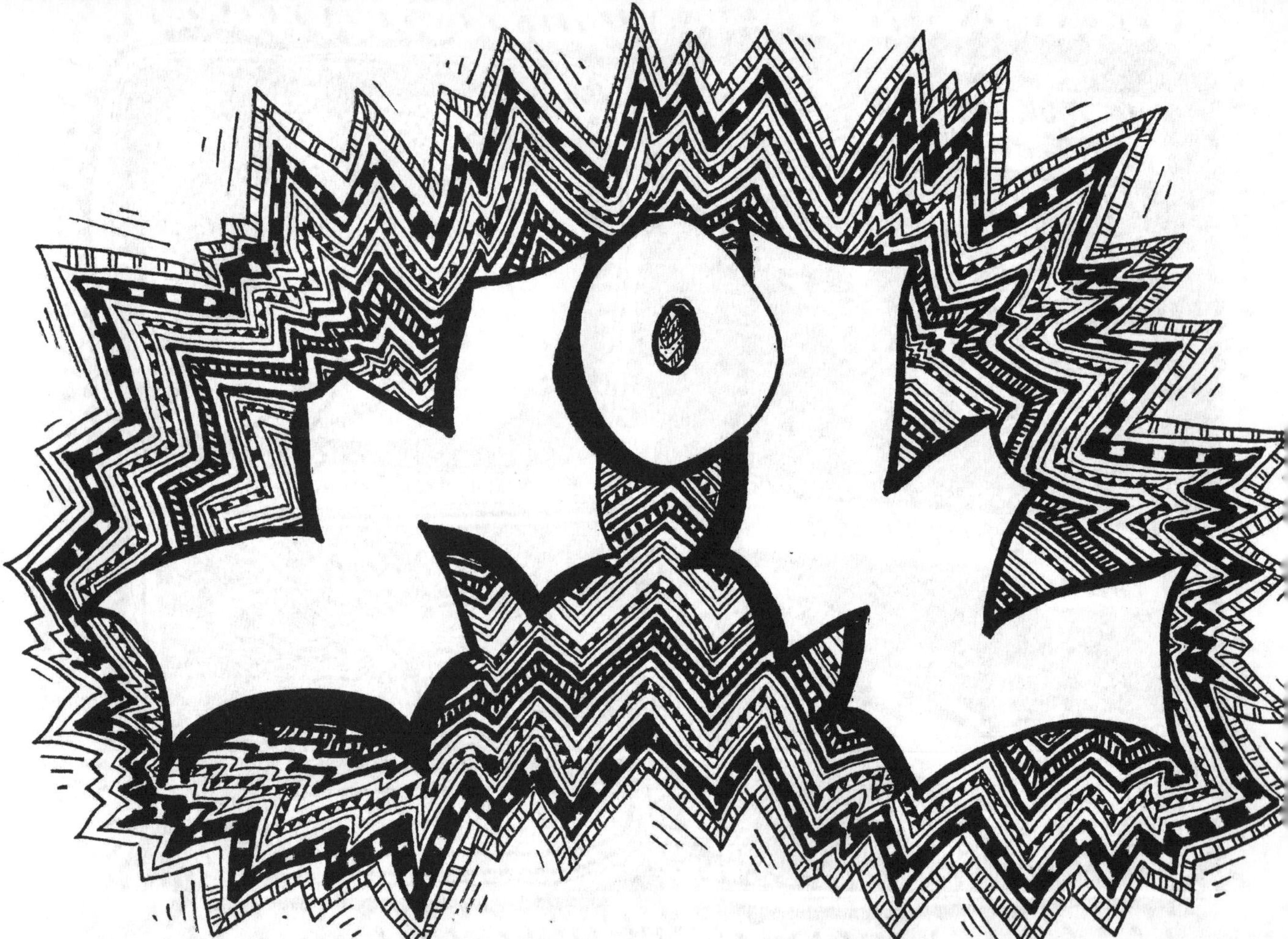

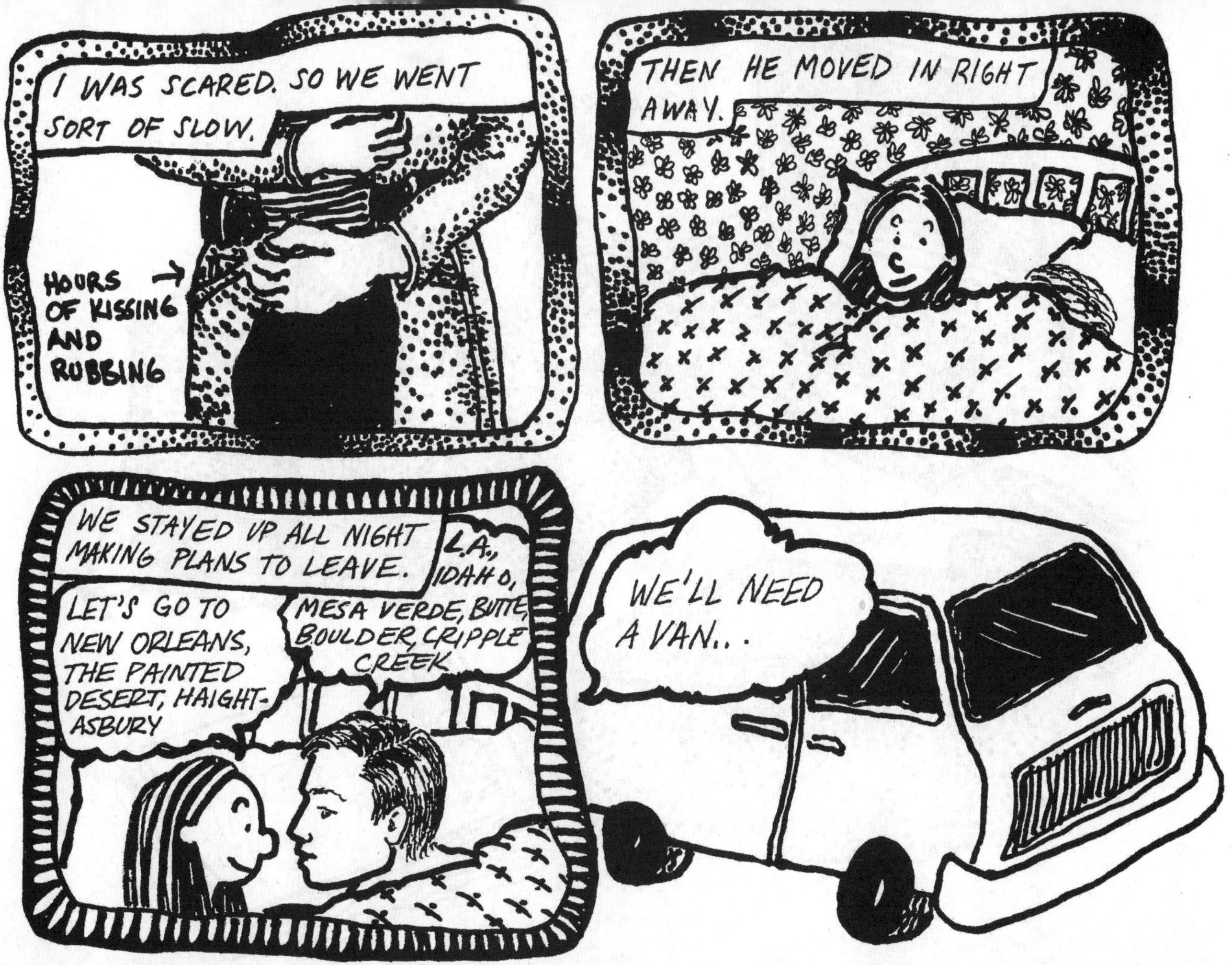
I WAS SCARED. SO WE WENT SORT OF SLOW.
HOURS OF KISSING AND RUBBING
THEN HE MOVED IN RIGHT AWAY.
WE STAYED UP ALL NIGHT MAKING PLANS TO LEAVE.
LET'S GO TO NEW ORLEANS, THE PAINTED DESERT, HAIGHT-ASBURY
MESA VERDE, BUTTE, BOULDER, CRIPPLE CREEK
L.A., IDAHO,
WE'LL NEED A VAN...

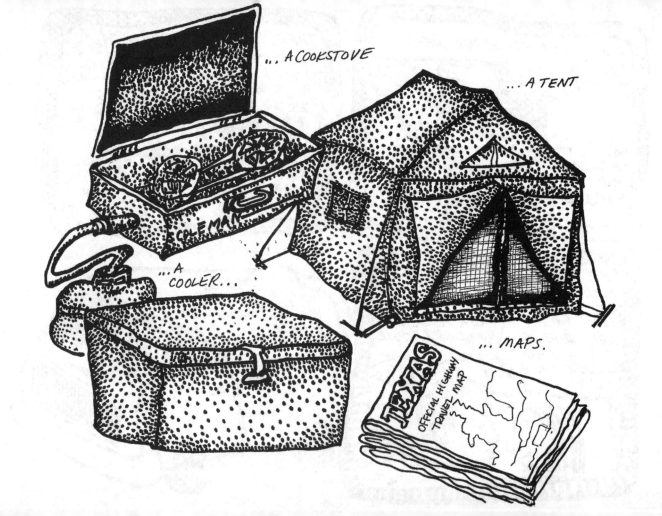

... A COOKSTOVE

... A TENT

...A
...COOLER...

COLEMAN

... MAPS.

TEXAS
OFFICIAL HIGHWAY
TRAVEL MAP

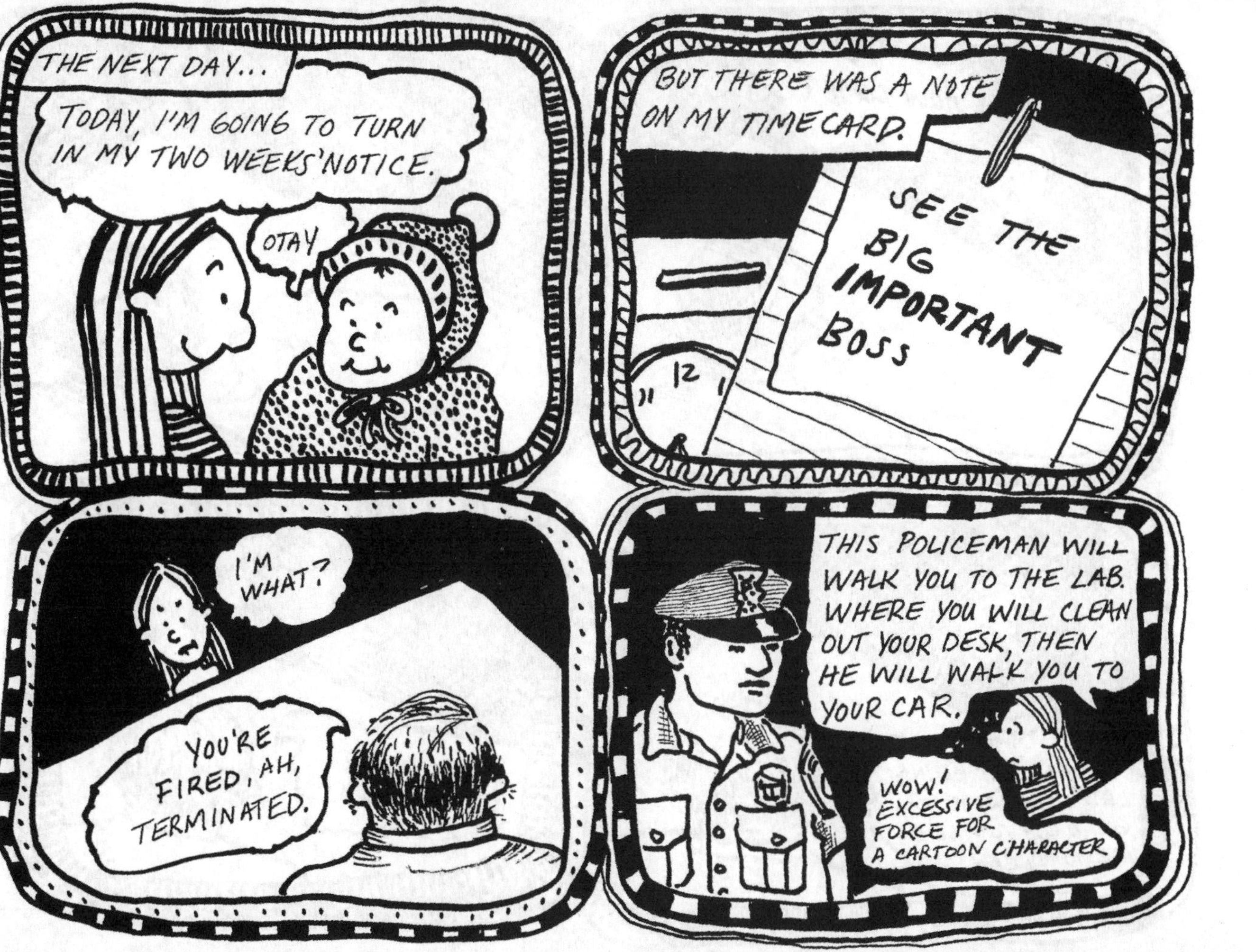
THE NEXT DAY...
TODAY, I'M GOING TO TURN IN MY TWO WEEKS' NOTICE.
OTAY
BUT THERE WAS A NOTE ON MY TIMECARD.
SEE THE BIG IMPORTANT BOSS
12
I'M WHAT?
YOU'RE FIRED, AH, TERMINATED.
THIS POLICEMAN WILL WALK YOU TO THE LAB. WHERE YOU WILL CLEAN OUT YOUR DESK, THEN HE WILL WALK YOU TO YOUR CAR.
WOW! EXCESSIVE FORCE FOR A CARTOON CHARACTER

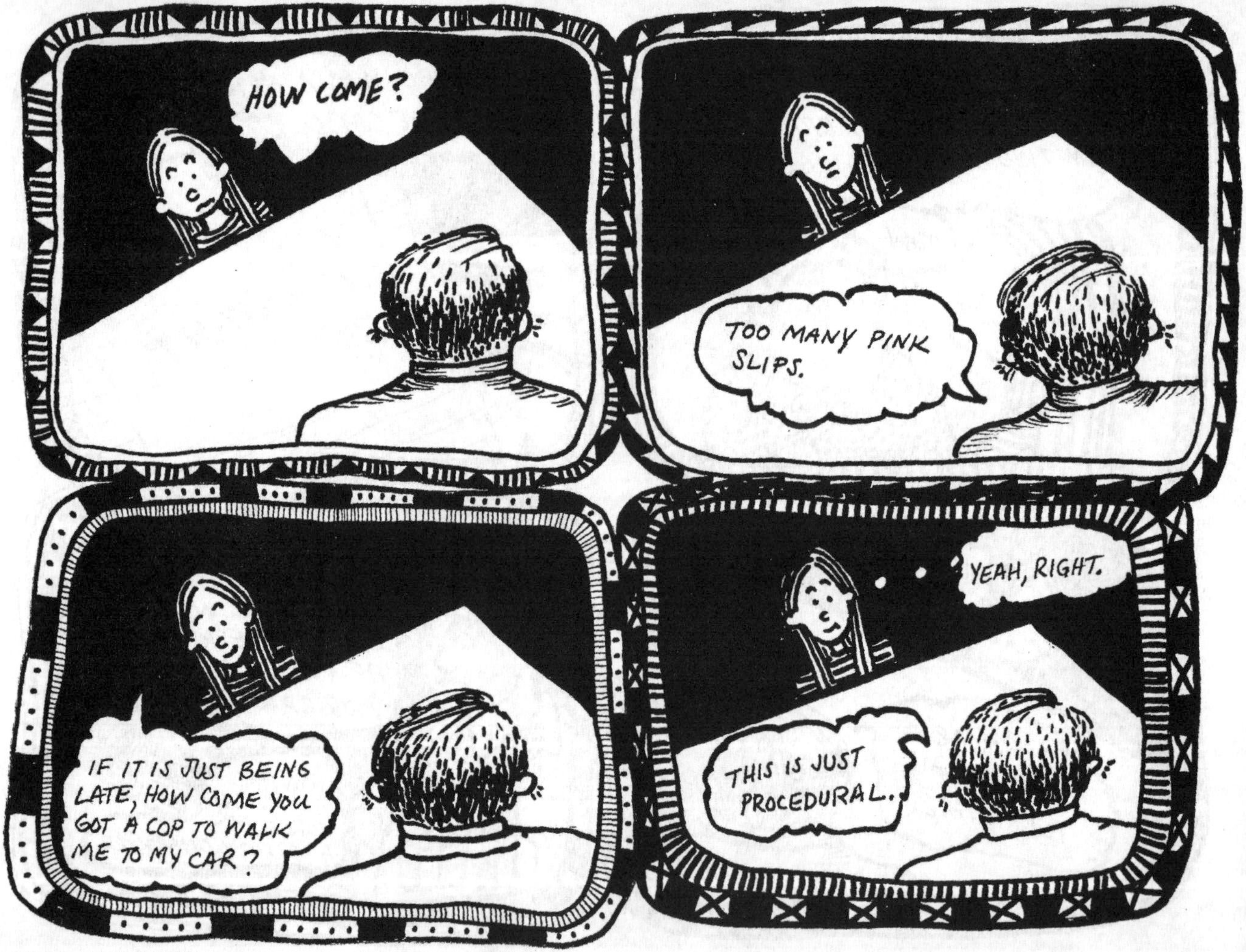
HOW COME?
TOO MANY PINK SLIPS.
IF IT IS JUST BEING LATE, HOW COME YOU GOT A COP TO WALK ME TO MY CAR?
YEAH, RIGHT.
THIS IS JUST PROCEDURAL.

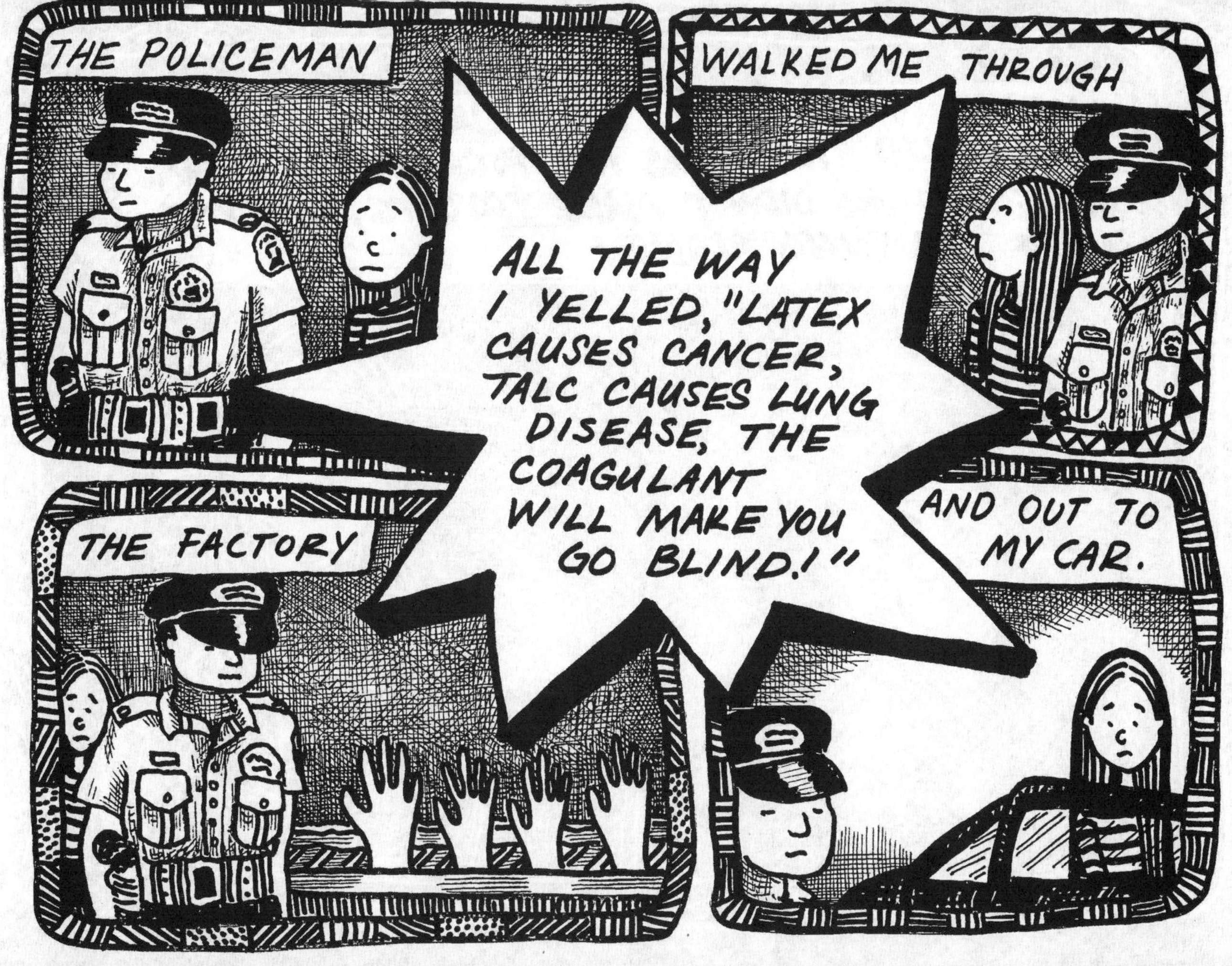
THE POLICEMAN
WALKED ME THROUGH
THE FACTORY
AND OUT TO MY CAR.
ALL THE WAY I YELLED, "LATEX CAUSES CANCER, TALC CAUSES LUNG DISEASE, THE COAGULANT WILL MAKE YOU GO BLIND!"

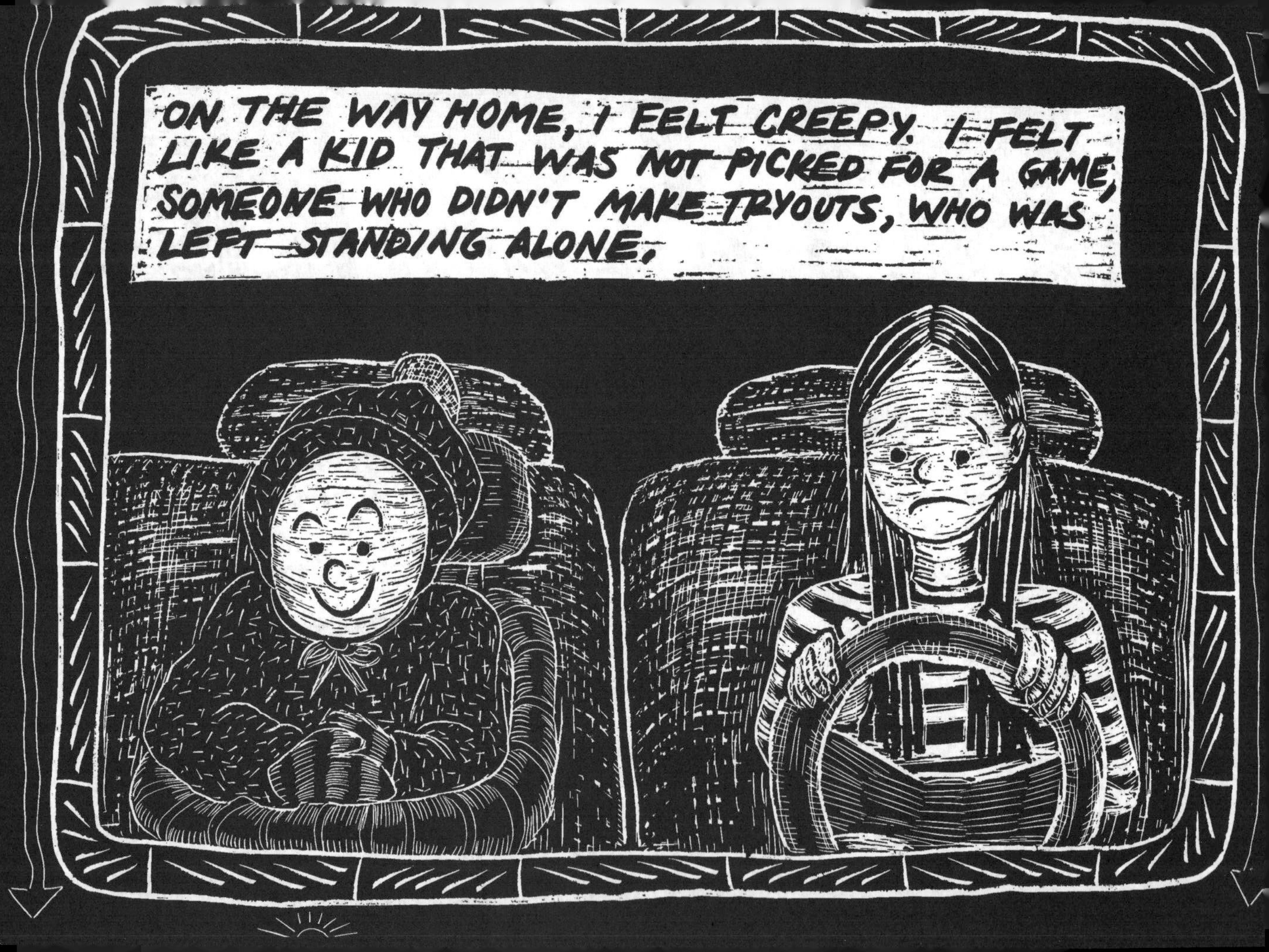
ON THE WAY HOME, I FELT CREEPY. I FELT LIKE A KID THAT WAS NOT PICKED FOR A GAME, SOMEONE WHO DIDN'T MAKE TRYOUTS, WHO WAS LEFT STANDING ALONE.

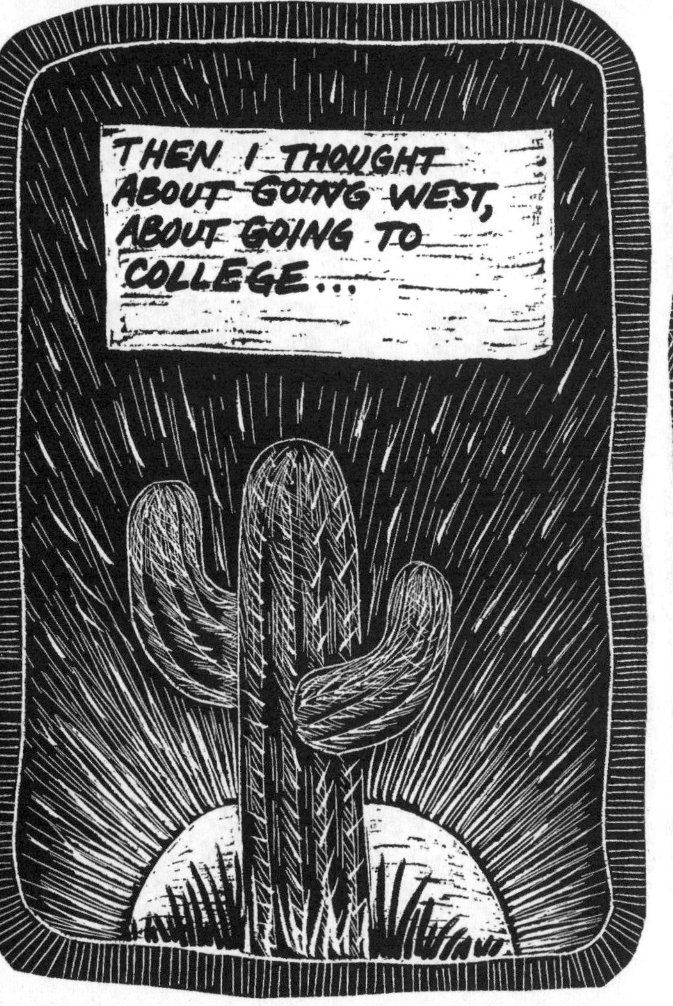
THEN I THOUGHT ABOUT GOING WEST, ABOUT GOING TO COLLEGE...

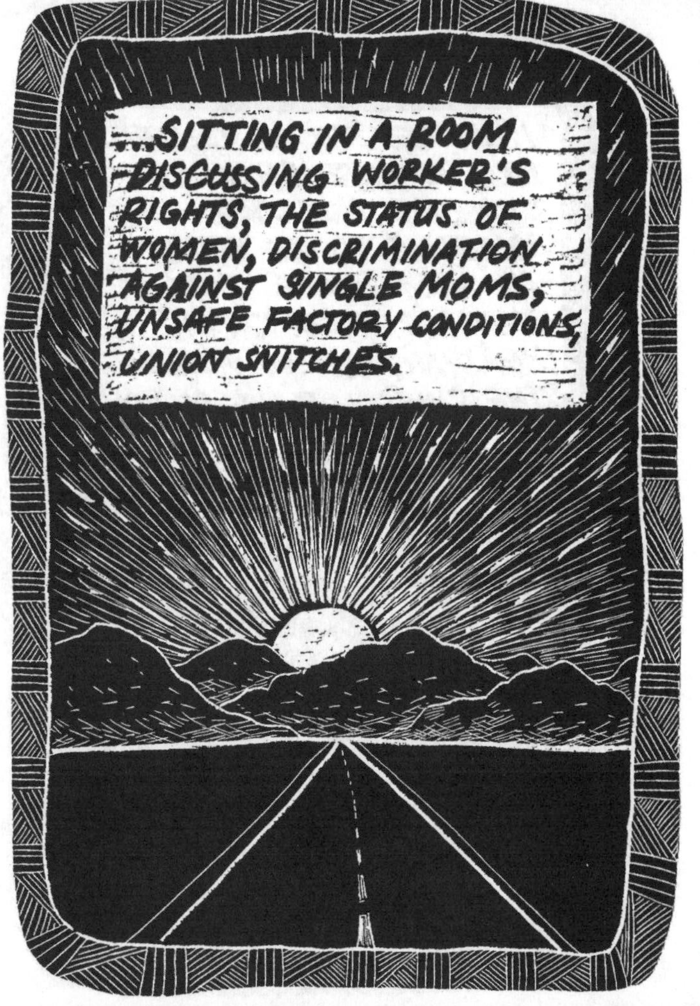
...SITTING IN A ROOM DISCUSSING WORKER'S RIGHTS, THE STATUS OF WOMEN, DISCRIMINATION AGAINST SINGLE MOMS, UNSAFE FACTORY CONDITIONS, UNION SNITCHES.

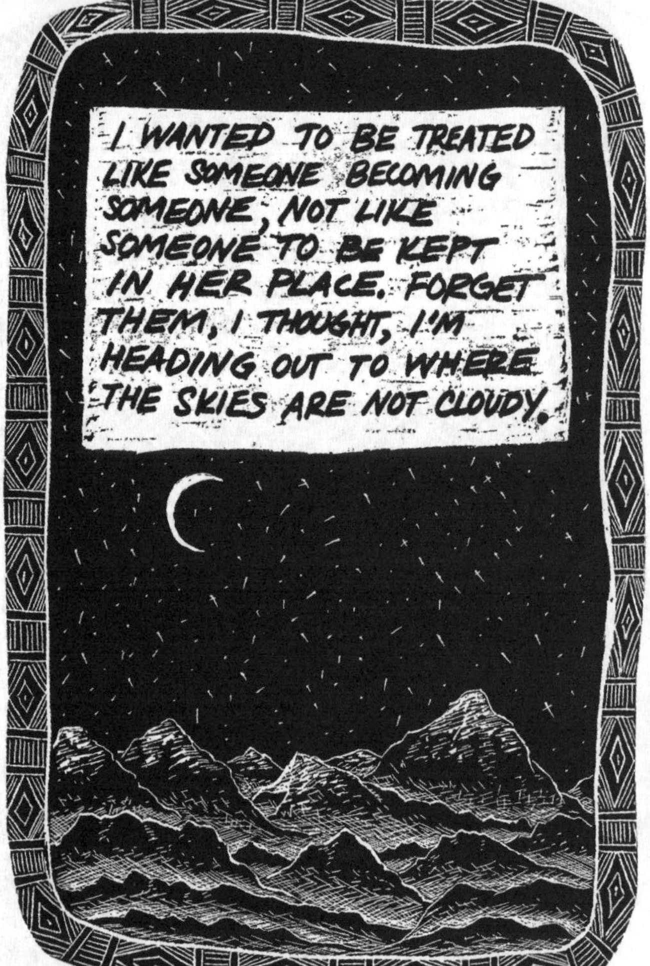
I WANTED TO BE TREATED LIKE SOMEONE BECOMING SOMEONE, NOT LIKE SOMEONE TO BE KEPT IN HER PLACE. FORGET THEM, I THOUGHT, I'M HEADING OUT TO WHERE THE SKIES ARE NOT CLOUDY.

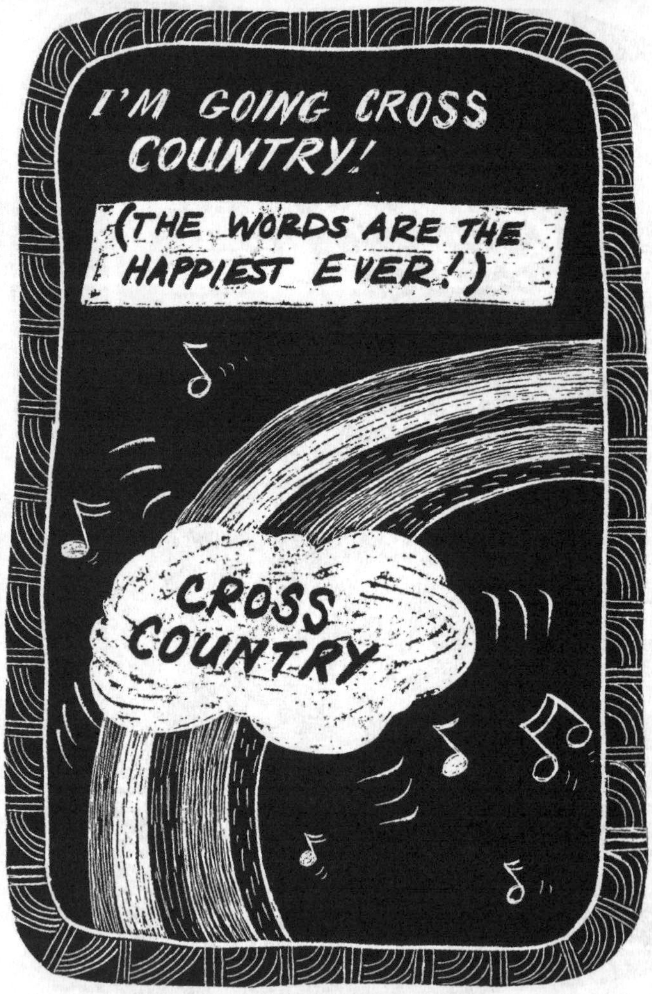
I'M GOING CROSS COUNTRY!
(THE WORDS ARE THE HAPPIEST EVER!)
CROSS COUNTRY

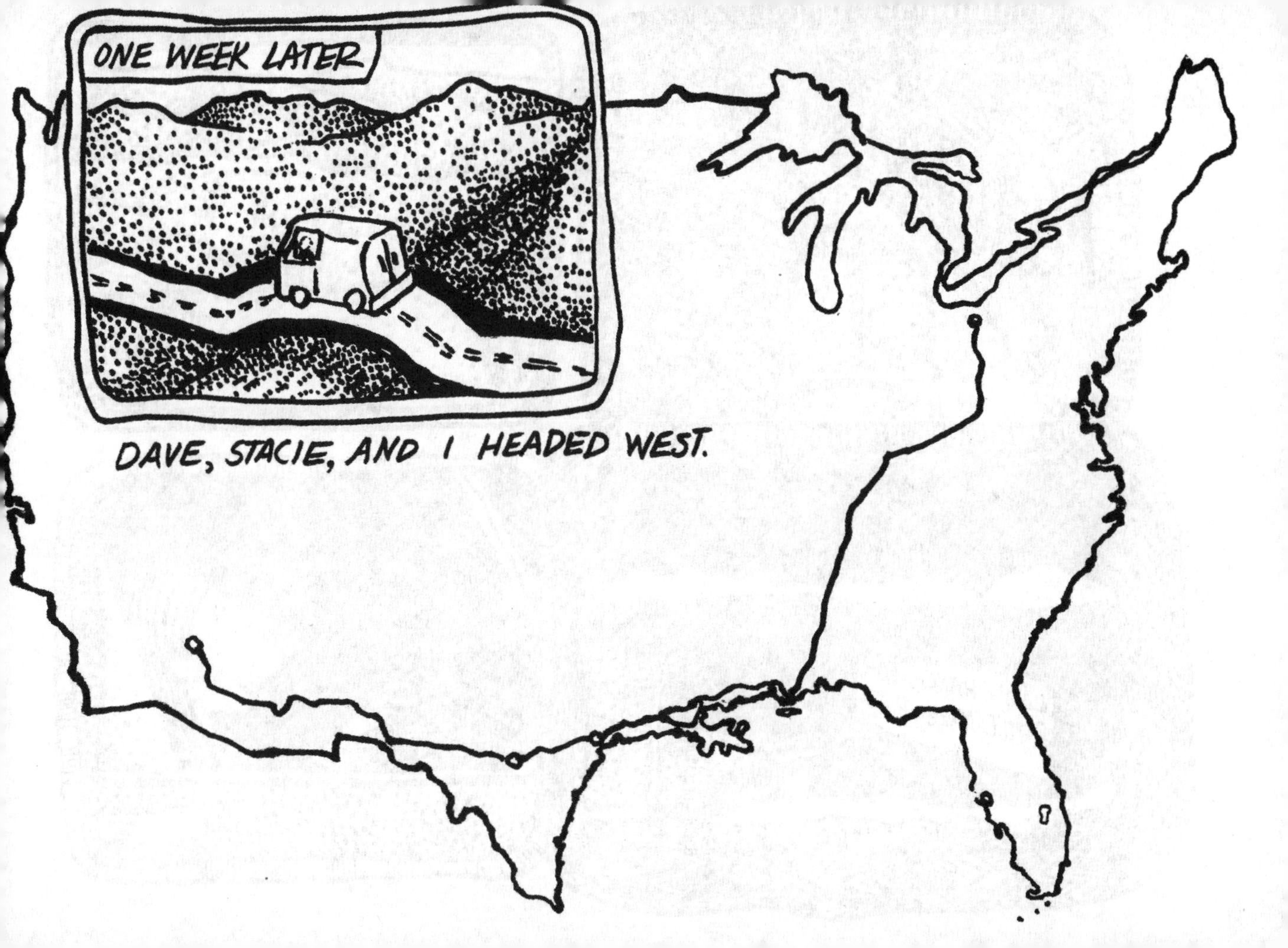
ONE WEEK LATER
DAVE, STACIE, AND I HEADED WEST.

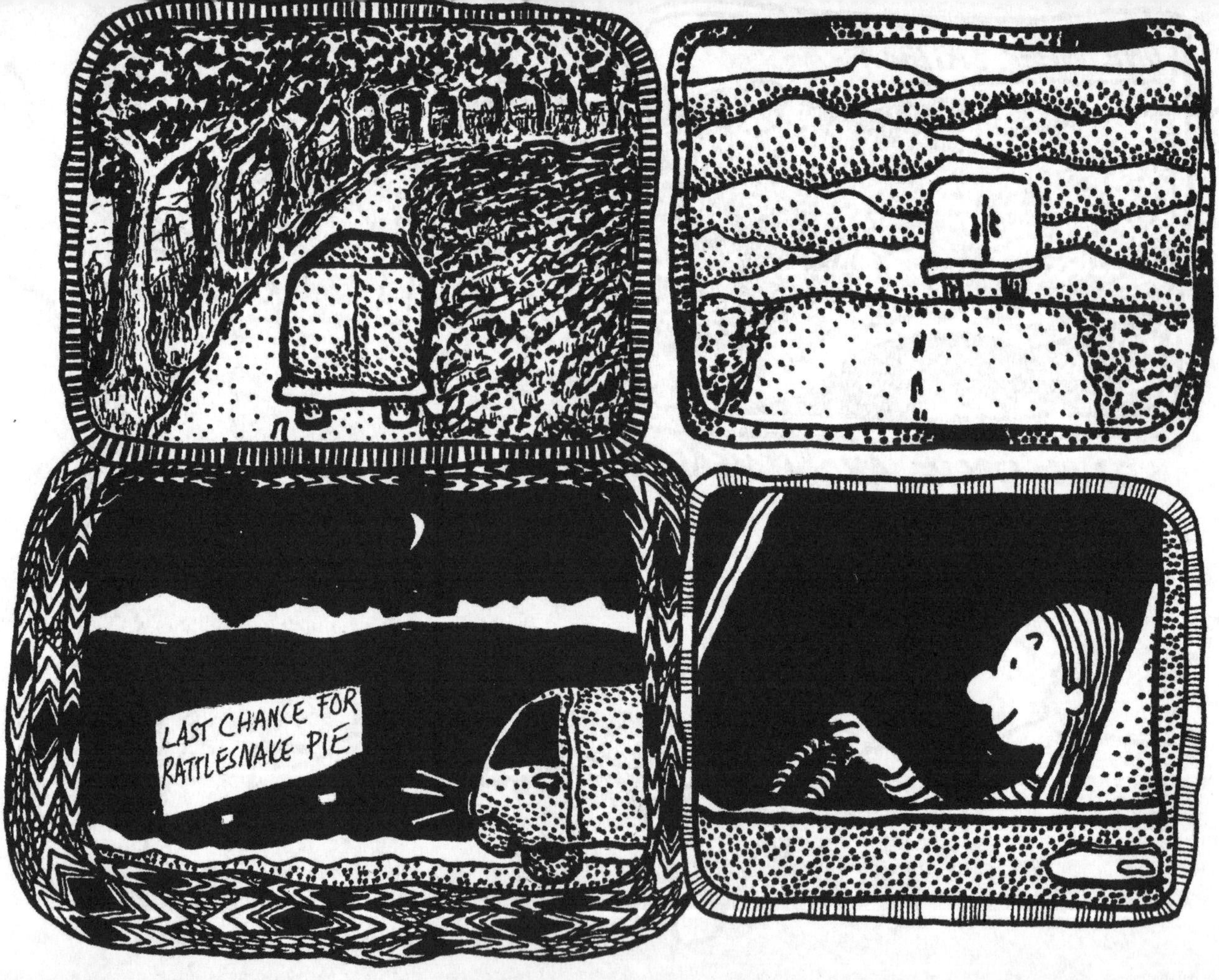
LAST CHANCE FOR
RATTLESNAKE PIE

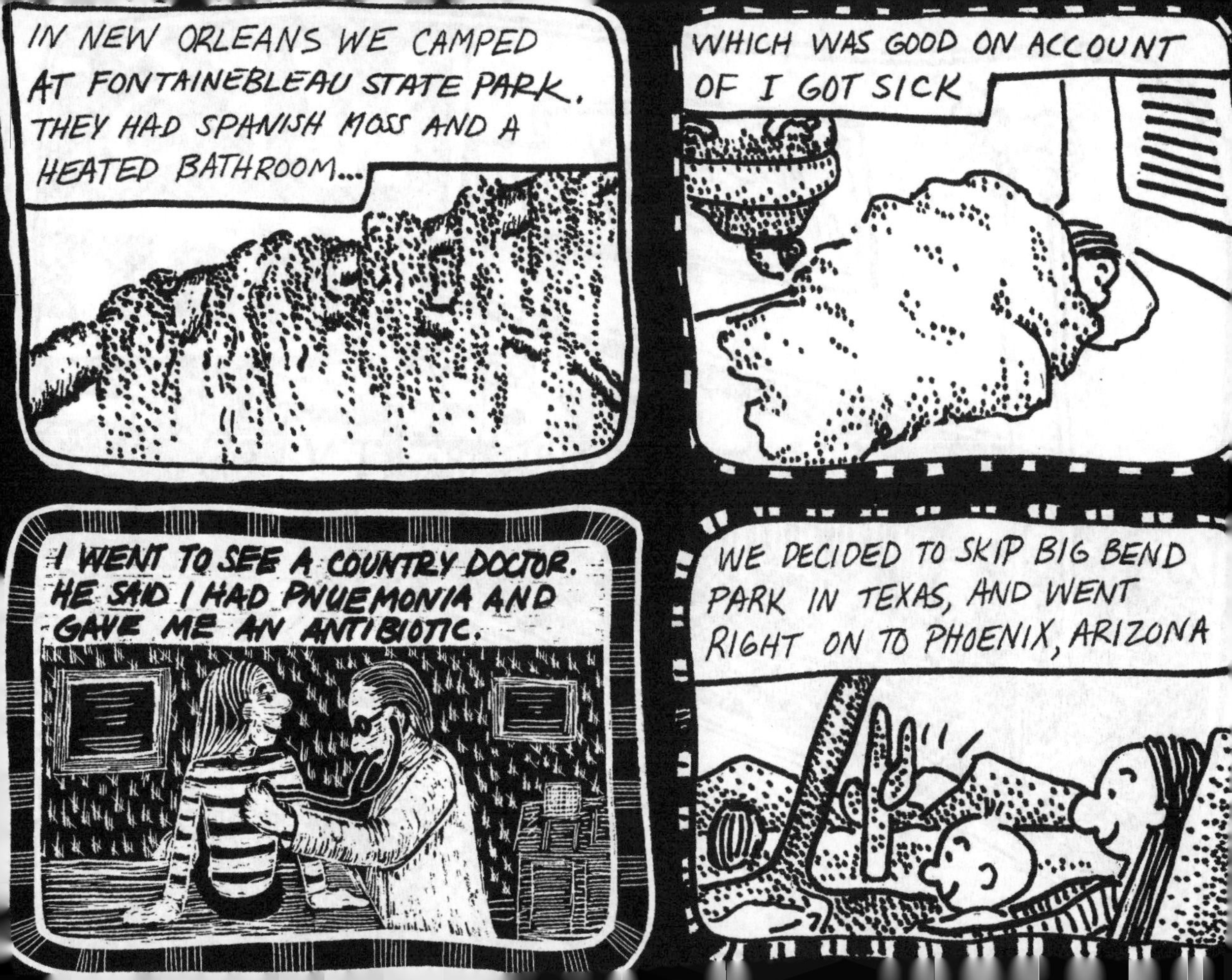
IN NEW ORLEANS WE CAMPED AT FONTAINEBLEAU STATE PARK. THEY HAD SPANISH MOSS AND A HEATED BATHROOM...
WHICH WAS GOOD ON ACCOUNT OF I GOT SICK
I WENT TO SEE A COUNTRY DOCTOR. HE SAID I HAD PNUEMONIA AND GAVE ME AN ANTIBIOTIC.
WE DECIDED TO SKIP BIG BEND PARK IN TEXAS, AND WENT RIGHT ON TO PHOENIX, ARIZONA

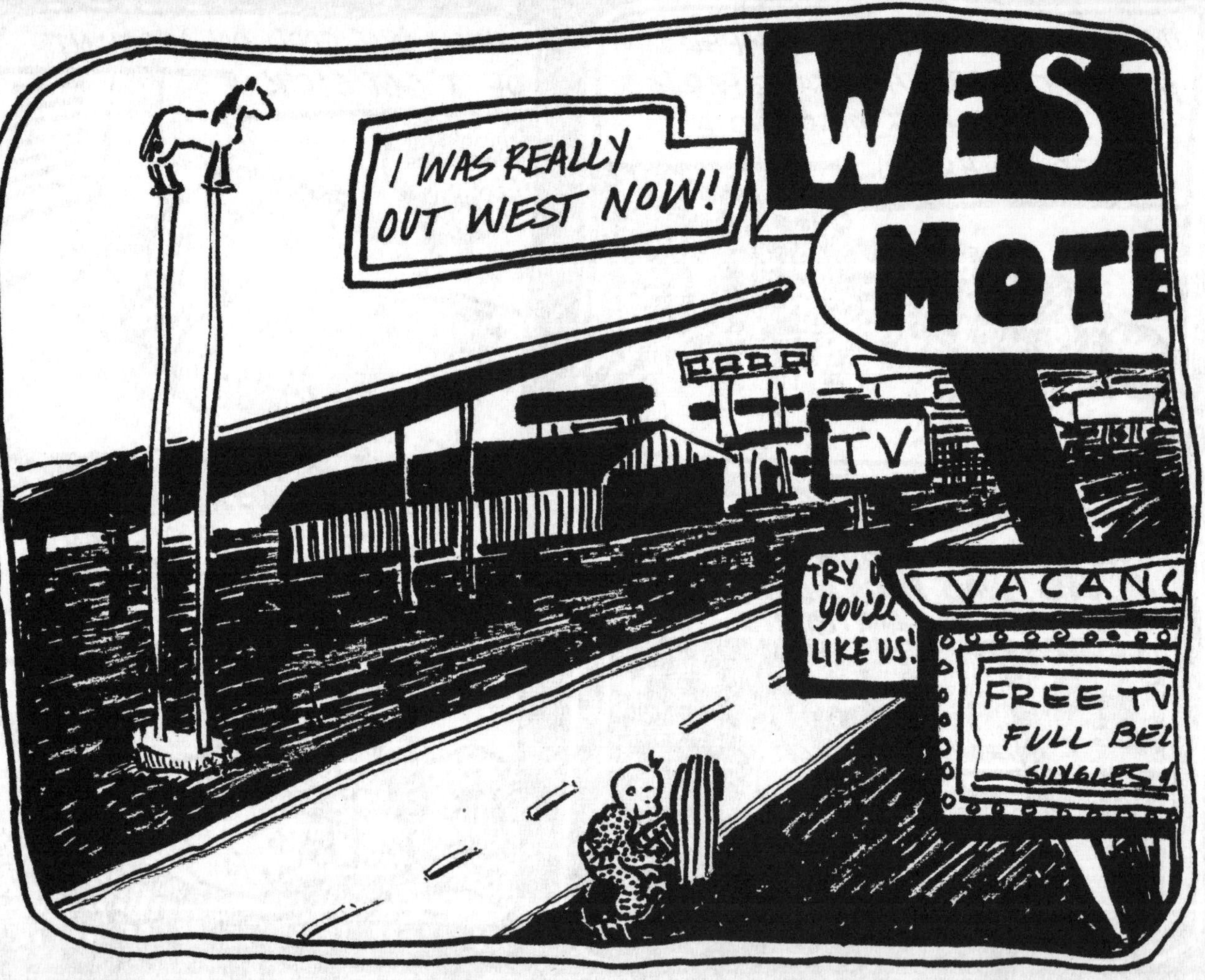
I WAS REALLY OUT WEST NOW!
WEST
MOTE
TV
TRY
you'll
LIKE US!
VACANC
FREE TV
FULL BE

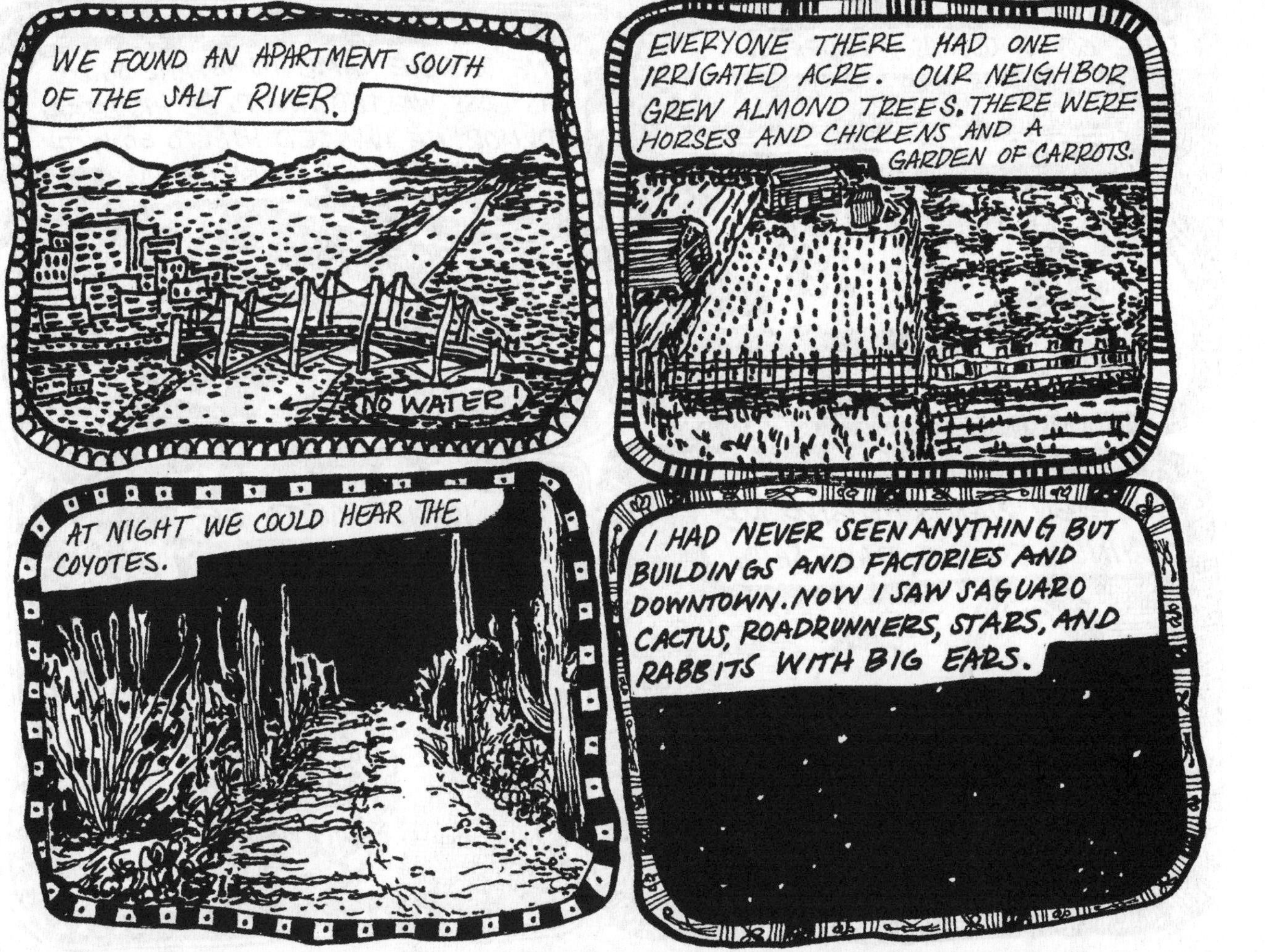
WE FOUND AN APARTMENT SOUTH OF THE SALT RIVER.
NO WATER!
EVERYONE THERE HAD ONE IRRIGATED ACRE. OUR NEIGHBOR GREW ALMOND TREES. THERE WERE HORSES AND CHICKENS AND A GARDEN OF CARROTS.
AT NIGHT WE COULD HEAR THE COYOTES.
I HAD NEVER SEEN ANYTHING BUT BUILDINGS AND FACTORIES AND DOWNTOWN. NOW I SAW SAGUARO CACTUS, ROADRUNNERS, STARS, AND RABBITS WITH BIG EARS.

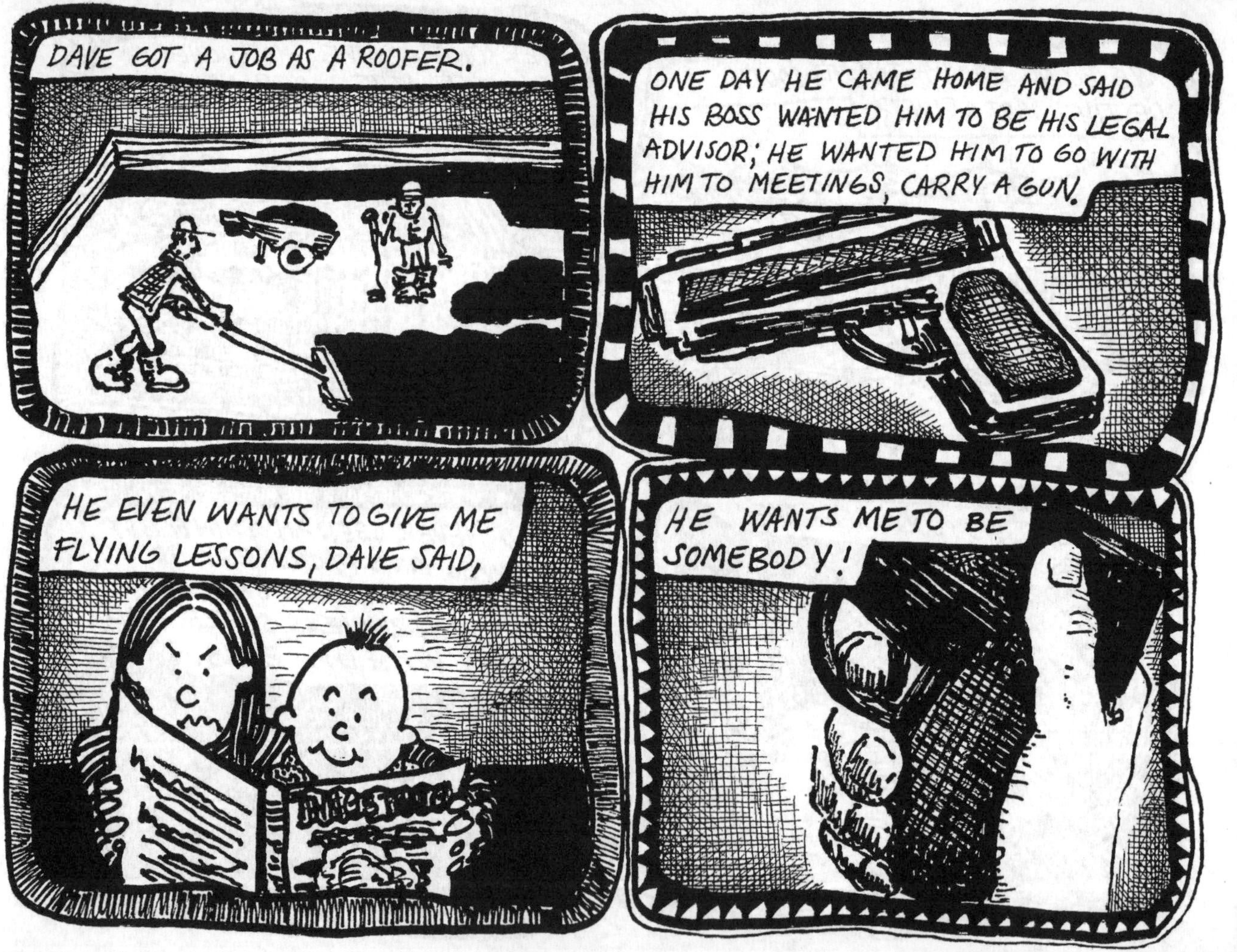
DAVE GOT A JOB AS A ROOFER.
ONE DAY HE CAME HOME AND SAID HIS BOSS WANTED HIM TO BE HIS LEGAL ADVISOR; HE WANTED HIM TO GO WITH HIM TO MEETINGS, CARRY A GUN.
HE EVEN WANTS TO GIVE ME FLYING LESSONS, DAVE SAID,
HE WANTS ME TO BE SOMEBODY!

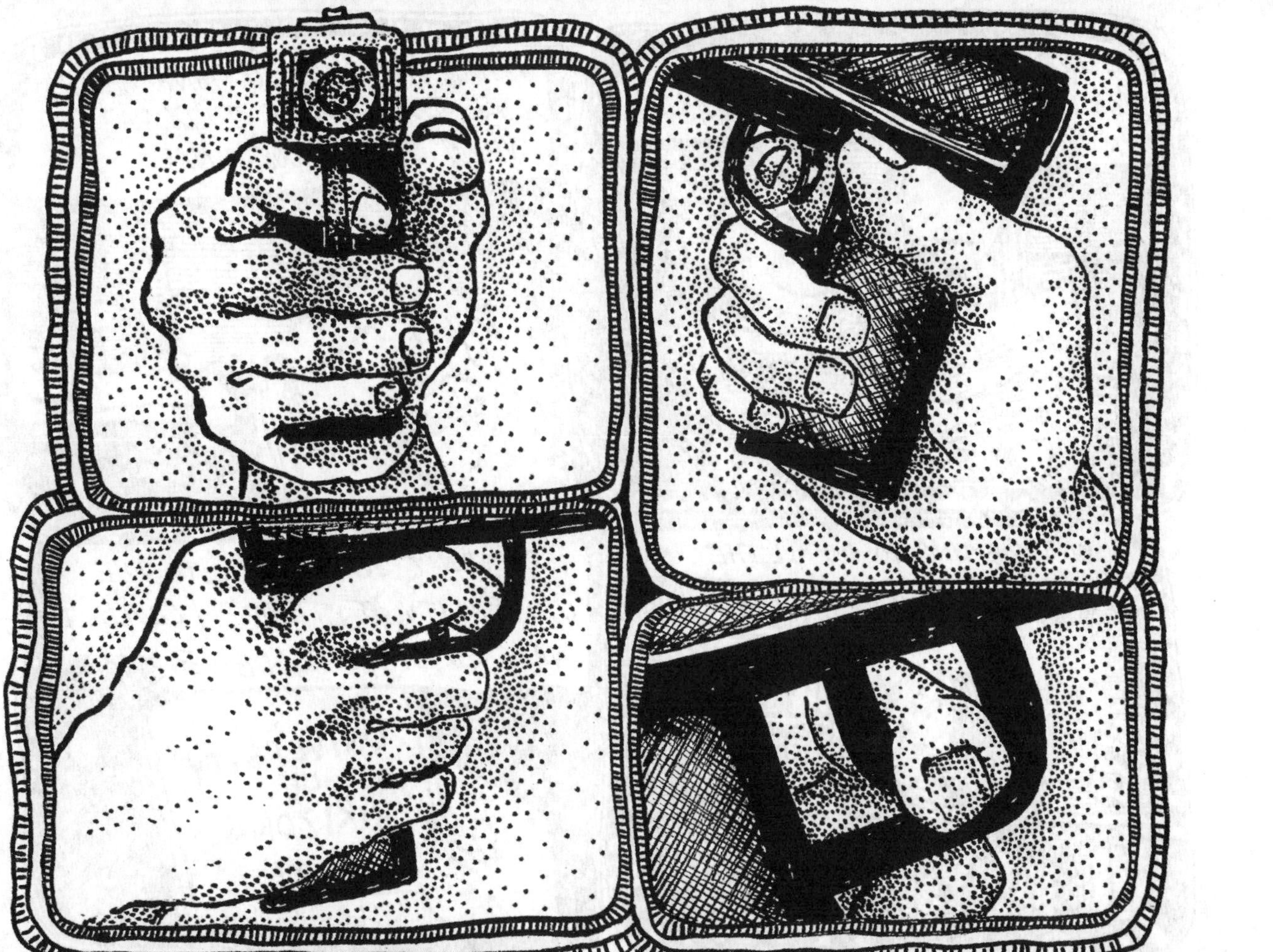

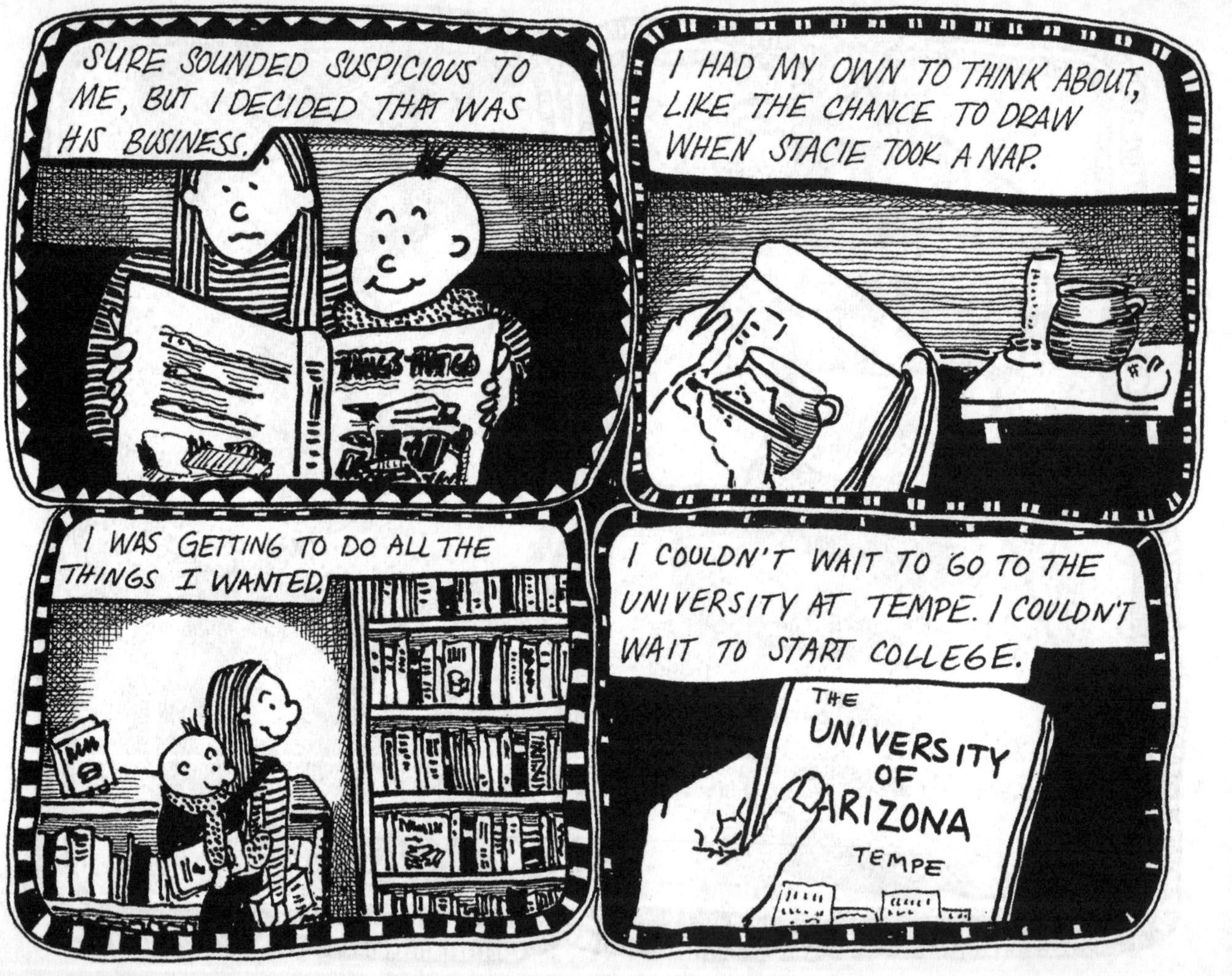
SURE SOUNDED SUSPICIOUS TO ME, BUT I DECIDED THAT WAS HIS BUSINESS.
I HAD MY OWN TO THINK ABOUT, LIKE THE CHANCE TO DRAW WHEN STACIE TOOK A NAP.
I WAS GETTING TO DO ALL THE THINGS I WANTED.
I COULDN'T WAIT TO GO TO THE UNIVERSITY AT TEMPE. I COULDN'T WAIT TO START COLLEGE.
THE UNIVERSITY OF ARIZONA
TEMPE

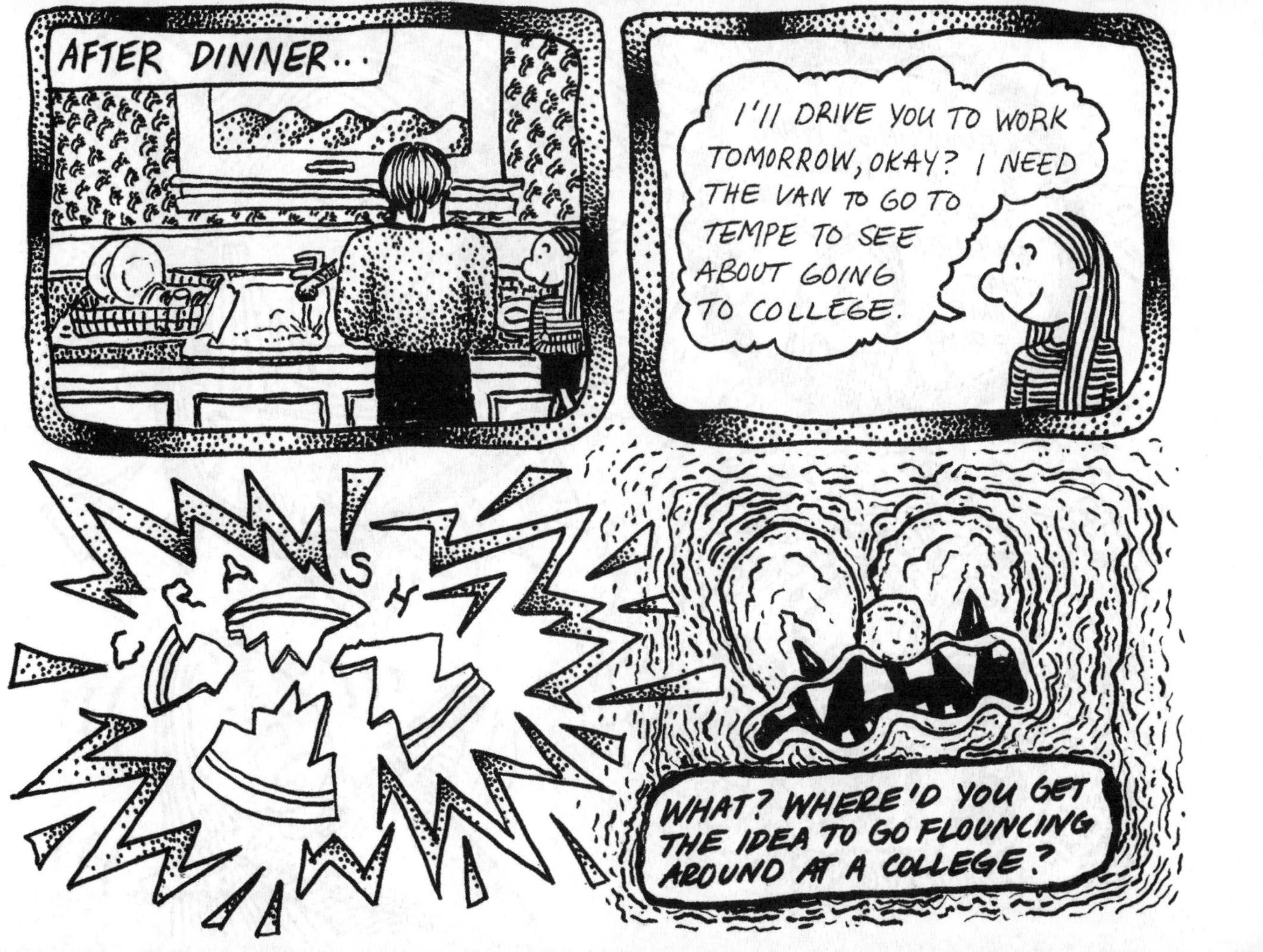
AFTER DINNER...
I'LL DRIVE YOU TO WORK TOMORROW, OKAY? I NEED THE VAN TO GO TO TEMPE TO SEE ABOUT GOING TO COLLEGE.
CRASH
WHAT? WHERE'D YOU GET THE IDEA TO GO FLOUNCING AROUND AT A COLLEGE?

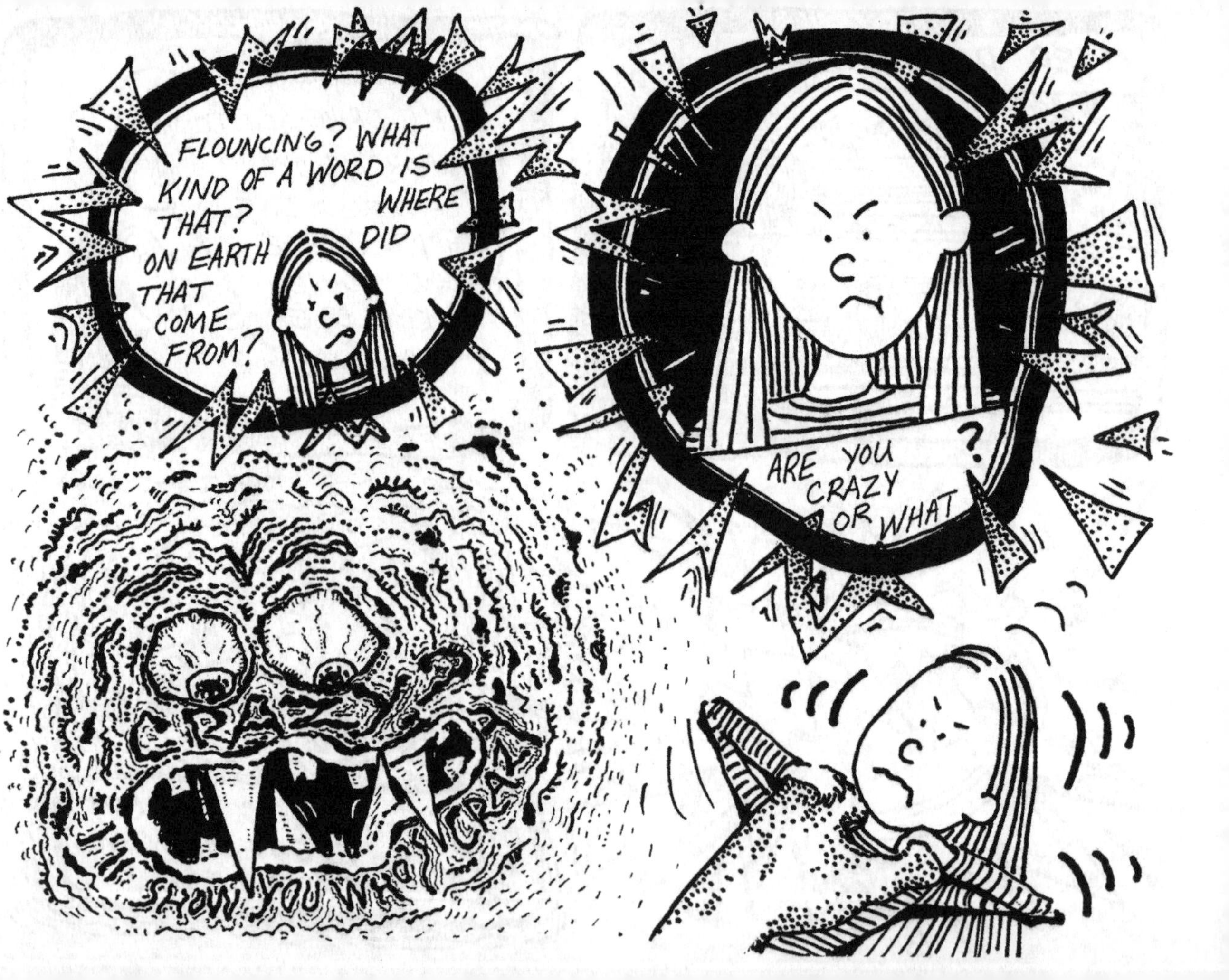
FLOUNCING? WHAT KIND OF A WORD IS THAT? WHERE ON EARTH DID THAT COME FROM?
ARE YOU CRAZY OR WHAT?
I'LL SHOW YOU WHO'S CRAZY

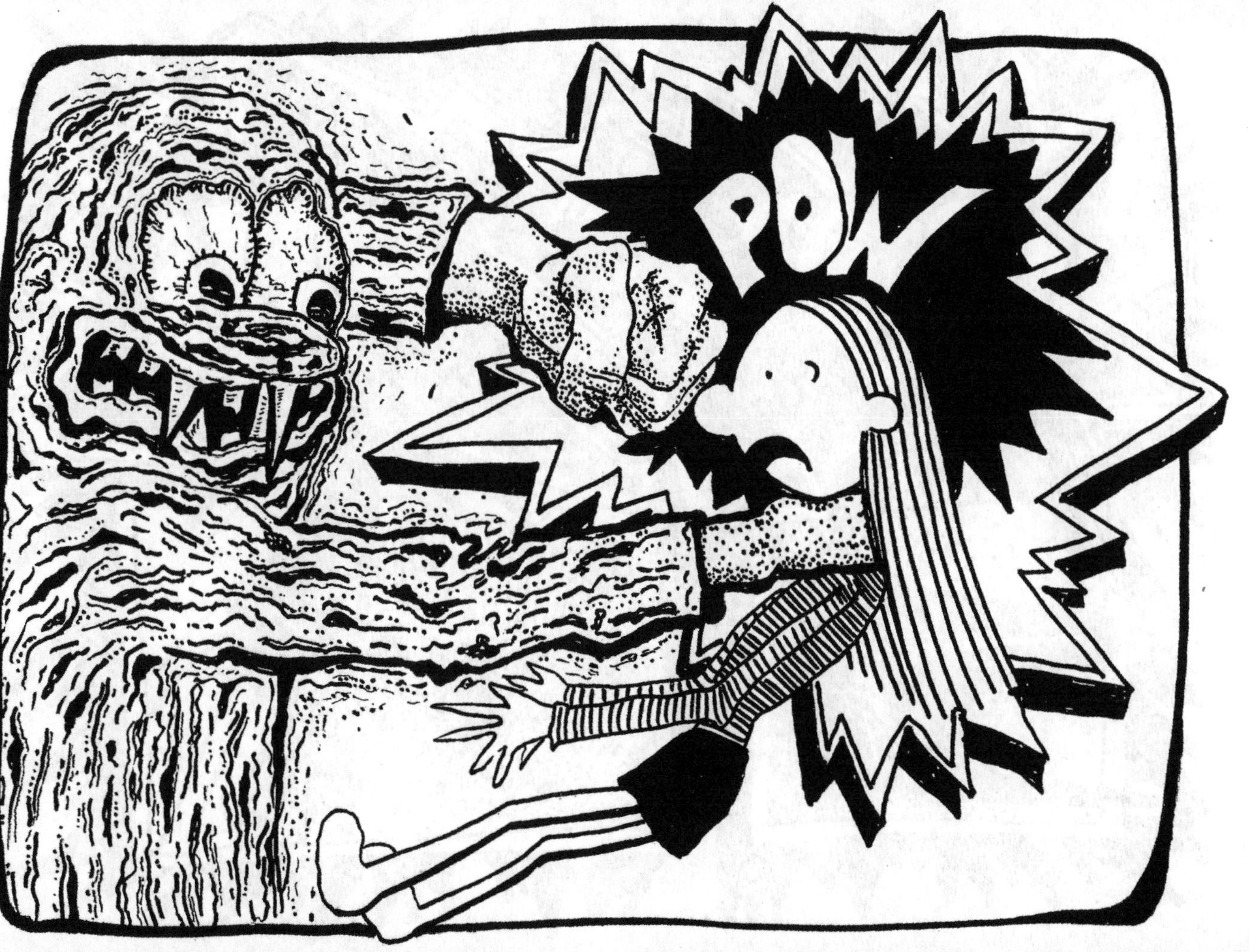
POW

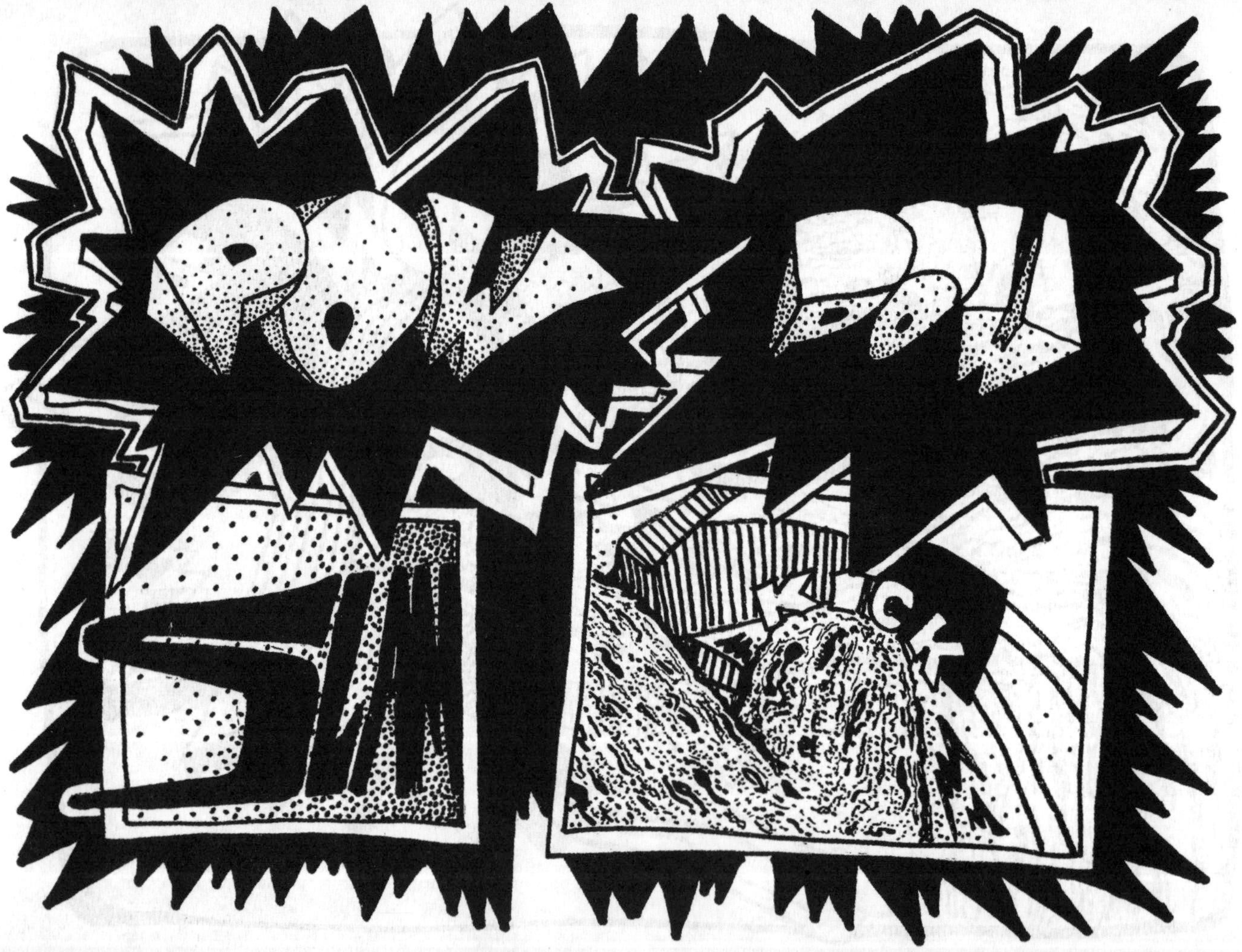
POW

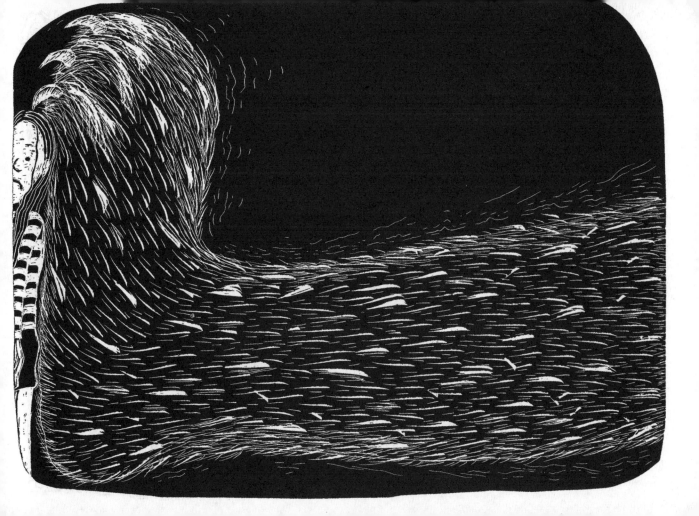

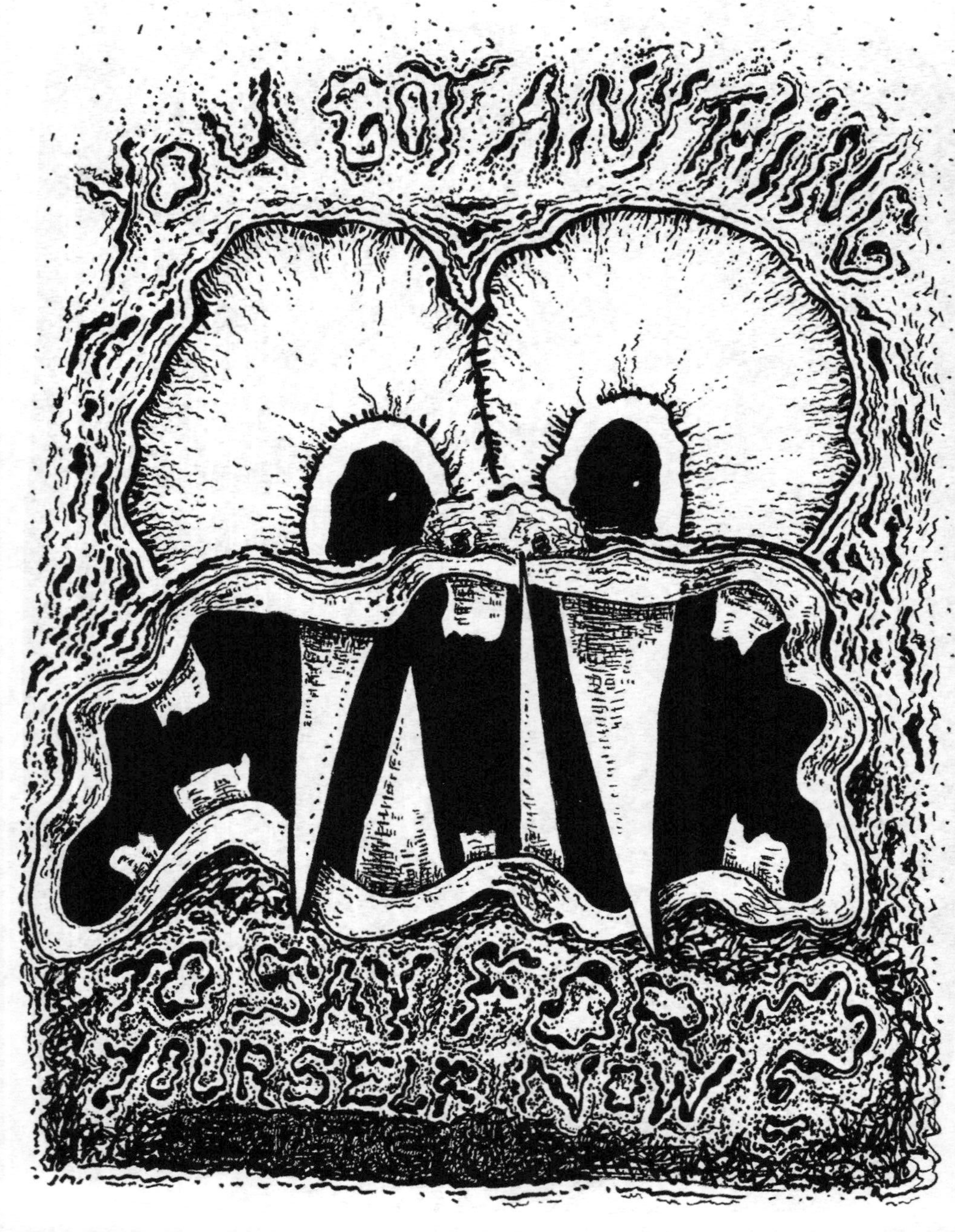
YOU GOT ANYTHING
TO SAY FOR
YOURSELF NOW

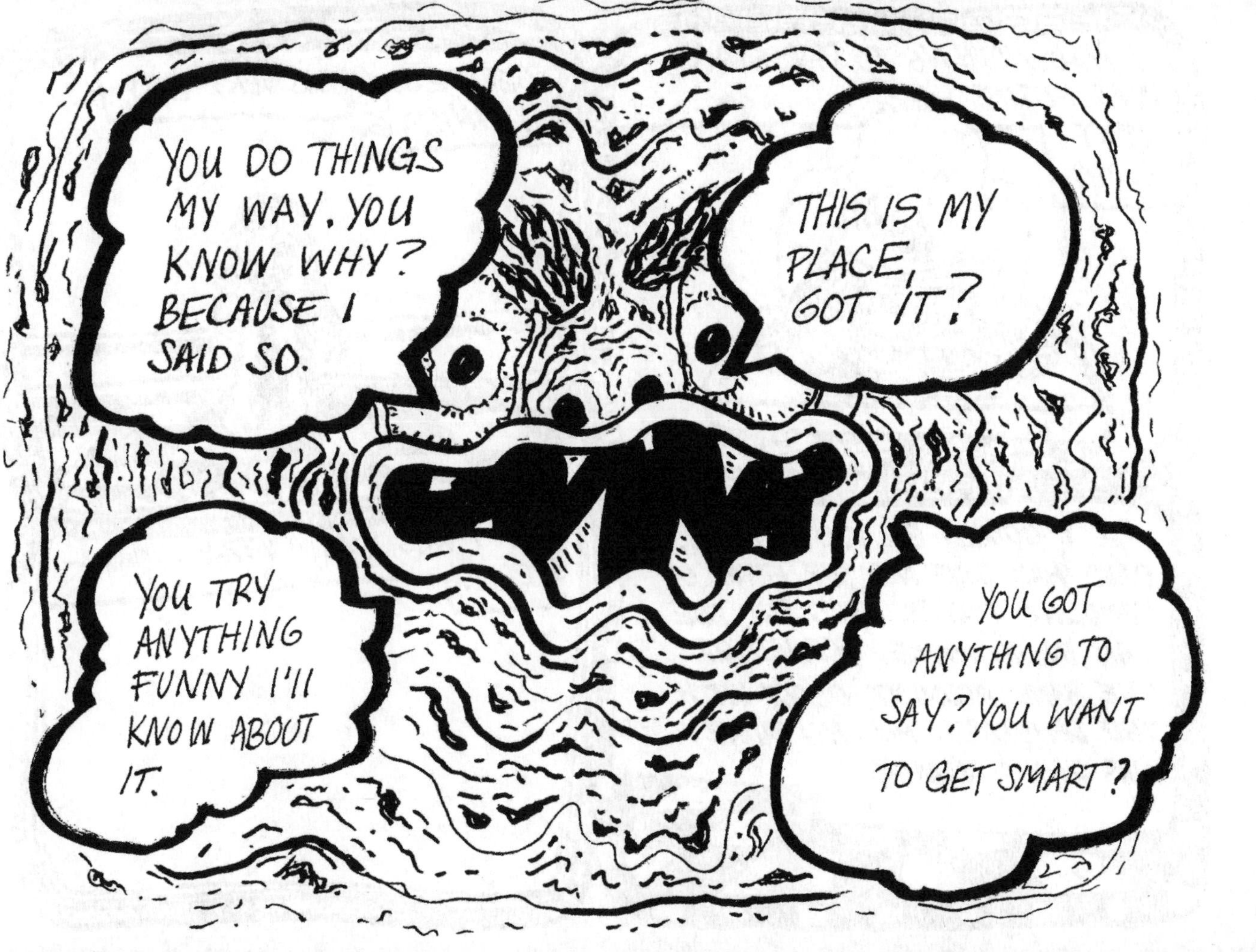
YOU DO THINGS MY WAY. YOU KNOW WHY? BECAUSE I SAID SO.
THIS IS MY PLACE, GOT IT?
YOU TRY ANYTHING FUNNY I'll KNOW ABOUT IT.
YOU GOT ANYTHING TO SAY? YOU WANT TO GET SMART?

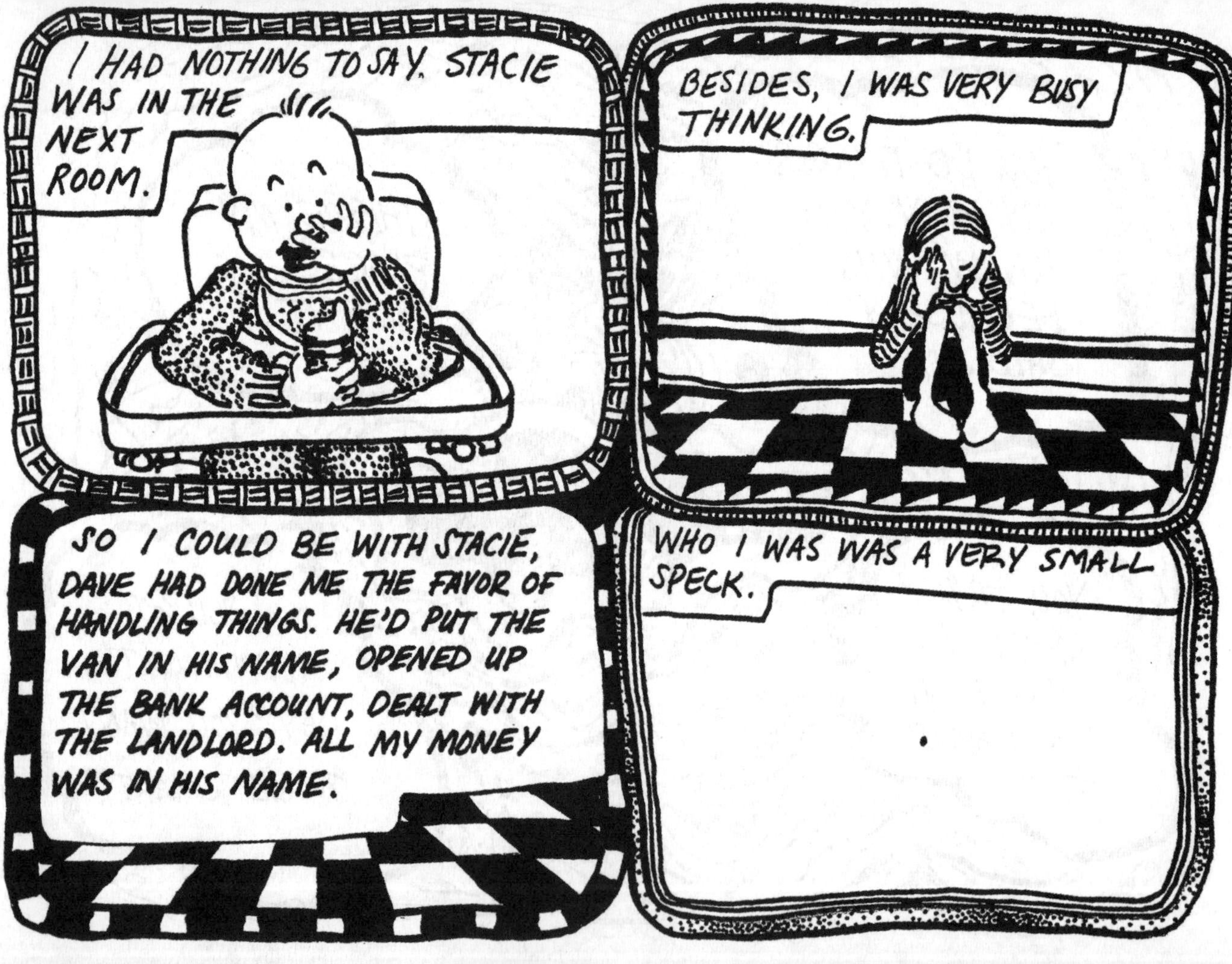
I HAD NOTHING TO SAY. STACIE WAS IN THE NEXT ROOM.
BESIDES, I WAS VERY BUSY THINKING.
SO I COULD BE WITH STACIE, DAVE HAD DONE ME THE FAVOR OF HANDLING THINGS. HE'D PUT THE VAN IN HIS NAME, OPENED UP THE BANK ACCOUNT, DEALT WITH THE LANDLORD. ALL MY MONEY WAS IN HIS NAME.
WHO I WAS WAS A VERY SMALL SPECK.

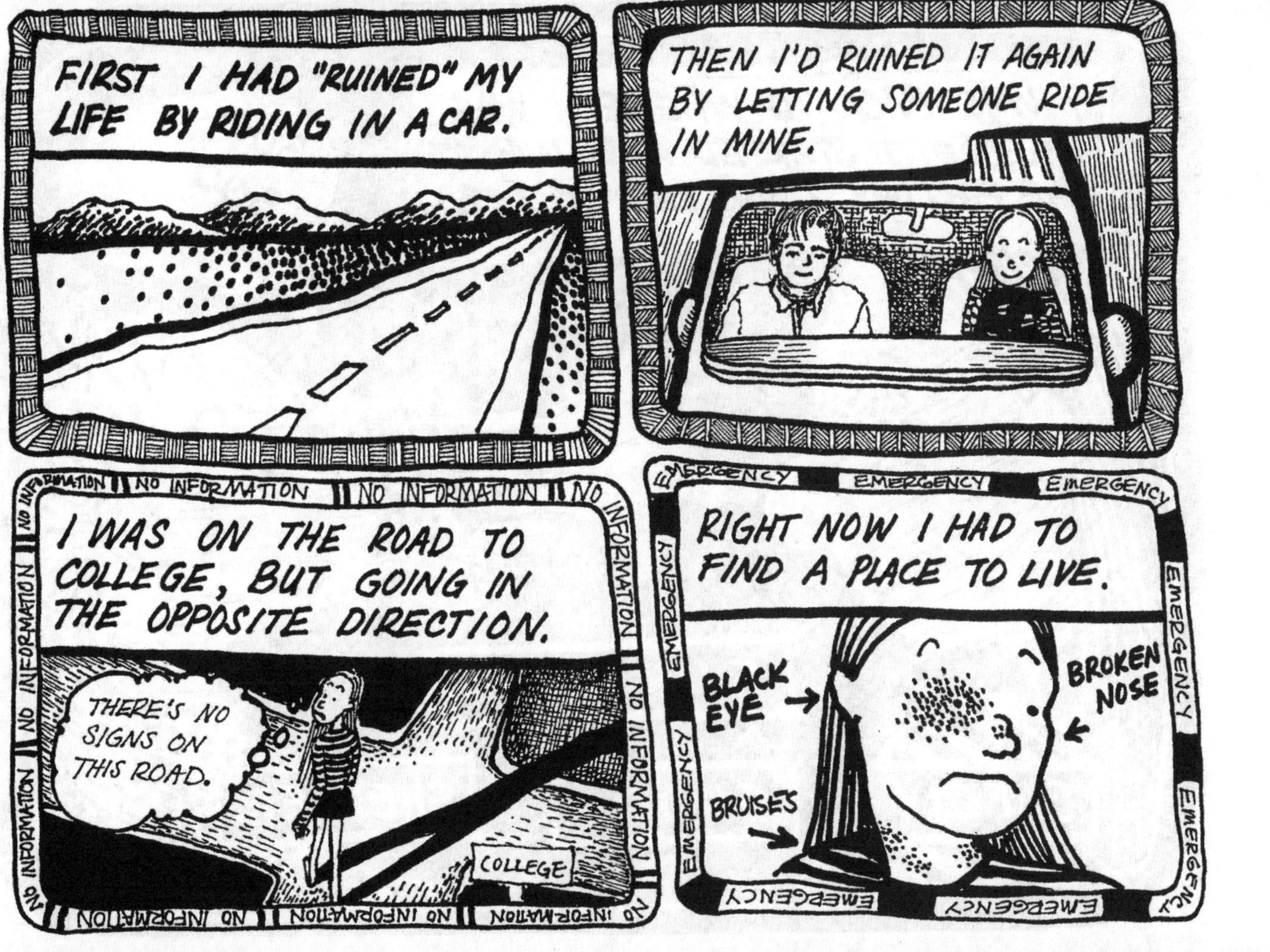
FIRST I HAD "RUINED" MY LIFE BY RIDING IN A CAR.
THEN I'D RUINED IT AGAIN BY LETTING SOMEONE RIDE IN MINE.
NO INFORMATION
I WAS ON THE ROAD TO COLLEGE, BUT GOING IN THE OPPOSITE DIRECTION.
THERE'S NO SIGNS ON THIS ROAD.
COLLEGE
EMERGENCY
RIGHT NOW I HAD TO FIND A PLACE TO LIVE.
BLACK EYE
BROKEN NOSE
BRUISES

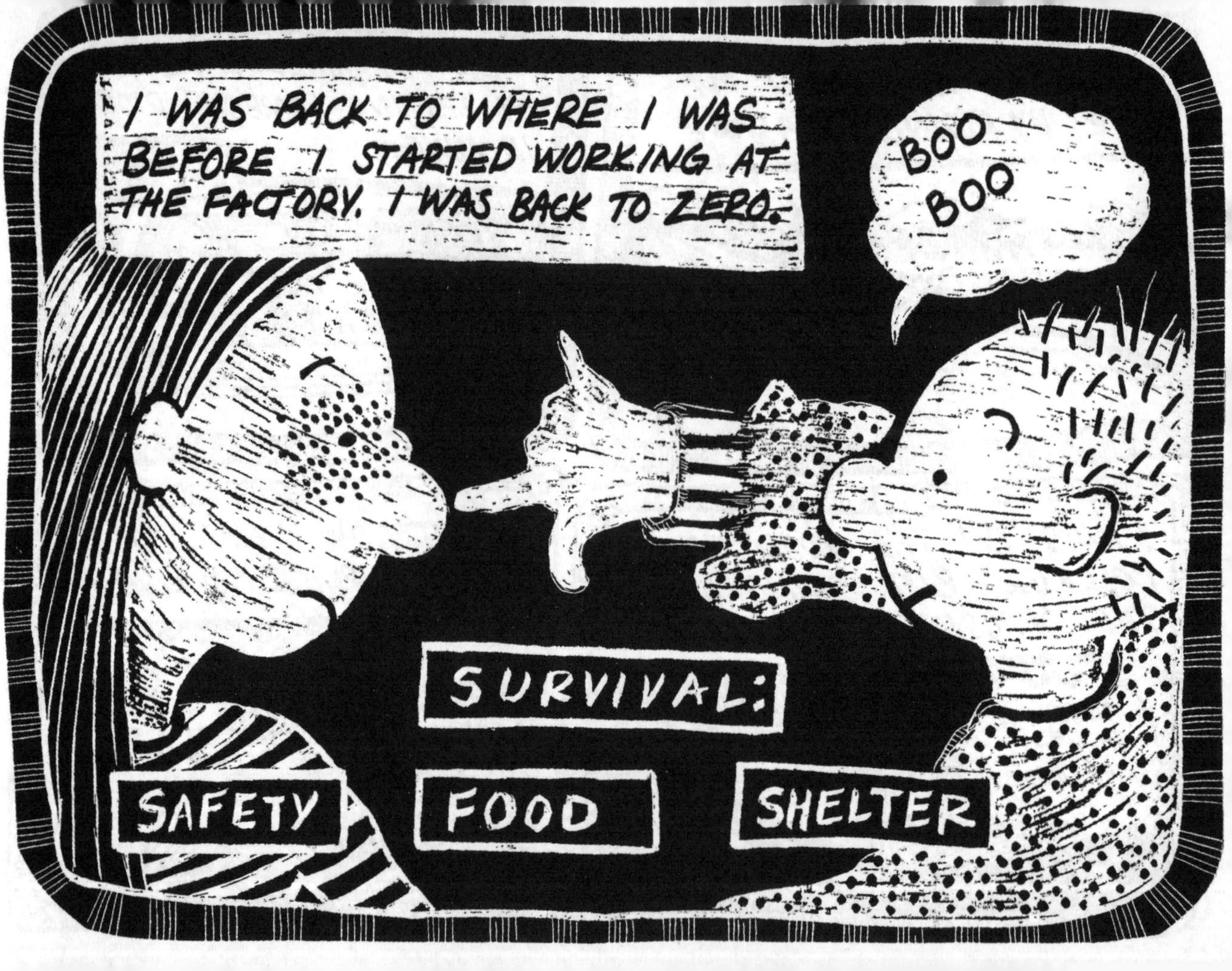
I WAS BACK TO WHERE I WAS BEFORE I STARTED WORKING AT THE FACTORY. I WAS BACK TO ZERO.
BOO BOO
SURVIVAL:
SAFETY
FOOD
SHELTER

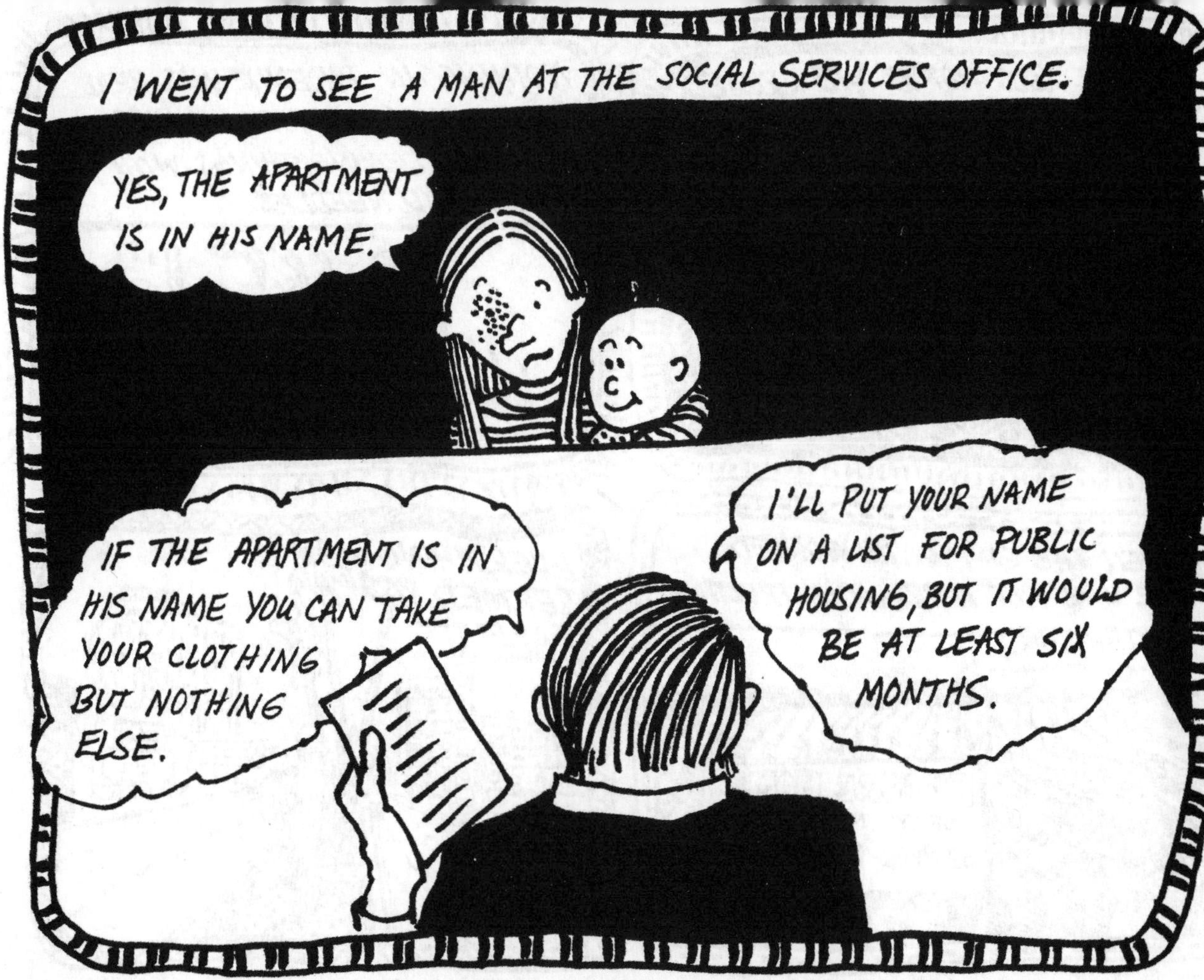
I WENT TO SEE A MAN AT THE SOCIAL SERVICES OFFICE.
YES, THE APARTMENT IS IN HIS NAME.
IF THE APARTMENT IS IN HIS NAME YOU CAN TAKE YOUR CLOTHING BUT NOTHING ELSE.
I'LL PUT YOUR NAME ON A LIST FOR PUBLIC HOUSING, BUT IT WOULD BE AT LEAST SIX MONTHS.

ON THE BUS HOME WE CROSSED THE SALT RIVER, WHICH IS REALLY NOT A RIVER AT ALL.

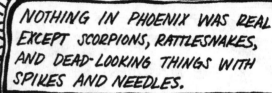

NOTHING IN PHOENIX WAS REAL EXCEPT SCORPIONS, RATTLESNAKES, AND DEAD-LOOKING THINGS WITH SPIKES AND NEEDLES.

EVEN THE GUY DAVE WORKED FOR WAS NOT A REAL CONSTRUCTION CONTRACTOR.

FUTURE HOME OF THE NEFARIOUS SHOPPING CENTER!

EVERYTHING SEEMED FAKE

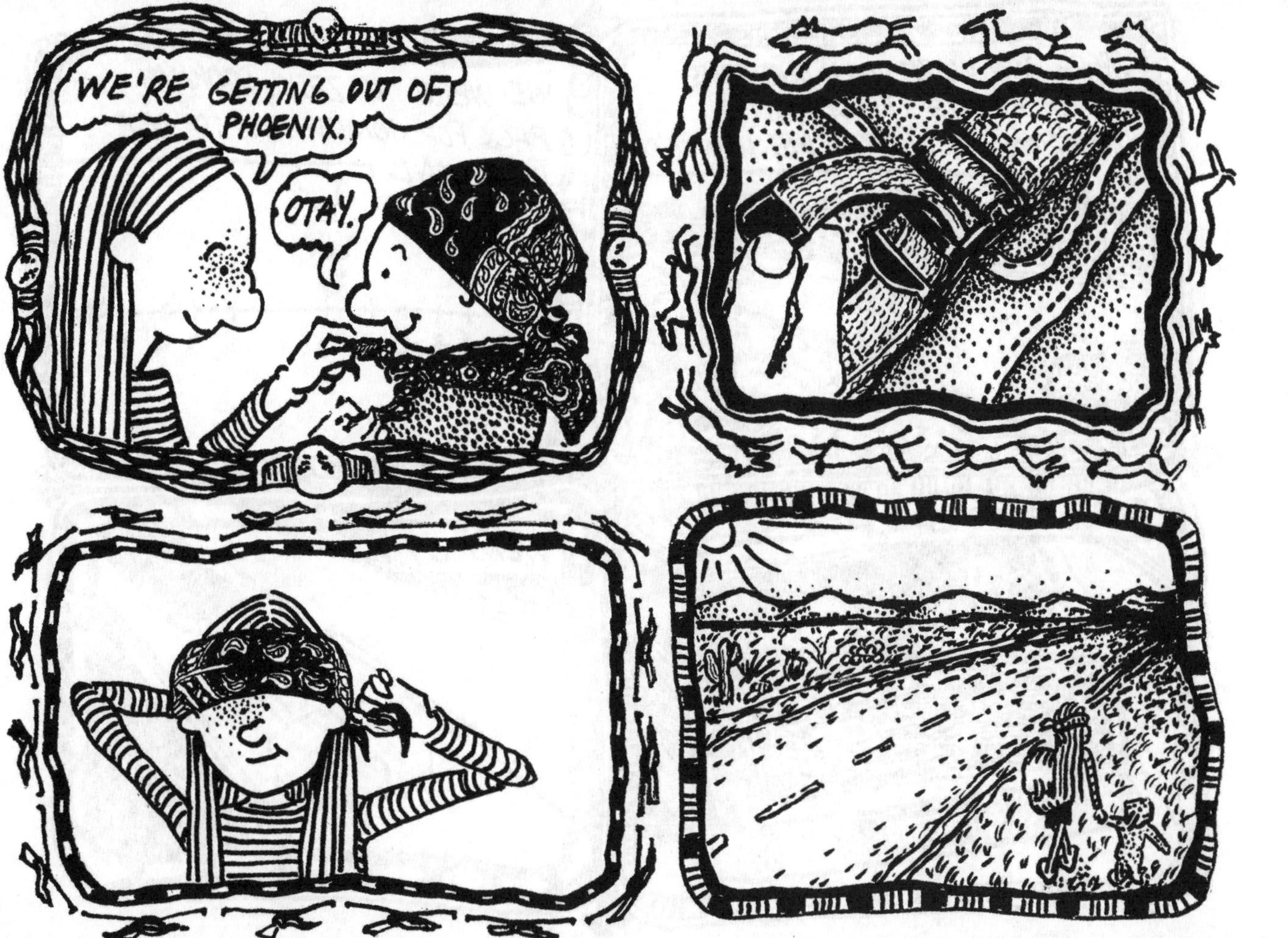
WE'RE GETTING OUT OF PHOENIX.
OTAY.

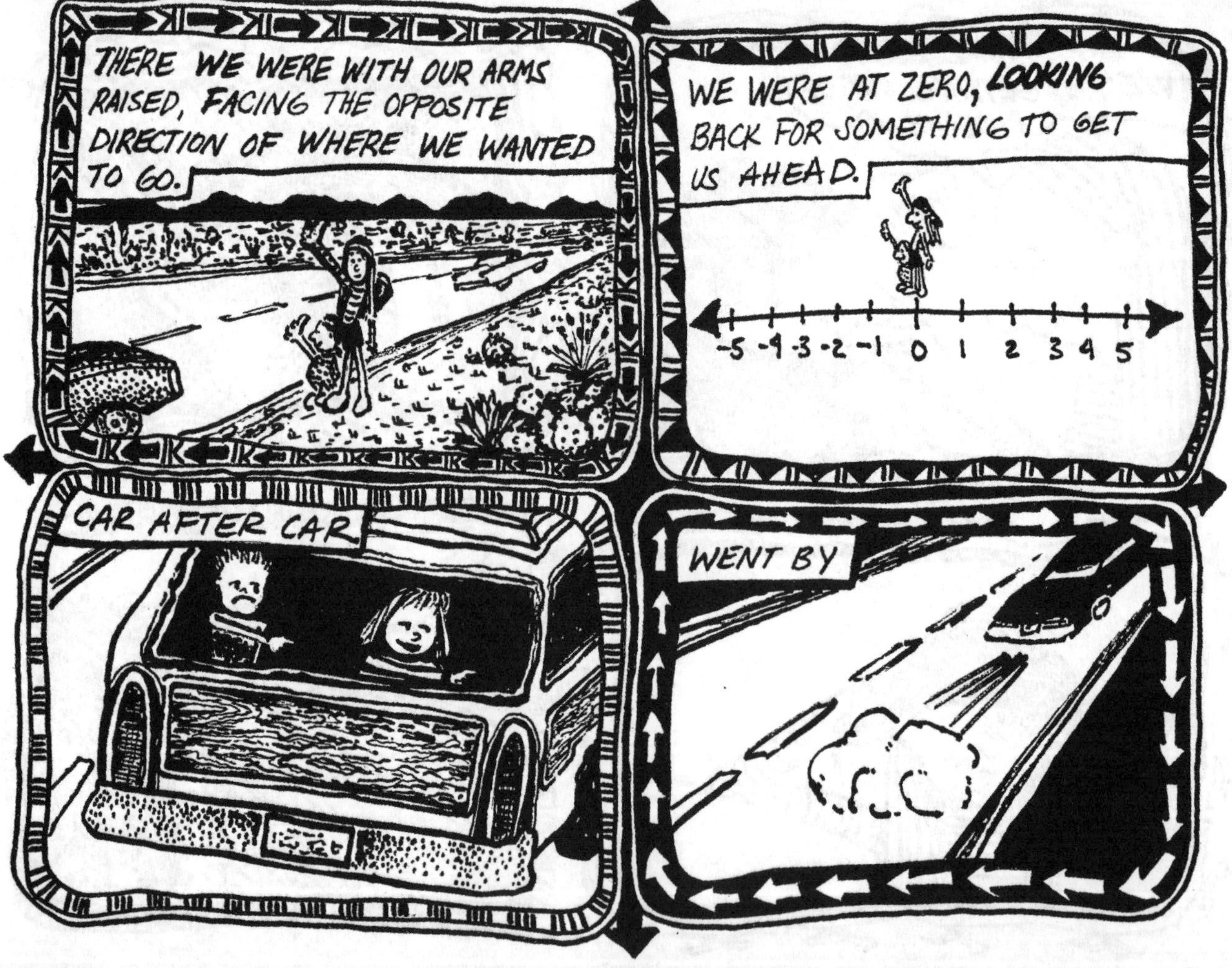
THERE WE WERE WITH OUR ARMS RAISED, FACING THE OPPOSITE DIRECTION OF WHERE WE WANTED TO GO.
WE WERE AT ZERO, LOOKING BACK FOR SOMETHING TO GET US AHEAD.
-5 -4 -3 -2 -1 0 1 2 3 4 5
CAR AFTER CAR
WENT BY

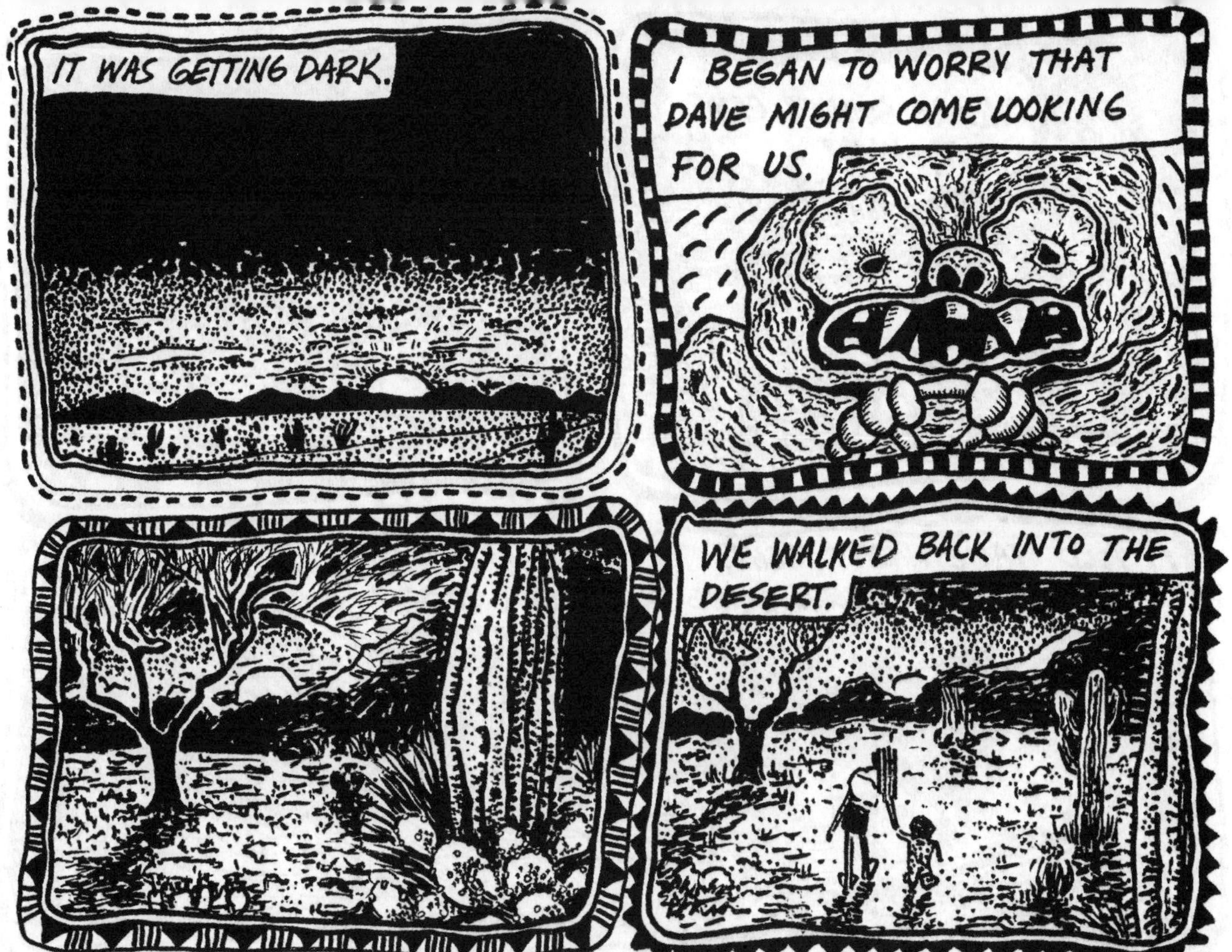
IT WAS GETTING DARK.
I BEGAN TO WORRY THAT DAVE MIGHT COME LOOKING FOR US.
WE WALKED BACK INTO THE DESERT.

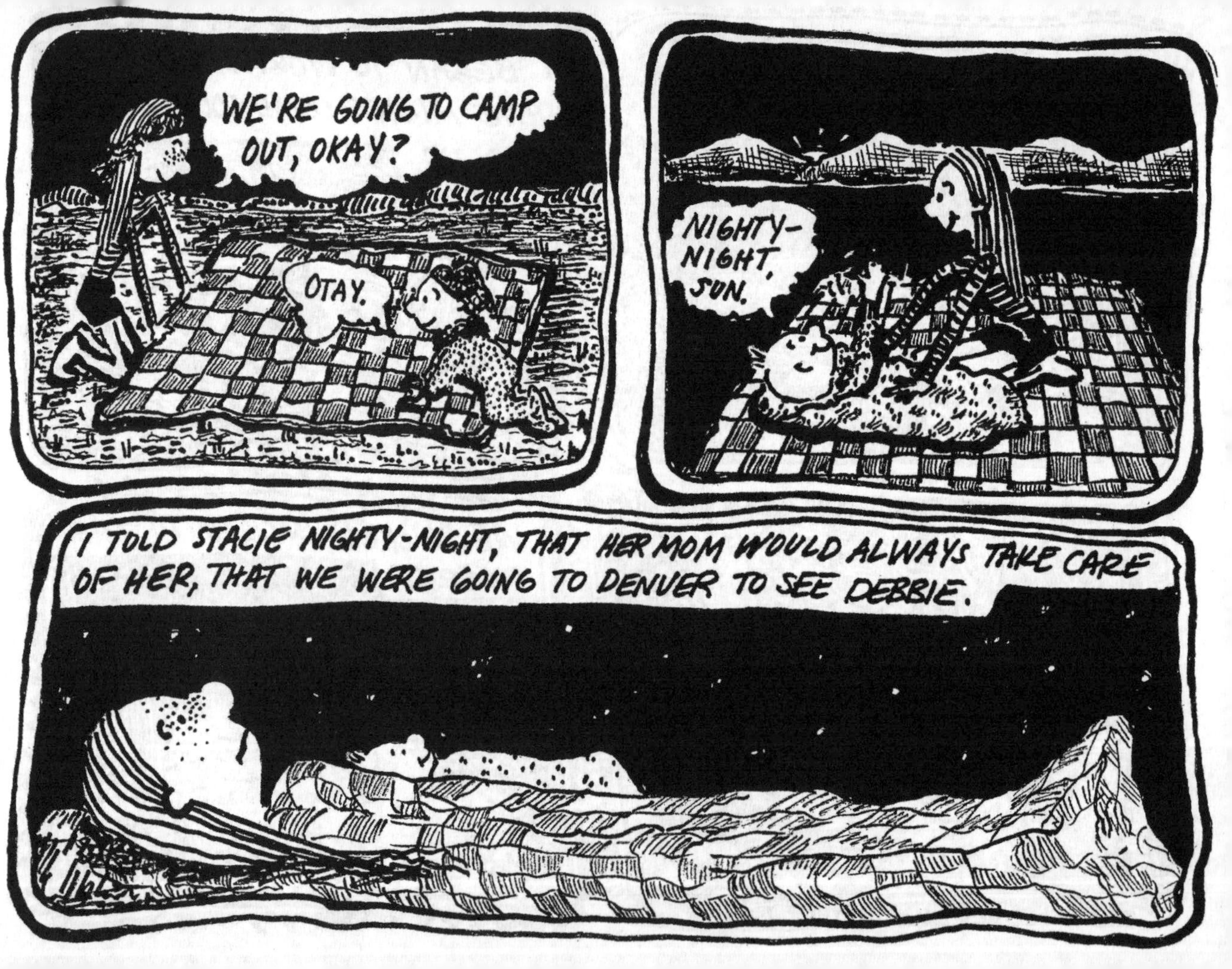
WE'RE GOING TO CAMP OUT, OKAY?
OTAY.
NIGHTY-NIGHT, SUN.
I TOLD STACIE NIGHTY-NIGHT, THAT HER MOM WOULD ALWAYS TAKE CARE OF HER, THAT WE WERE GOING TO DENVER TO SEE DEBBIE.

BUT THAT WAS NOT HOW I FELT AT ALL.

INSTEAD, ALL I COULD THINK ABOUT WERE ALL THE BAD THINGS THAT HAD EVER HAPPENED TO ME.

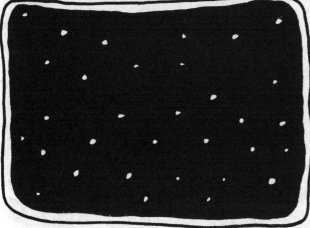

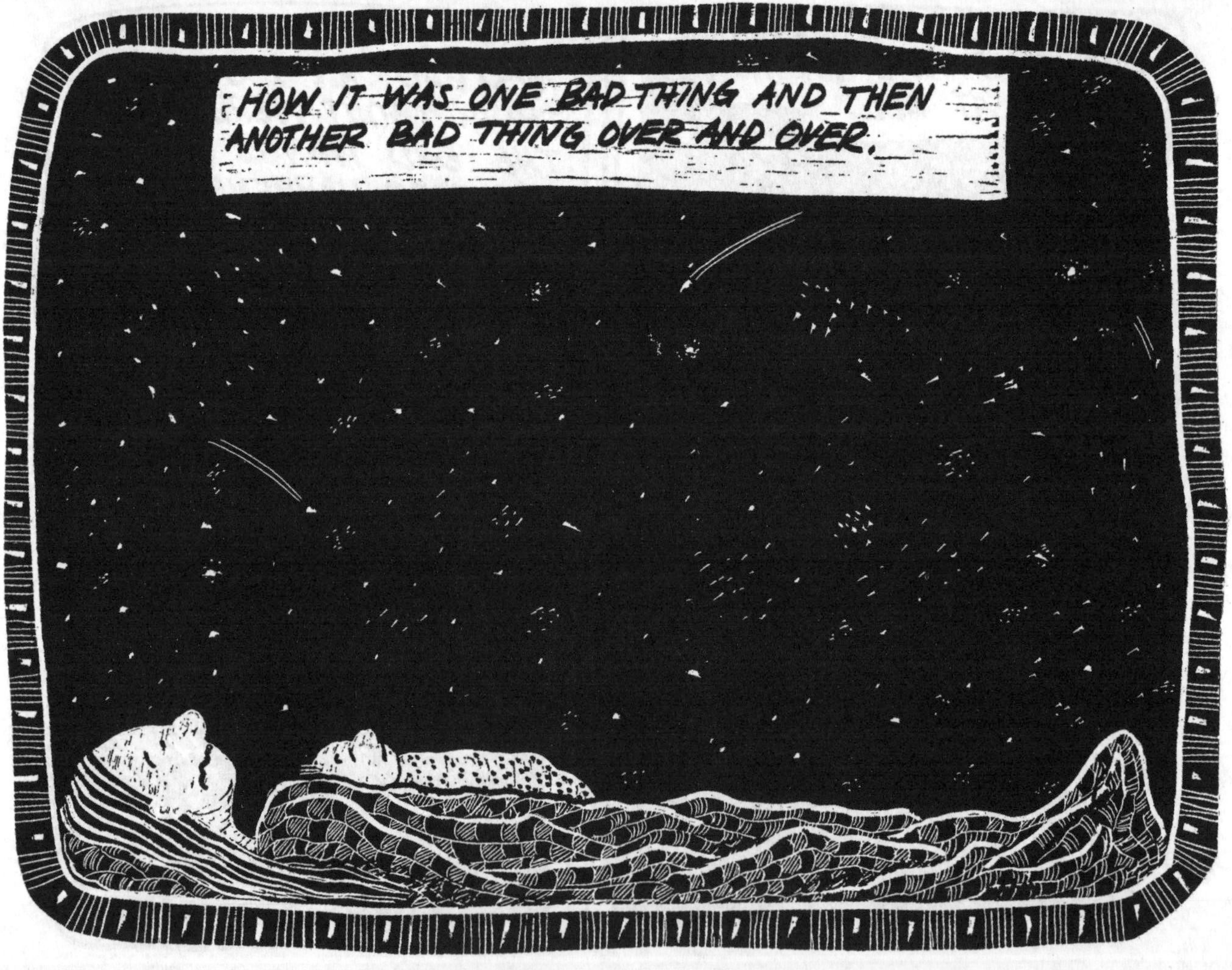
HOW IT WAS ONE BAD THING AND THEN ANOTHER BAD THING OVER AND OVER.

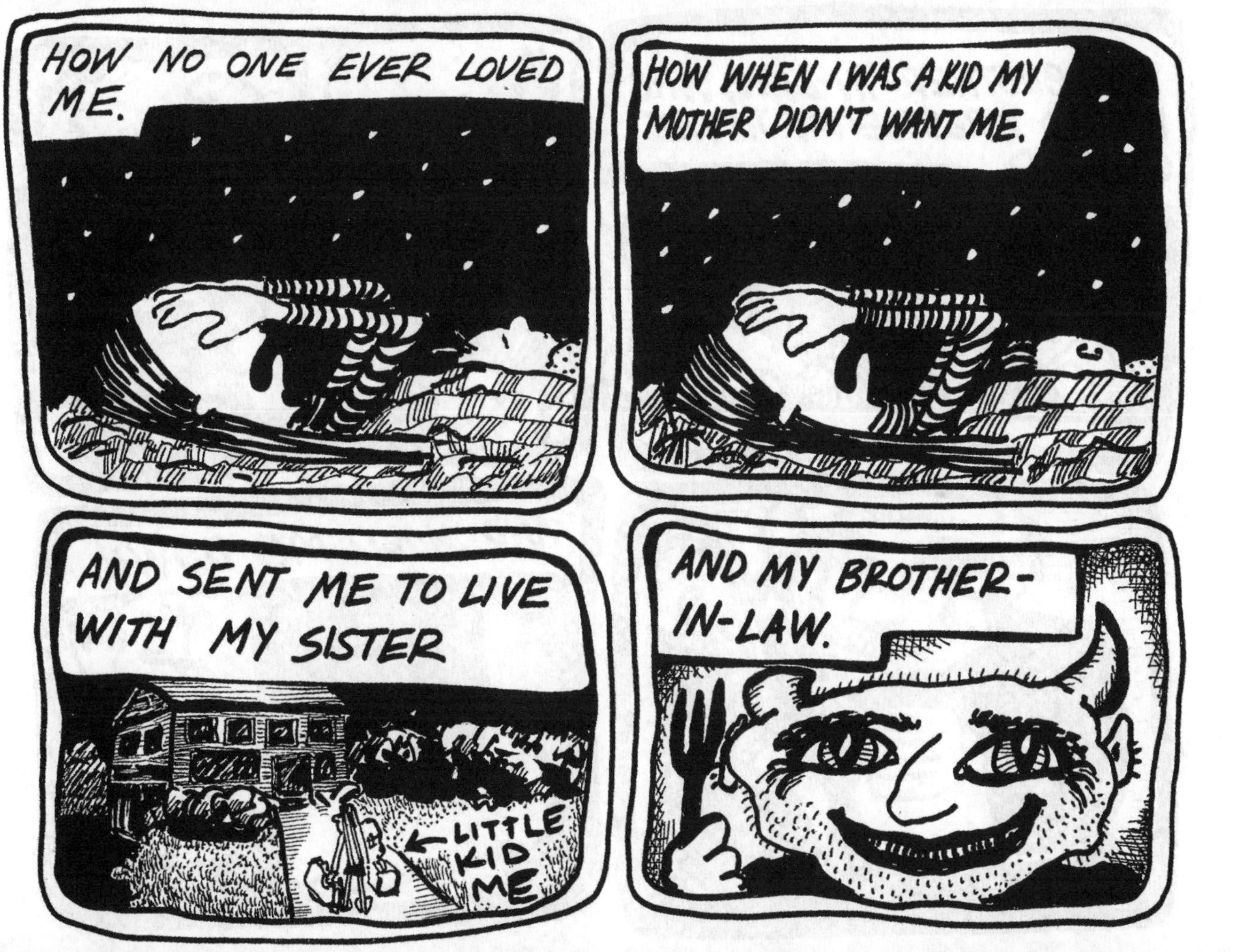
HOW NO ONE EVER LOVED ME.
HOW WHEN I WAS A KID MY MOTHER DIDN'T WANT ME.
AND SENT ME TO LIVE WITH MY SISTER
LITTLE KID ME
AND MY BROTHER-IN-LAW.

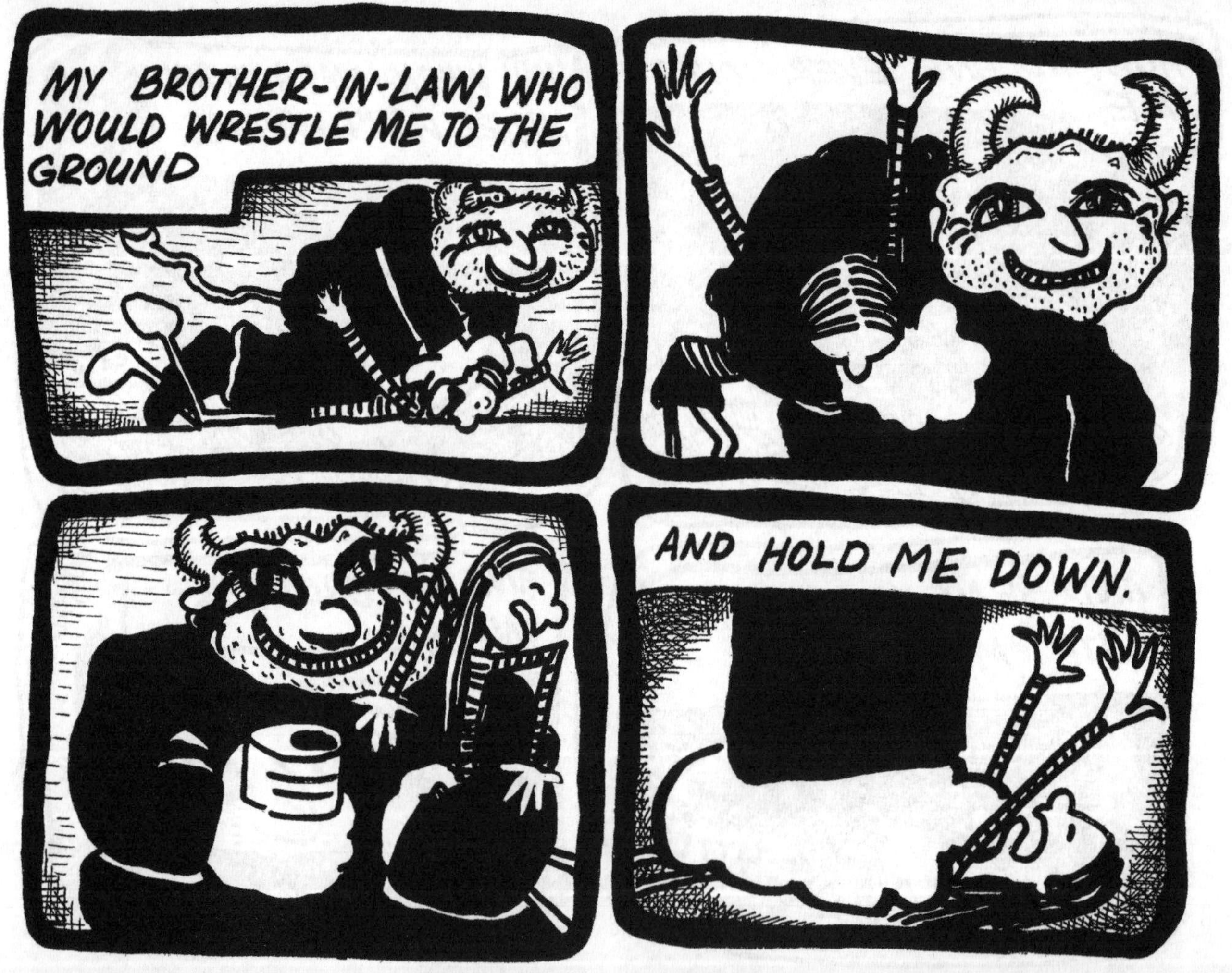
MY BROTHER-IN-LAW, WHO WOULD WRESTLE ME TO THE GROUND
AND HOLD ME DOWN.

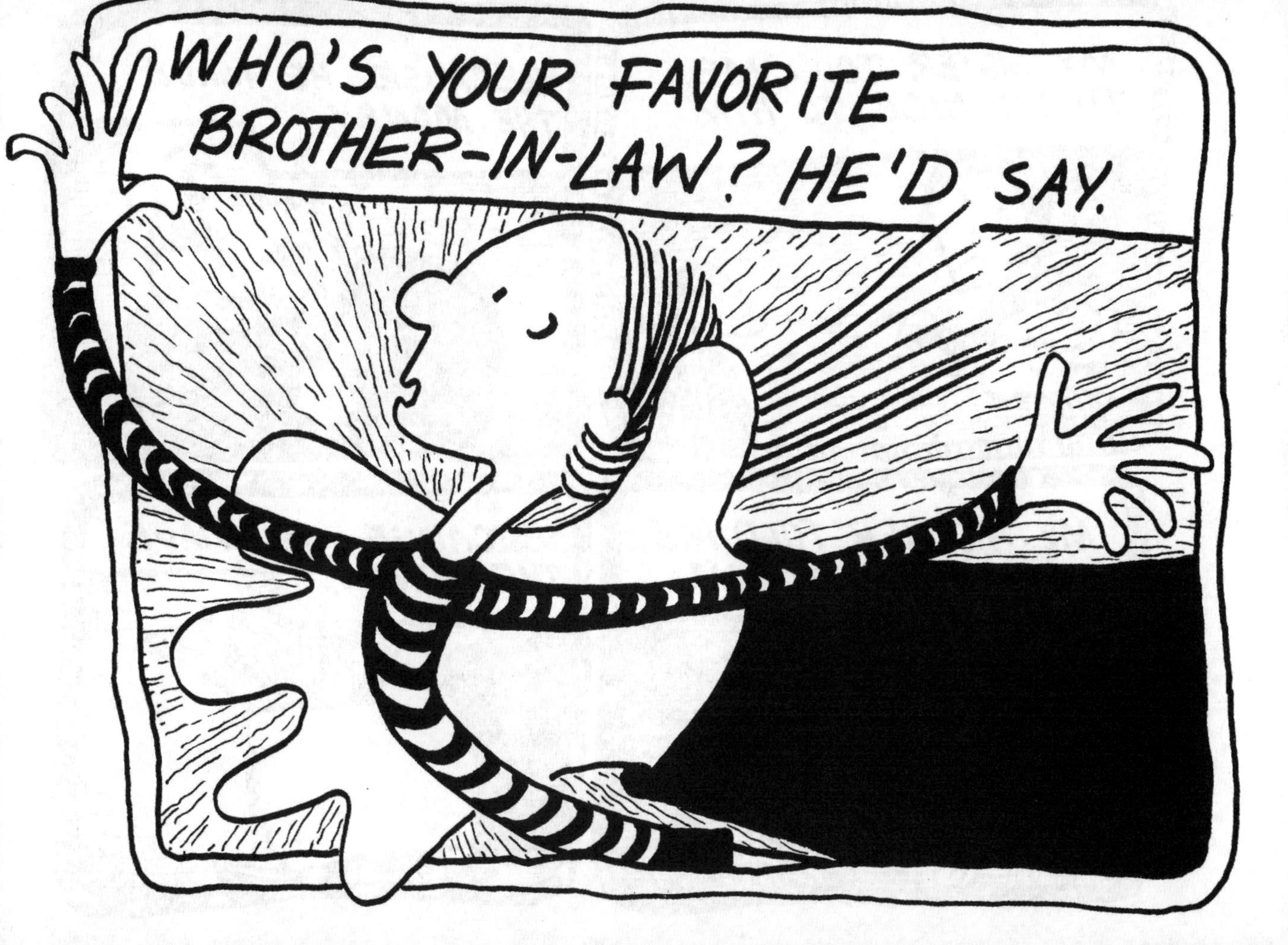
WHO'S YOUR FAVORITE BROTHER-IN-LAW? HE'D SAY.

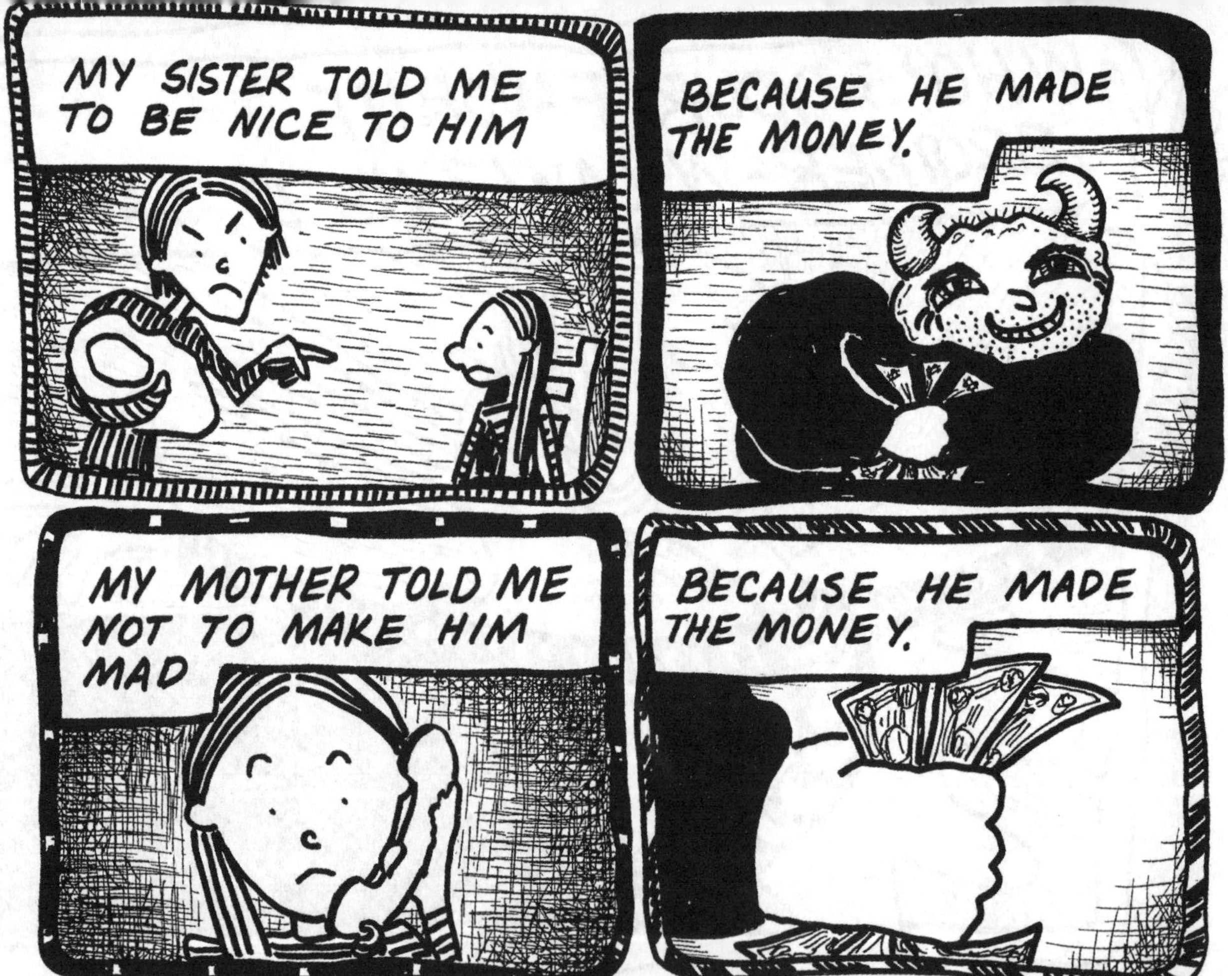
MY SISTER TOLD ME TO BE NICE TO HIM
BECAUSE HE MADE THE MONEY.
MY MOTHER TOLD ME NOT TO MAKE HIM MAD
BECAUSE HE MADE THE MONEY.

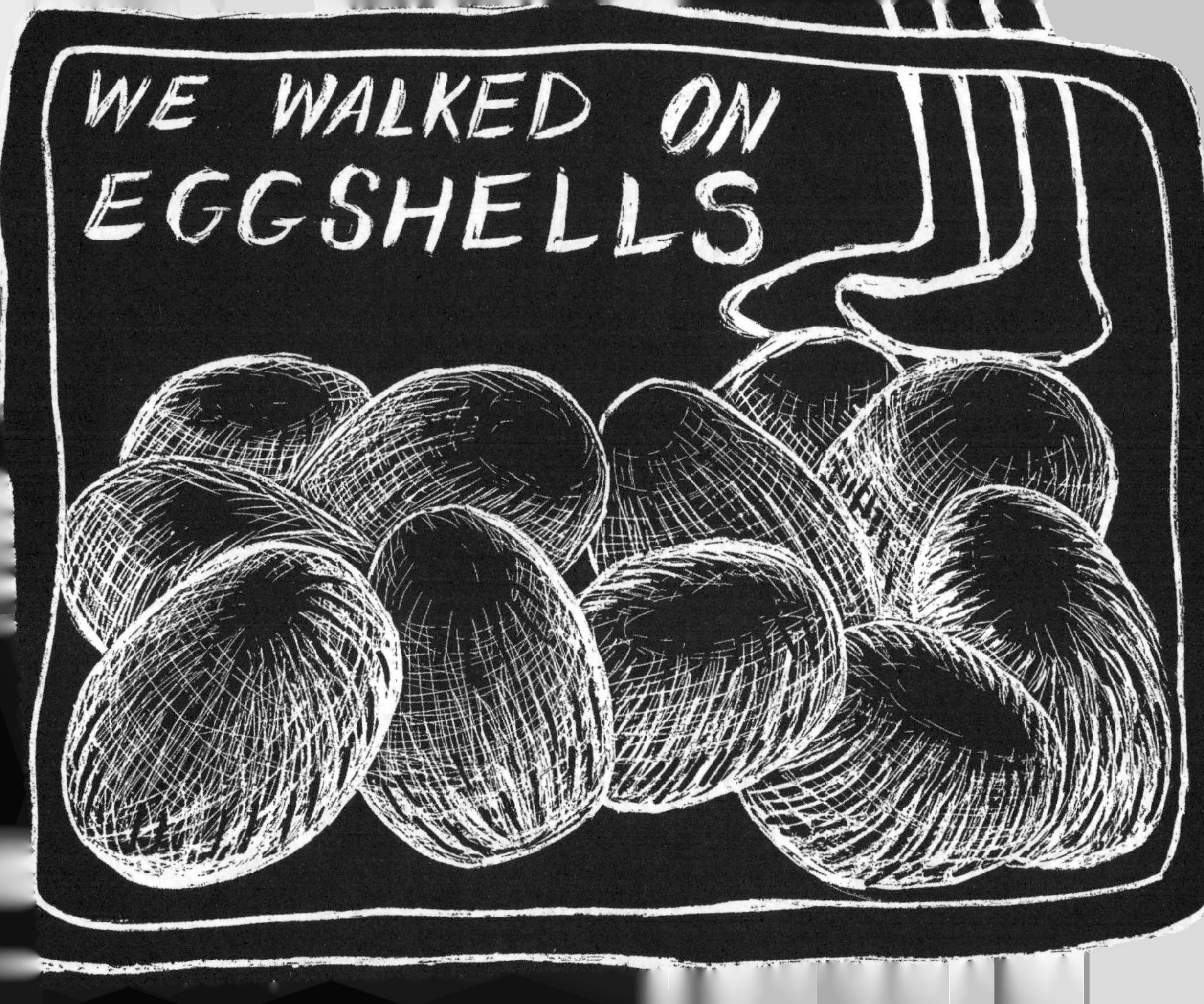
WE WALKED ON
EGGSHELLS

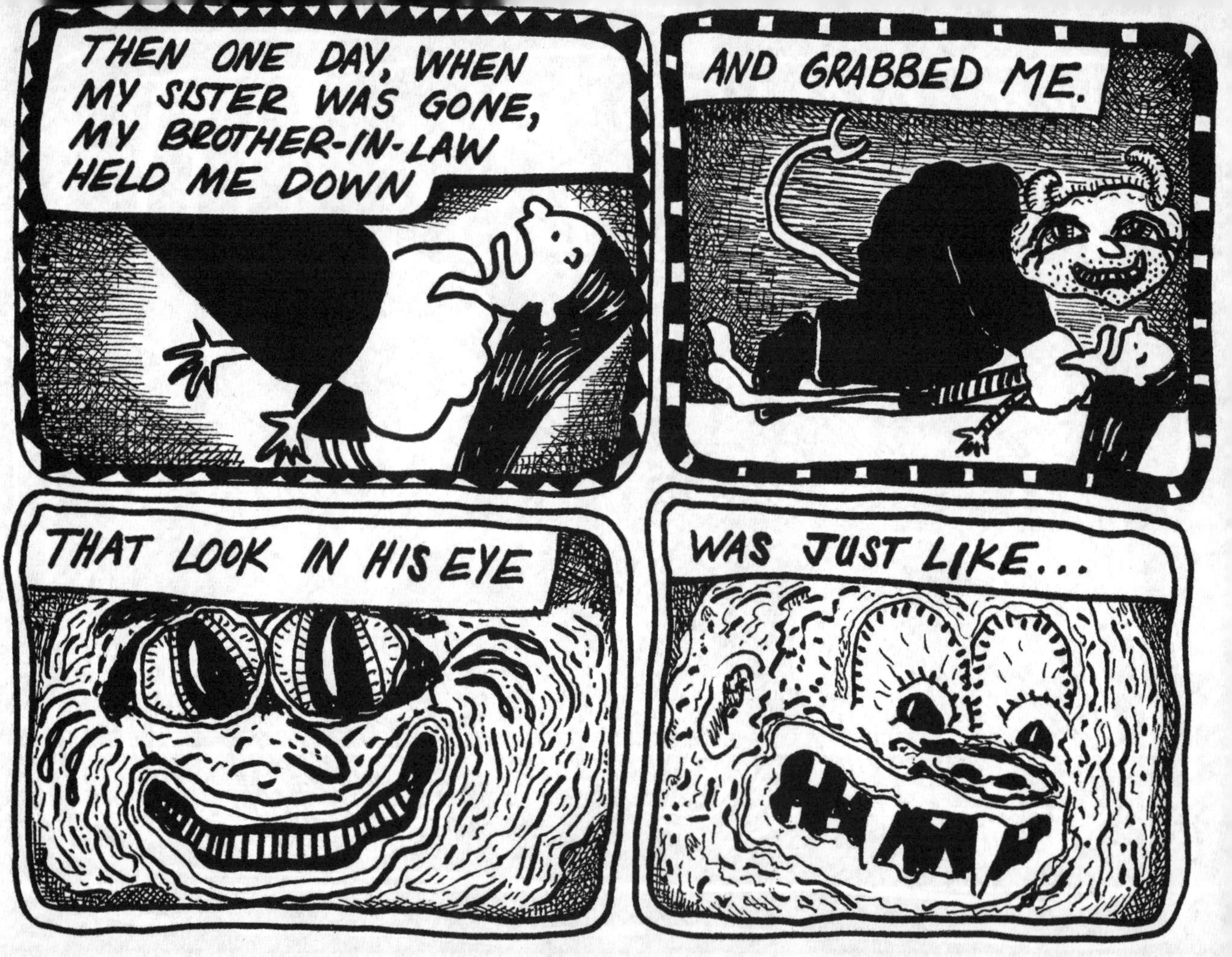
THEN ONE DAY, WHEN MY SISTER WAS GONE, MY BROTHER-IN-LAW HELD ME DOWN
AND GRABBED ME.
THAT LOOK IN HIS EYE
WAS JUST LIKE...

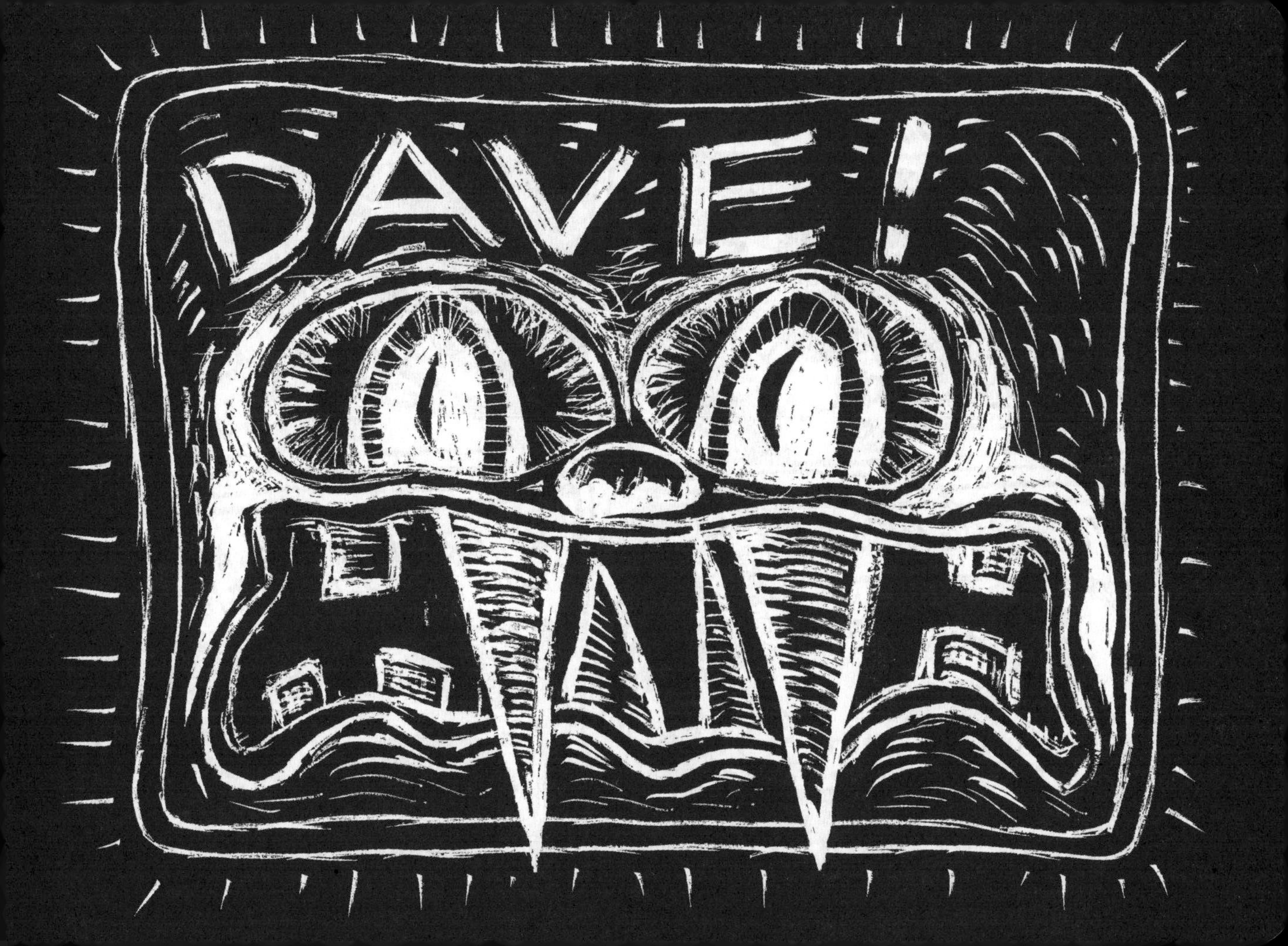
DAVE!

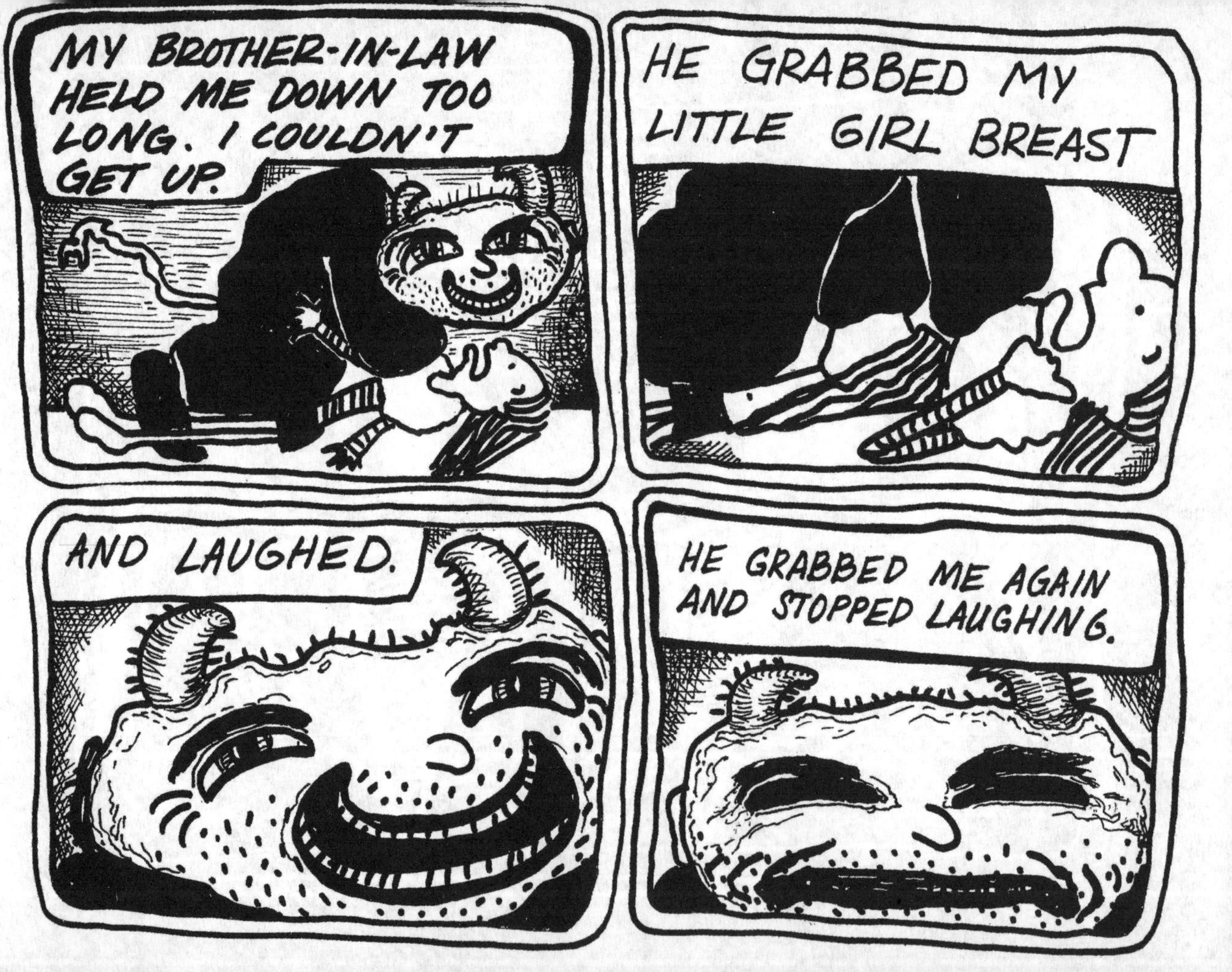
MY BROTHER-IN-LAW HELD ME DOWN TOO LONG. I COULDN'T GET UP.
HE GRABBED MY LITTLE GIRL BREAST
AND LAUGHED.
HE GRABBED ME AGAIN AND STOPPED LAUGHING.

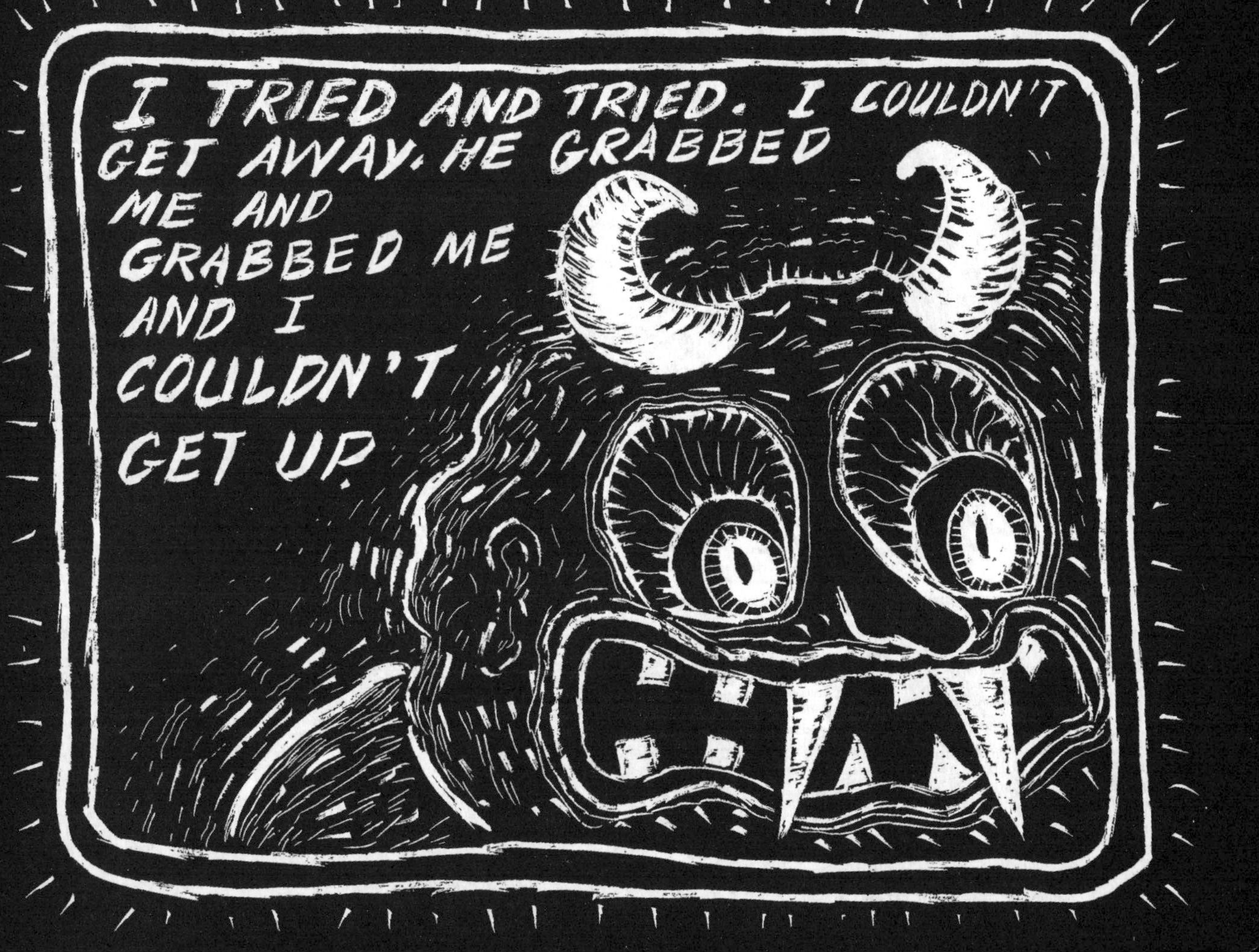
I TRIED AND TRIED. I COULDN'T GET AWAY. HE GRABBED ME AND GRABBED ME AND I COULDN'T GET UP.

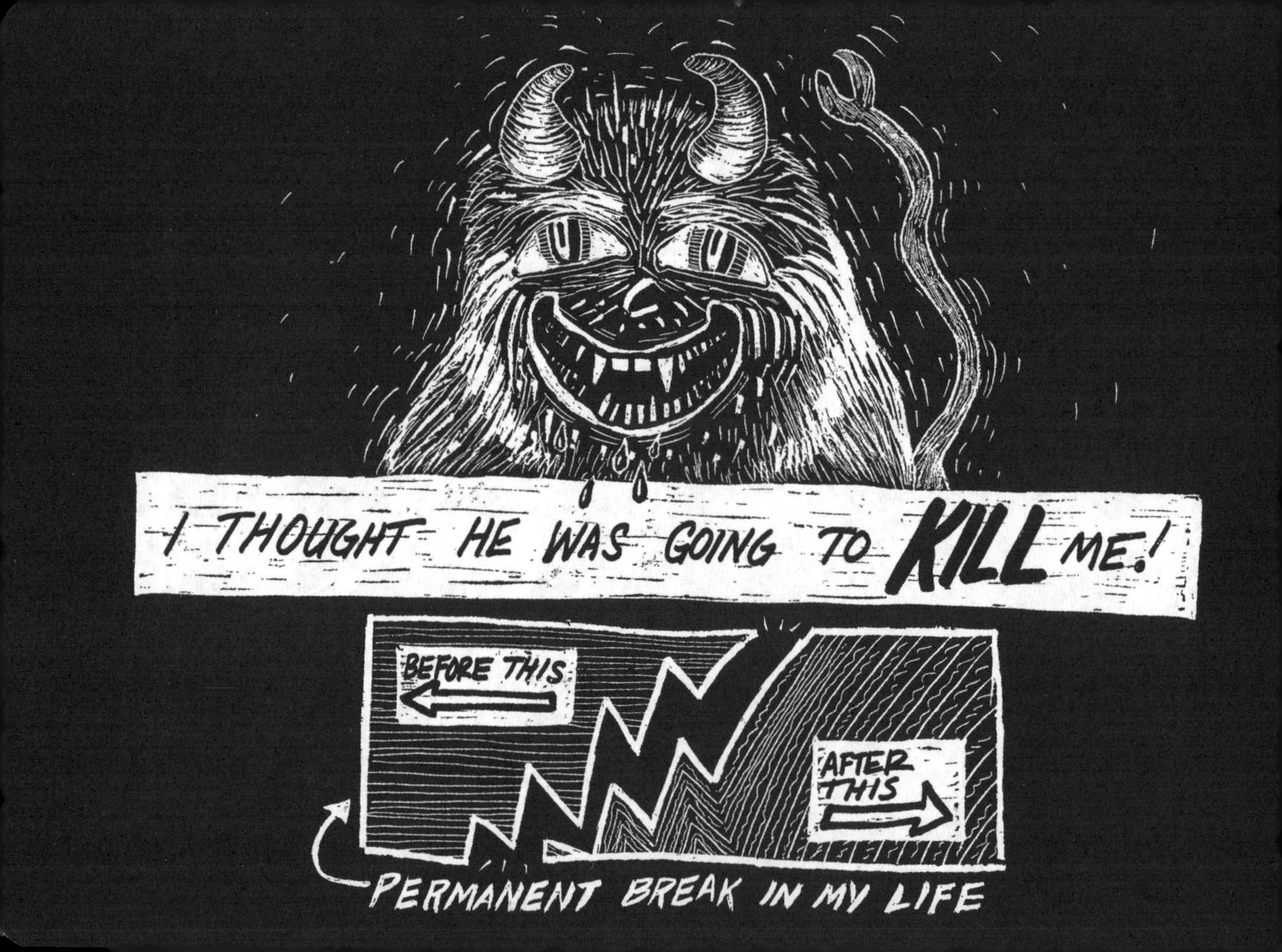
I THOUGHT HE WAS GOING TO KILL ME!
BEFORE THIS
AFTER THIS
PERMANENT BREAK IN MY LIFE

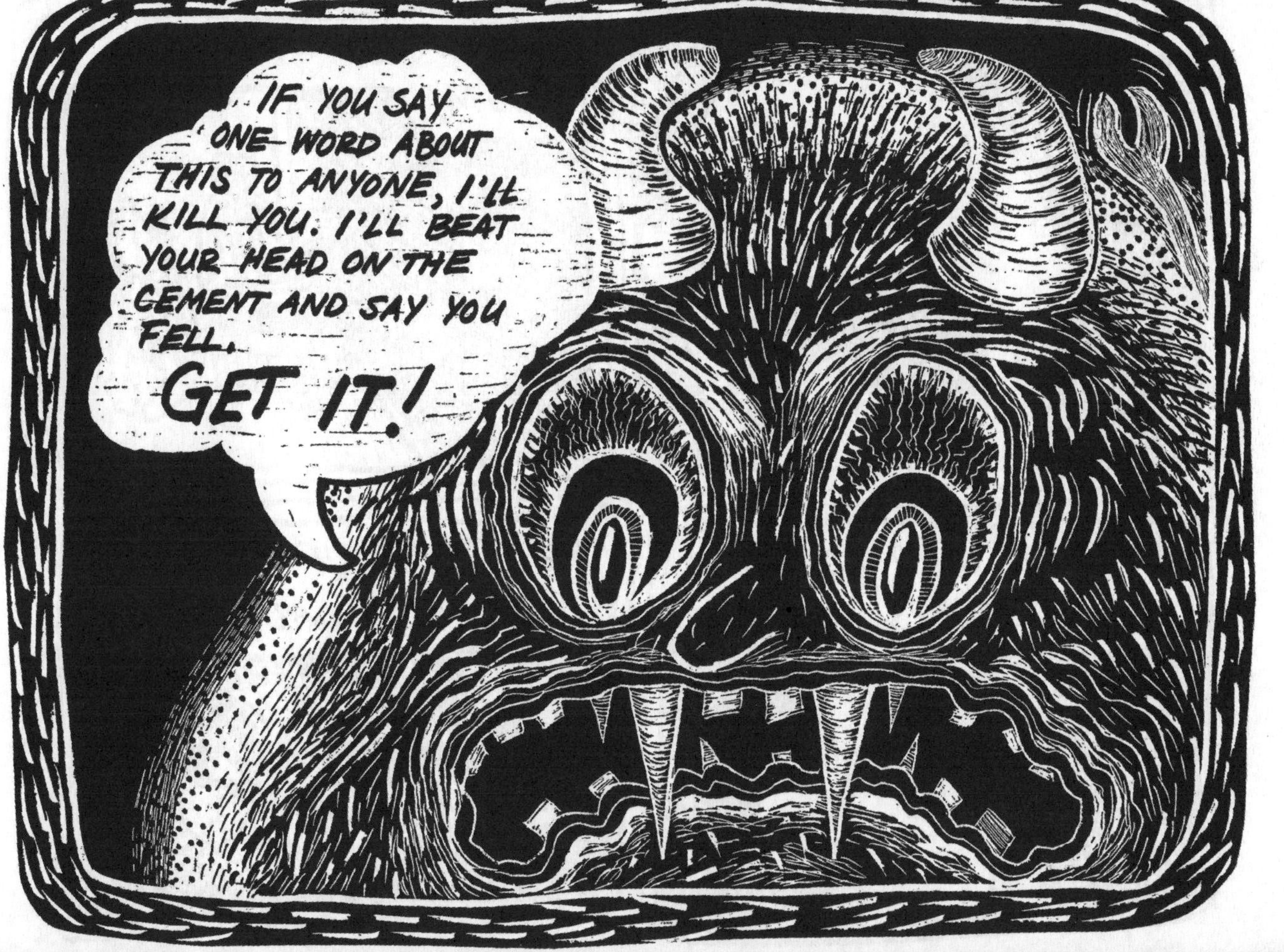
IF YOU SAY ONE WORD ABOUT THIS TO ANYONE, I'LL KILL YOU. I'LL BEAT YOUR HEAD ON THE CEMENT AND SAY YOU FELL.
GET IT!

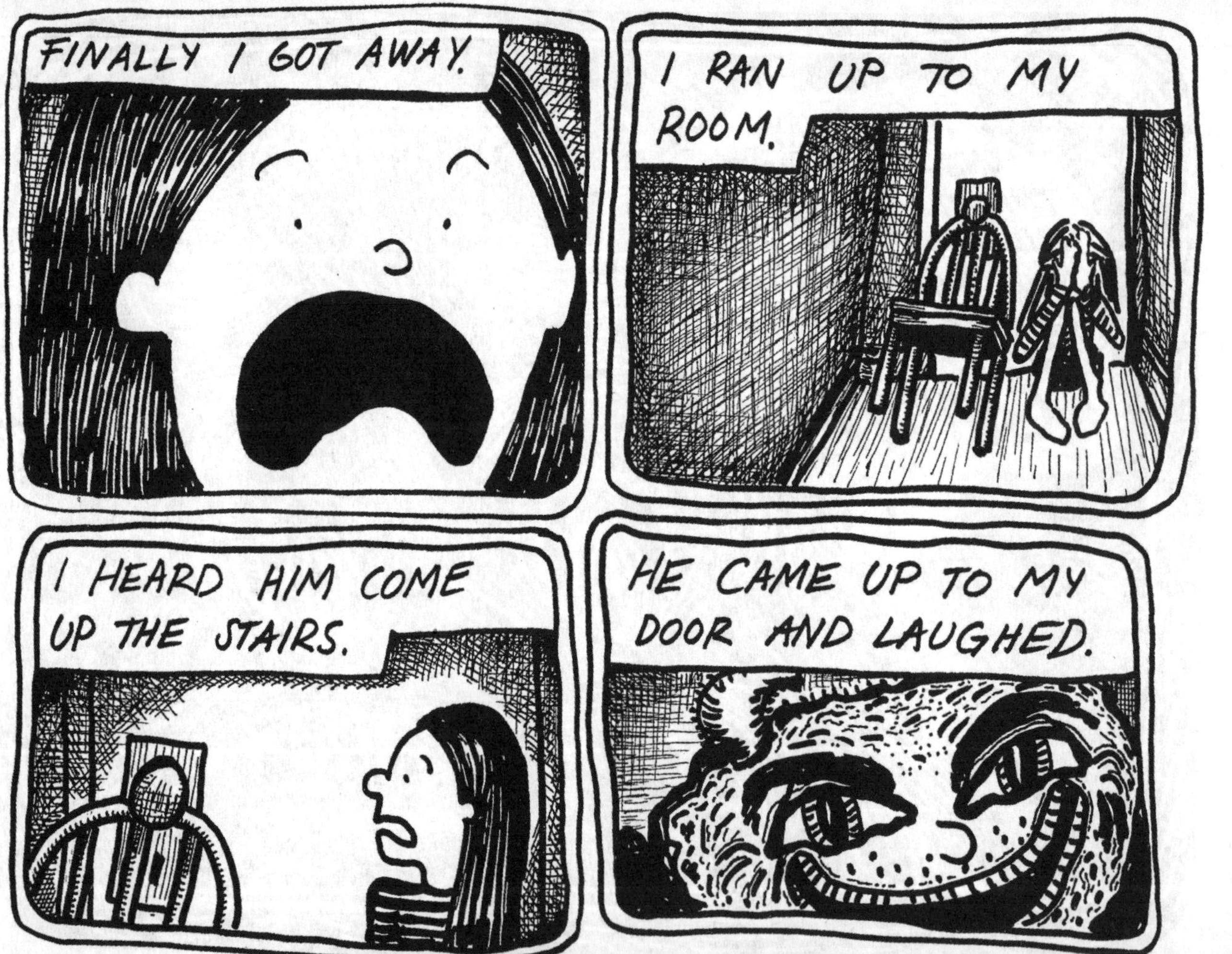
FINALLY I GOT AWAY.
I RAN UP TO MY ROOM.
I HEARD HIM COME UP THE STAIRS.
HE CAME UP TO MY DOOR AND LAUGHED.

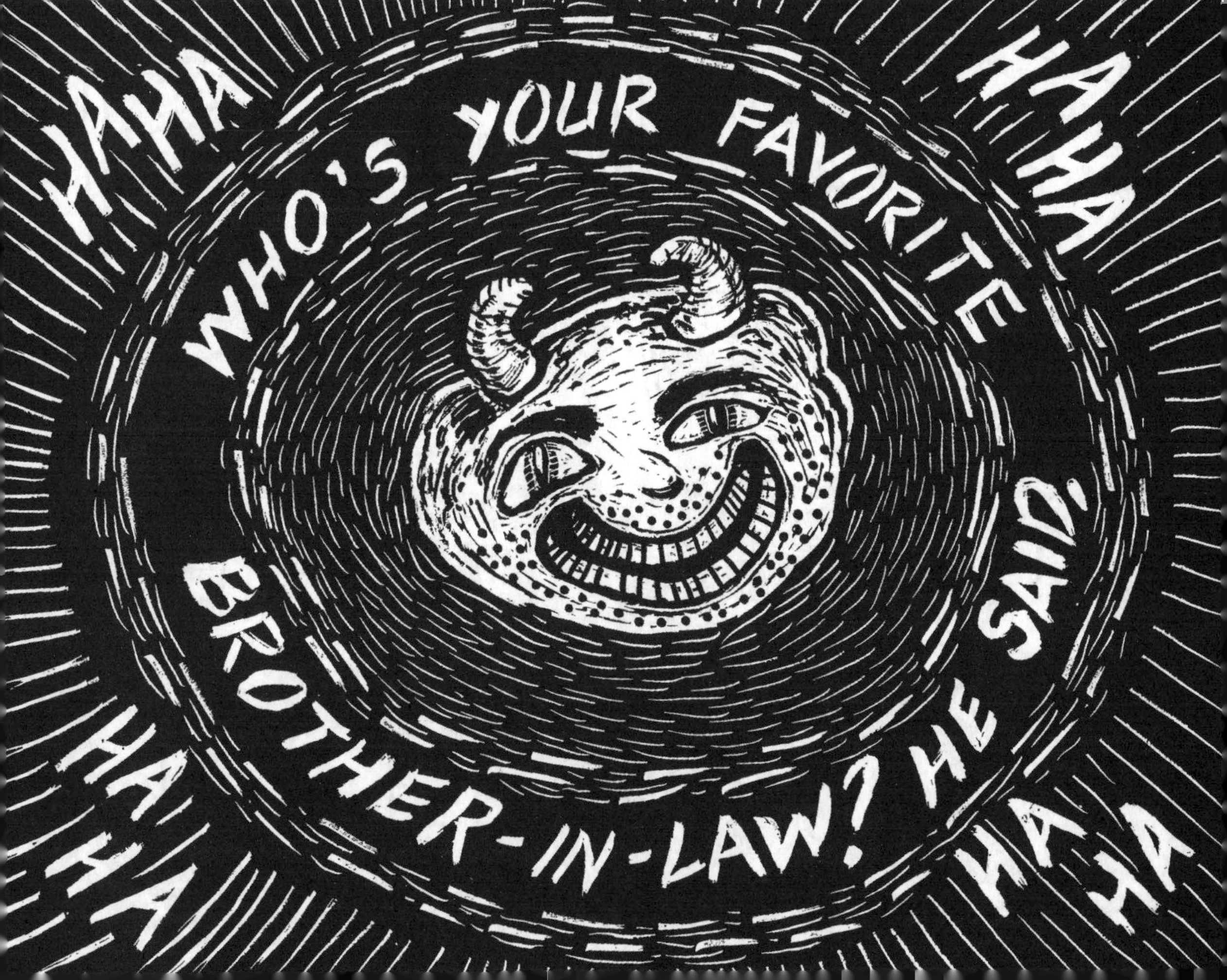
HAHA
WHO'S YOUR FAVORITE
HAHA
BROTHER-IN-LAW? HE SAID,
HAHA
HAHA

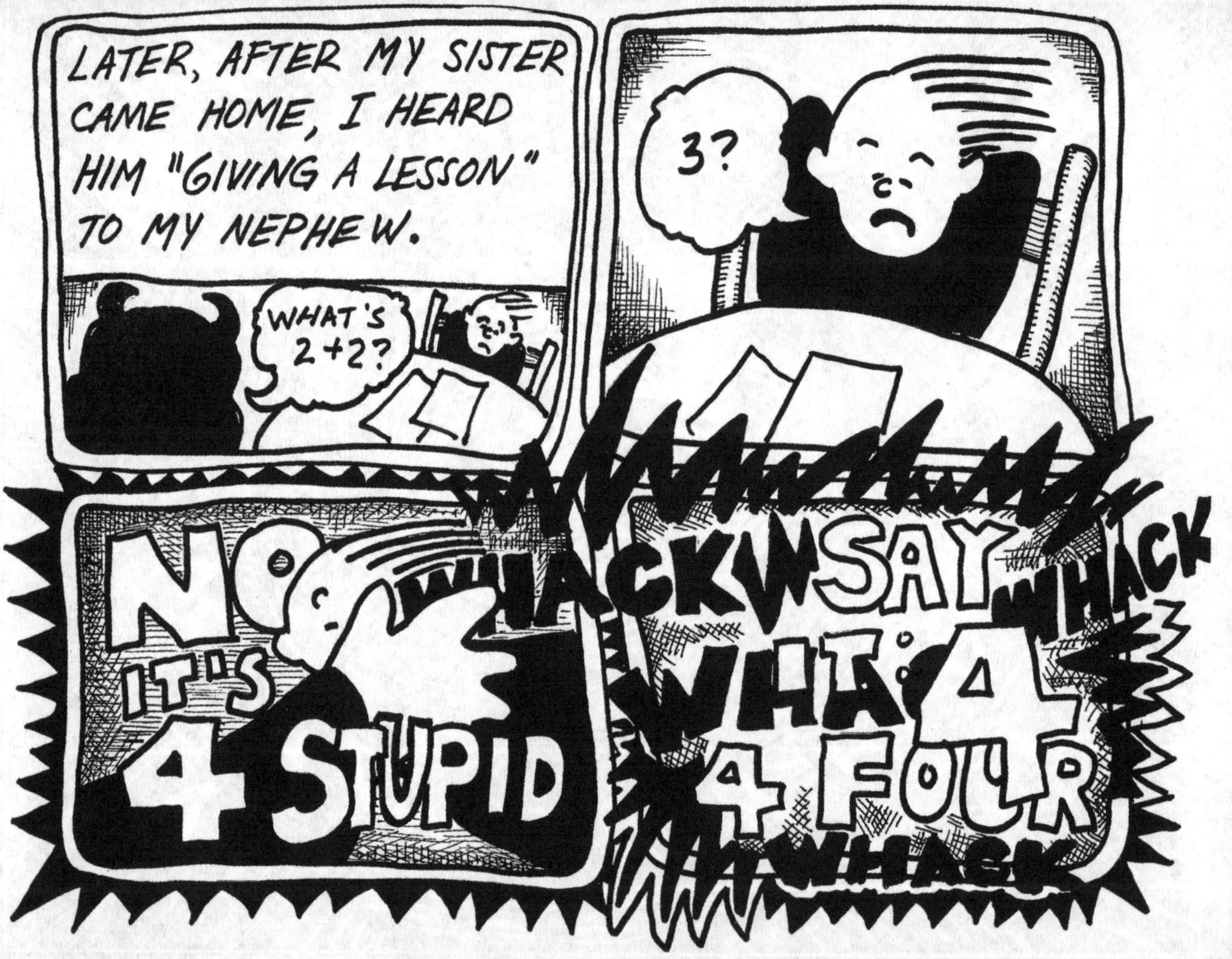
LATER, AFTER MY SISTER CAME HOME, I HEARD HIM "GIVING A LESSON" TO MY NEPHEW.
WHAT'S 2+2?
3?
NO
IT'S 4 STUPID
WHACK
SAY WHAT 4
4 FOUR
WHACK
WHACK

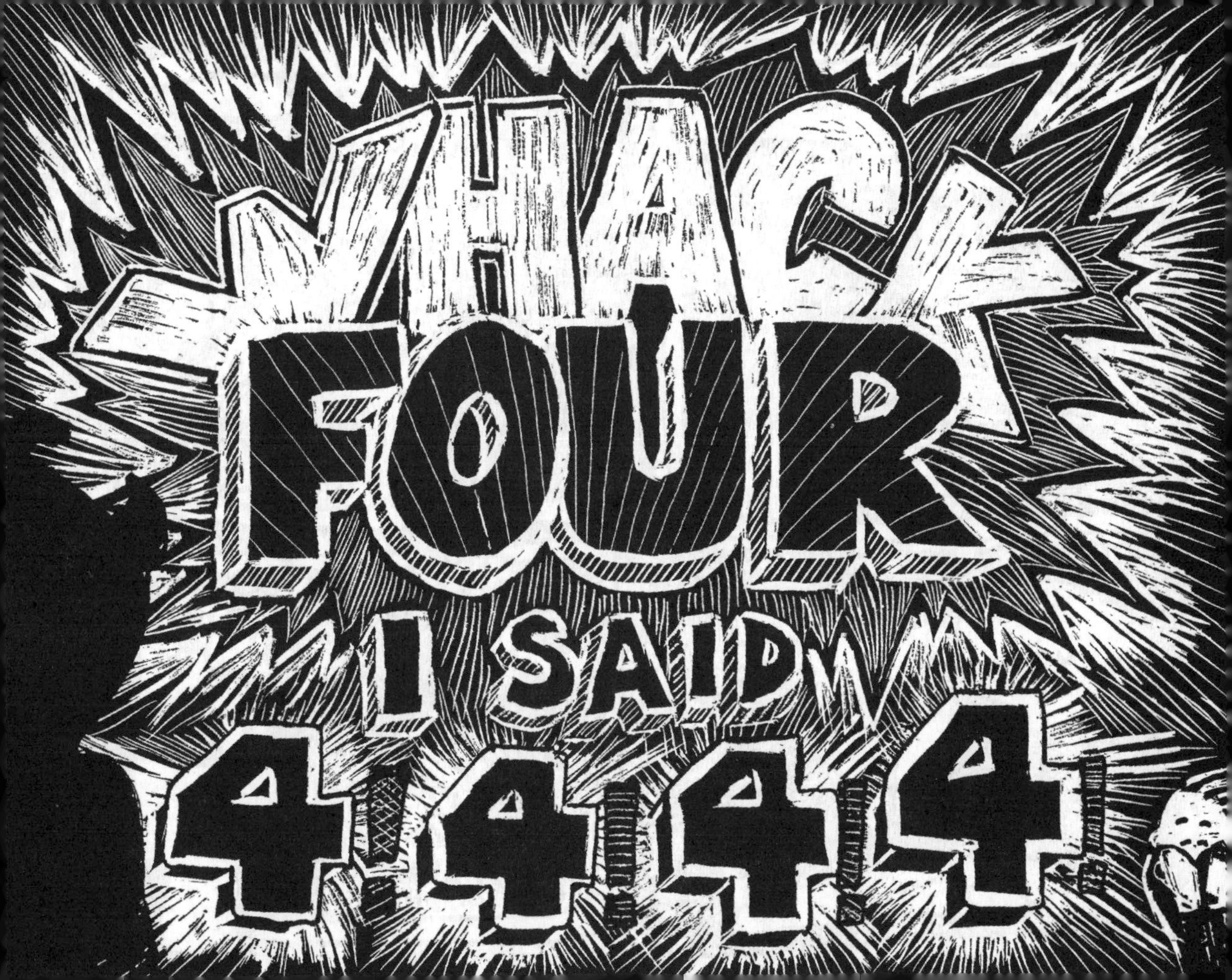
FOUR
I SAID
4! 4! 4! 4!

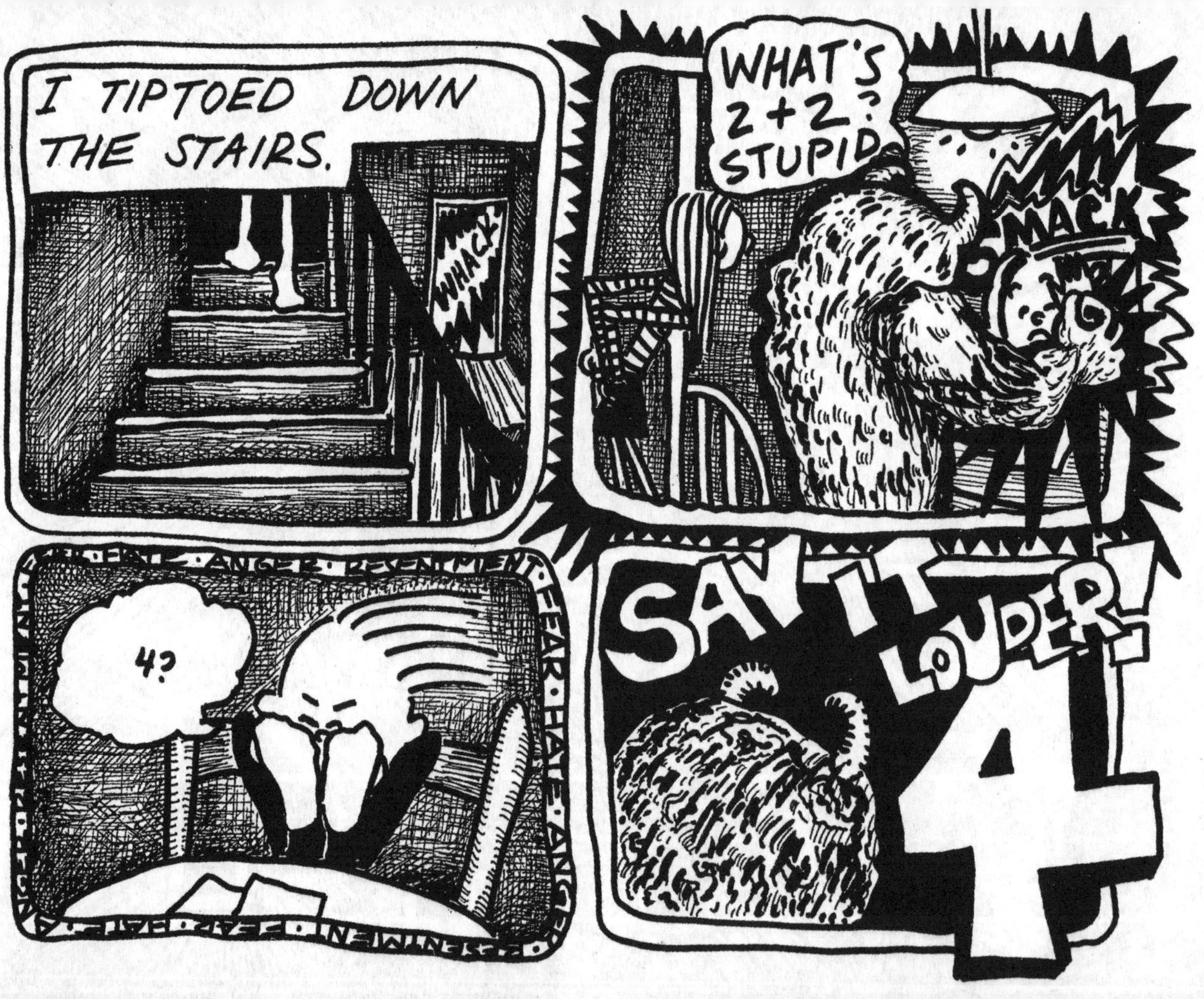
I TIPTOED DOWN THE STAIRS.
WHACK
WHAT'S 2+2? STUPID
SMACK
HATE · ANGER · RESENTMENT · FEAR · HATE · ANGER
4?
SAY IT LOUDER!
4

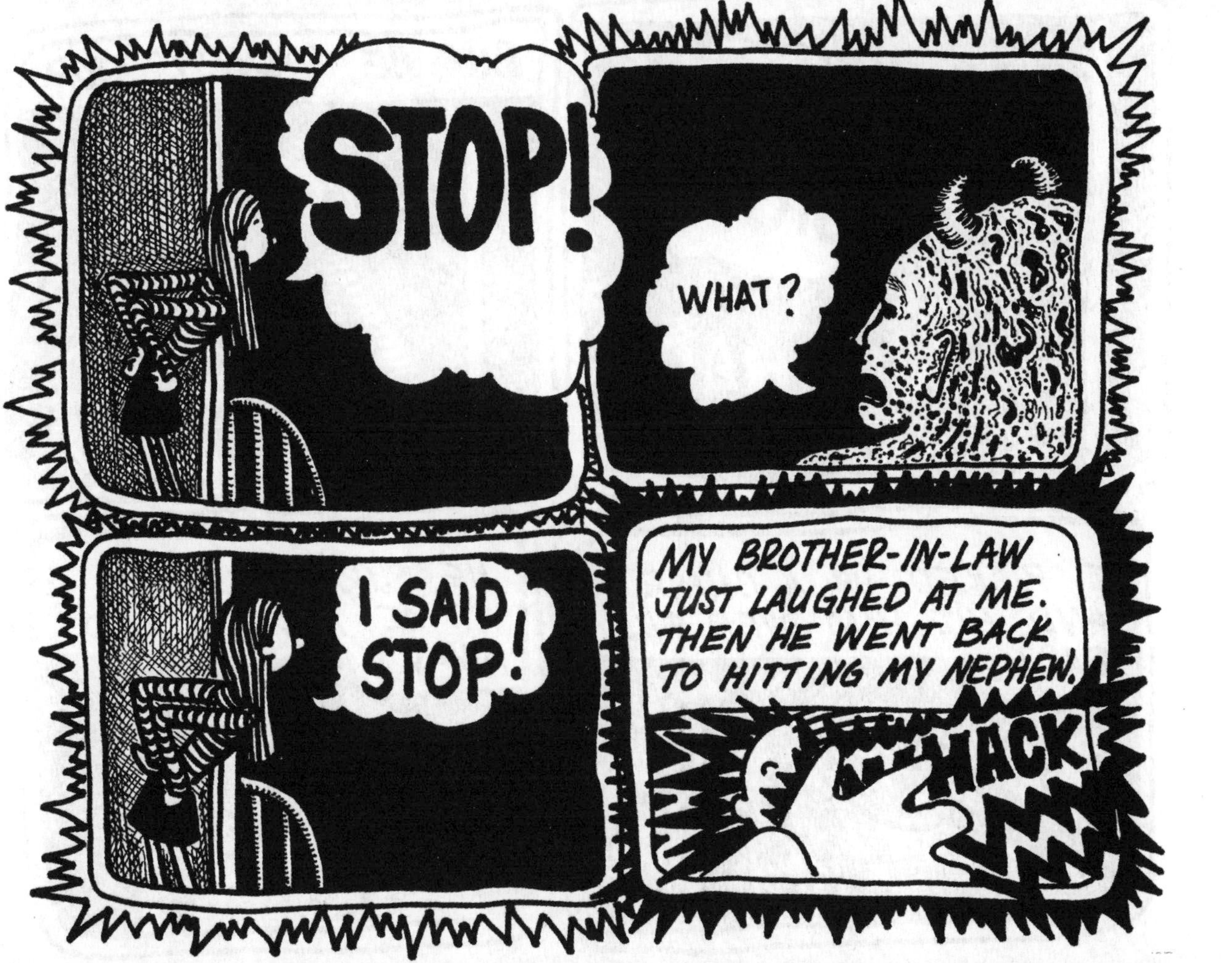
STOP!
WHAT?
I SAID STOP!
MY BROTHER-IN-LAW JUST LAUGHED AT ME. THEN HE WENT BACK TO HITTING MY NEPHEW.
HACK

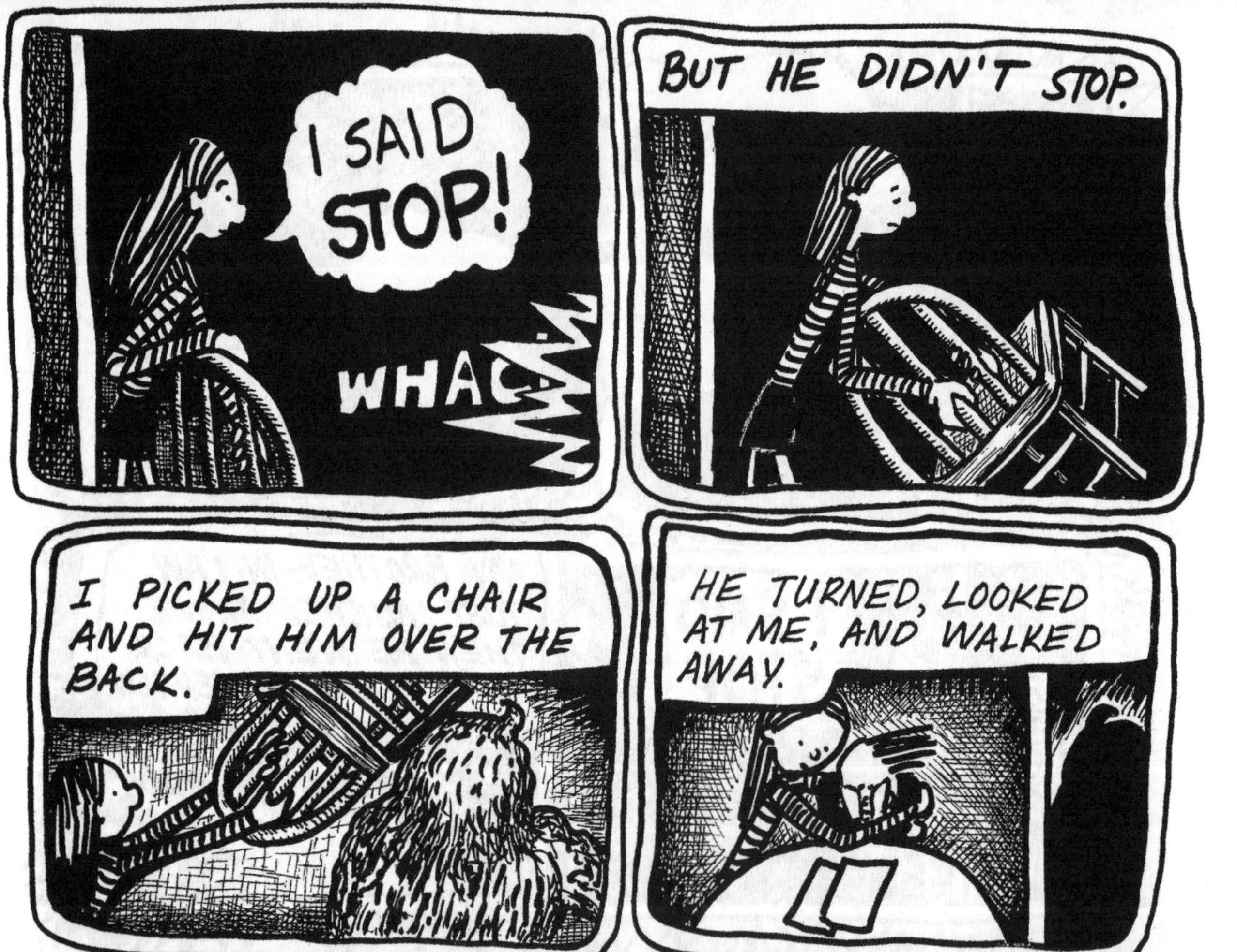
I SAID STOP!
WHAC
BUT HE DIDN'T STOP.
I PICKED UP A CHAIR AND HIT HIM OVER THE BACK.
HE TURNED, LOOKED AT ME, AND WALKED AWAY.

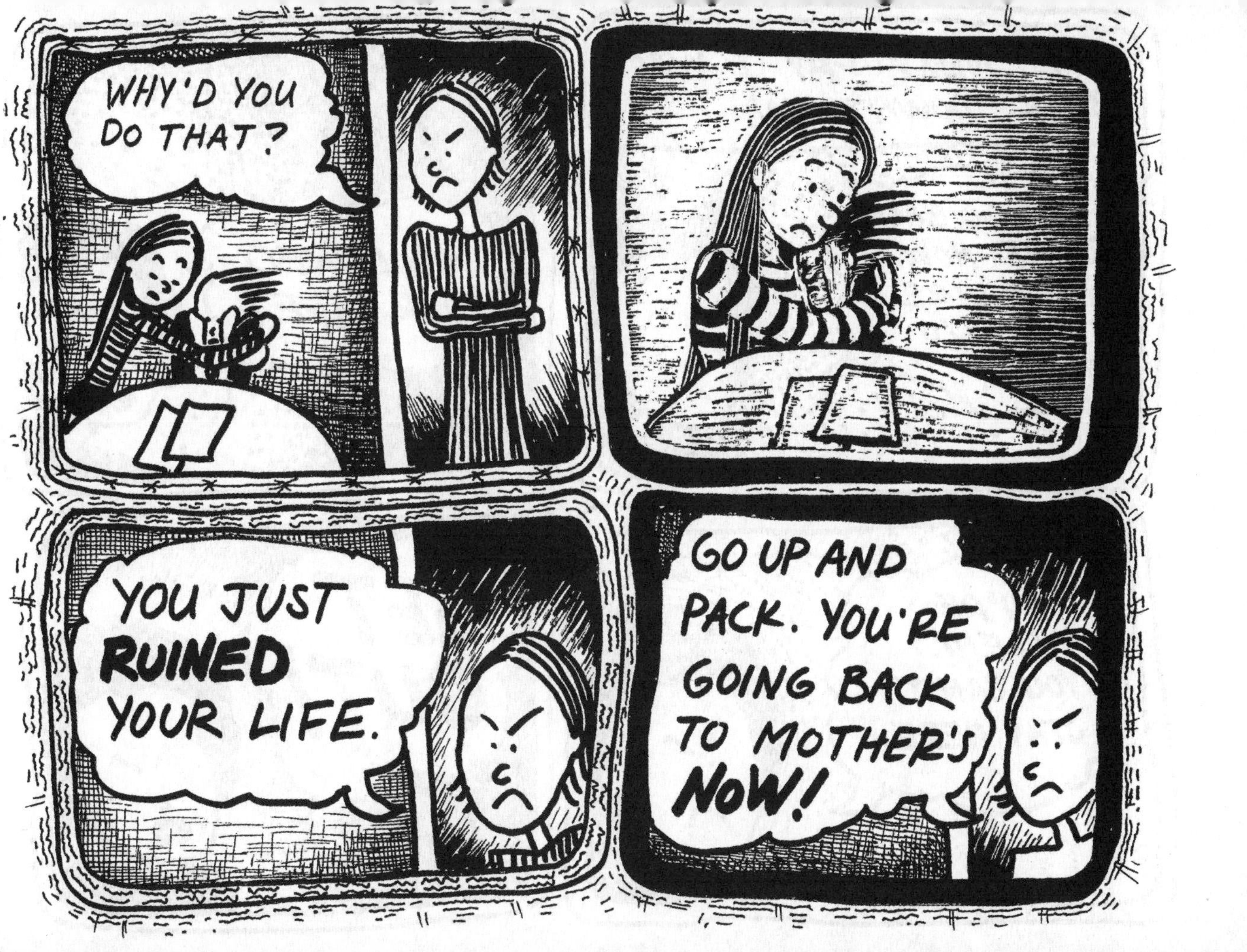
WHY'D YOU DO THAT?
YOU JUST **RUINED** YOUR LIFE.
GO UP AND PACK. YOU'RE GOING BACK TO MOTHER'S **NOW!**

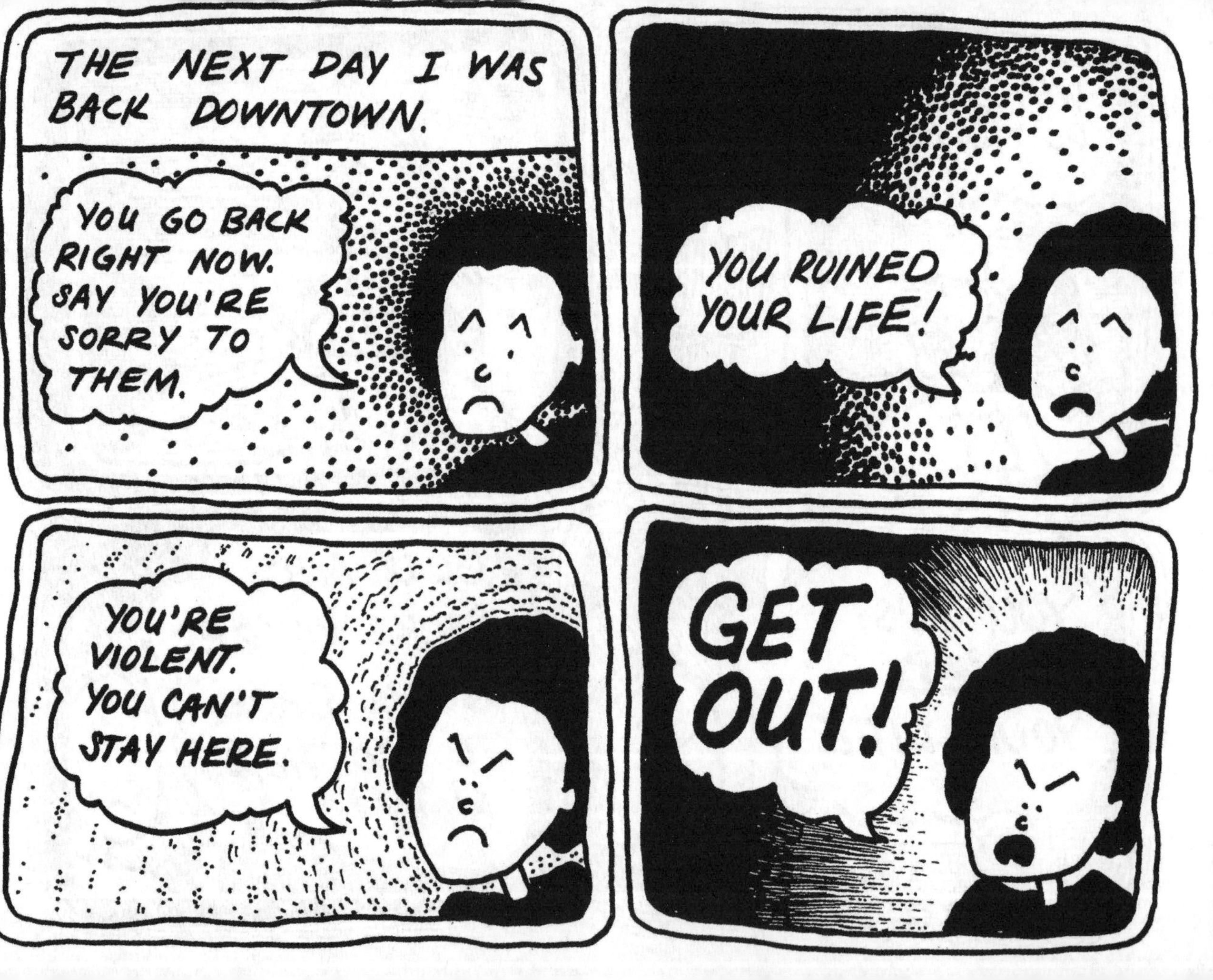
THE NEXT DAY I WAS BACK DOWNTOWN.
YOU GO BACK RIGHT NOW. SAY YOU'RE SORRY TO THEM.
YOU RUINED YOUR LIFE!
YOU'RE VIOLENT. YOU CAN'T STAY HERE.
GET OUT!

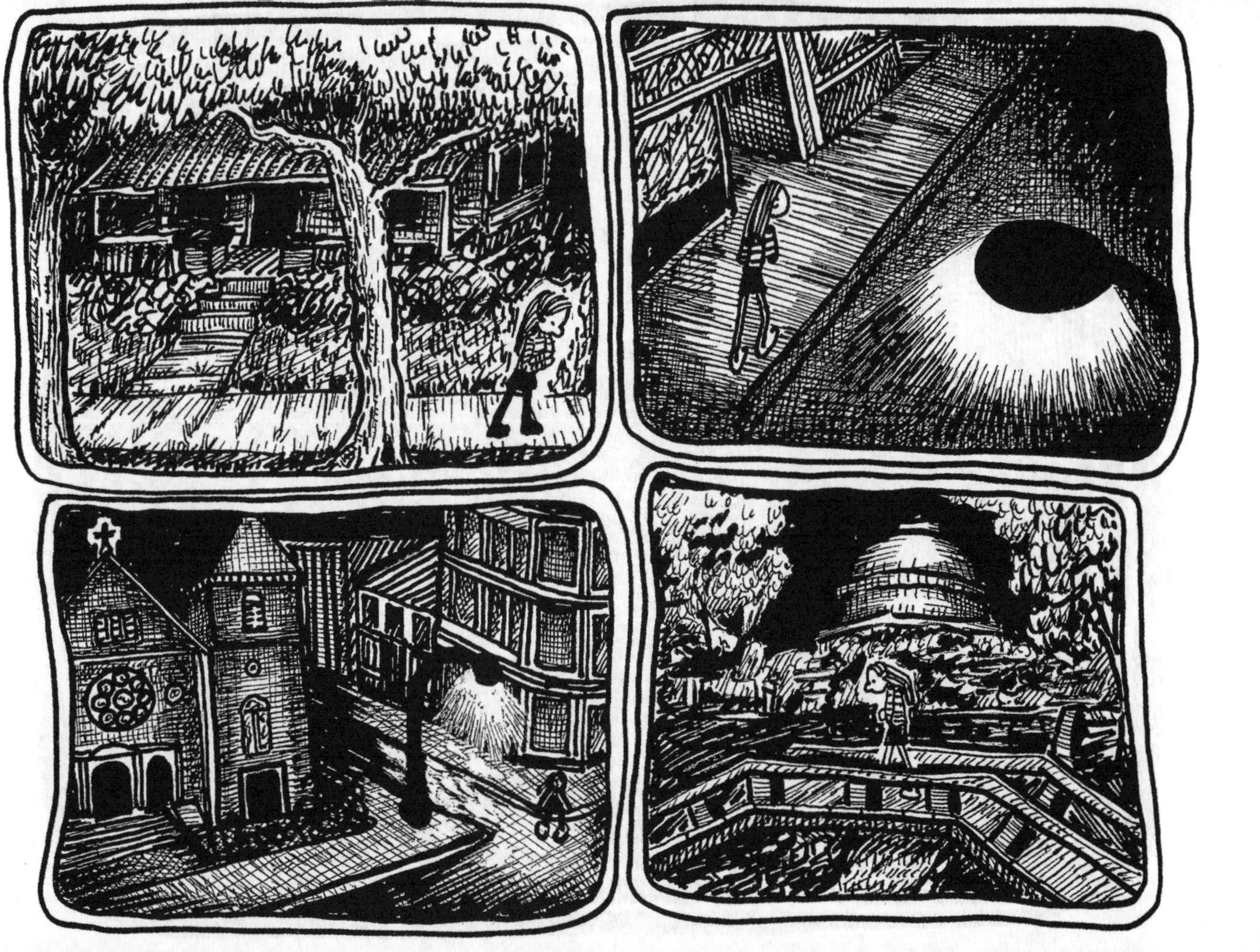

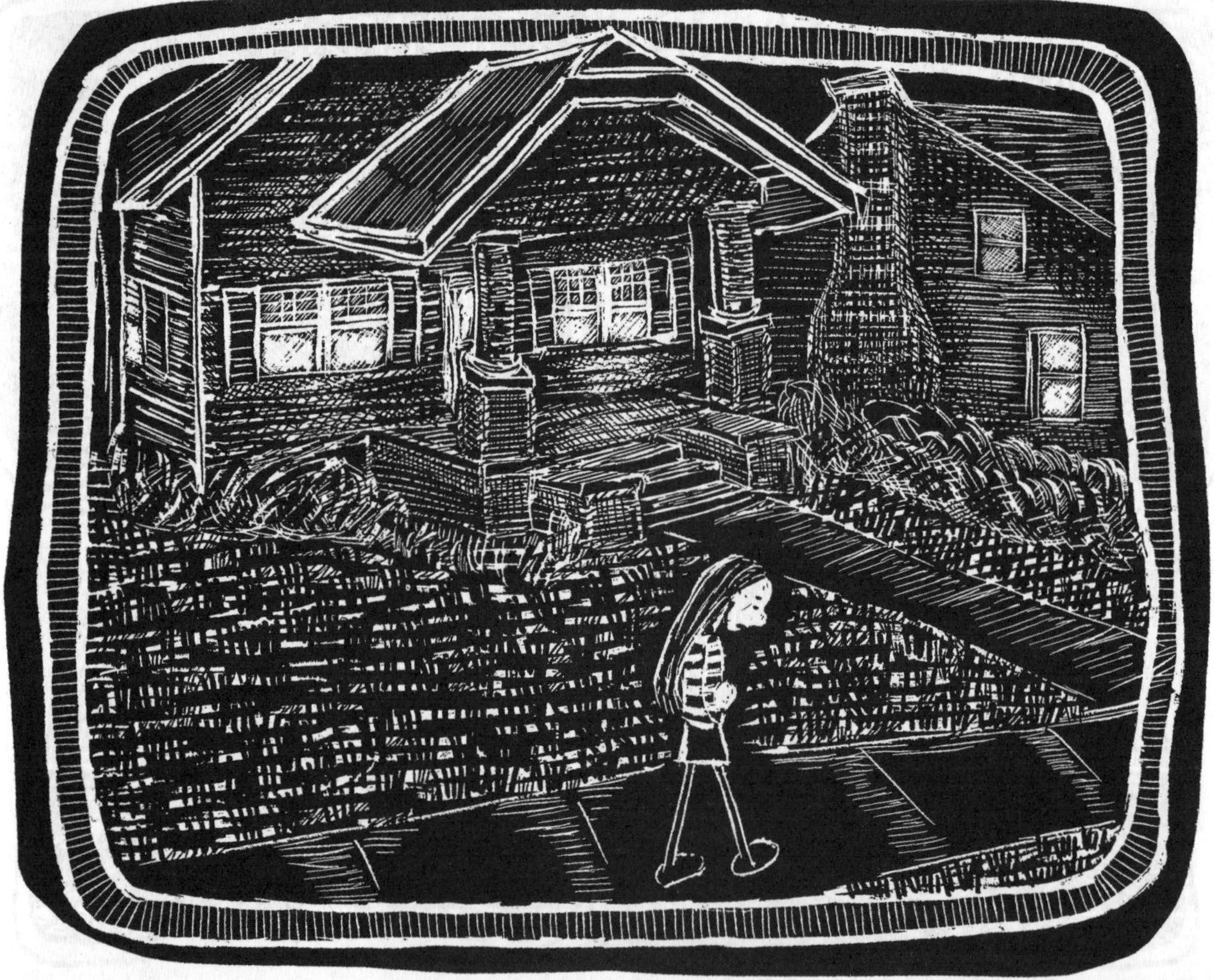

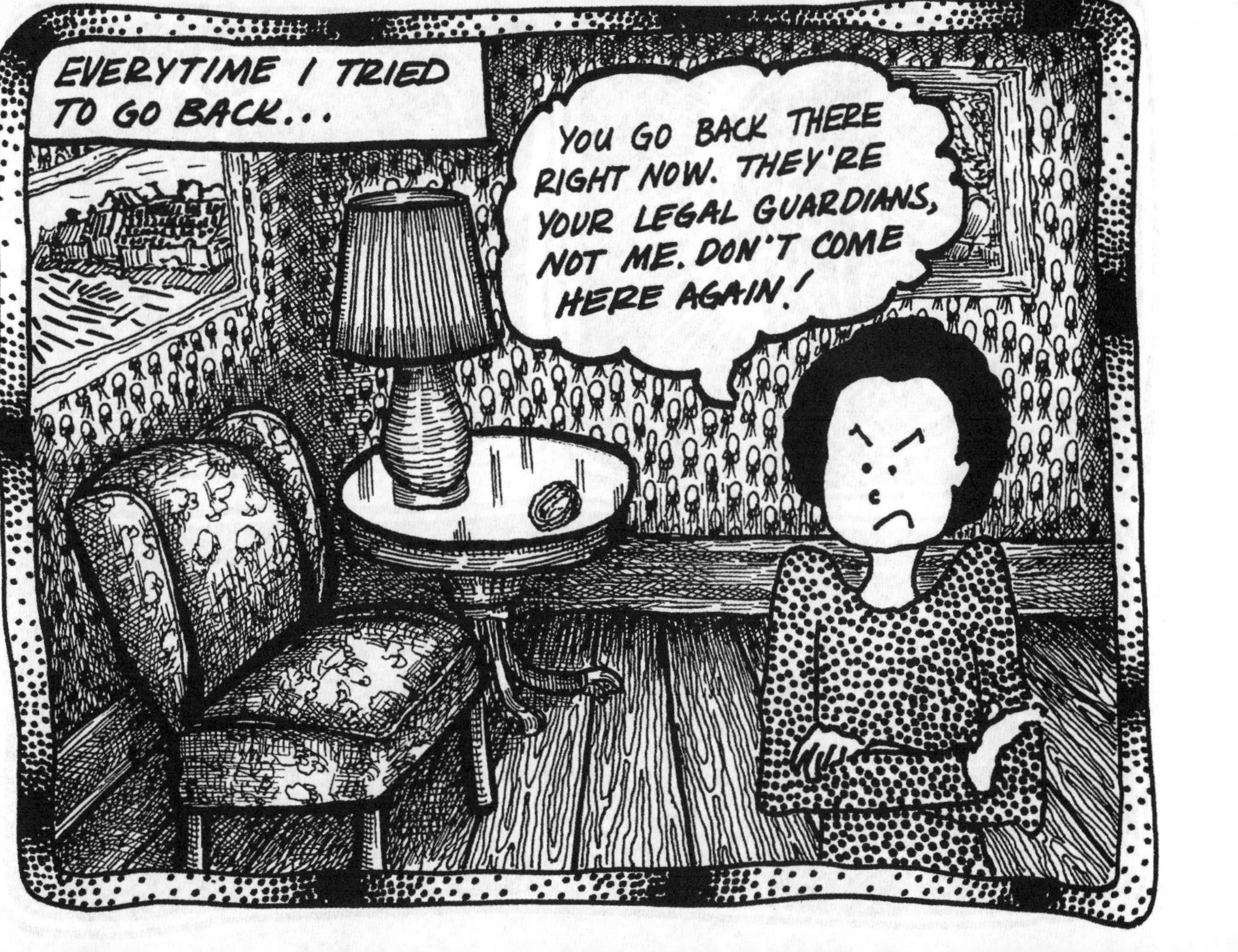
EVERYTIME I TRIED TO GO BACK...
YOU GO BACK THERE RIGHT NOW. THEY'RE YOUR LEGAL GUARDIANS, NOT ME. DON'T COME HERE AGAIN!

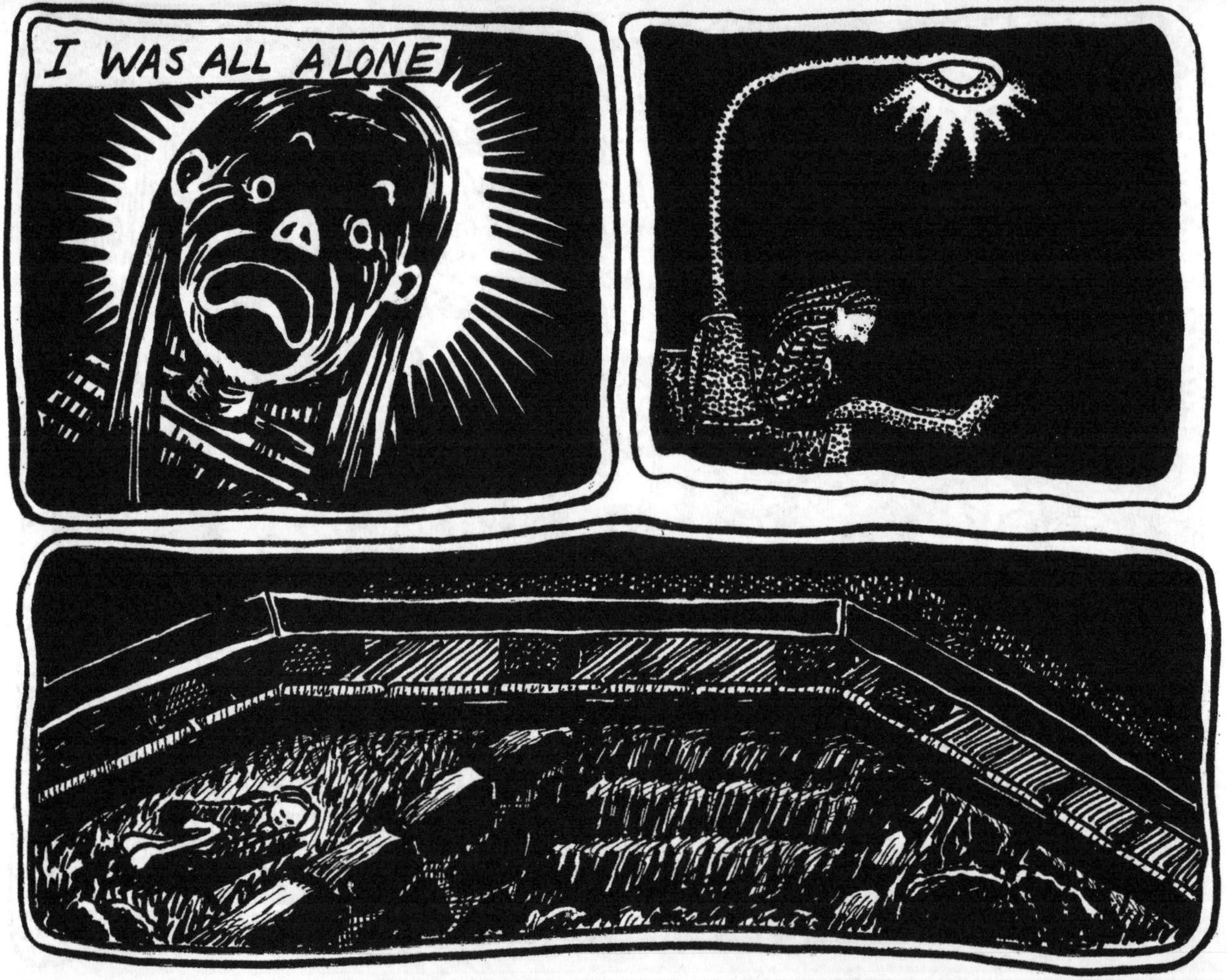
I WAS ALL ALONE

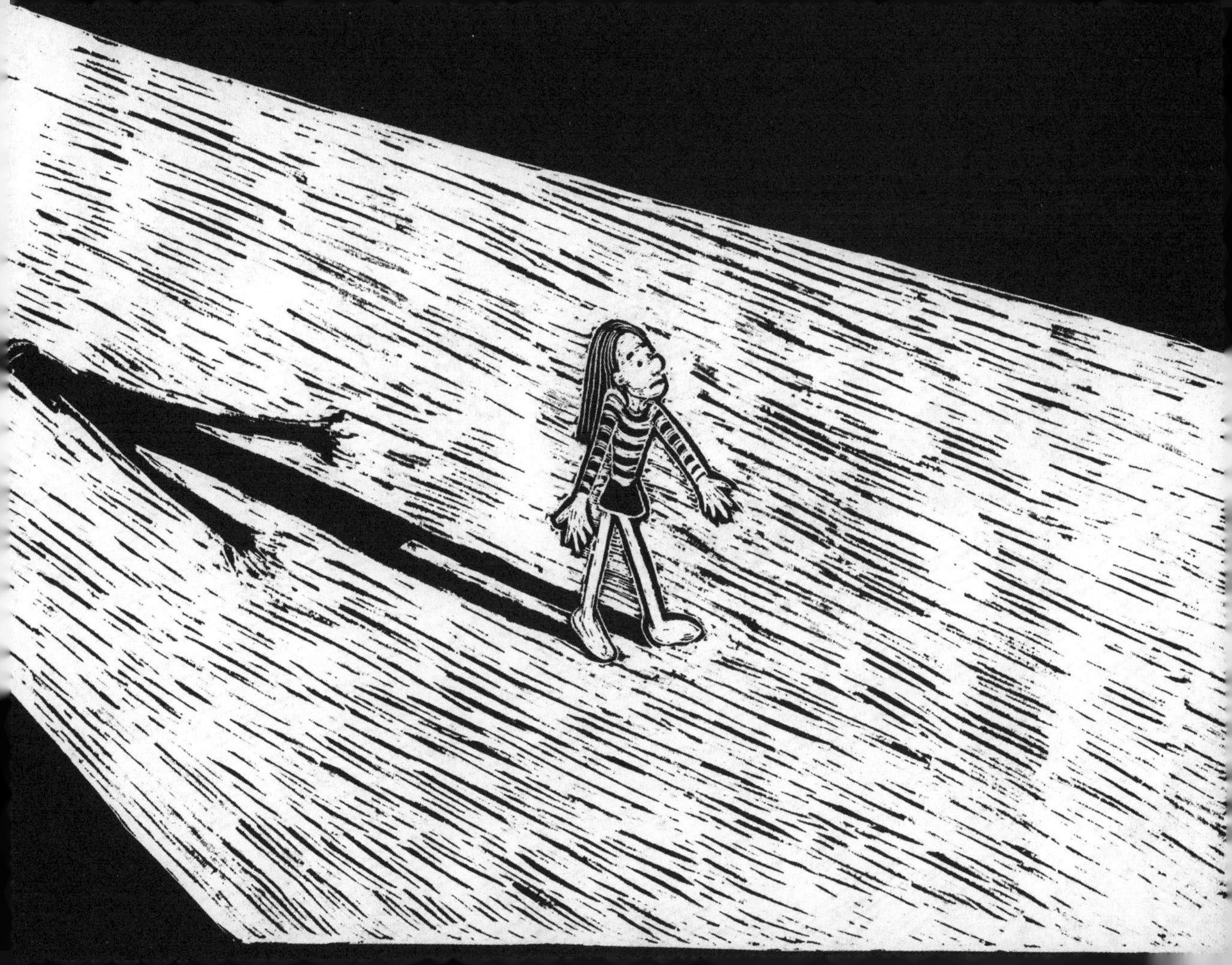

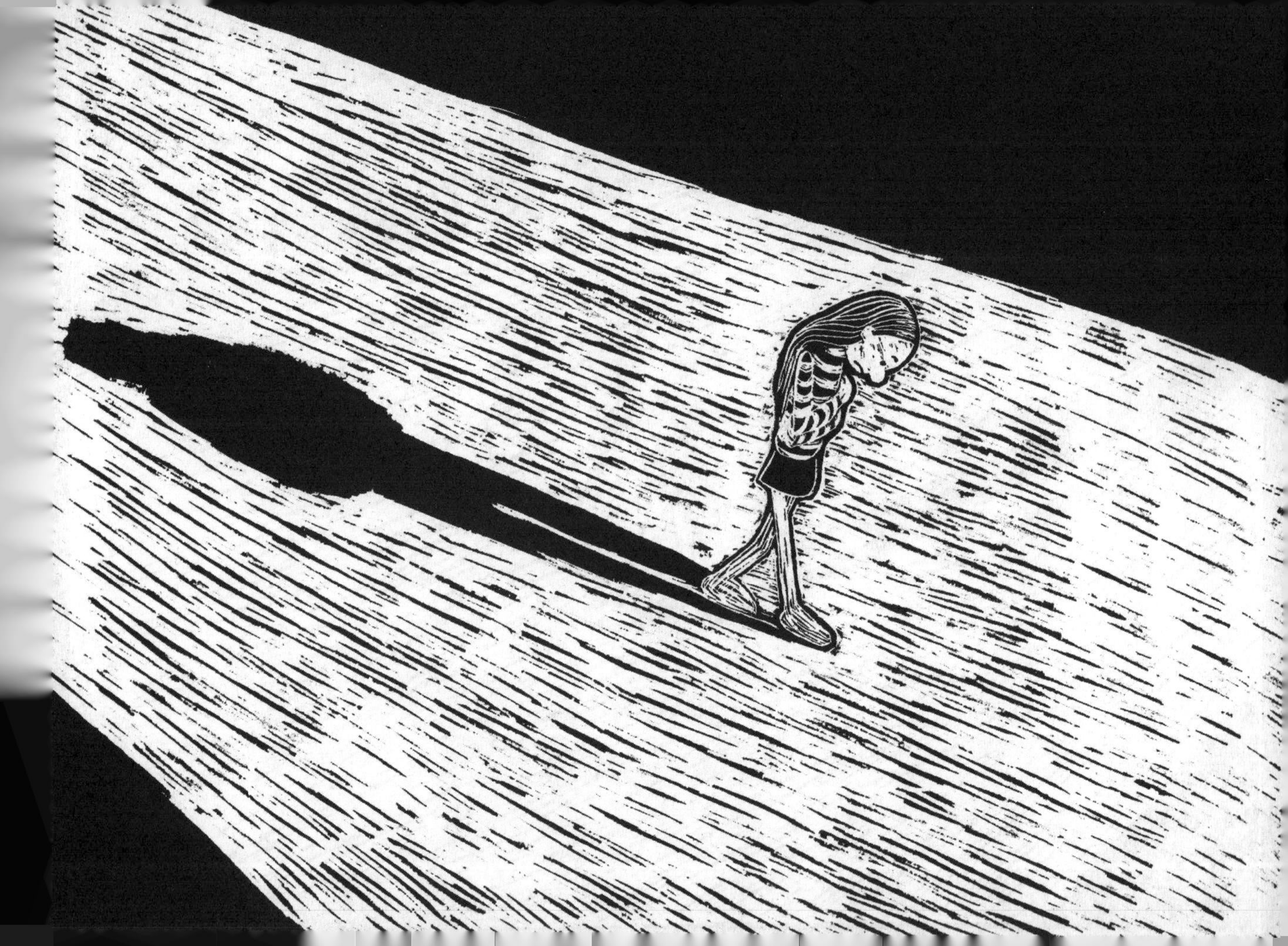

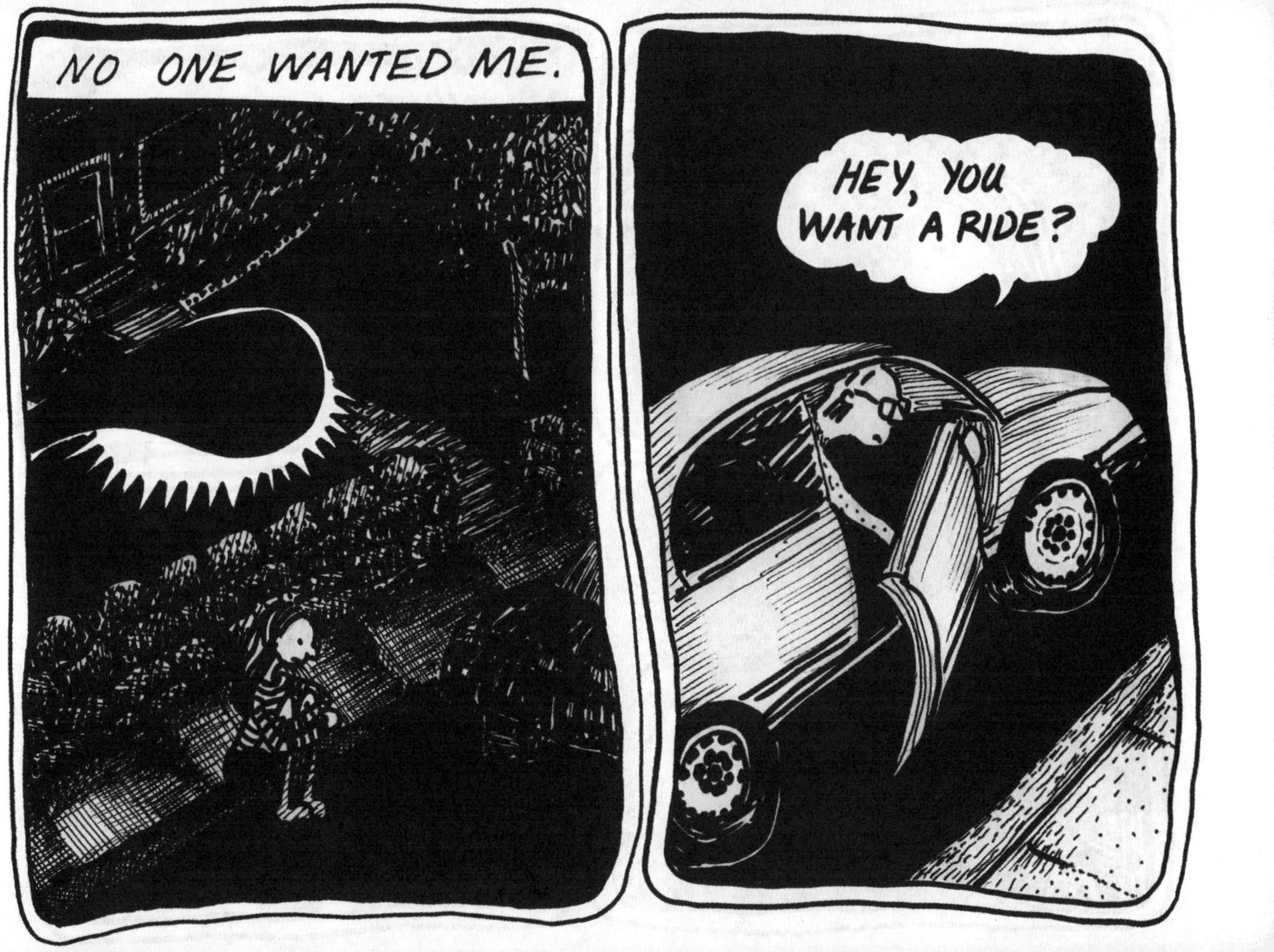
NO ONE WANTED ME.
HEY, YOU WANT A RIDE?

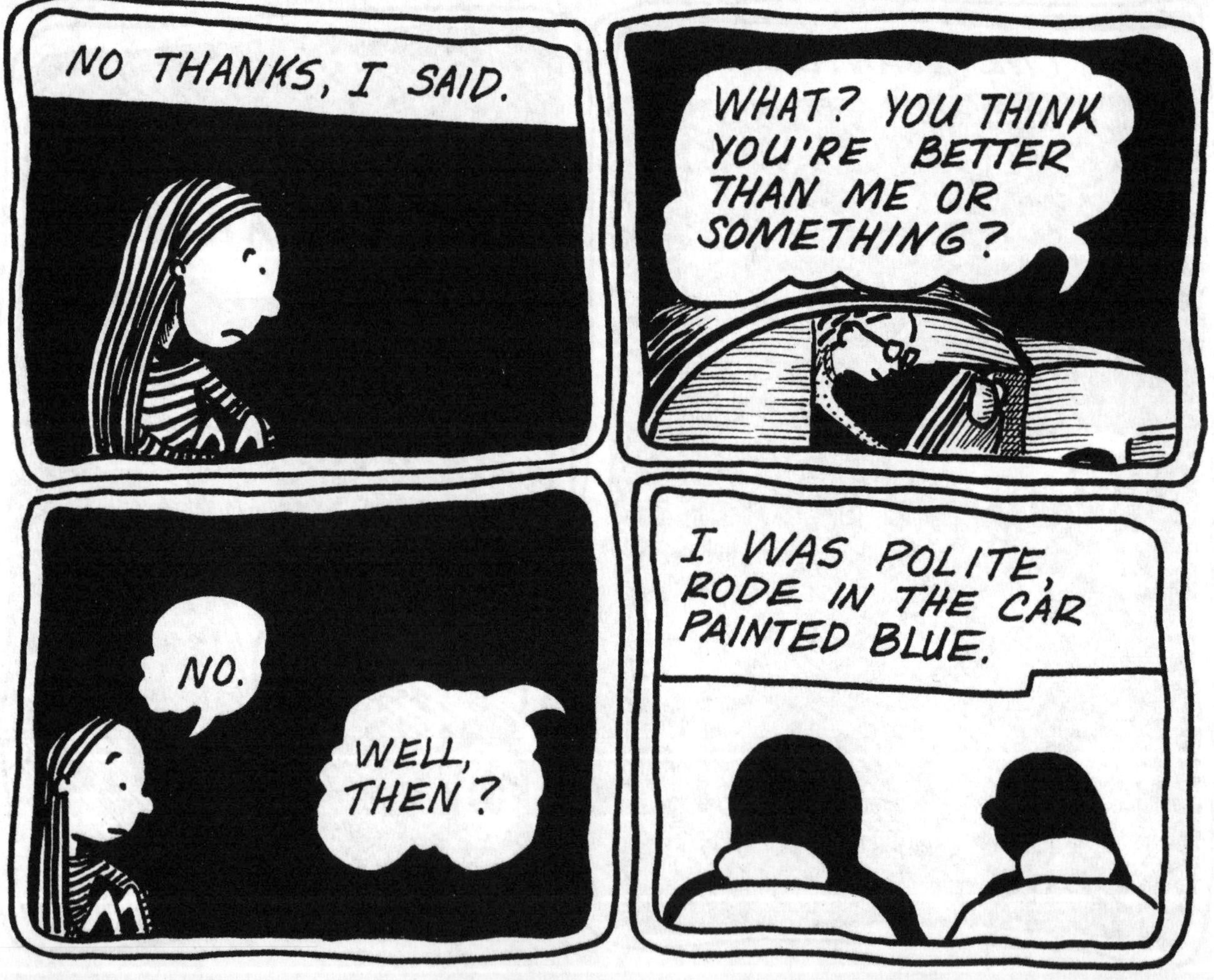
NO THANKS, I SAID.
WHAT? YOU THINK YOU'RE BETTER THAN ME OR SOMETHING?
NO.
WELL, THEN?
I WAS POLITE, RODE IN THE CAR PAINTED BLUE.

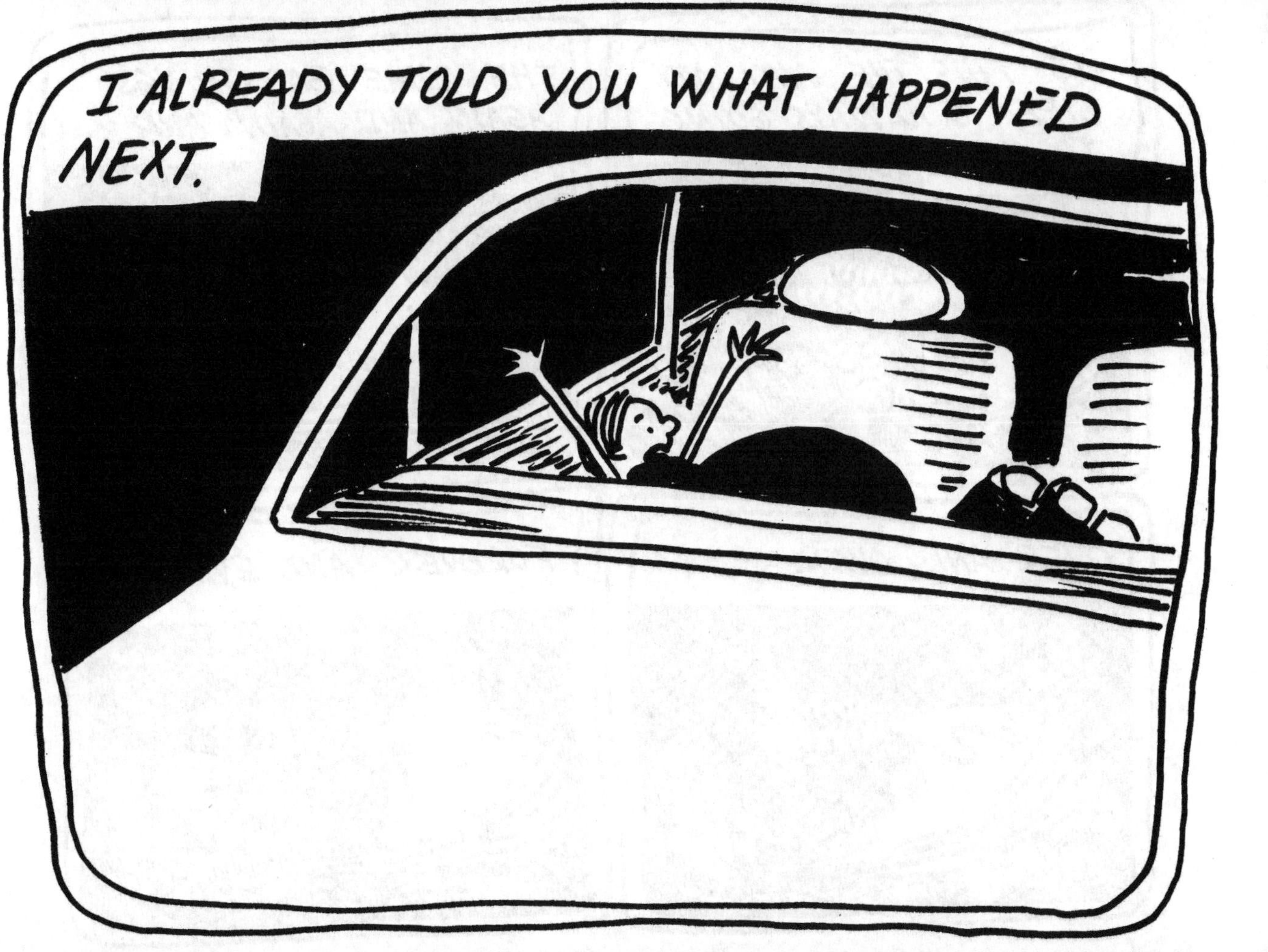
I ALREADY TOLD YOU WHAT HAPPENED NEXT.

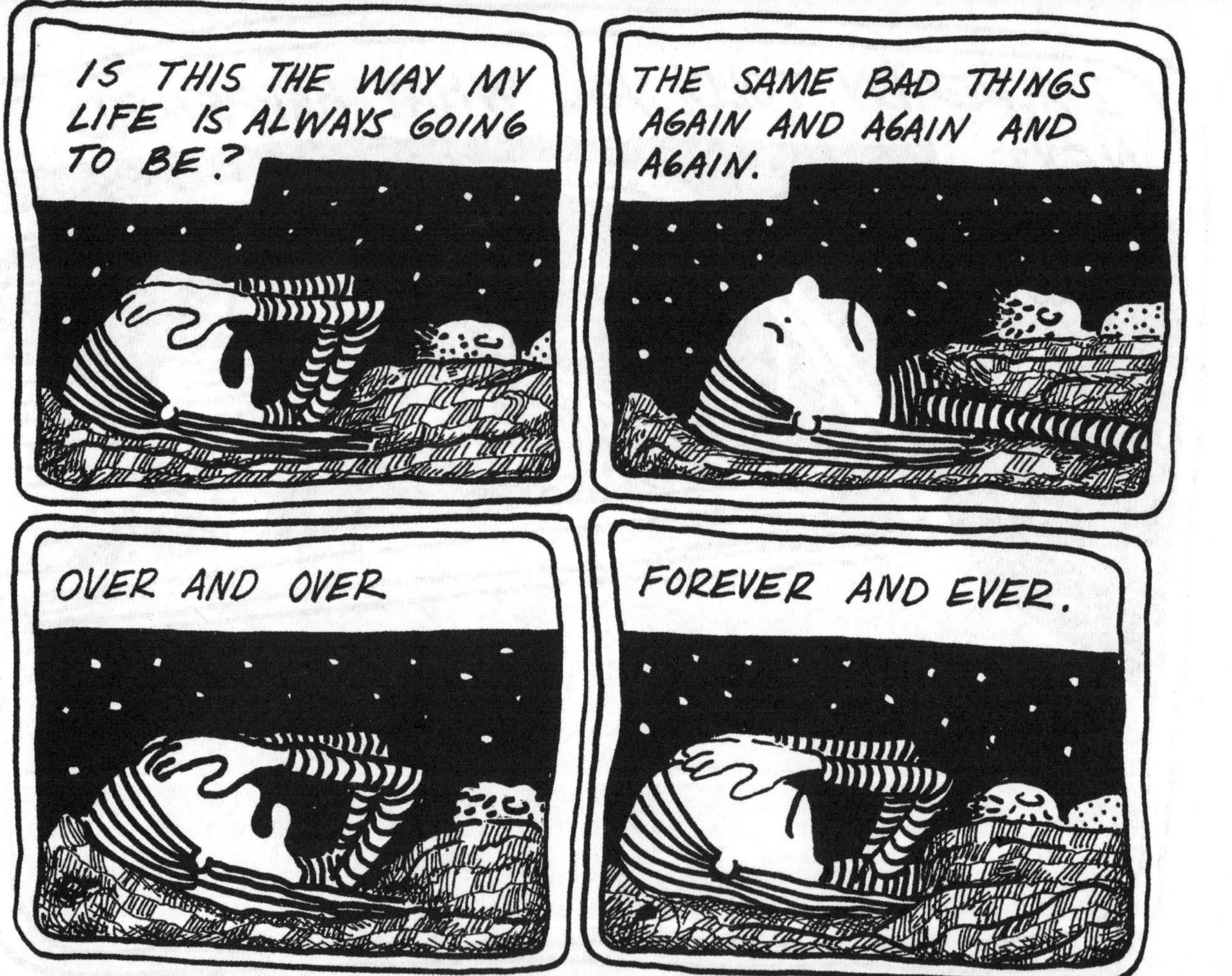
IS THIS THE WAY MY LIFE IS ALWAYS GOING TO BE?
THE SAME BAD THINGS AGAIN AND AGAIN AND AGAIN.
OVER AND OVER
FOREVER AND EVER.

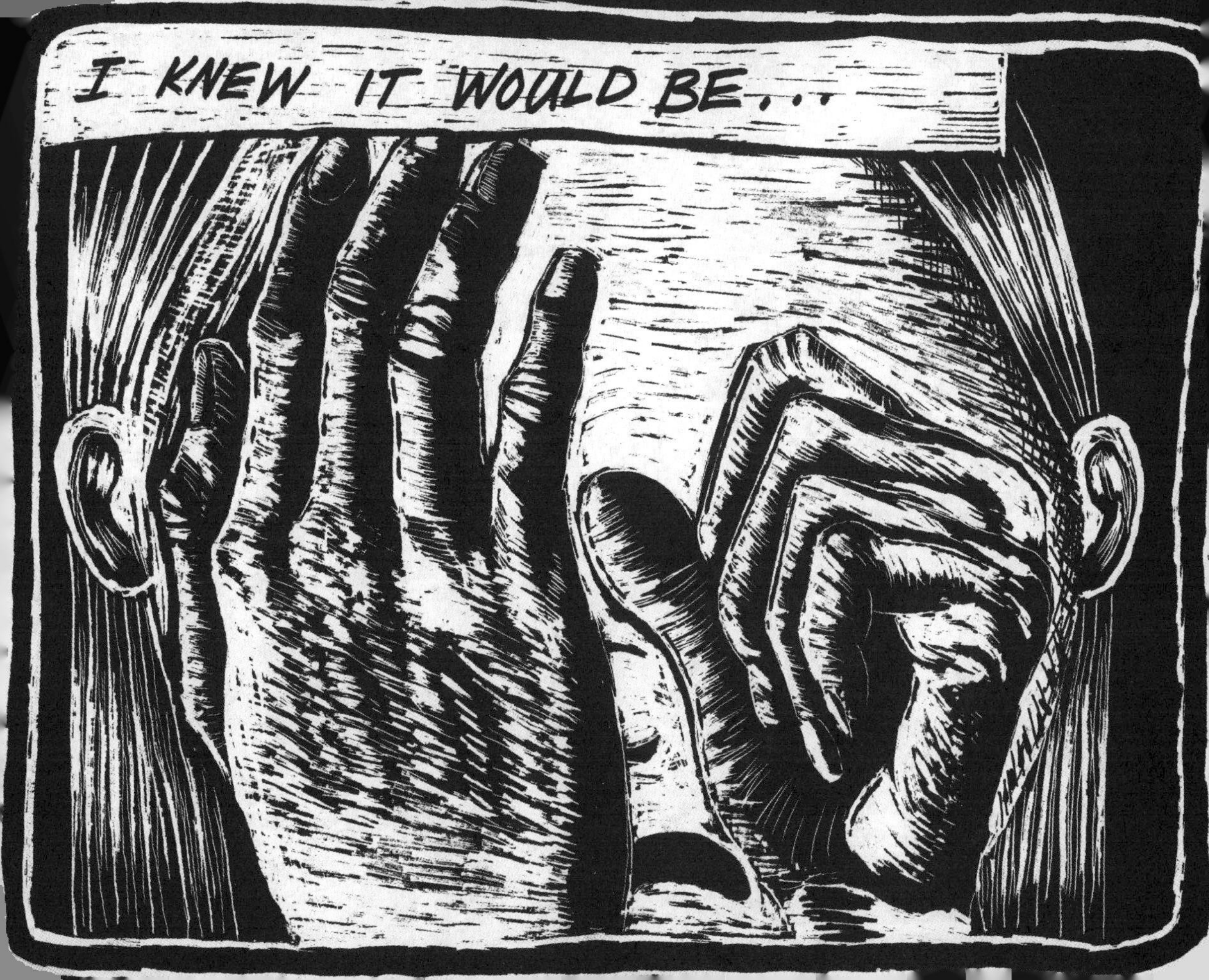
I KNEW IT WOULD BE...

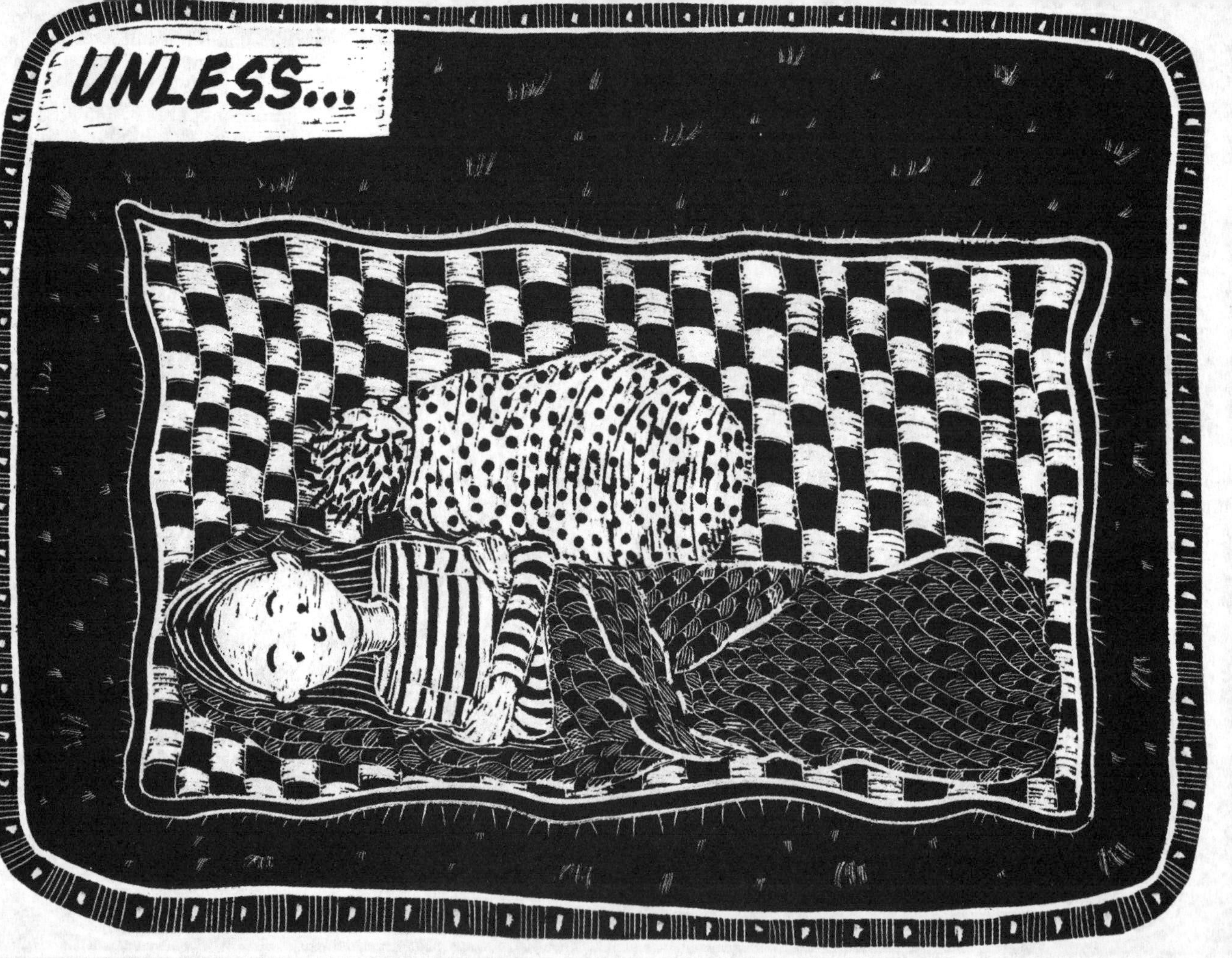
UNLESS...

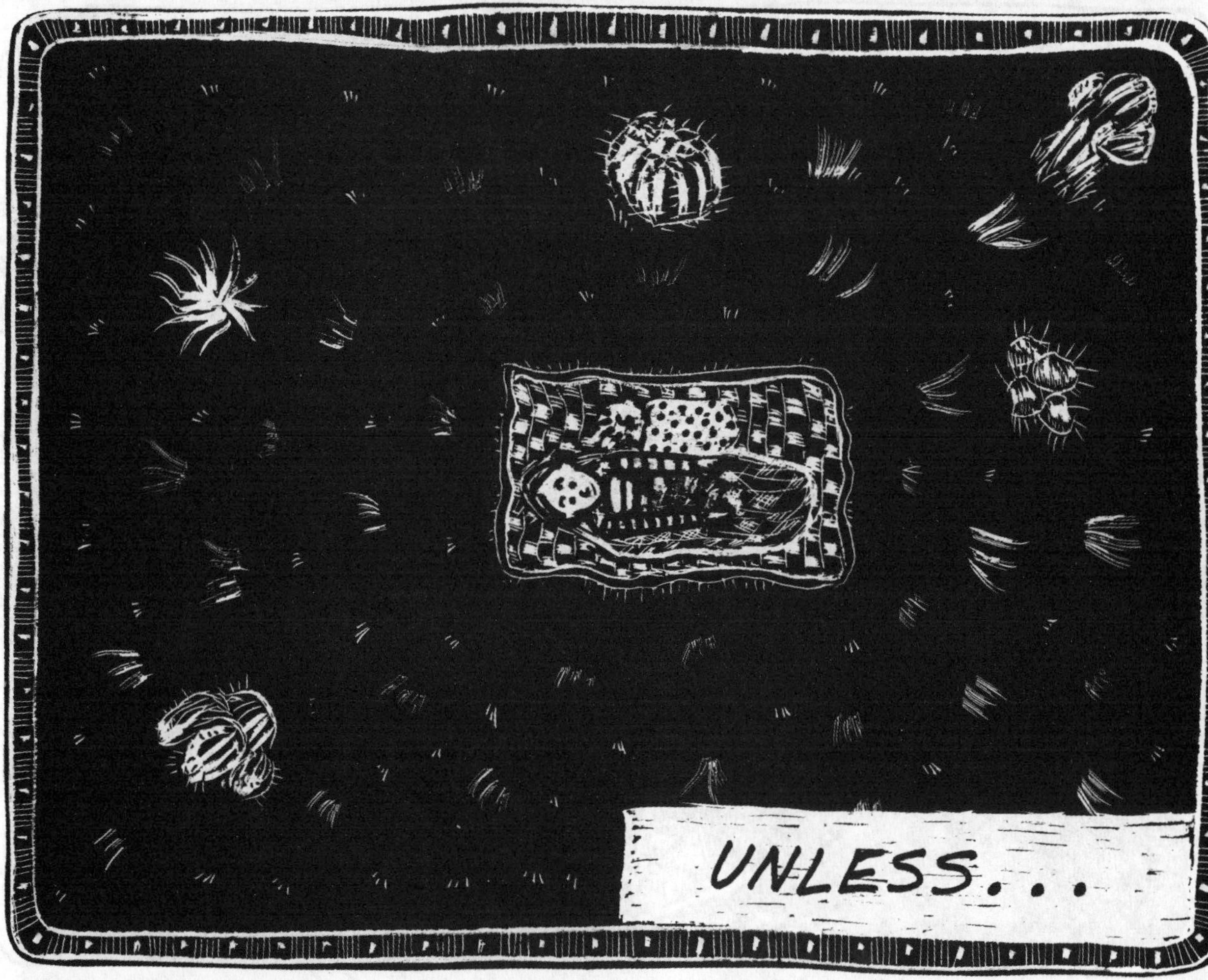
UNLESS...

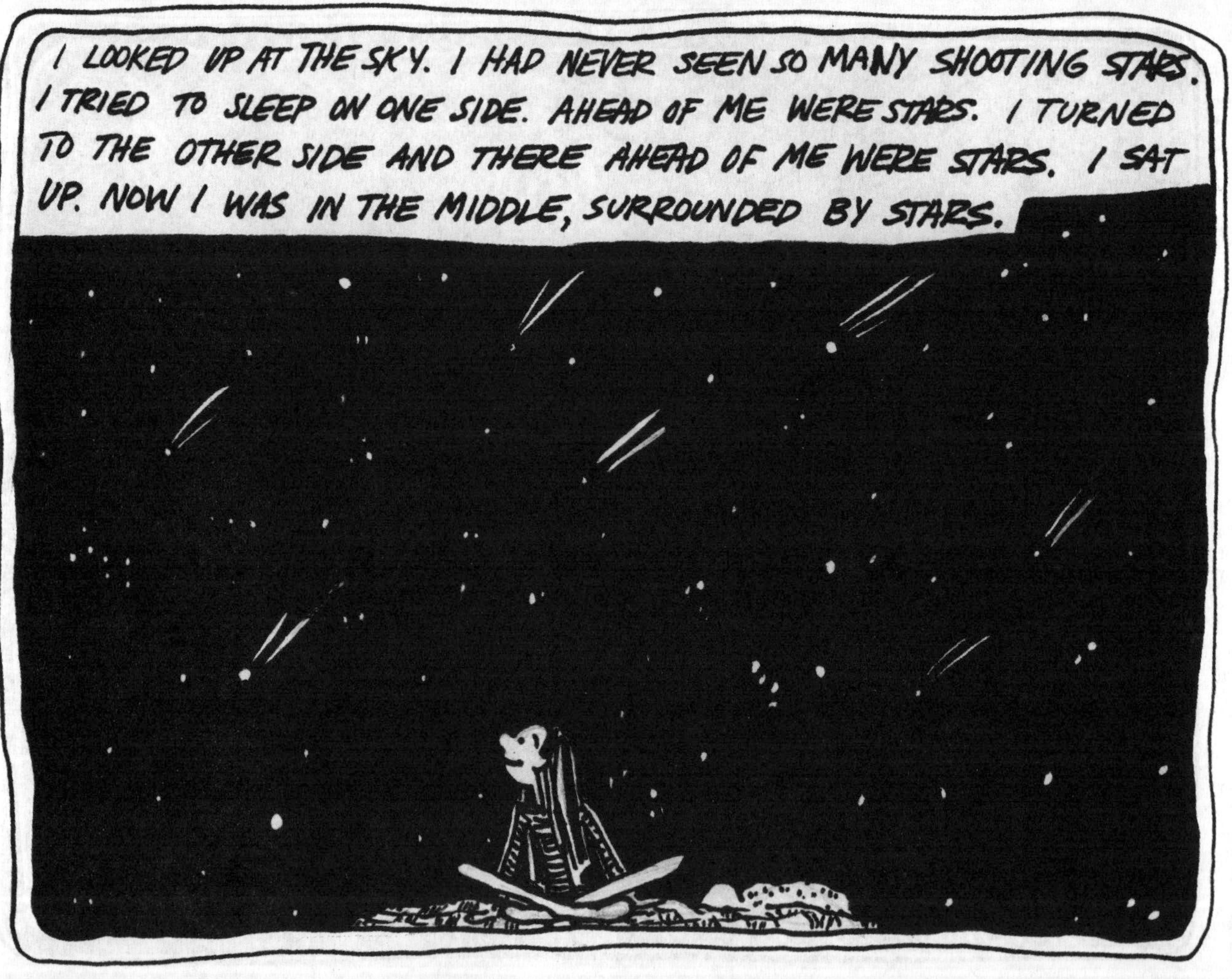
I LOOKED UP AT THE SKY. I HAD NEVER SEEN SO MANY SHOOTING STARS. I TRIED TO SLEEP ON ONE SIDE. AHEAD OF ME WERE STARS. I TURNED TO THE OTHER SIDE AND THERE AHEAD OF ME WERE STARS. I SAT UP. NOW I WAS IN THE MIDDLE, SURROUNDED BY STARS.

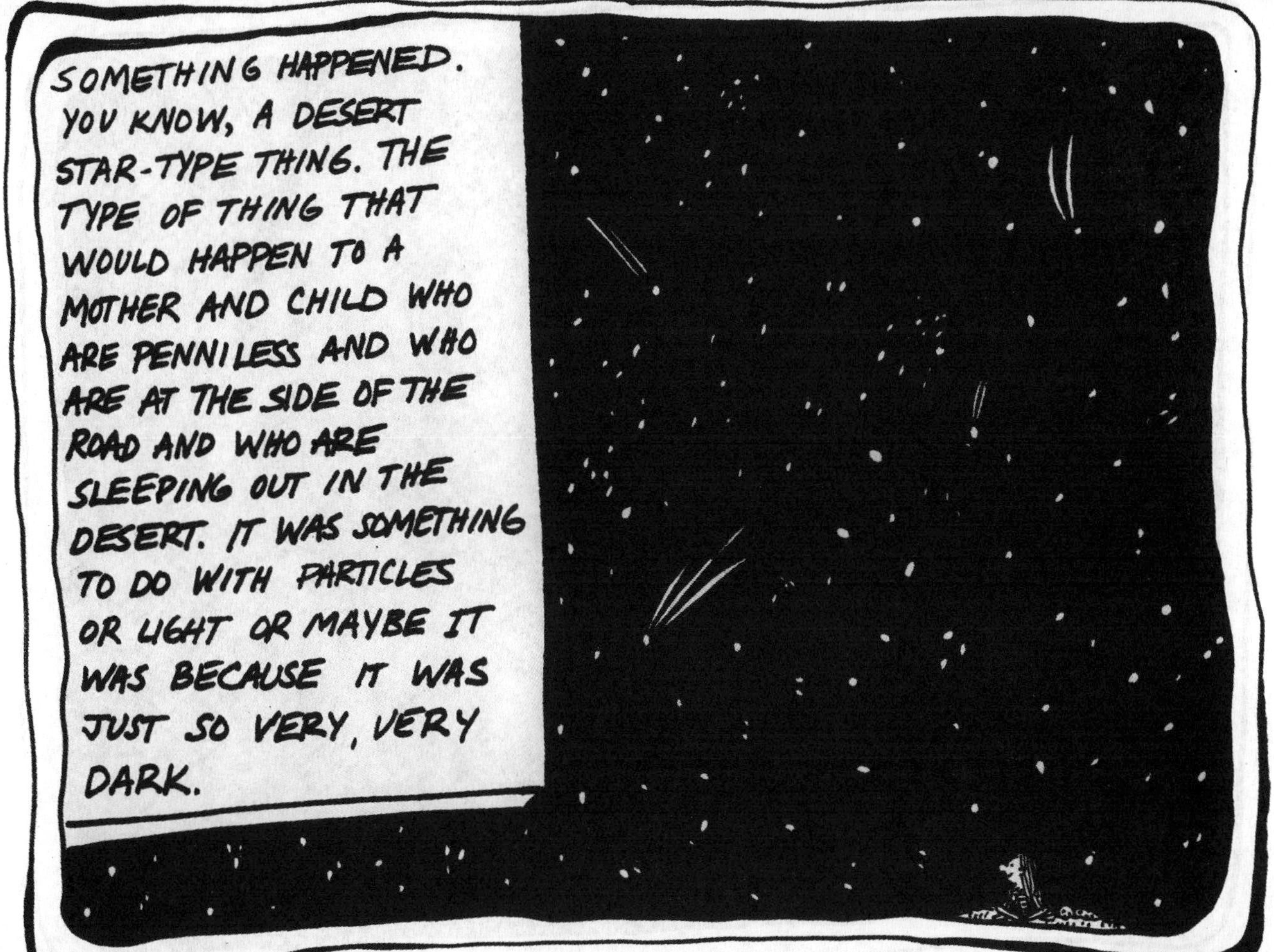
SOMETHING HAPPENED. YOU KNOW, A DESERT STAR-TYPE THING. THE TYPE OF THING THAT WOULD HAPPEN TO A MOTHER AND CHILD WHO ARE PENNILESS AND WHO ARE AT THE SIDE OF THE ROAD AND WHO ARE SLEEPING OUT IN THE DESERT. IT WAS SOMETHING TO DO WITH PARTICLES OR LIGHT OR MAYBE IT WAS BECAUSE IT WAS JUST SO VERY, VERY DARK.

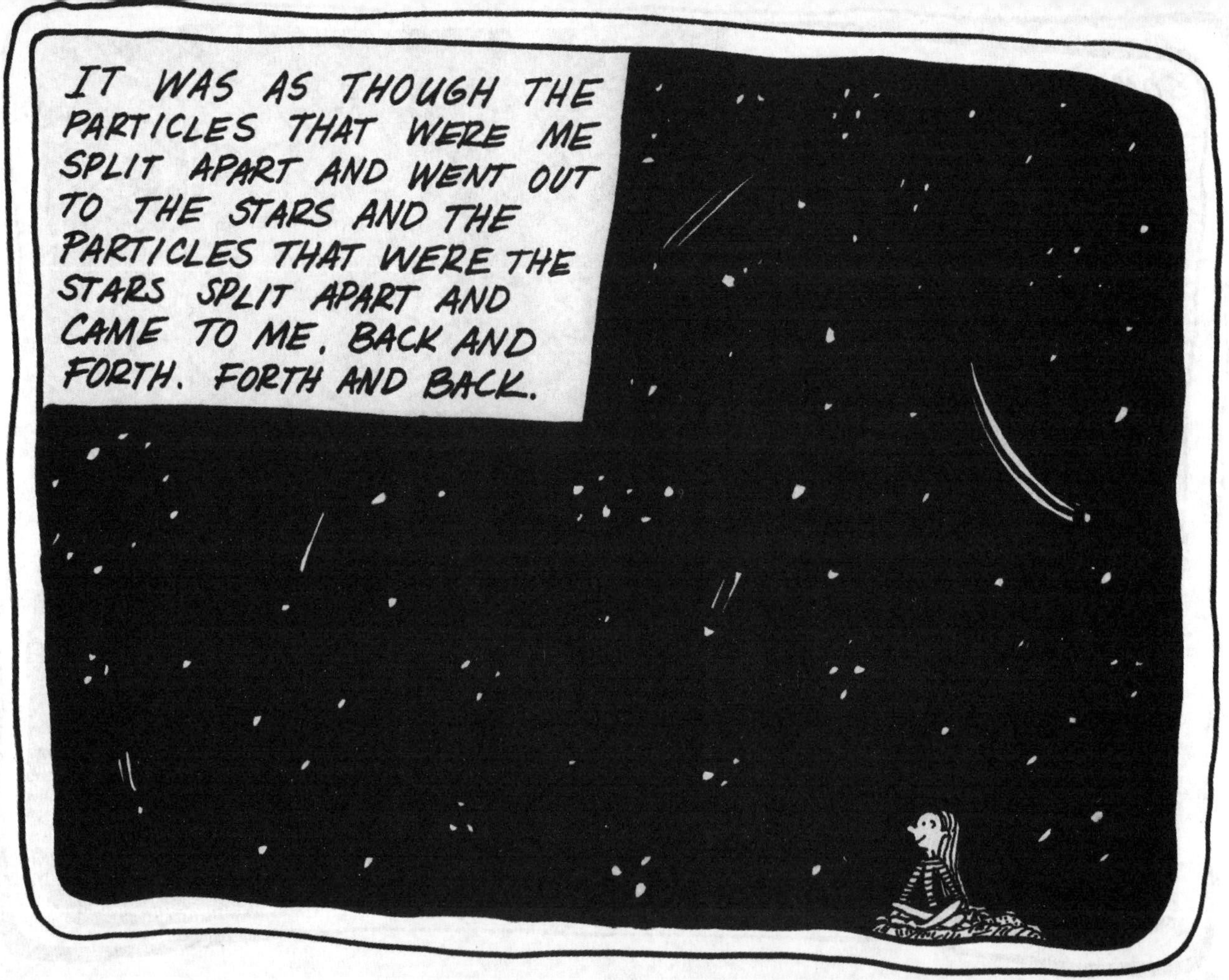
IT WAS AS THOUGH THE PARTICLES THAT WERE ME SPLIT APART AND WENT OUT TO THE STARS AND THE PARTICLES THAT WERE THE STARS SPLIT APART AND CAME TO ME. BACK AND FORTH. FORTH AND BACK.

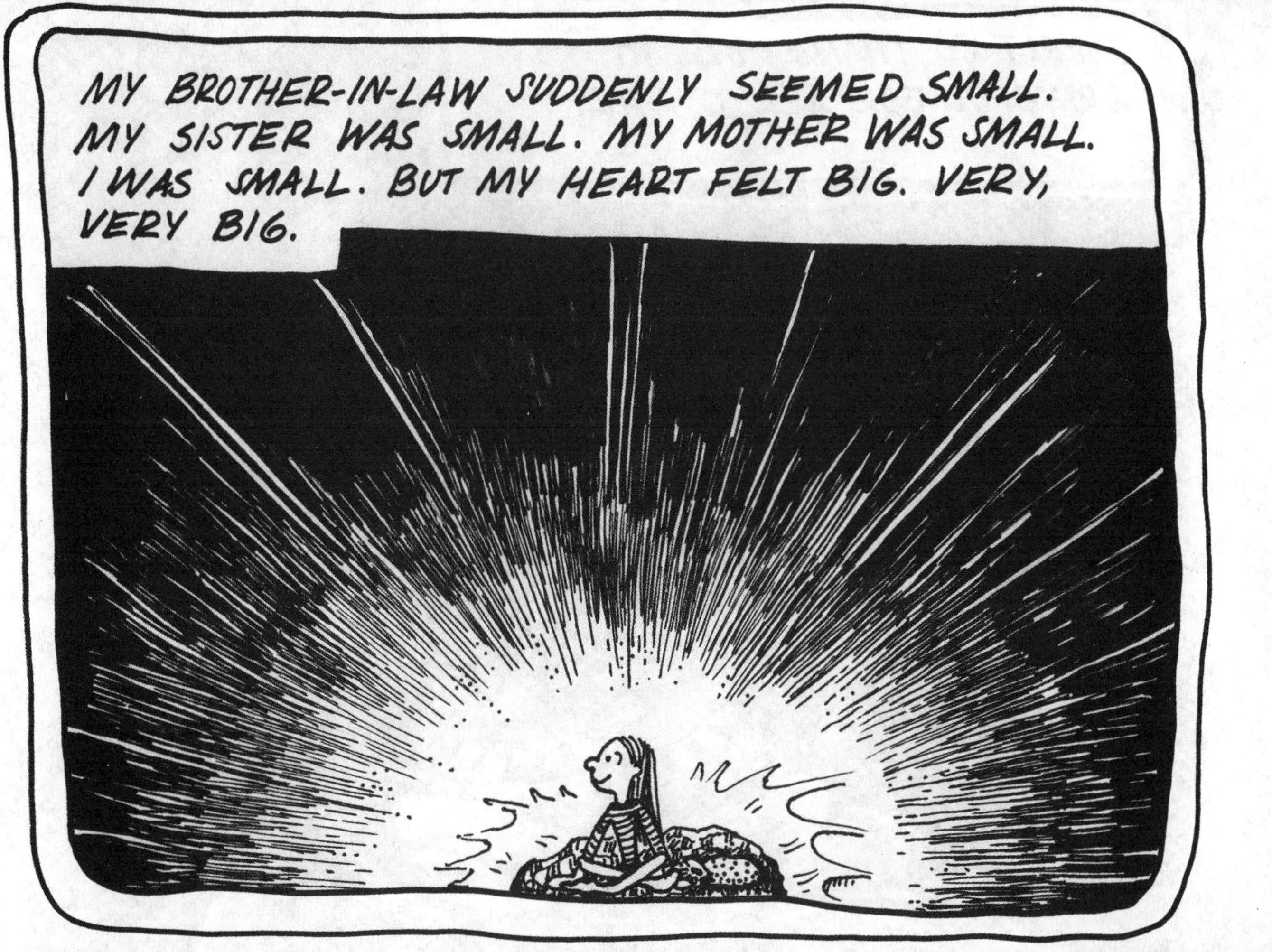
MY BROTHER-IN-LAW SUDDENLY SEEMED SMALL. MY SISTER WAS SMALL. MY MOTHER WAS SMALL. I WAS SMALL. BUT MY HEART FELT BIG. VERY, VERY BIG.

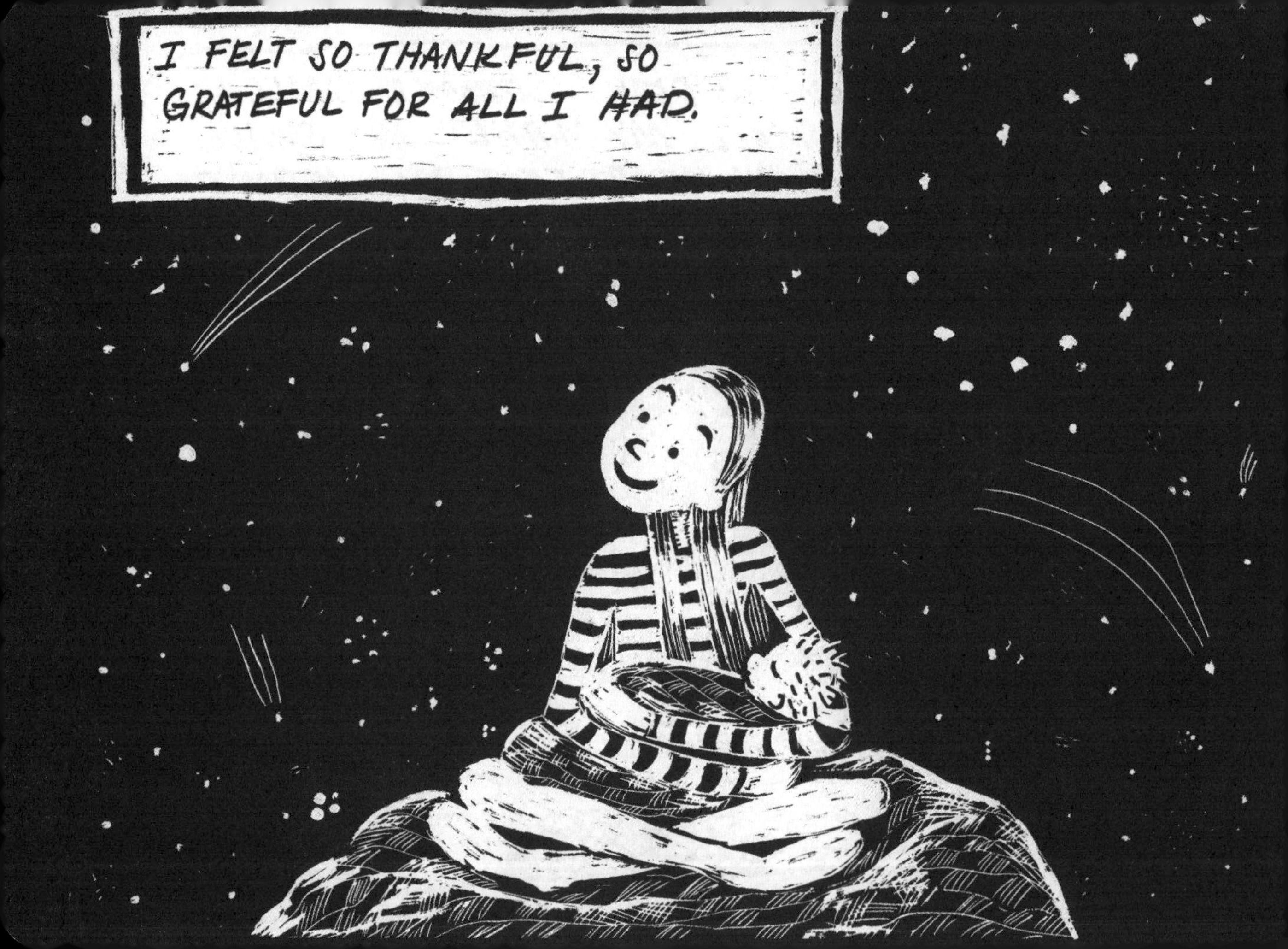
I FELT SO THANKFUL, SO GRATEFUL FOR ALL I HAD.

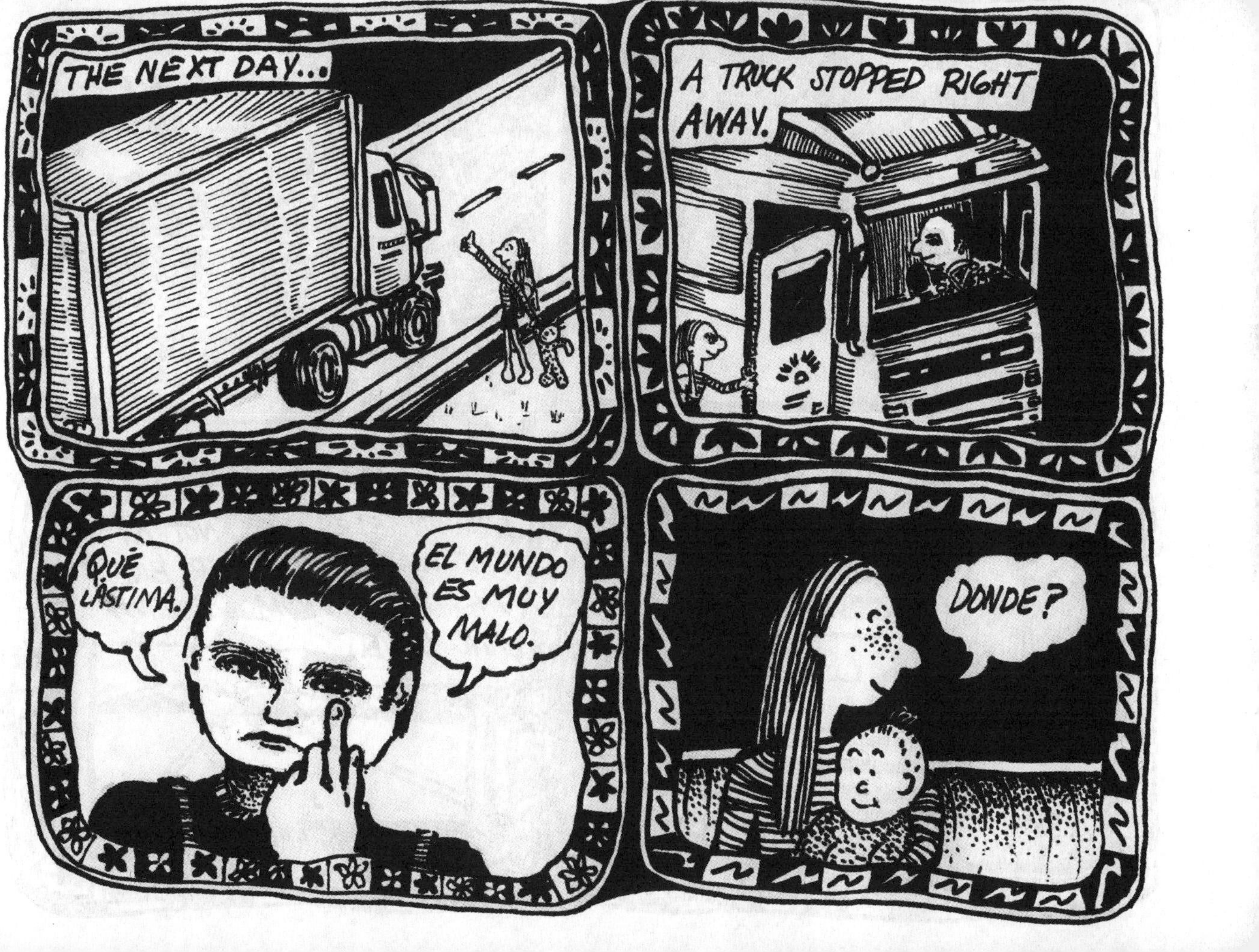
THE NEXT DAY...
A TRUCK STOPPED RIGHT AWAY.
QUÉ LÁSTIMA.
EL MUNDO ES MUY MALO.
DONDE?

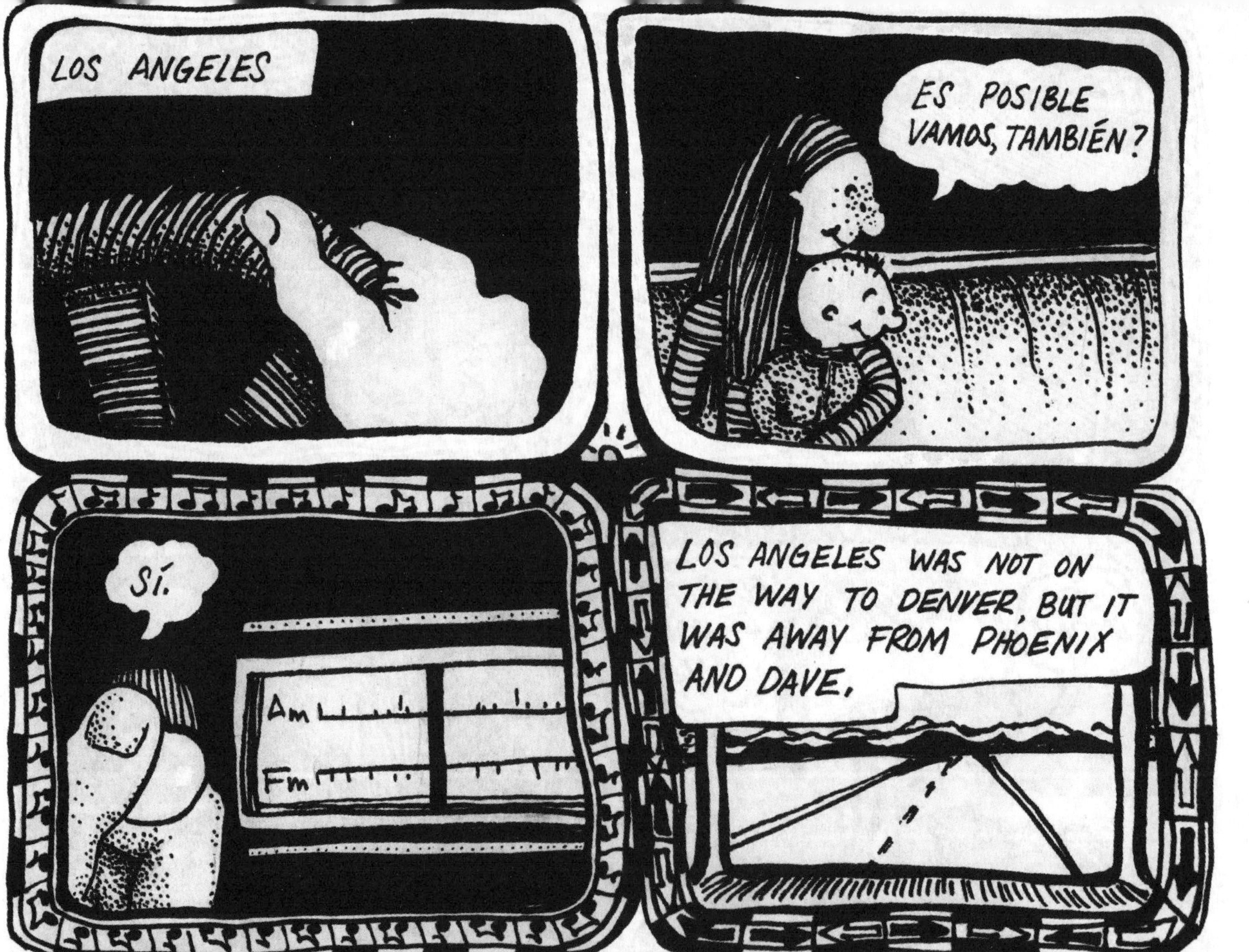
LOS ANGELES
ES POSIBLE VAMOS, TAMBIÉN?
SÍ.
Am
Fm
LOS ANGELES WAS NOT ON THE WAY TO DENVER, BUT IT WAS AWAY FROM PHOENIX AND DAVE.

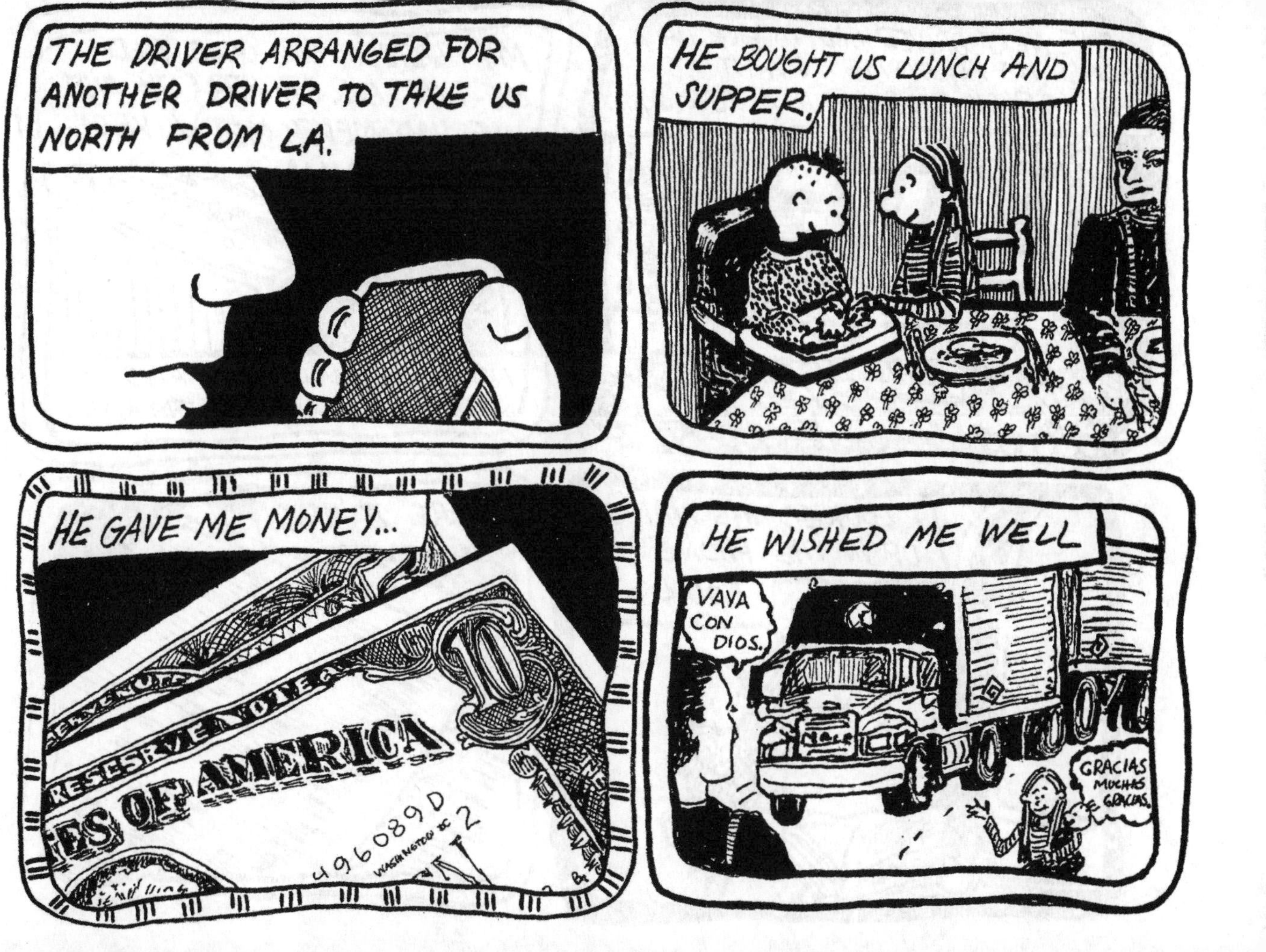
THE DRIVER ARRANGED FOR ANOTHER DRIVER TO TAKE US NORTH FROM L.A.
HE BOUGHT US LUNCH AND SUPPER.
HE GAVE ME MONEY...
HE WISHED ME WELL
VAYA CON DIOS.
GRACIAS MUCHAS GRACIAS.

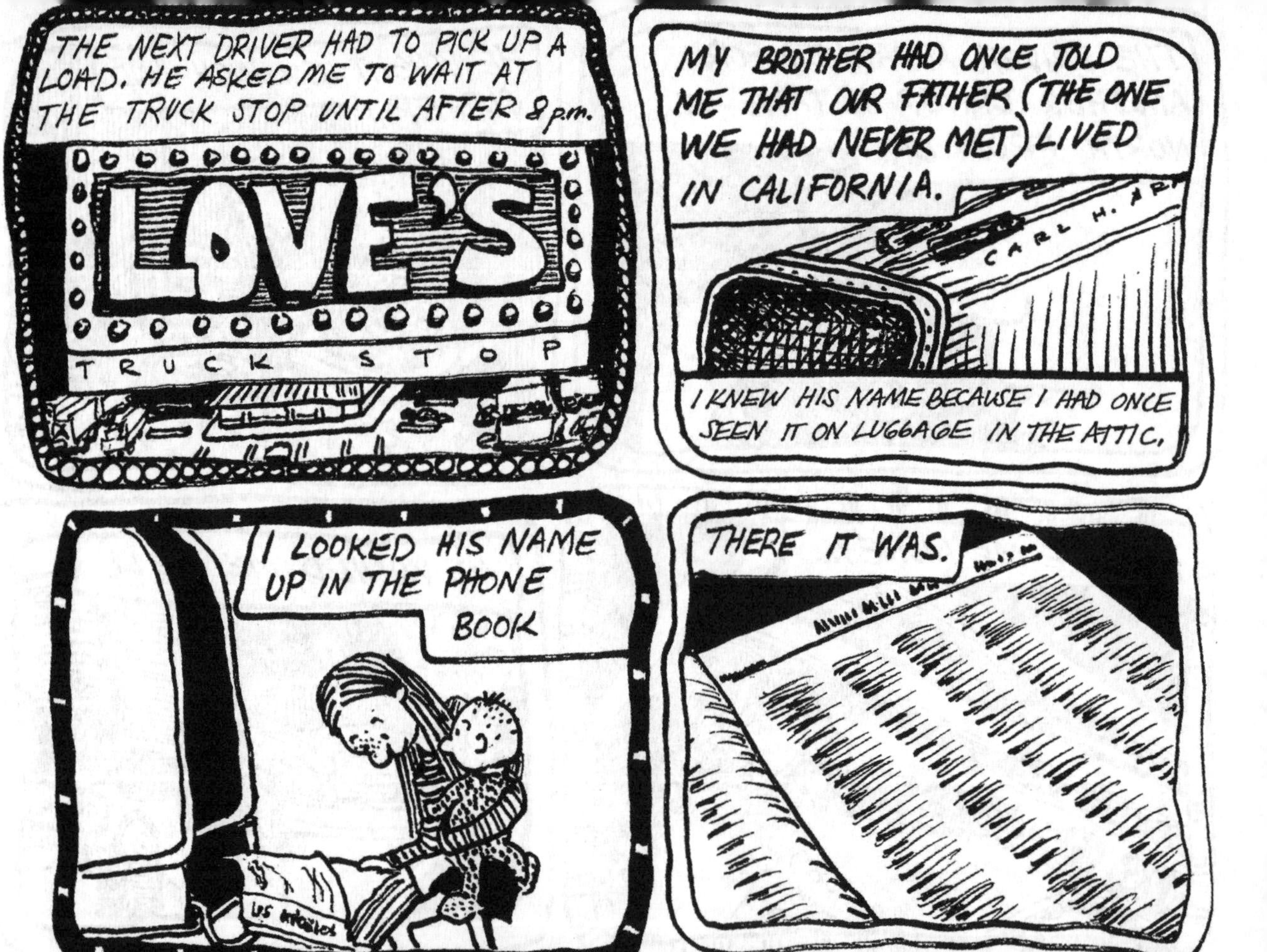
THE NEXT DRIVER HAD TO PICK UP A LOAD. HE ASKED ME TO WAIT AT THE TRUCK STOP UNTIL AFTER 8 p.m.
LOVE'S
TRUCK STOP
MY BROTHER HAD ONCE TOLD ME THAT OUR FATHER (THE ONE WE HAD NEVER MET) LIVED IN CALIFORNIA.
CARL H.
I KNEW HIS NAME BECAUSE I HAD ONCE SEEN IT ON LUGGAGE IN THE ATTIC.
I LOOKED HIS NAME UP IN THE PHONE BOOK
THERE IT WAS.

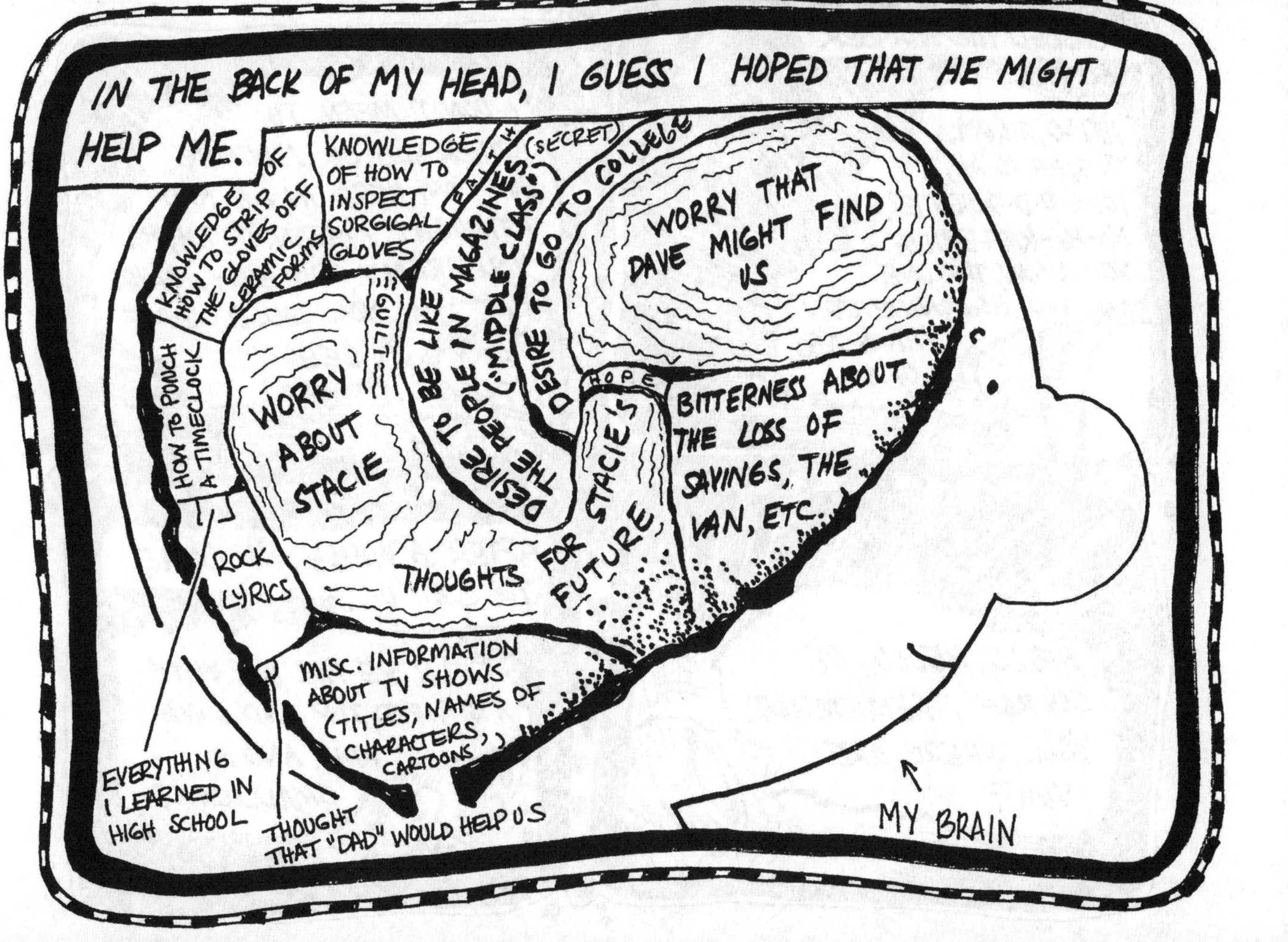
IN THE BACK OF MY HEAD, I GUESS I HOPED THAT HE MIGHT HELP ME.
KNOWLEDGE HOW TO STRIP OF THE GLOVES OFF CERAMIC FORMS
KNOWLEDGE OF HOW TO INSPECT SURGICAL GLOVES
FAITH
(SECRET) DESIRE TO BE LIKE THE PEOPLE IN MAGAZINES ("MIDDLE CLASS")
DESIRE TO GO TO COLLEGE
WORRY THAT DAVE MIGHT FIND US
GUILT
HOW TO PUNCH A TIMECLOCK
WORRY ABOUT STACIE
HOPE
BITTERNESS ABOUT THE LOSS OF SAVINGS, THE VAN, ETC.
STACIE'S FUTURE
THOUGHTS FOR
ROCK LYRICS
MISC. INFORMATION ABOUT TV SHOWS (TITLES, NAMES OF CHARACTERS, CARTOONS)
EVERYTHING I LEARNED IN HIGH SCHOOL
THOUGHT THAT "DAD" WOULD HELP US
MY BRAIN

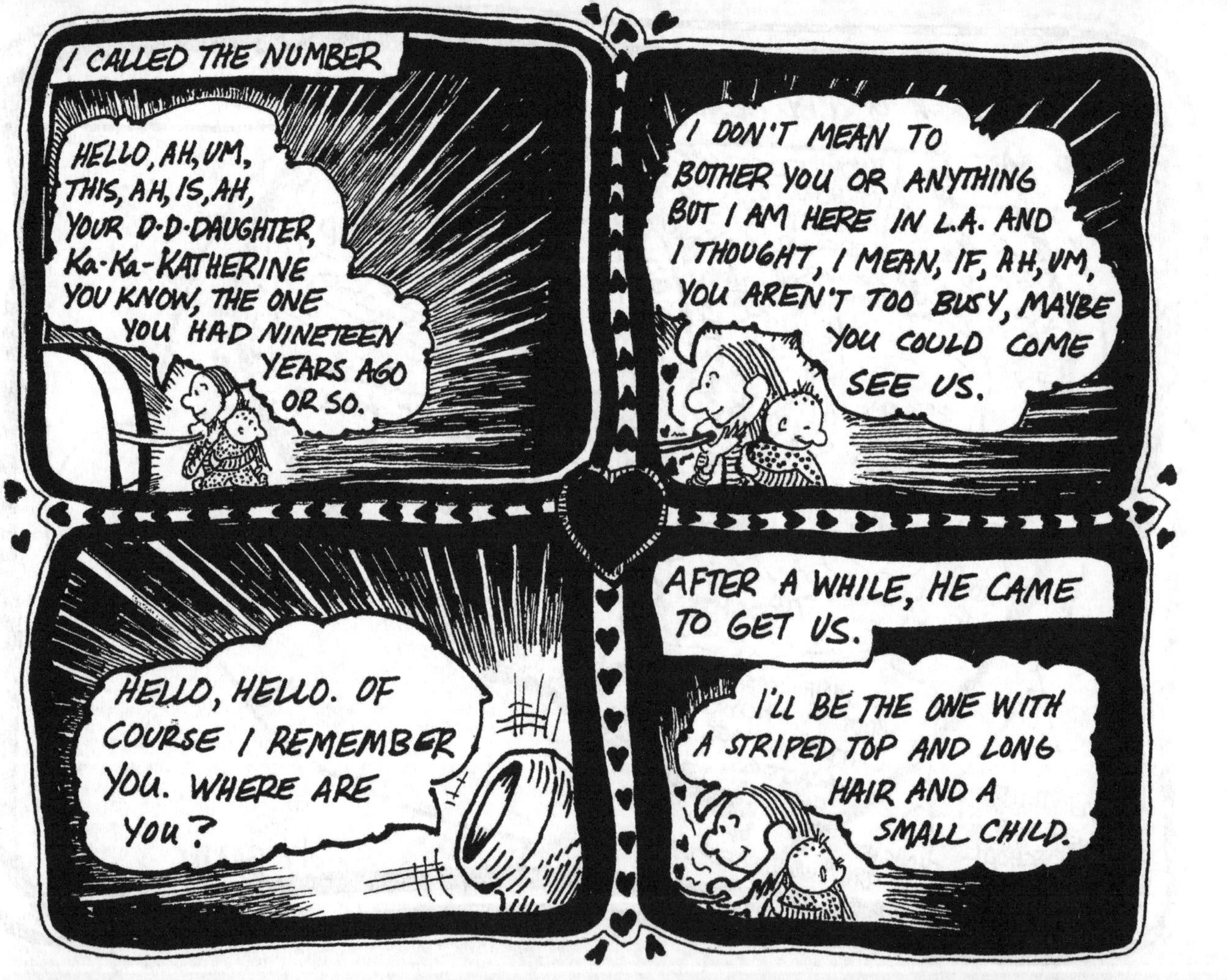
I CALLED THE NUMBER
HELLO, AH, UM, THIS, AH, IS, AH, YOUR D-D-DAUGHTER, Ka-Ka-KATHERINE YOU KNOW, THE ONE YOU HAD NINETEEN YEARS AGO OR SO.
I DON'T MEAN TO BOTHER YOU OR ANYTHING BUT I AM HERE IN L.A. AND I THOUGHT, I MEAN, IF, AH, UM, YOU AREN'T TOO BUSY, MAYBE YOU COULD COME SEE US.
HELLO, HELLO. OF COURSE I REMEMBER YOU. WHERE ARE YOU?
AFTER A WHILE, HE CAME TO GET US.
I'LL BE THE ONE WITH A STRIPED TOP AND LONG HAIR AND A SMALL CHILD.

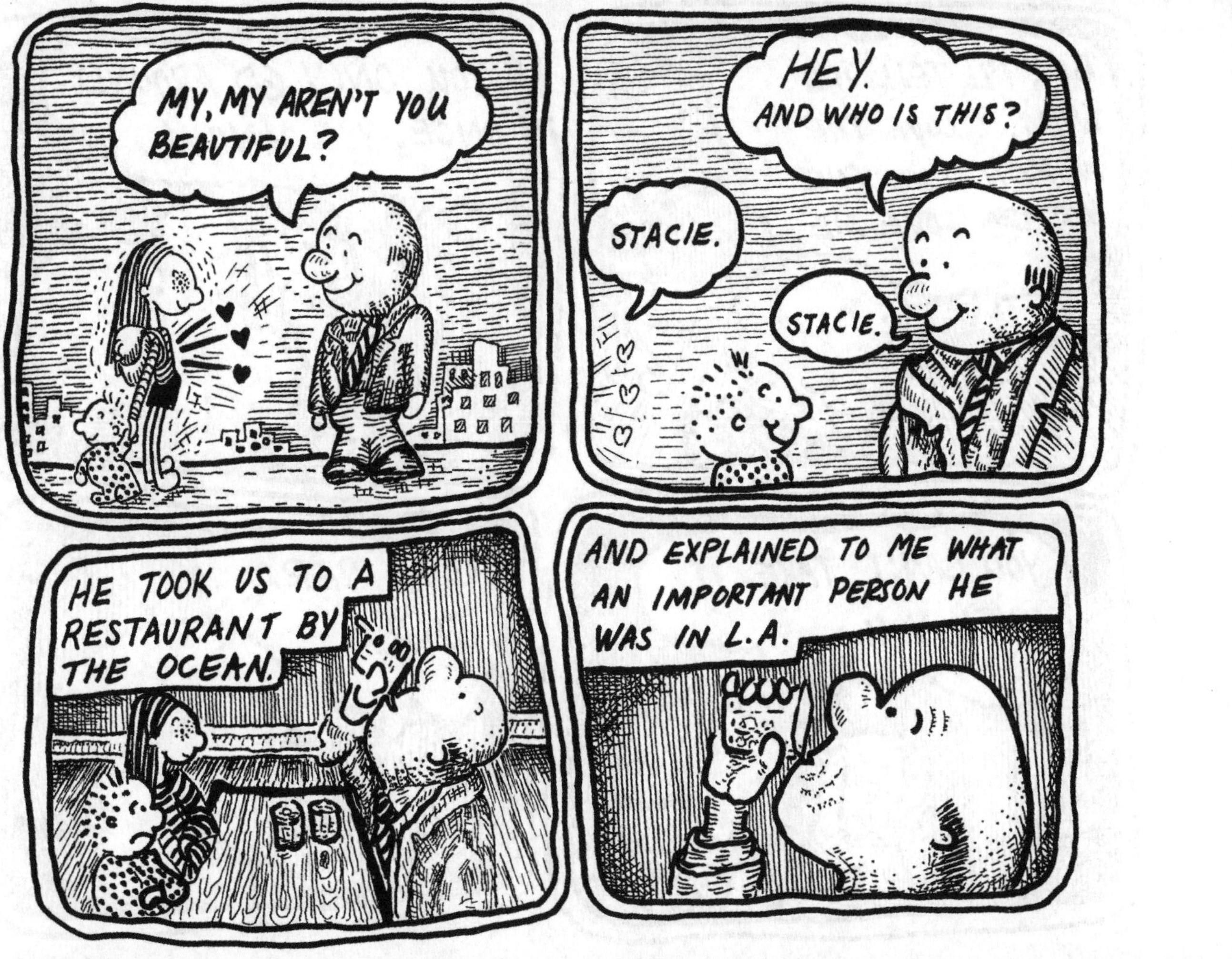
MY, MY AREN'T YOU BEAUTIFUL?
HEY. AND WHO IS THIS?
STACIE.
STACIE.
HE TOOK US TO A RESTAURANT BY THE OCEAN.
AND EXPLAINED TO ME WHAT AN IMPORTANT PERSON HE WAS IN L.A.

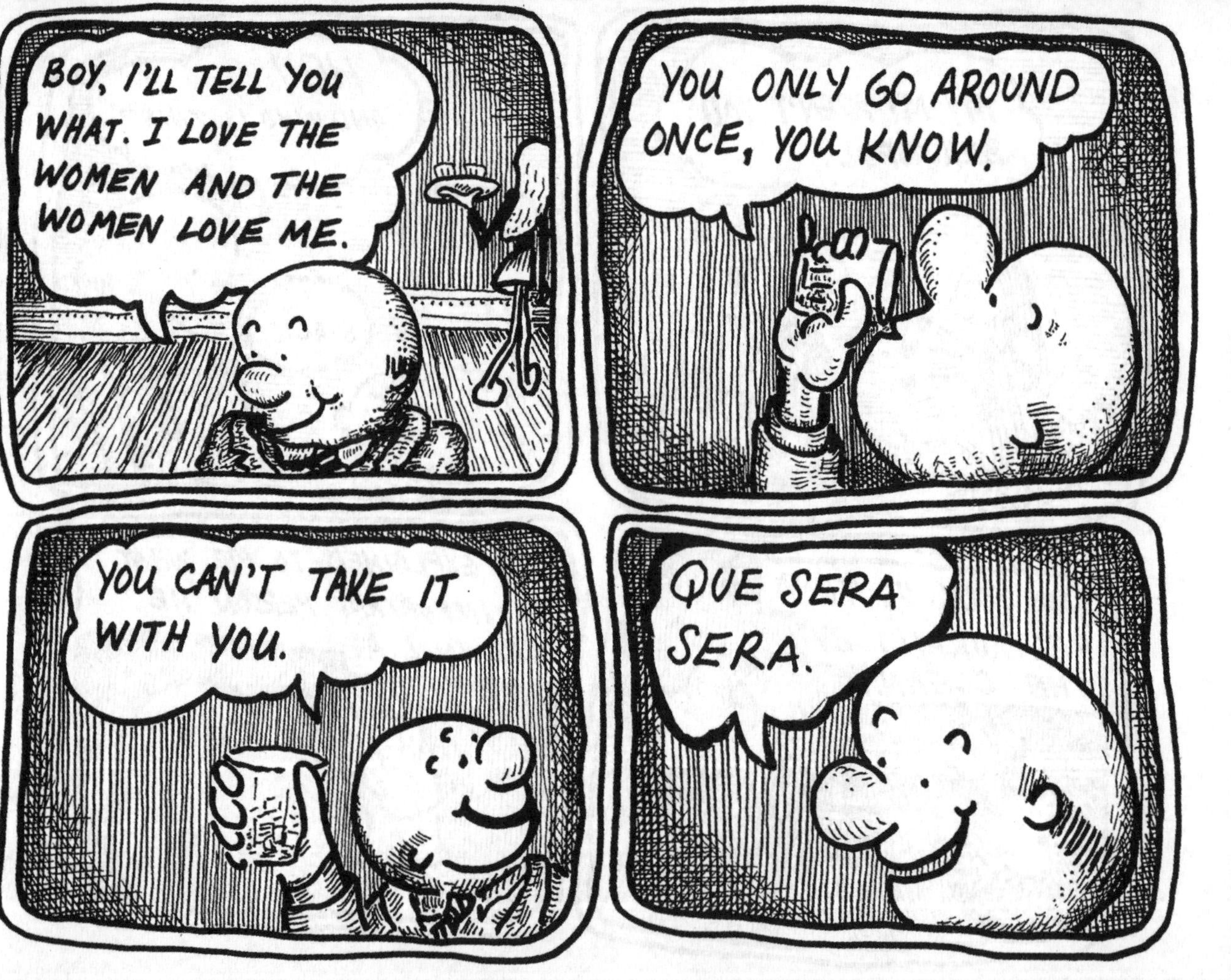
BOY, I'LL TELL YOU WHAT. I LOVE THE WOMEN AND THE WOMEN LOVE ME.
YOU ONLY GO AROUND ONCE, YOU KNOW.
YOU CAN'T TAKE IT WITH YOU.
QUE SERA SERA.

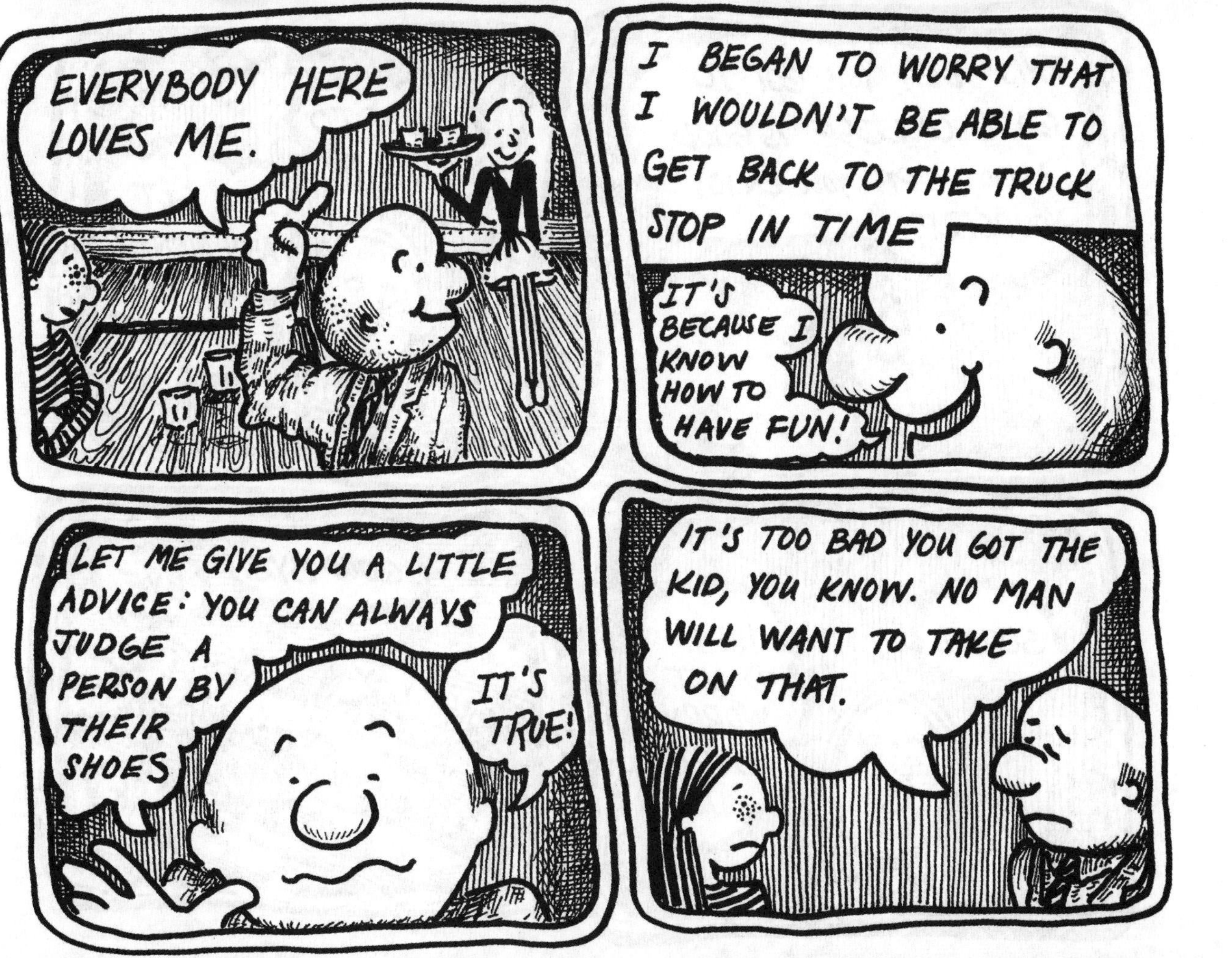
EVERYBODY HERE LOVES ME.
I BEGAN TO WORRY THAT I WOULDN'T BE ABLE TO GET BACK TO THE TRUCK STOP IN TIME
IT'S BECAUSE I KNOW HOW TO HAVE FUN!
LET ME GIVE YOU A LITTLE ADVICE: YOU CAN ALWAYS JUDGE A PERSON BY THEIR SHOES
IT'S TRUE!
IT'S TOO BAD YOU GOT THE KID, YOU KNOW. NO MAN WILL WANT TO TAKE ON THAT.

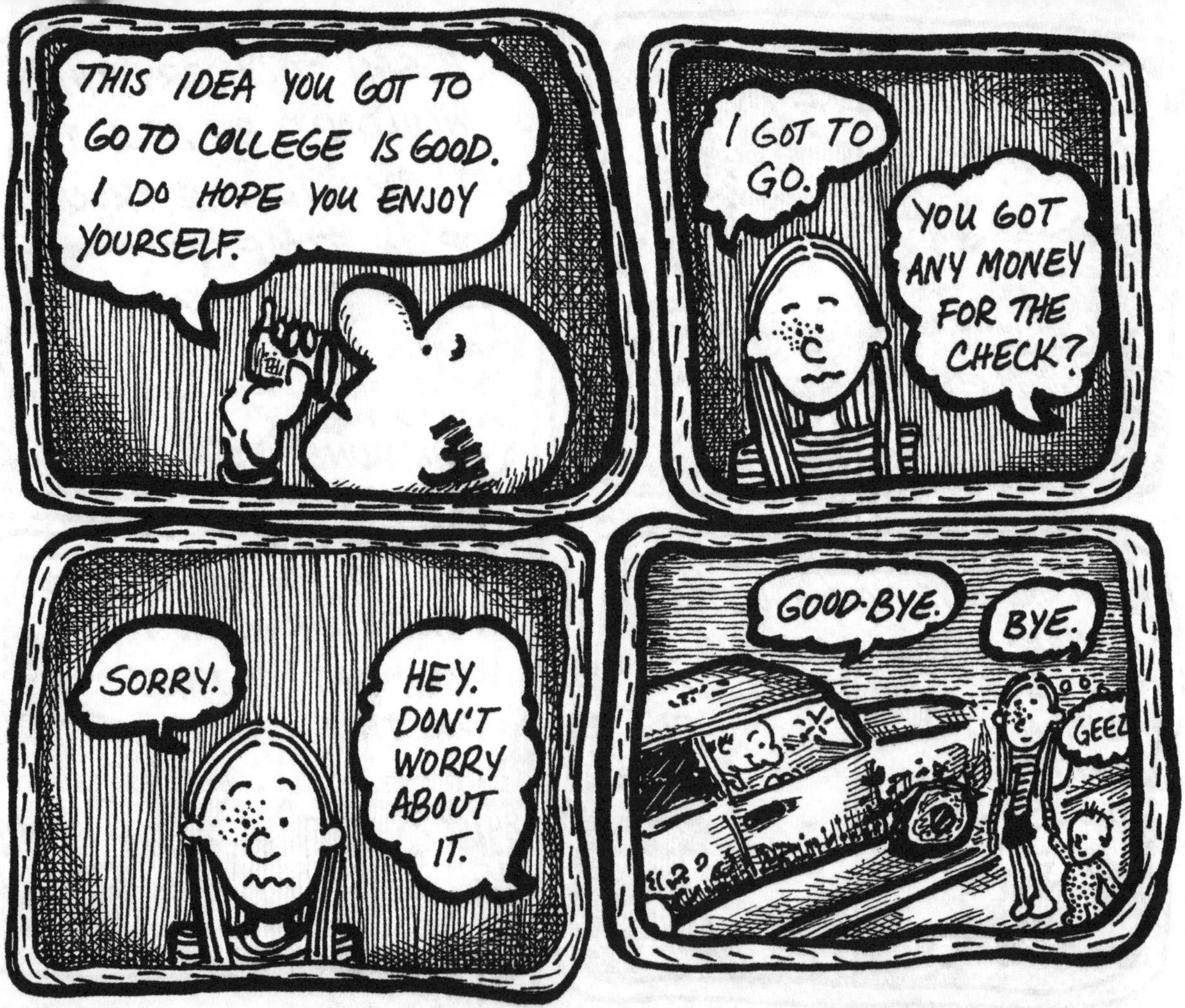
THIS IDEA YOU GOT TO GO TO COLLEGE IS GOOD. I DO HOPE YOU ENJOY YOURSELF.
I GOT TO GO.
YOU GOT ANY MONEY FOR THE CHECK?
SORRY.
HEY. DON'T WORRY ABOUT IT.
GOOD-BYE.
BYE.
GEEZ

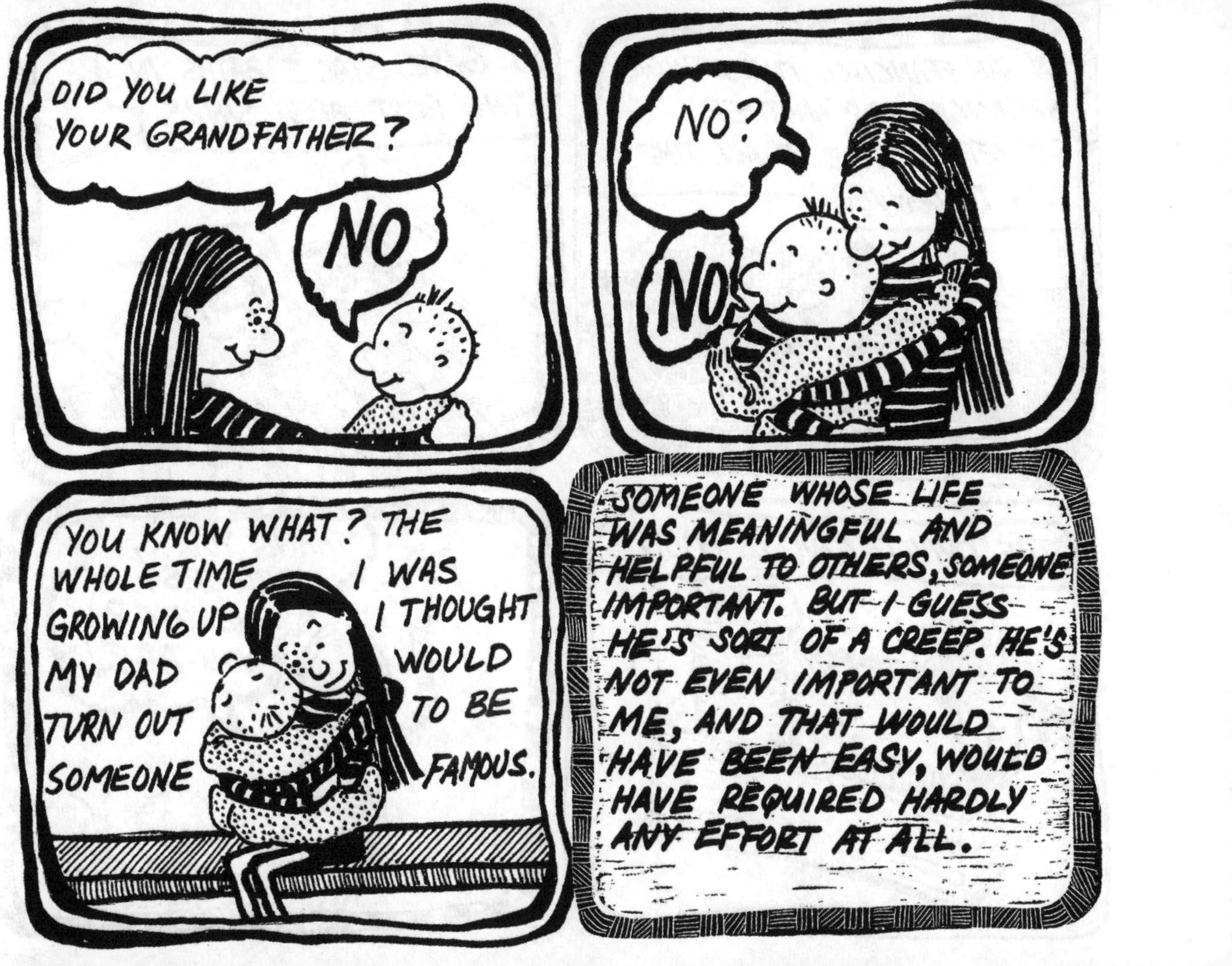
DID YOU LIKE YOUR GRANDFATHER?
NO
NO?
NO
YOU KNOW WHAT? THE WHOLE TIME I WAS GROWING UP I THOUGHT MY DAD WOULD TURN OUT TO BE SOMEONE FAMOUS.
SOMEONE WHOSE LIFE WAS MEANINGFUL AND HELPFUL TO OTHERS, SOMEONE IMPORTANT. BUT I GUESS HE'S SORT OF A CREEP. HE'S NOT EVEN IMPORTANT TO ME, AND THAT WOULD HAVE BEEN EASY, WOULD HAVE REQUIRED HARDLY ANY EFFORT AT ALL.

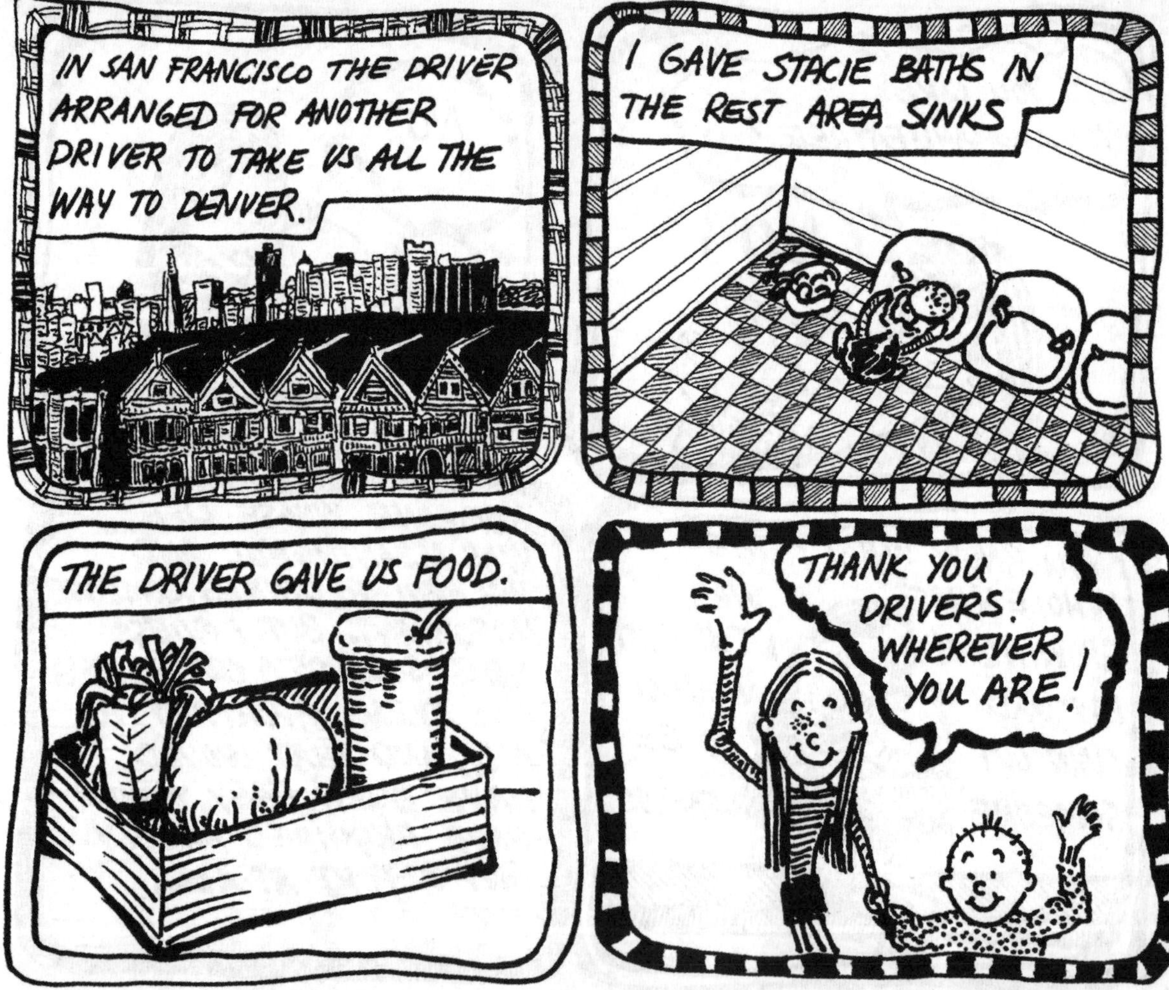
IN SAN FRANCISCO THE DRIVER ARRANGED FOR ANOTHER DRIVER TO TAKE US ALL THE WAY TO DENVER.
I GAVE STACIE BATHS IN THE REST AREA SINKS
THE DRIVER GAVE US FOOD.
THANK YOU DRIVERS! WHEREVER YOU ARE!

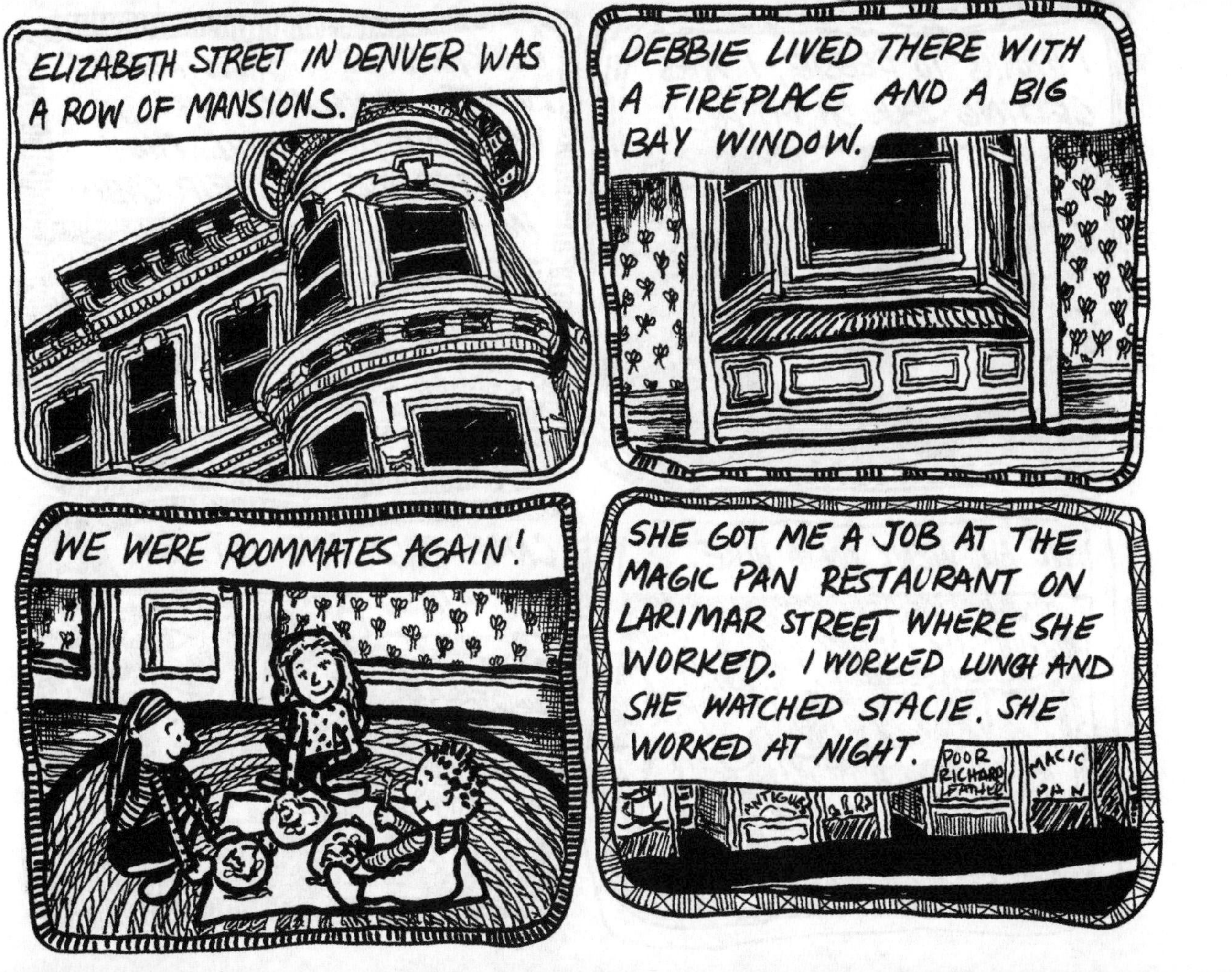
ELIZABETH STREET IN DENVER WAS A ROW OF MANSIONS.
DEBBIE LIVED THERE WITH A FIREPLACE AND A BIG BAY WINDOW.
WE WERE ROOMMATES AGAIN!
SHE GOT ME A JOB AT THE MAGIC PAN RESTAURANT ON LARIMAR STREET WHERE SHE WORKED. I WORKED LUNCH AND SHE WATCHED STACIE. SHE WORKED AT NIGHT.
POOR RICHARD LEATHER
MAGIC PAN
ANTIQUES

THANKS TO DEBBIE, I WAS GETTING BACK ON MY FEET.

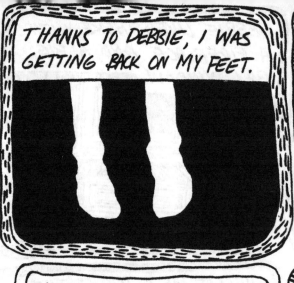

EVERYONE AT THE RESTAURANT LOOKED YOUNG AND (WELL, IT WAS TRUE) BEAUTIFUL. THEY INVITED ME TO THEIR CABIN IN IDAHO SPRINGS.

WE ALL WENT ON A HIKE,

CAME BACK AND SAT BY THE FIRE.

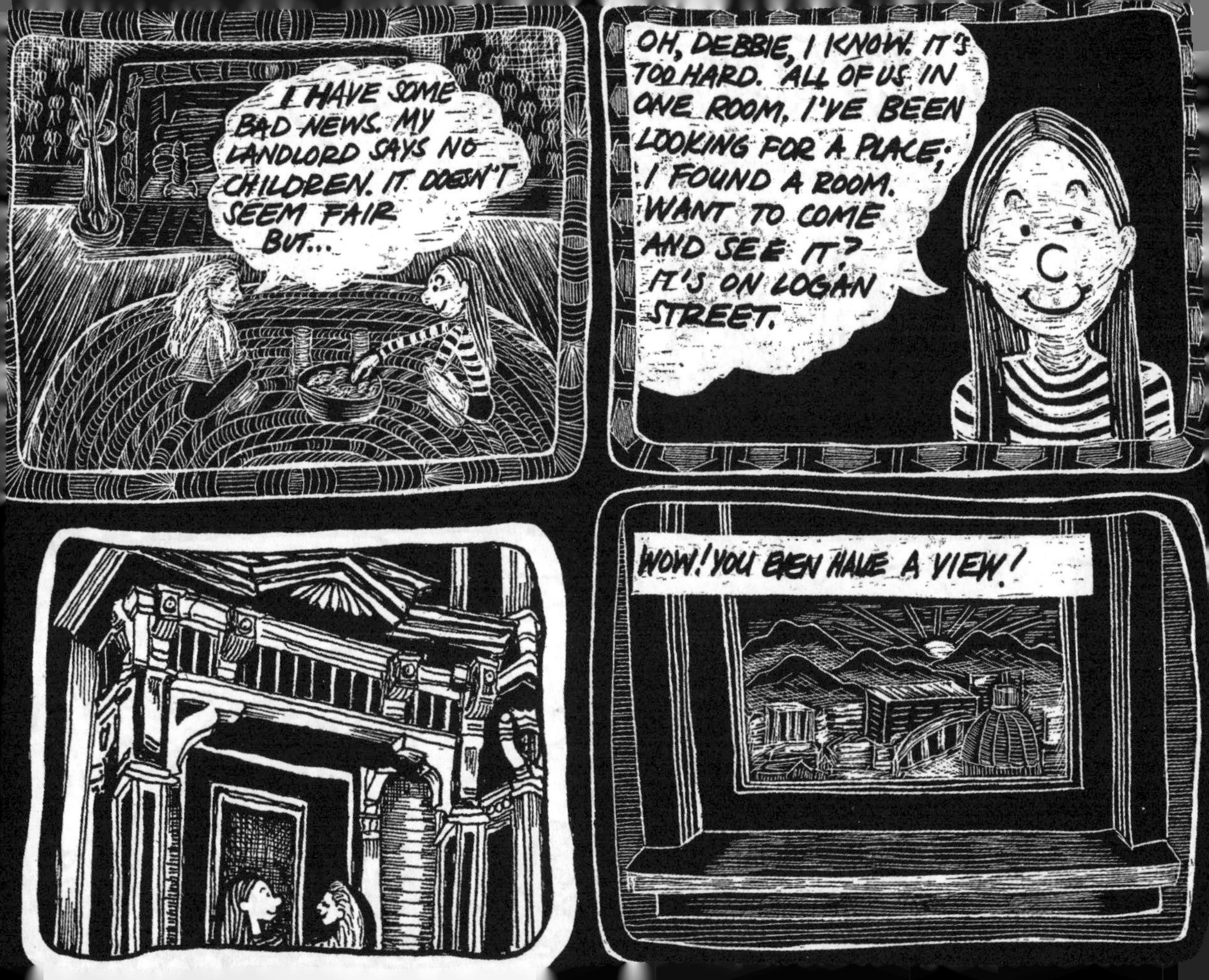
I HAVE SOME BAD NEWS. MY LANDLORD SAYS NO CHILDREN. IT DOESN'T SEEM FAIR BUT...
OH, DEBBIE, I KNOW. IT'S TOO HARD. ALL OF US IN ONE ROOM. I'VE BEEN LOOKING FOR A PLACE; I FOUND A ROOM. WANT TO COME AND SEE IT? IT'S ON LOGAN STREET.
WOW! YOU EVEN HAVE A VIEW!

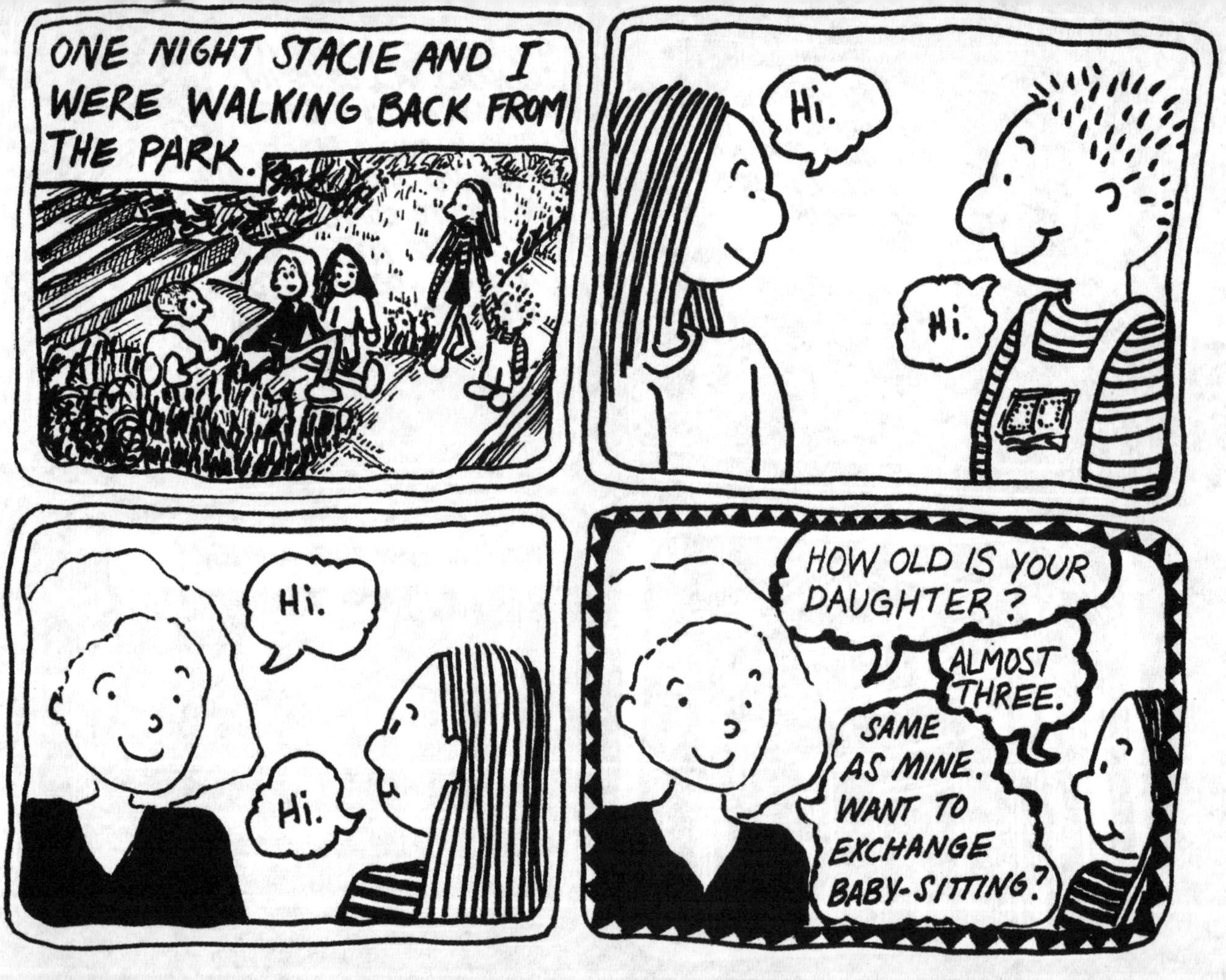
ONE NIGHT STACIE AND I WERE WALKING BACK FROM THE PARK.
Hi.
Hi.
Hi.
Hi.
HOW OLD IS YOUR DAUGHTER?
ALMOST THREE.
SAME AS MINE. WANT TO EXCHANGE BABY-SITTING?

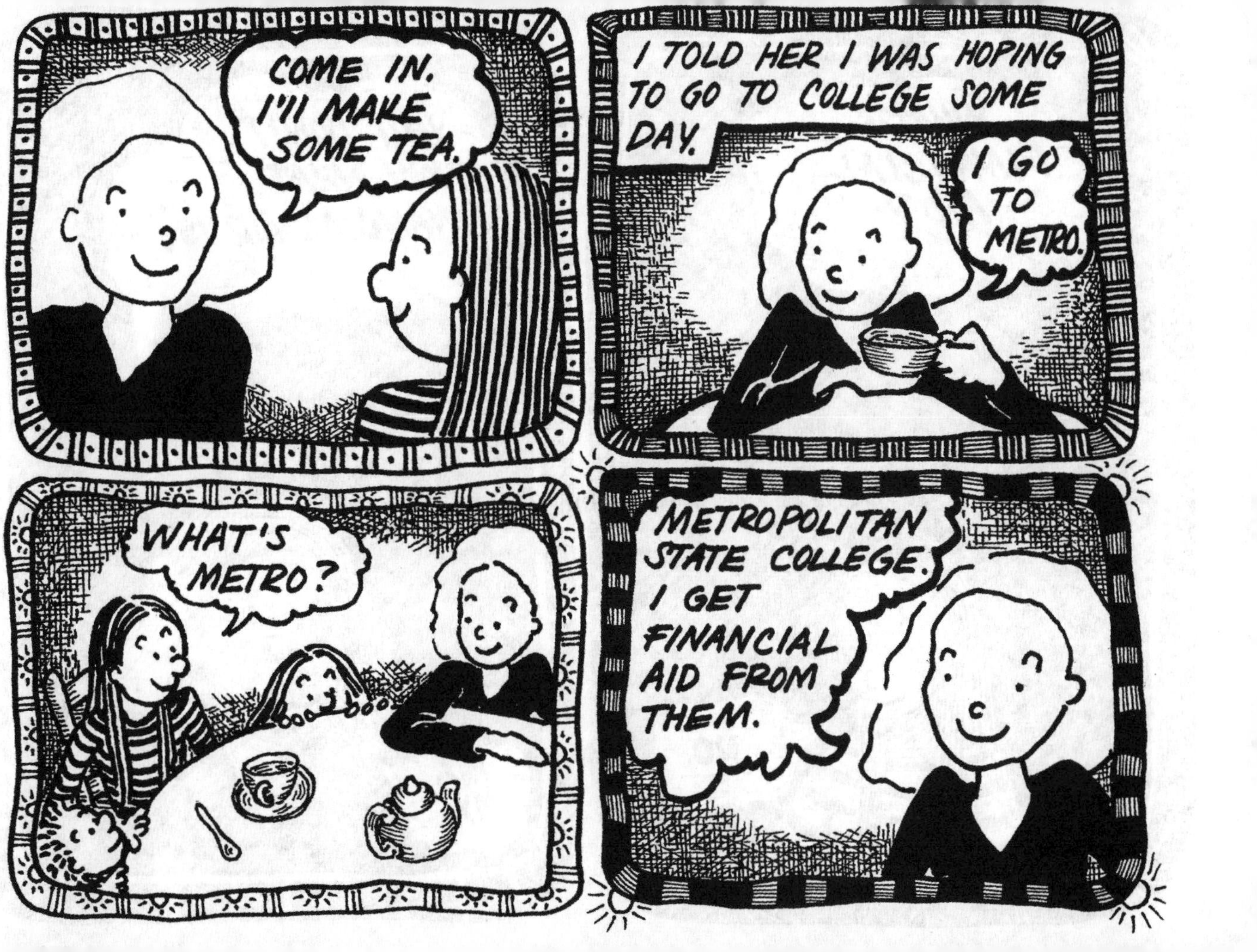
COME IN. I'll MAKE SOME TEA.
I TOLD HER I WAS HOPING TO GO TO COLLEGE SOME DAY.
I GO TO METRO.
WHAT'S METRO?
METROPOLITAN STATE COLLEGE. I GET FINANCIAL AID FROM THEM.

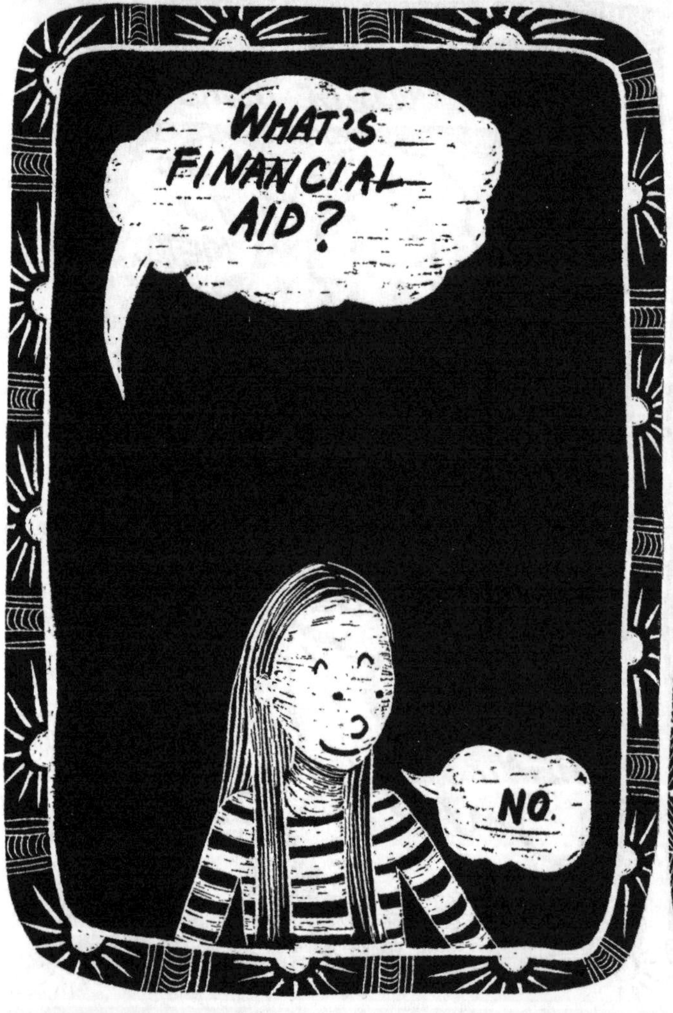
WHAT'S FINANCIAL AID?
NO.

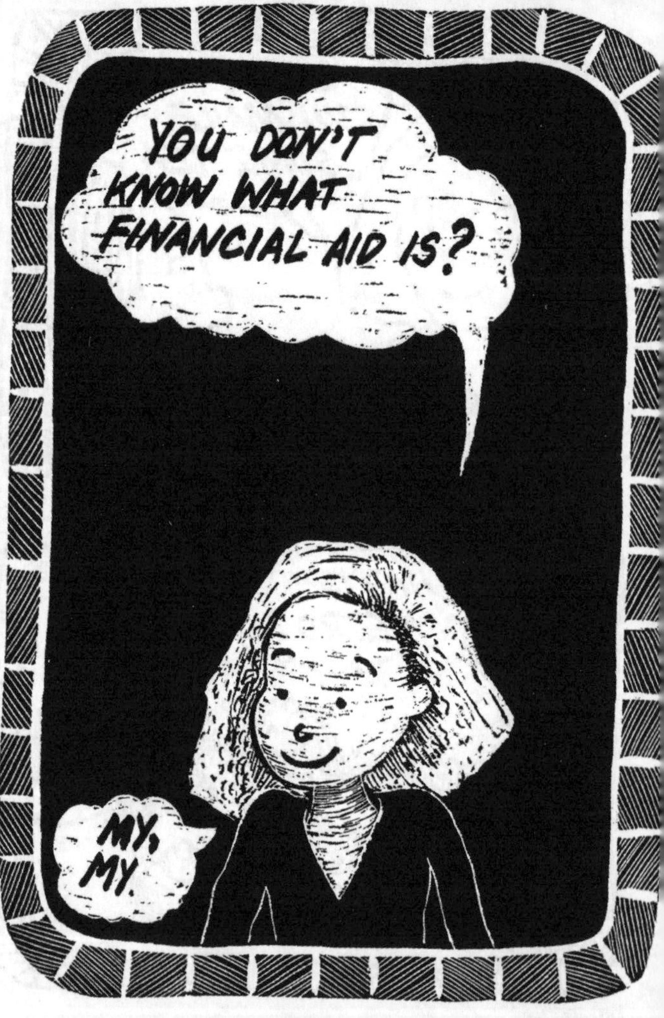
YOU DON'T KNOW WHAT FINANCIAL AID IS?
MY, MY.

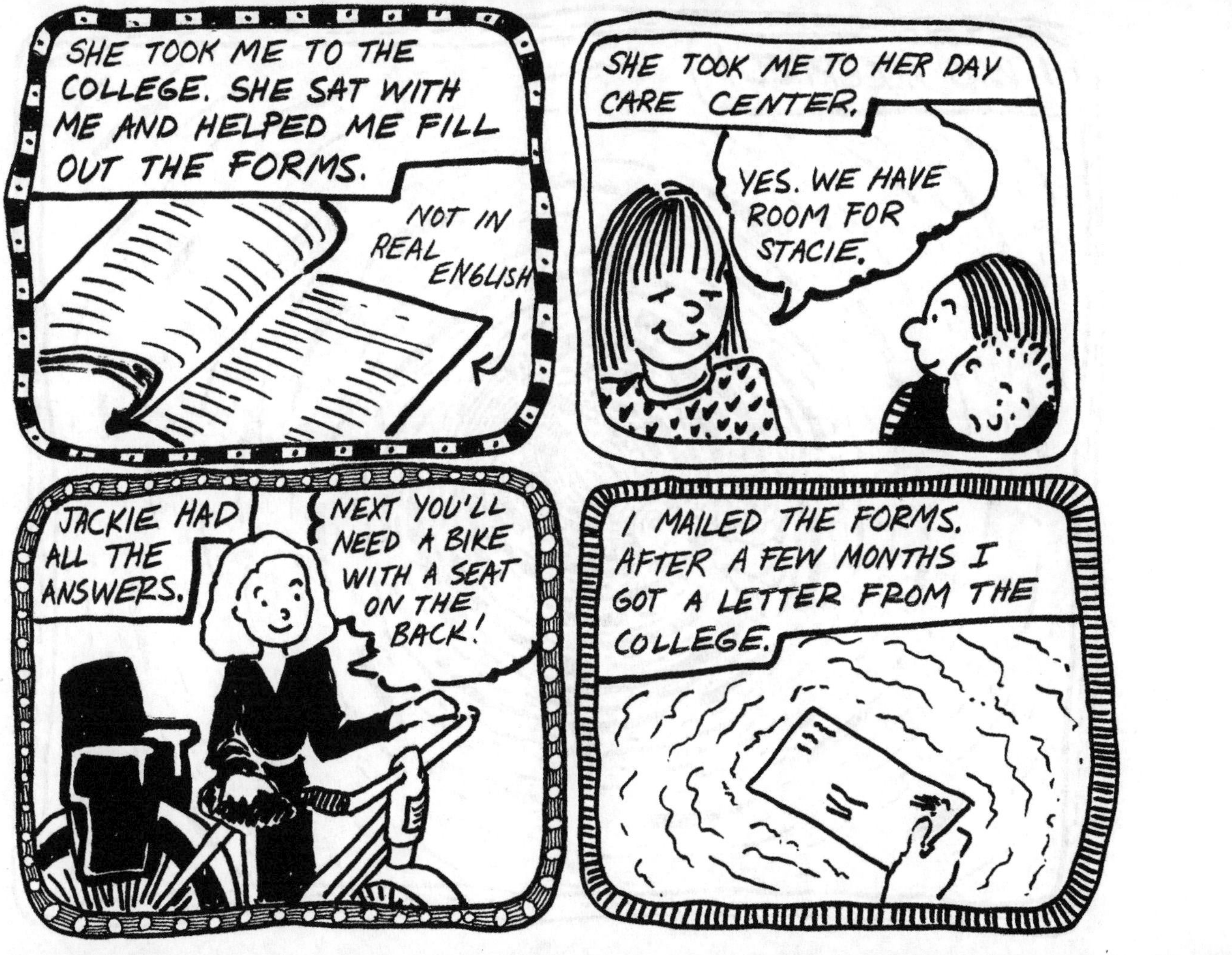

SHE TOOK ME TO THE COLLEGE. SHE SAT WITH ME AND HELPED ME FILL OUT THE FORMS.
NOT IN REAL ENGLISH
SHE TOOK ME TO HER DAY CARE CENTER.
YES. WE HAVE ROOM FOR STACIE.
JACKIE HAD ALL THE ANSWERS.
NEXT YOU'LL NEED A BIKE WITH A SEAT ON THE BACK!
I MAILED THE FORMS. AFTER A FEW MONTHS I GOT A LETTER FROM THE COLLEGE.

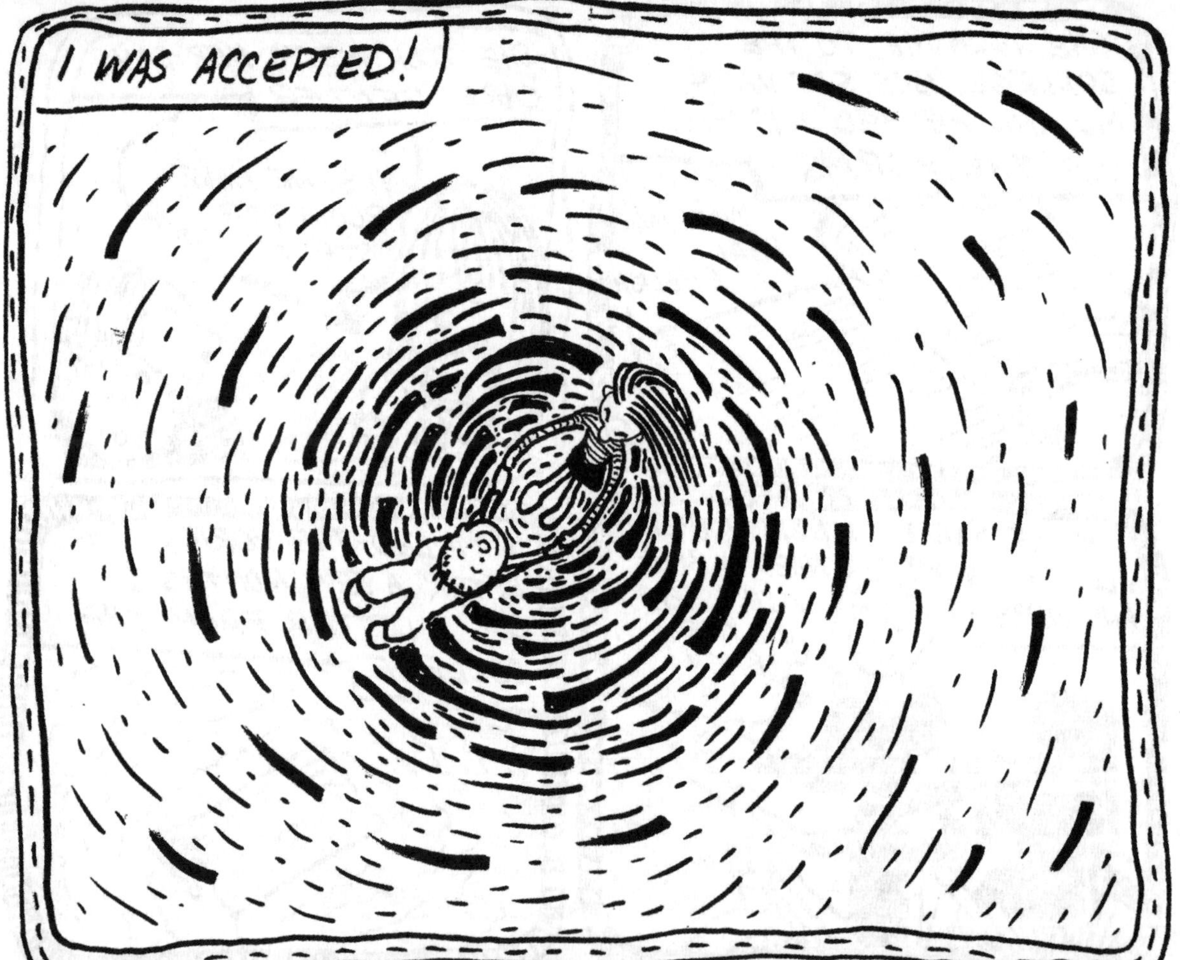
I WAS ACCEPTED!

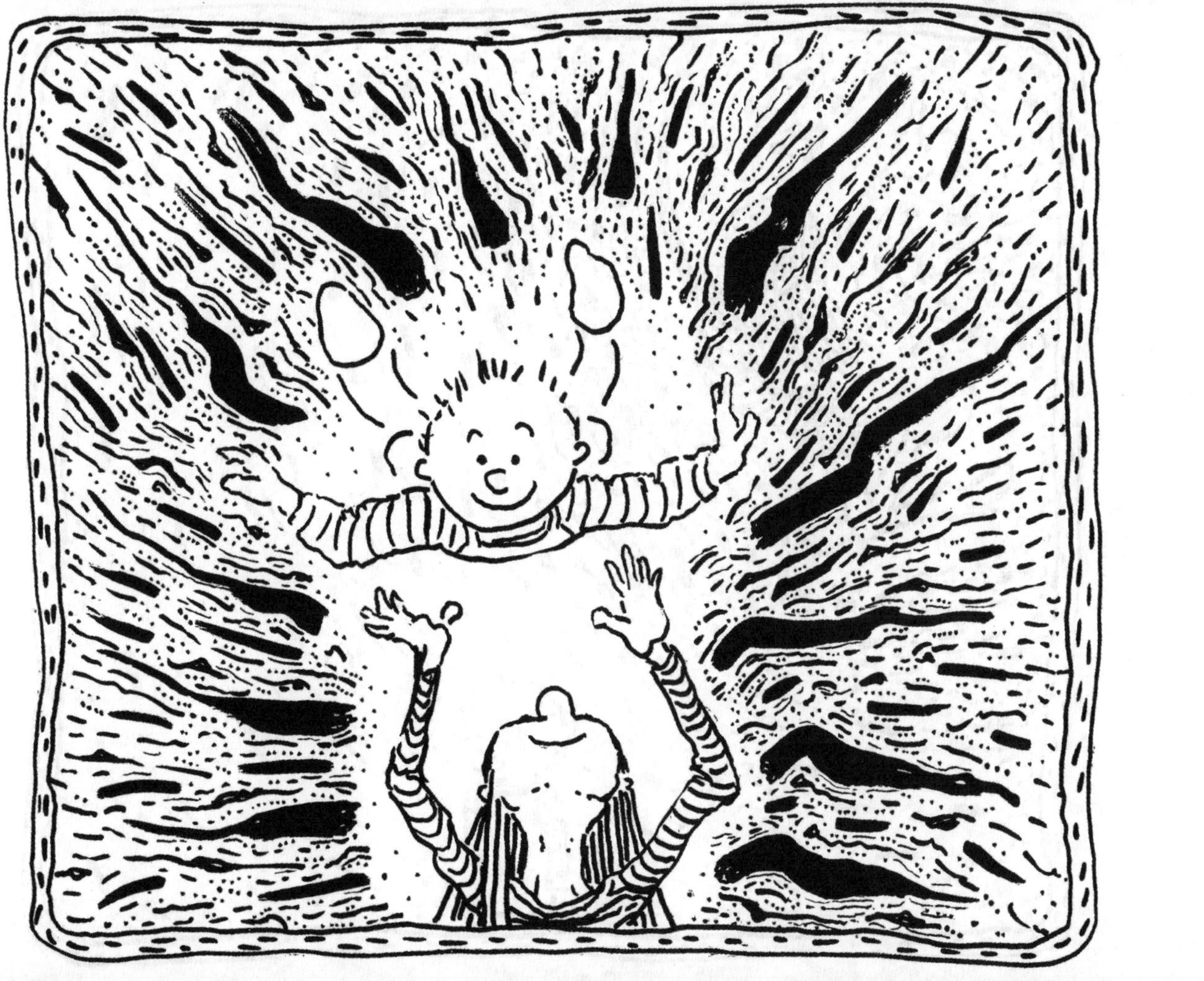

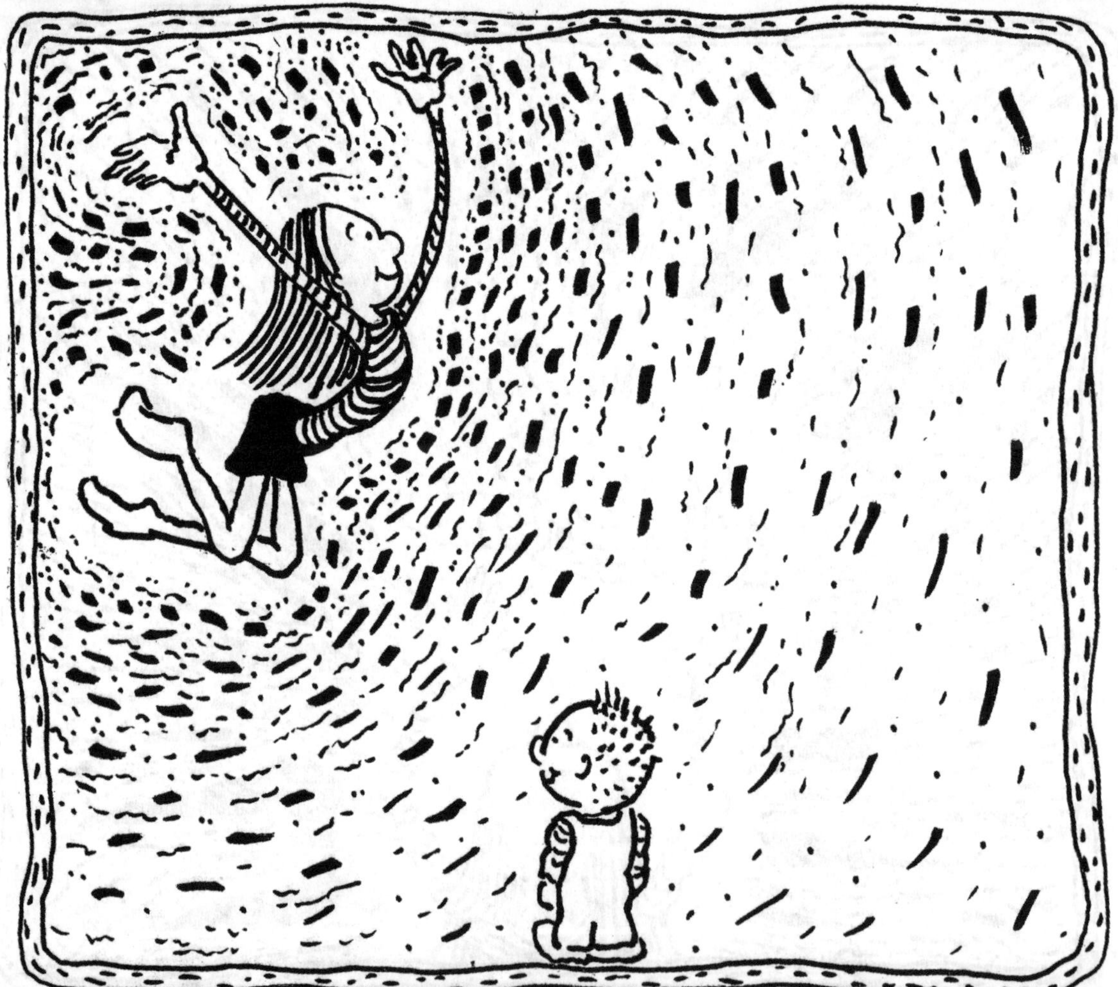

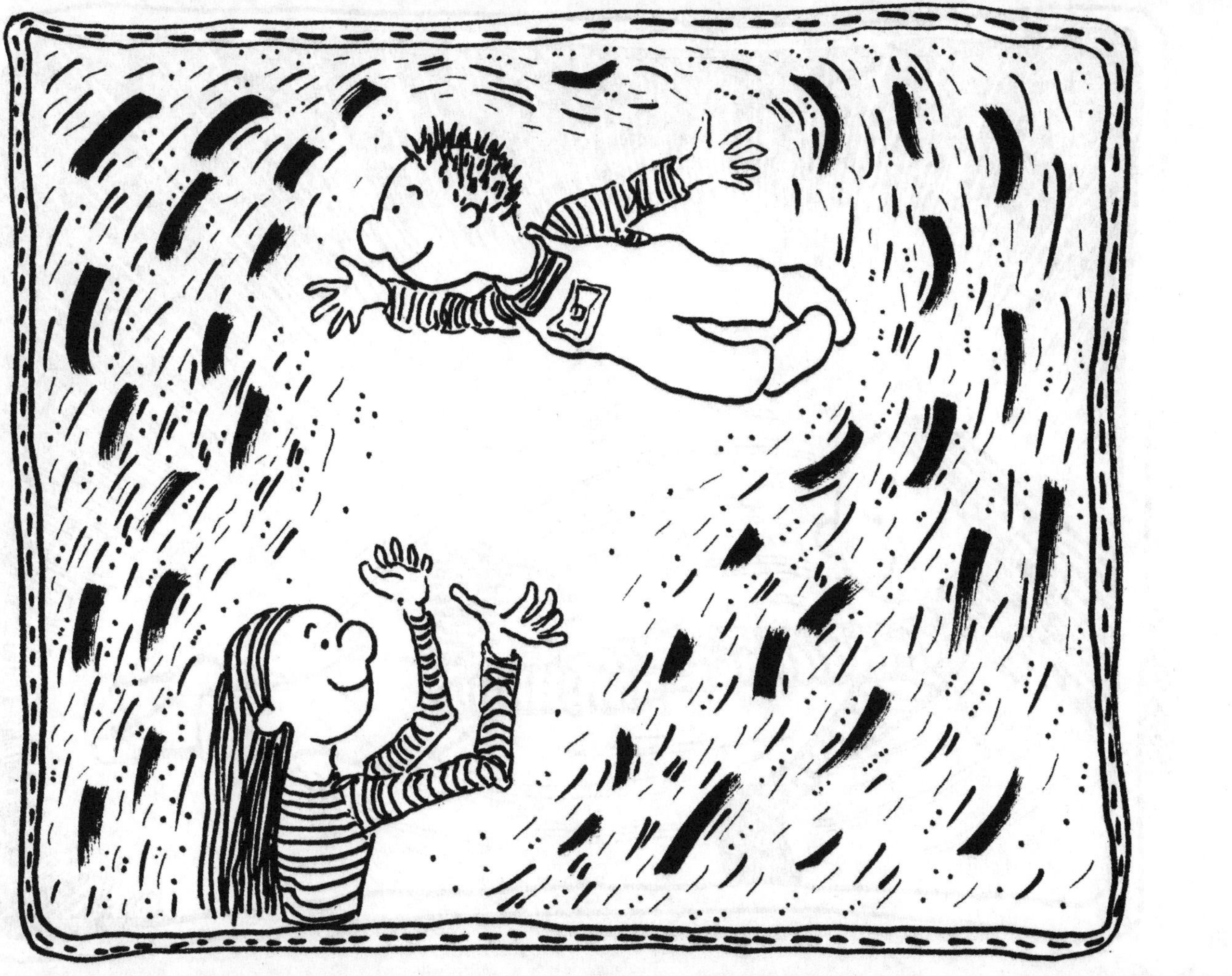

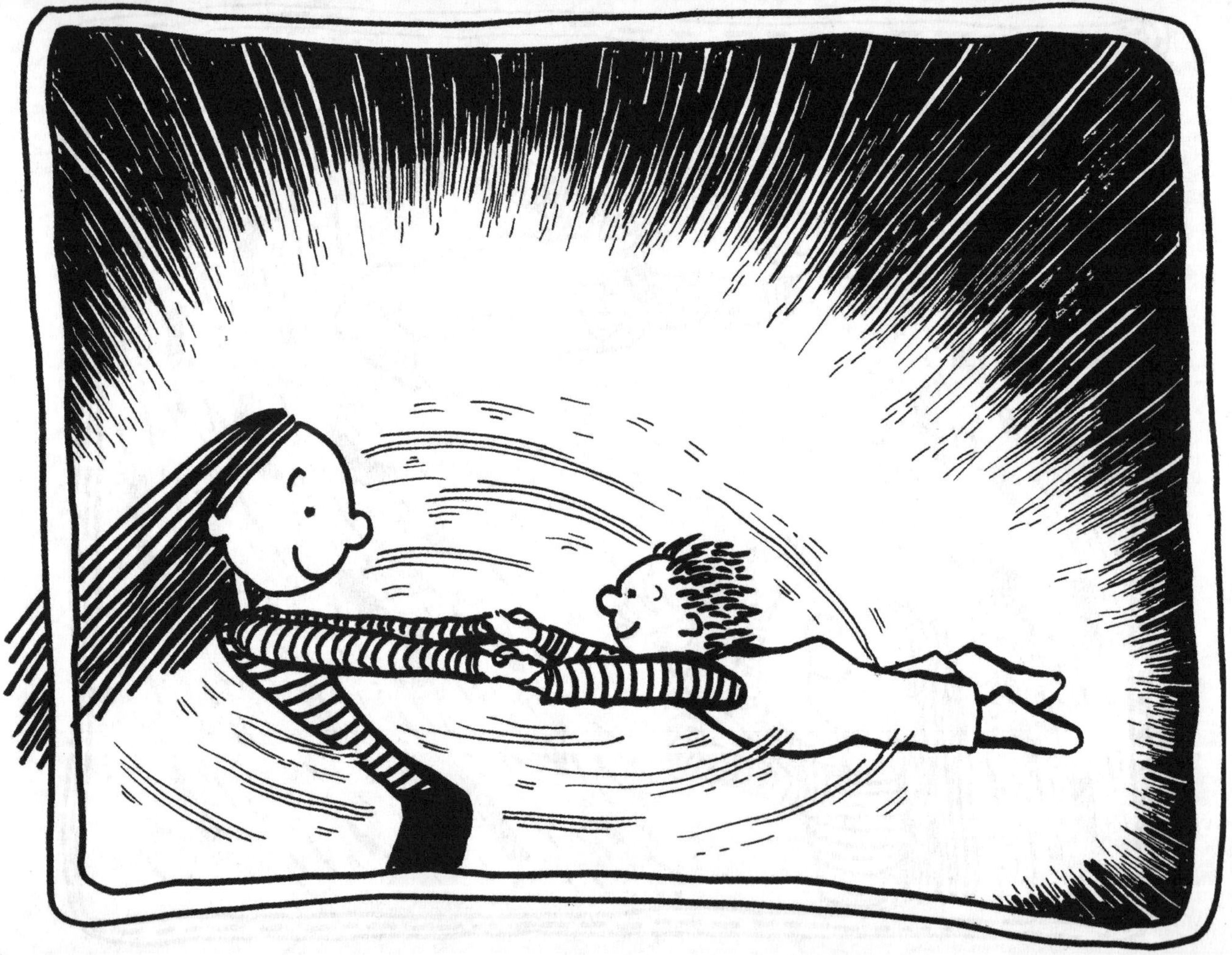

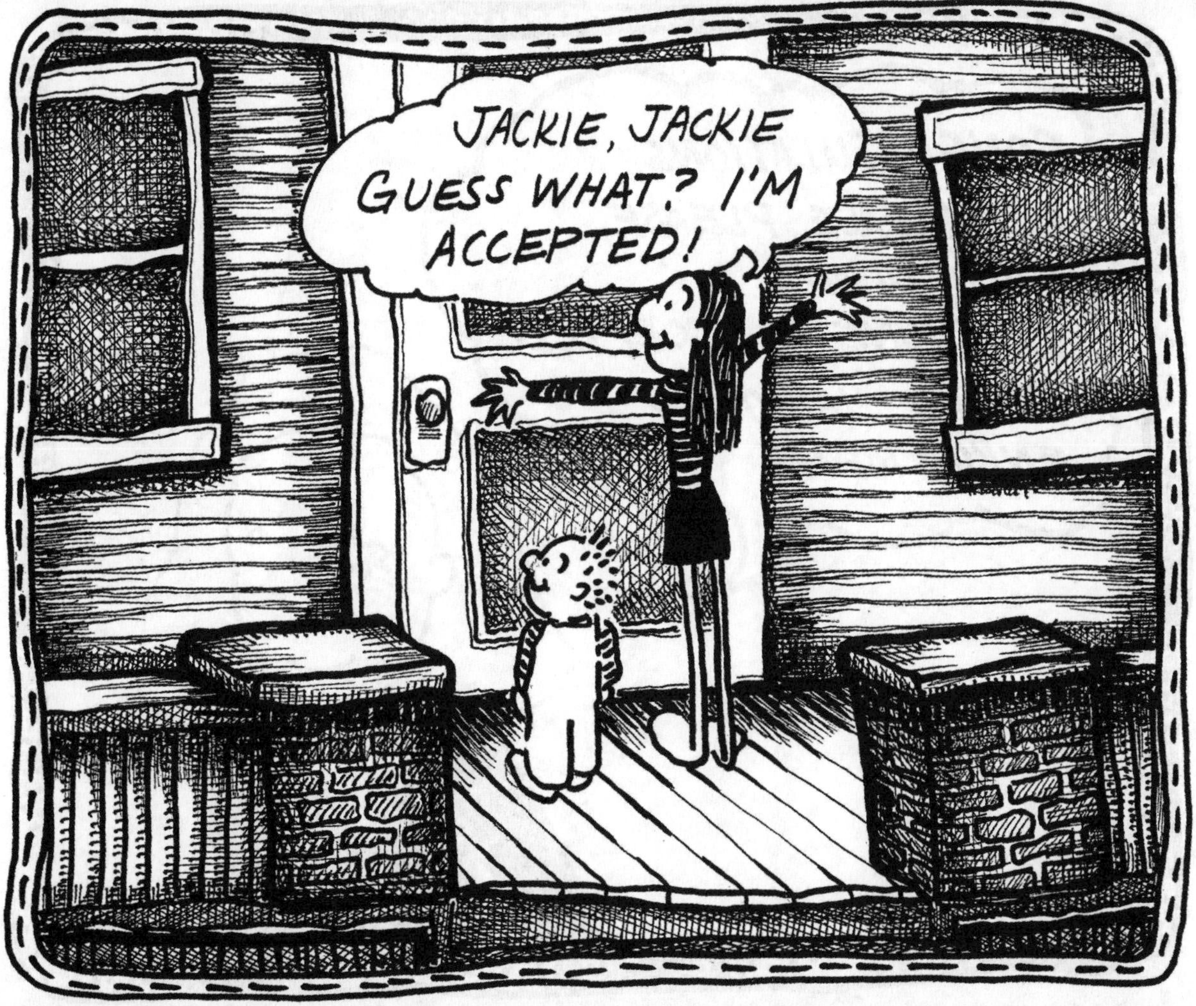
JACKIE, JACKIE GUESS WHAT? I'M ACCEPTED!

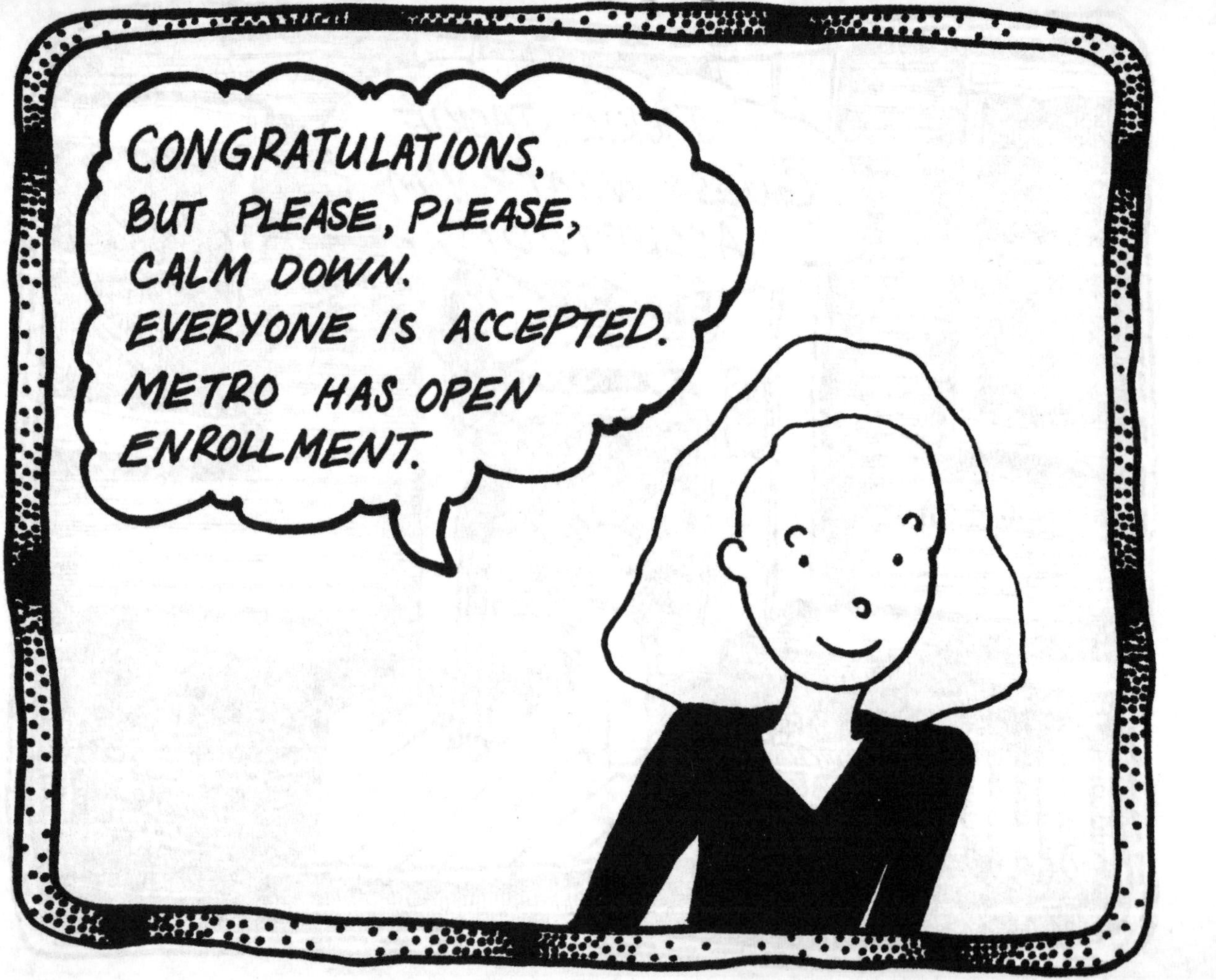
CONGRATULATIONS, BUT PLEASE, PLEASE, CALM DOWN. EVERYONE IS ACCEPTED. METRO HAS OPEN ENROLLMENT.

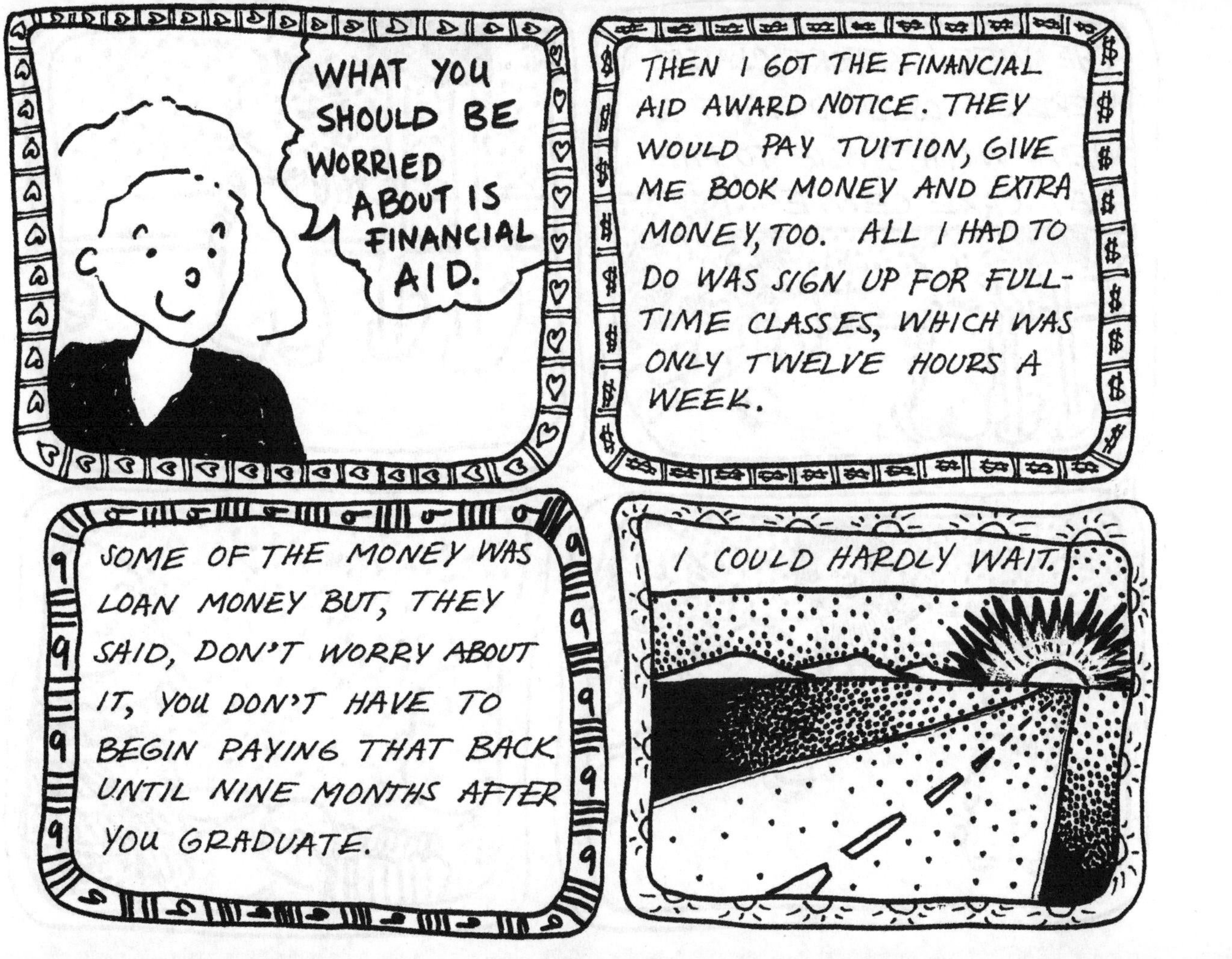
WHAT YOU SHOULD BE WORRIED ABOUT IS FINANCIAL AID.
THEN I GOT THE FINANCIAL AID AWARD NOTICE. THEY WOULD PAY TUITION, GIVE ME BOOK MONEY AND EXTRA MONEY, TOO. ALL I HAD TO DO WAS SIGN UP FOR FULL-TIME CLASSES, WHICH WAS ONLY TWELVE HOURS A WEEK.
SOME OF THE MONEY WAS LOAN MONEY BUT, THEY SAID, DON'T WORRY ABOUT IT, YOU DON'T HAVE TO BEGIN PAYING THAT BACK UNTIL NINE MONTHS AFTER YOU GRADUATE.
I COULD HARDLY WAIT.

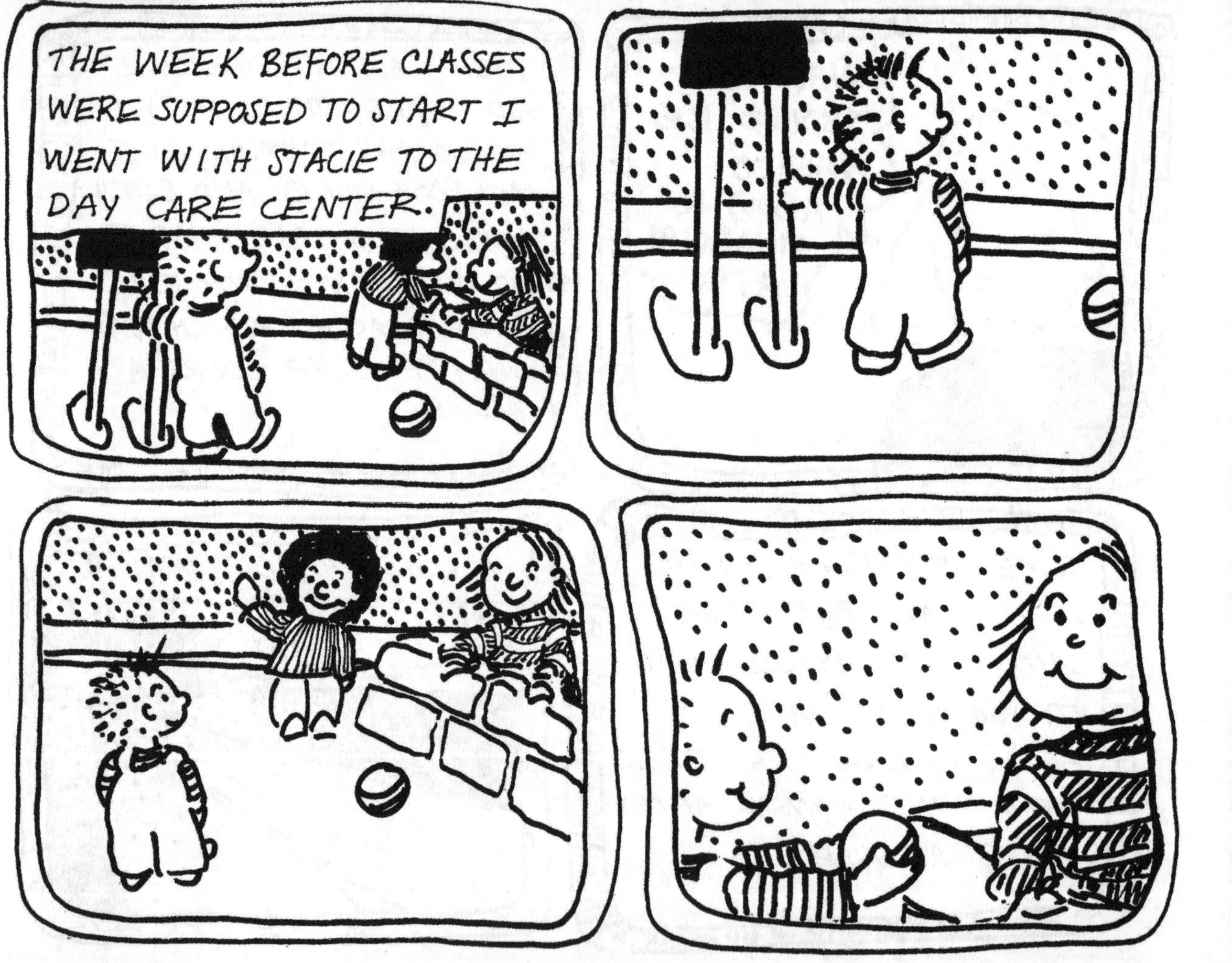
THE WEEK BEFORE CLASSES WERE SUPPOSED TO START I WENT WITH STACIE TO THE DAY CARE CENTER.

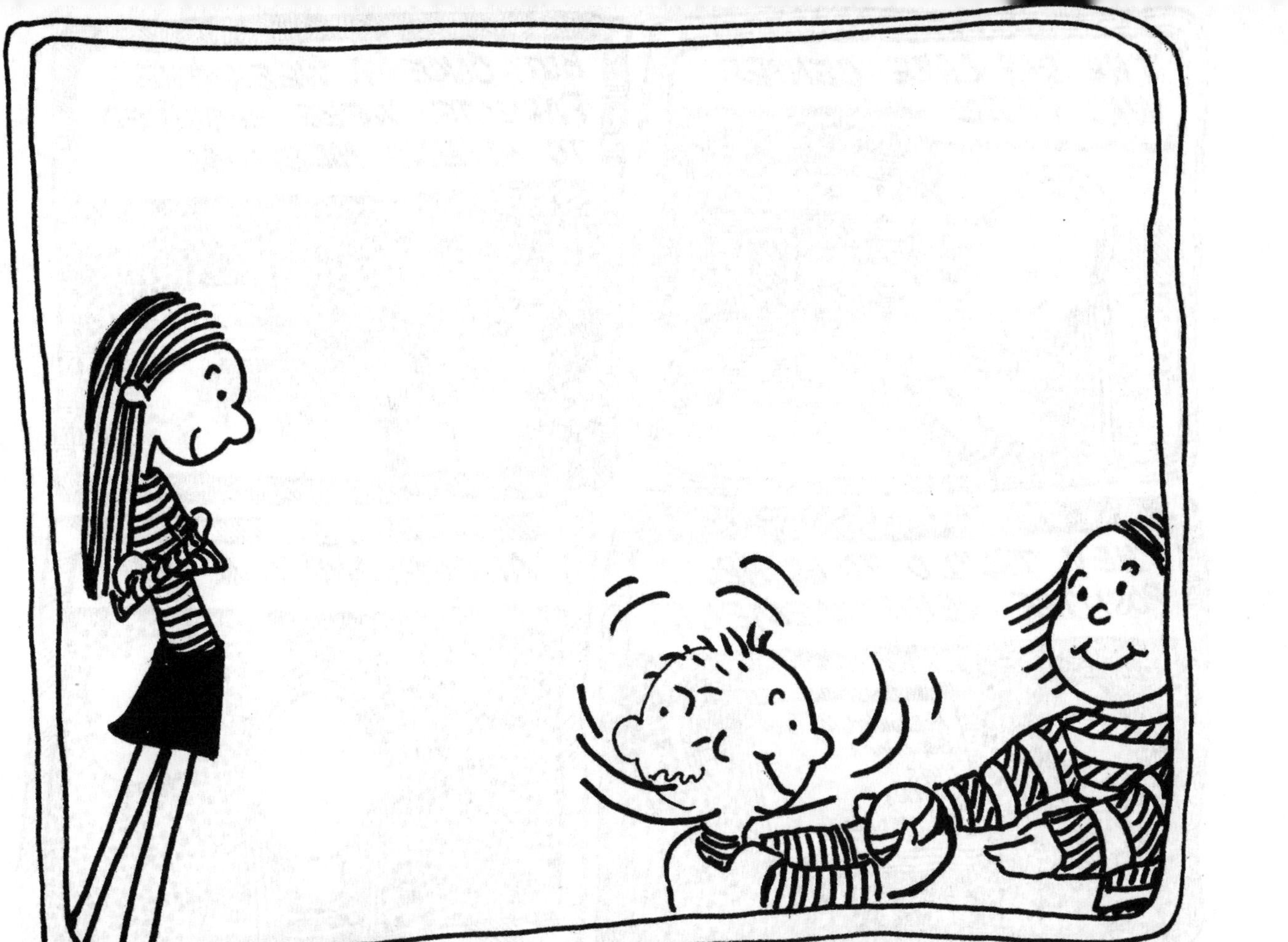

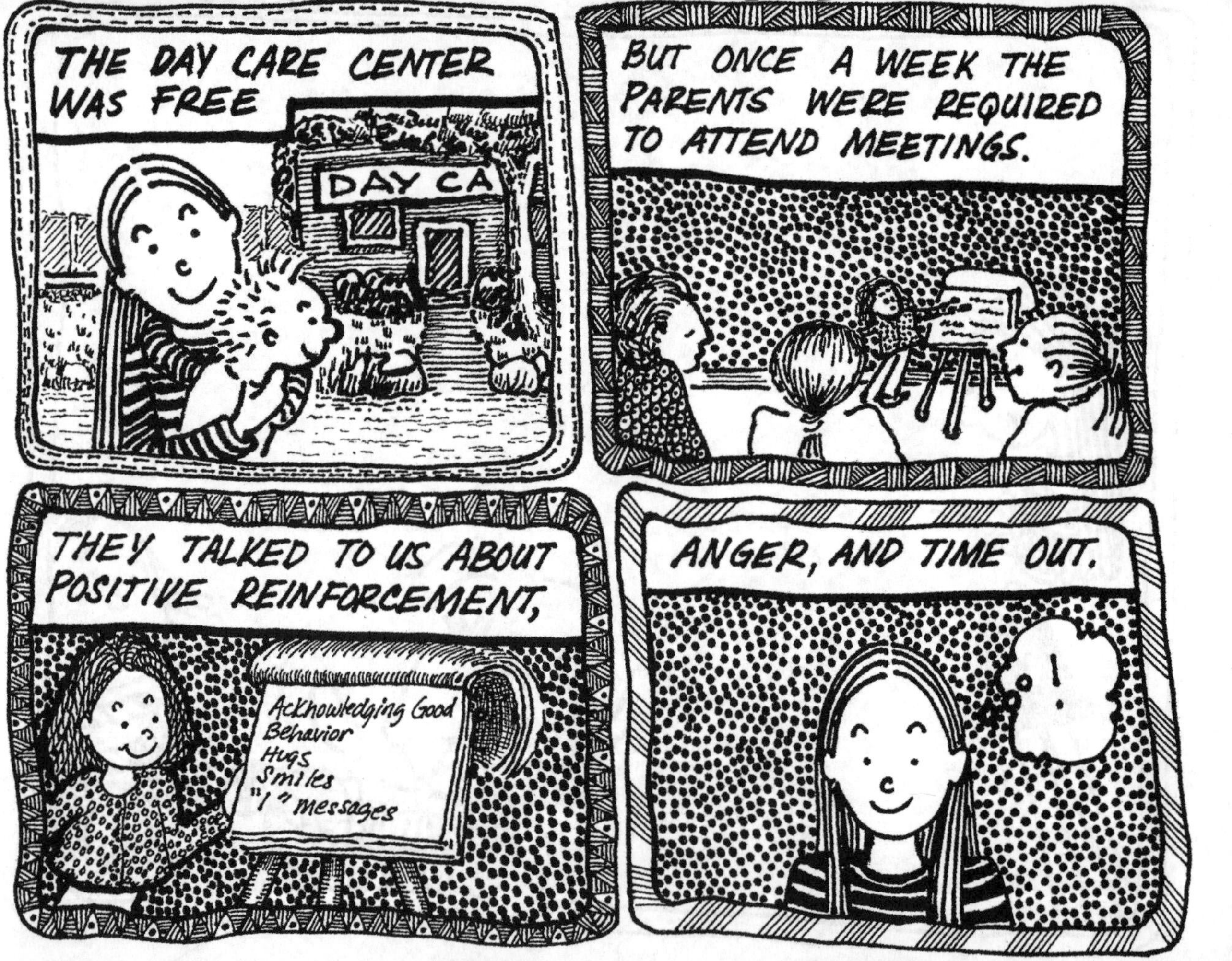
THE DAY CARE CENTER WAS FREE
DAY CA
BUT ONCE A WEEK THE PARENTS WERE REQUIRED TO ATTEND MEETINGS.
THEY TALKED TO US ABOUT POSITIVE REINFORCEMENT,
Acknowledging Good Behavior
Hugs
Smiles
"I" messages
ANGER, AND TIME OUT.
!

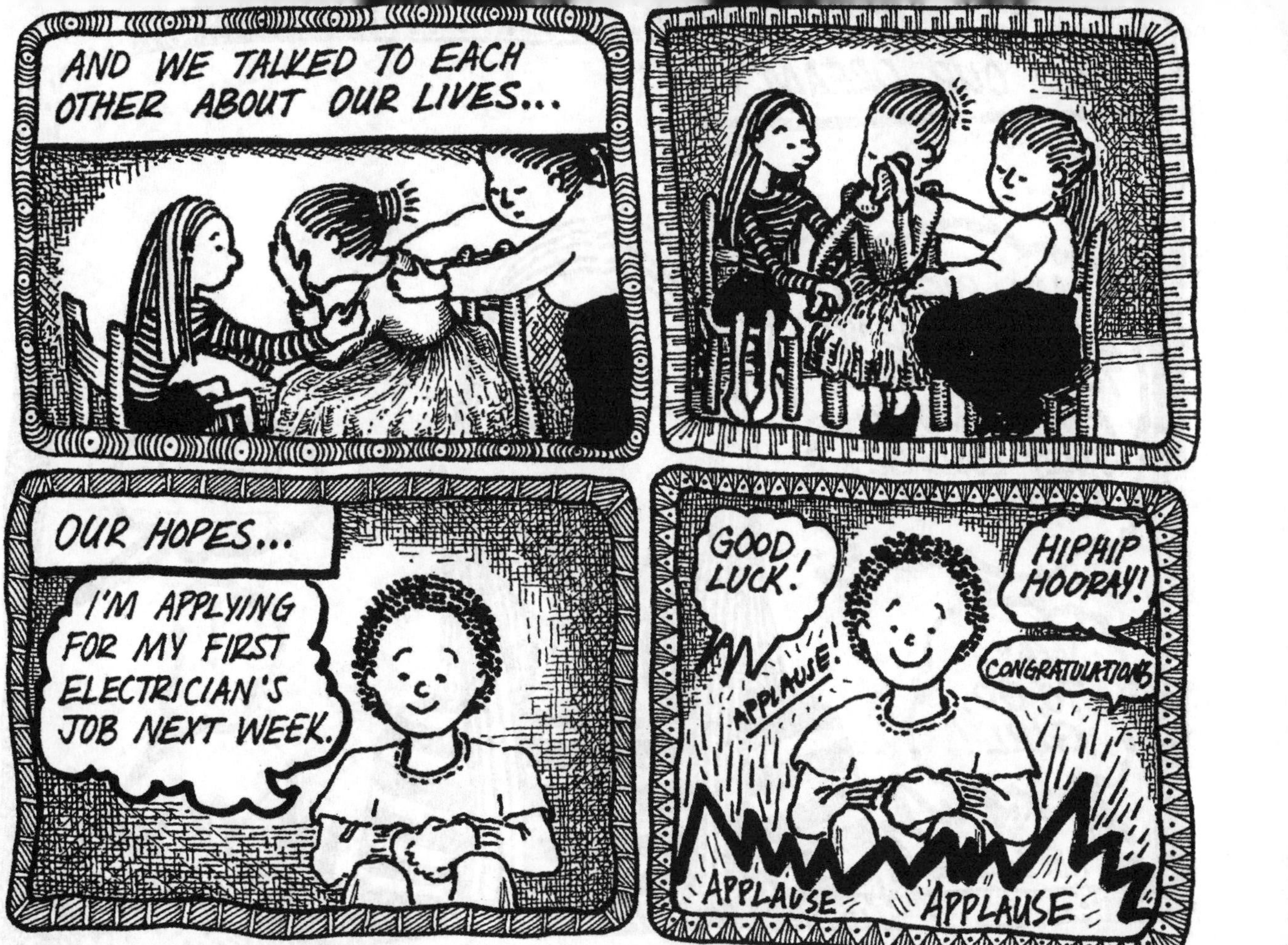
AND WE TALKED TO EACH OTHER ABOUT OUR LIVES...
OUR HOPES...
I'M APPLYING FOR MY FIRST ELECTRICIAN'S JOB NEXT WEEK.
GOOD LUCK!
HIPHIP HOORAY!
APPLAUSE!
CONGRATULATIONS
APPLAUSE
APPLAUSE

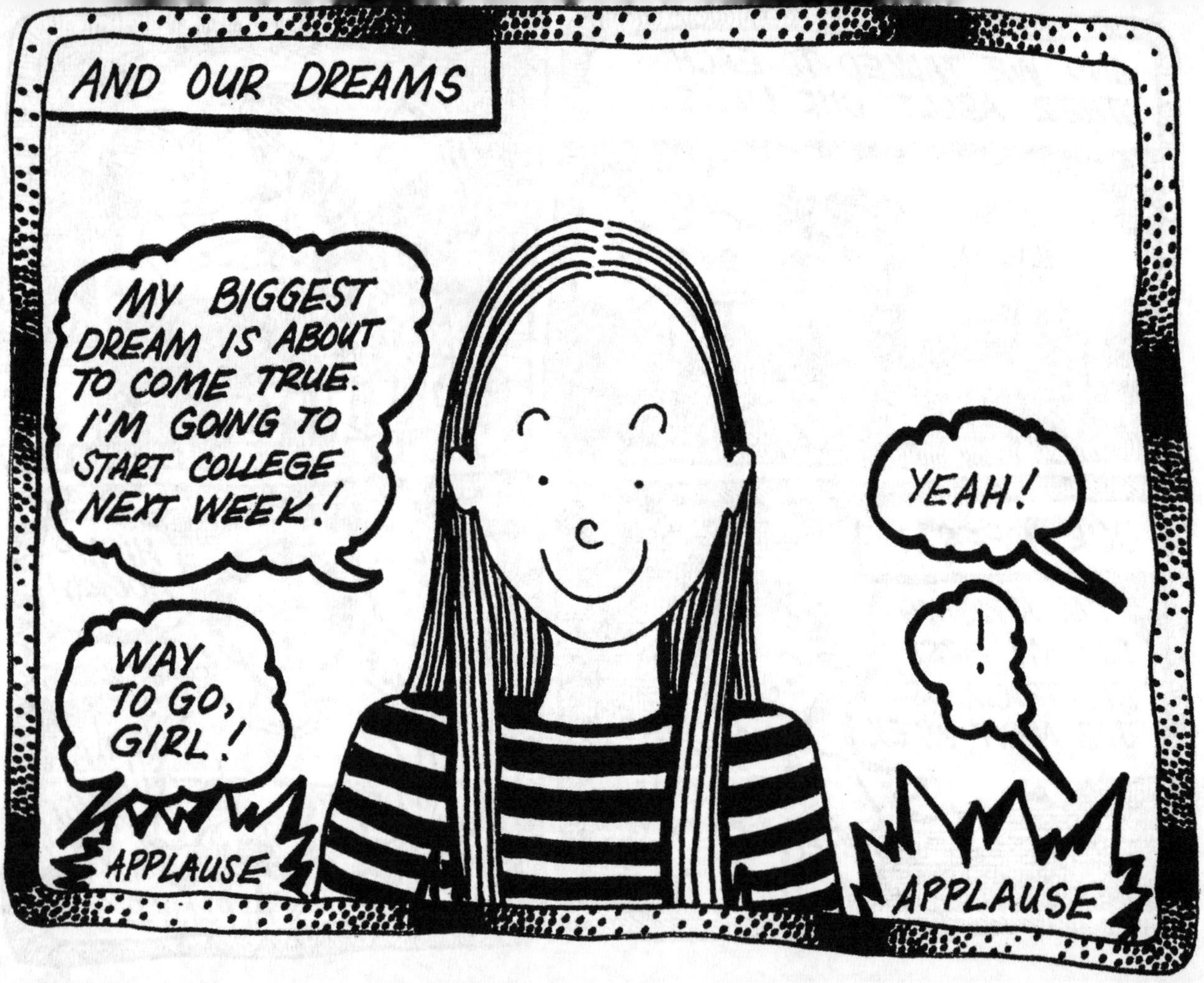
AND OUR DREAMS
MY BIGGEST DREAM IS ABOUT TO COME TRUE. I'M GOING TO START COLLEGE NEXT WEEK!
WAY TO GO, GIRL!
YEAH!
!
APPLAUSE
APPLAUSE

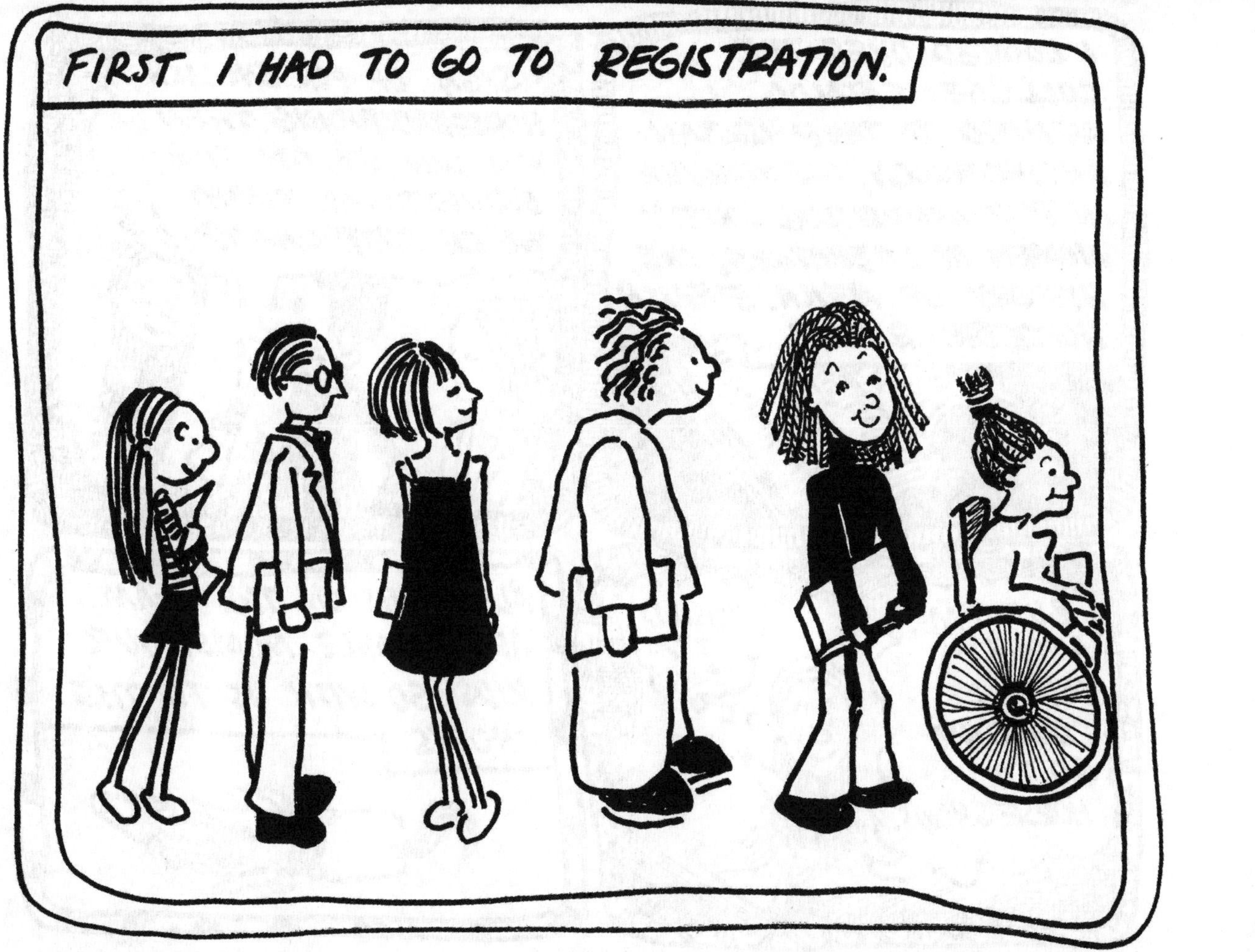
FIRST I HAD TO GO TO REGISTRATION.

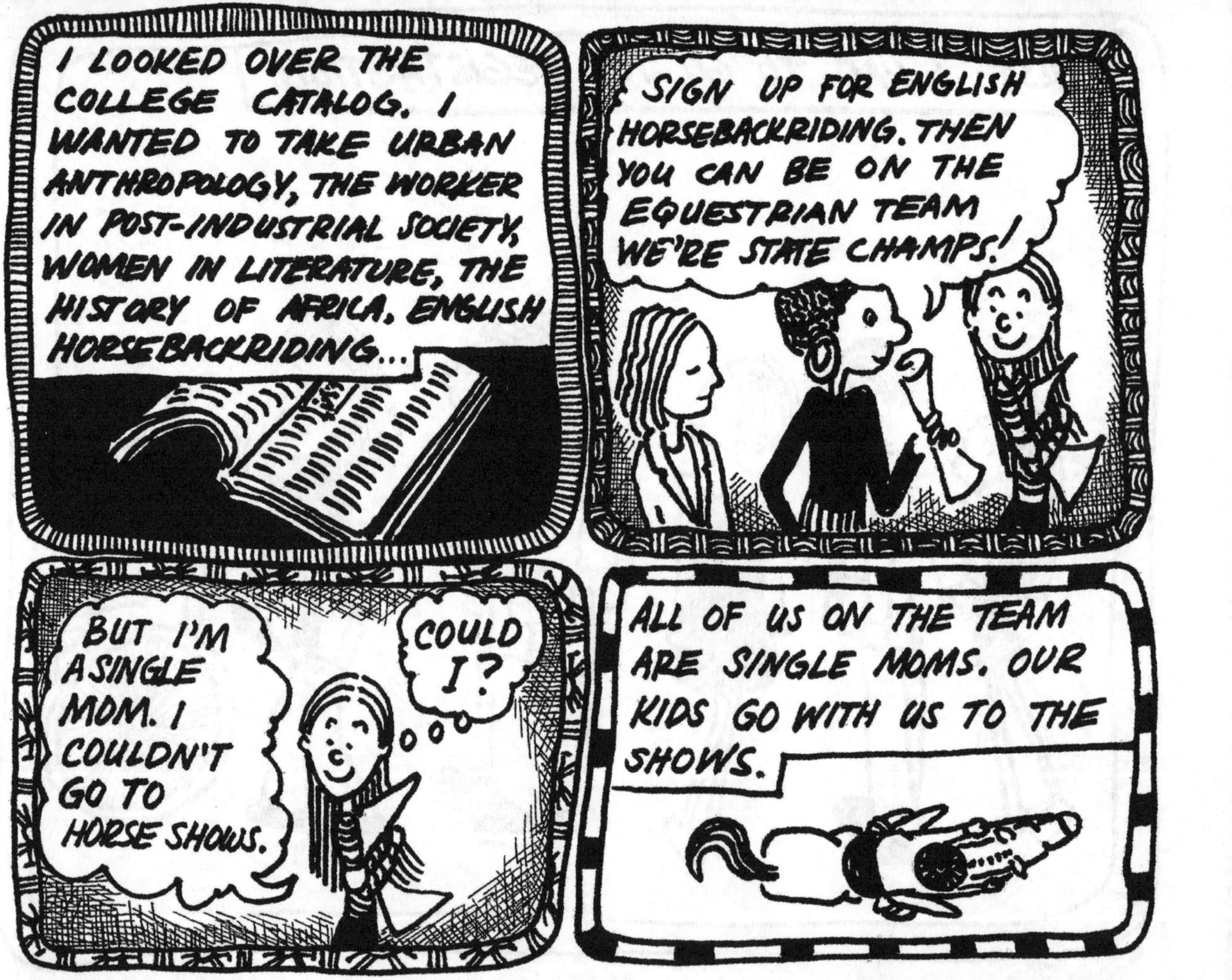
I LOOKED OVER THE COLLEGE CATALOG. I WANTED TO TAKE URBAN ANTHROPOLOGY, THE WORKER IN POST-INDUSTRIAL SOCIETY, WOMEN IN LITERATURE, THE HISTORY OF AFRICA, ENGLISH HORSEBACKRIDING...
SIGN UP FOR ENGLISH HORSEBACKRIDING. THEN YOU CAN BE ON THE EQUESTRIAN TEAM WE'RE STATE CHAMPS!
BUT I'M A SINGLE MOM. I COULDN'T GO TO HORSE SHOWS.
COULD I?
ALL OF US ON THE TEAM ARE SINGLE MOMS. OUR KIDS GO WITH US TO THE SHOWS.

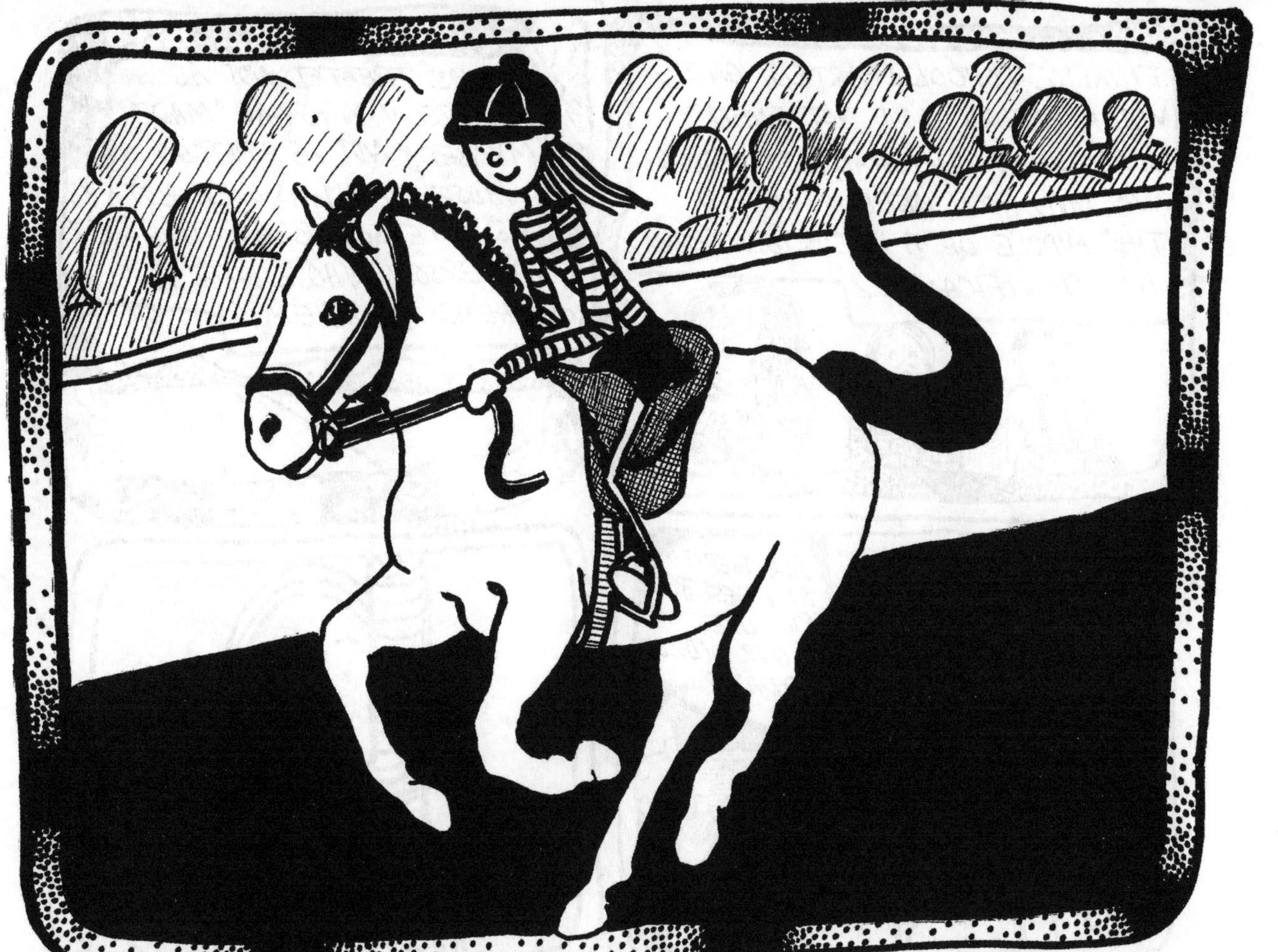

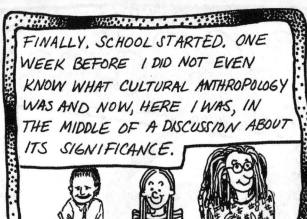

FINALLY, SCHOOL STARTED. ONE WEEK BEFORE I DID NOT EVEN KNOW WHAT CULTURAL ANTHROPOLOGY WAS AND NOW, HERE I WAS, IN THE MIDDLE OF A DISCUSSION ABOUT ITS SIGNIFICANCE.

I WAS TREATED NOT AS A PERSON WHO HAD "MADE MY BED," NOT AS A PERSON WHOSE LIFE WAS OVER, BUT AS A PERSON BECOMING, A PERSON WHOSE LIFE IS AHEAD OF THEM.

IN ENGLISH CLASS:

The Scarlet Letter

ARE THERE ANY HESTER PRYNNES IN OUR WORLD TODAY?

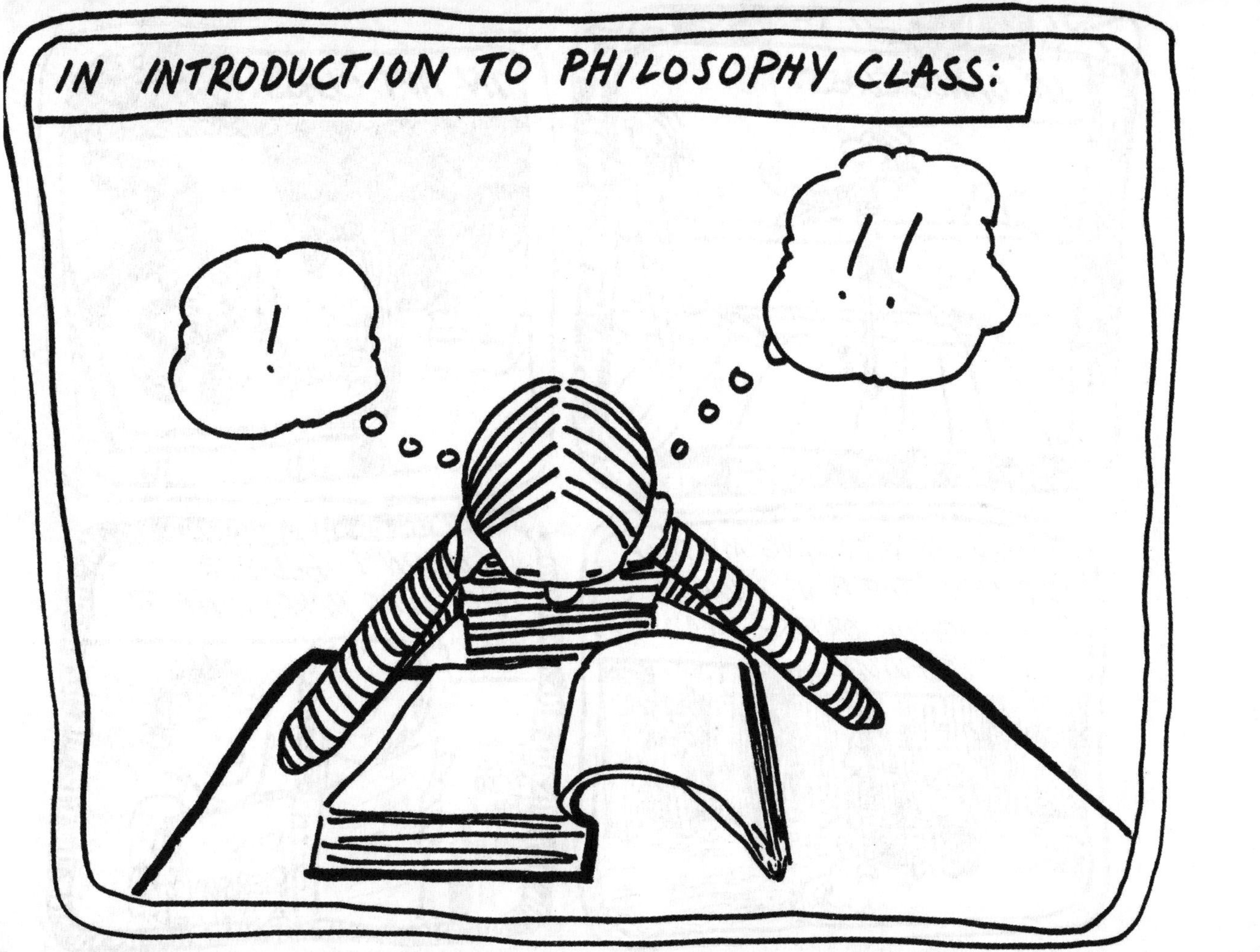
IN INTRODUCTION TO PHILOSOPHY CLASS:
!
!!

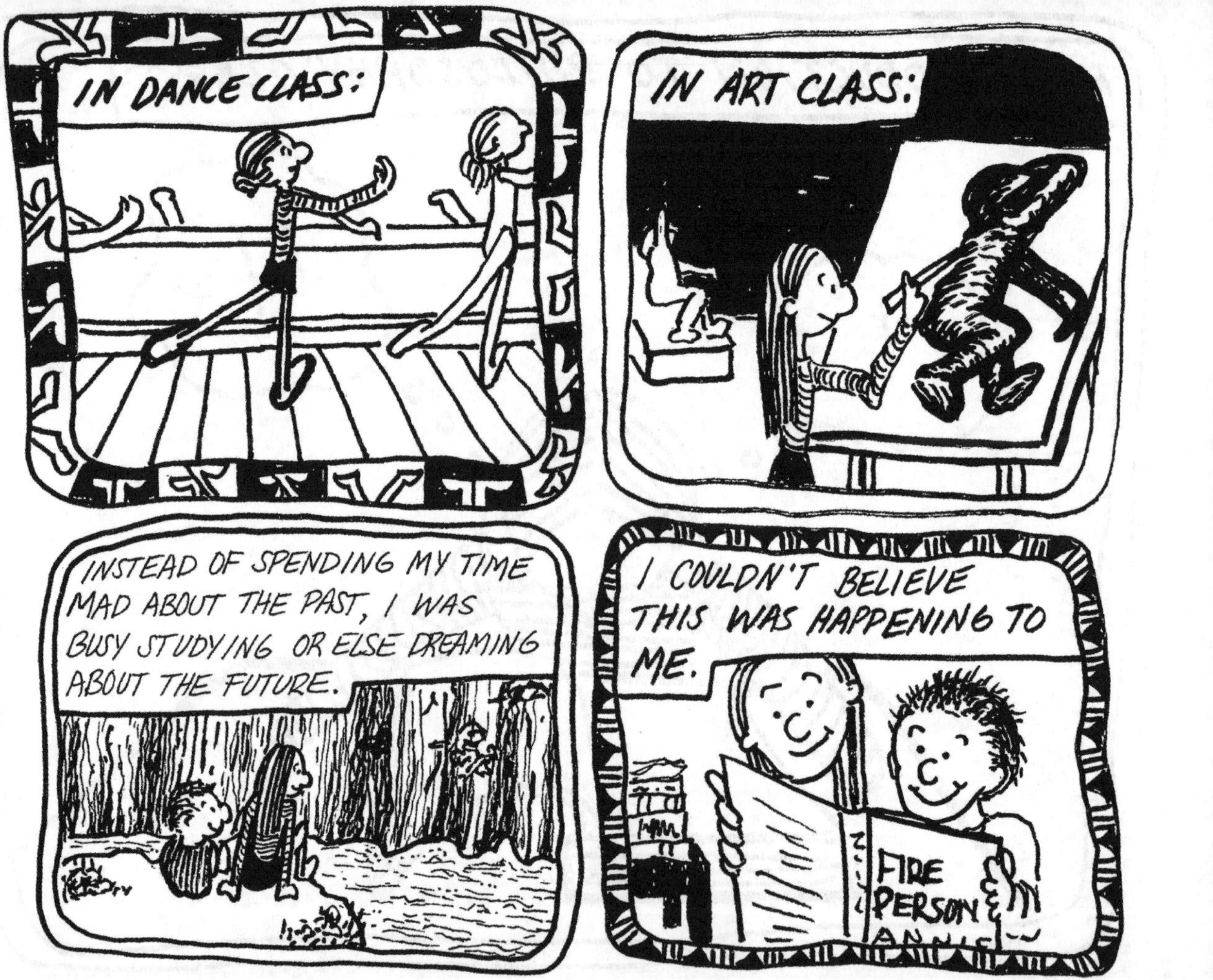
IN DANCE CLASS:
IN ART CLASS:
INSTEAD OF SPENDING MY TIME MAD ABOUT THE PAST, I WAS BUSY STUDYING OR ELSE DREAMING ABOUT THE FUTURE.
I COULDN'T BELIEVE THIS WAS HAPPENING TO ME.
FIRE PERSON

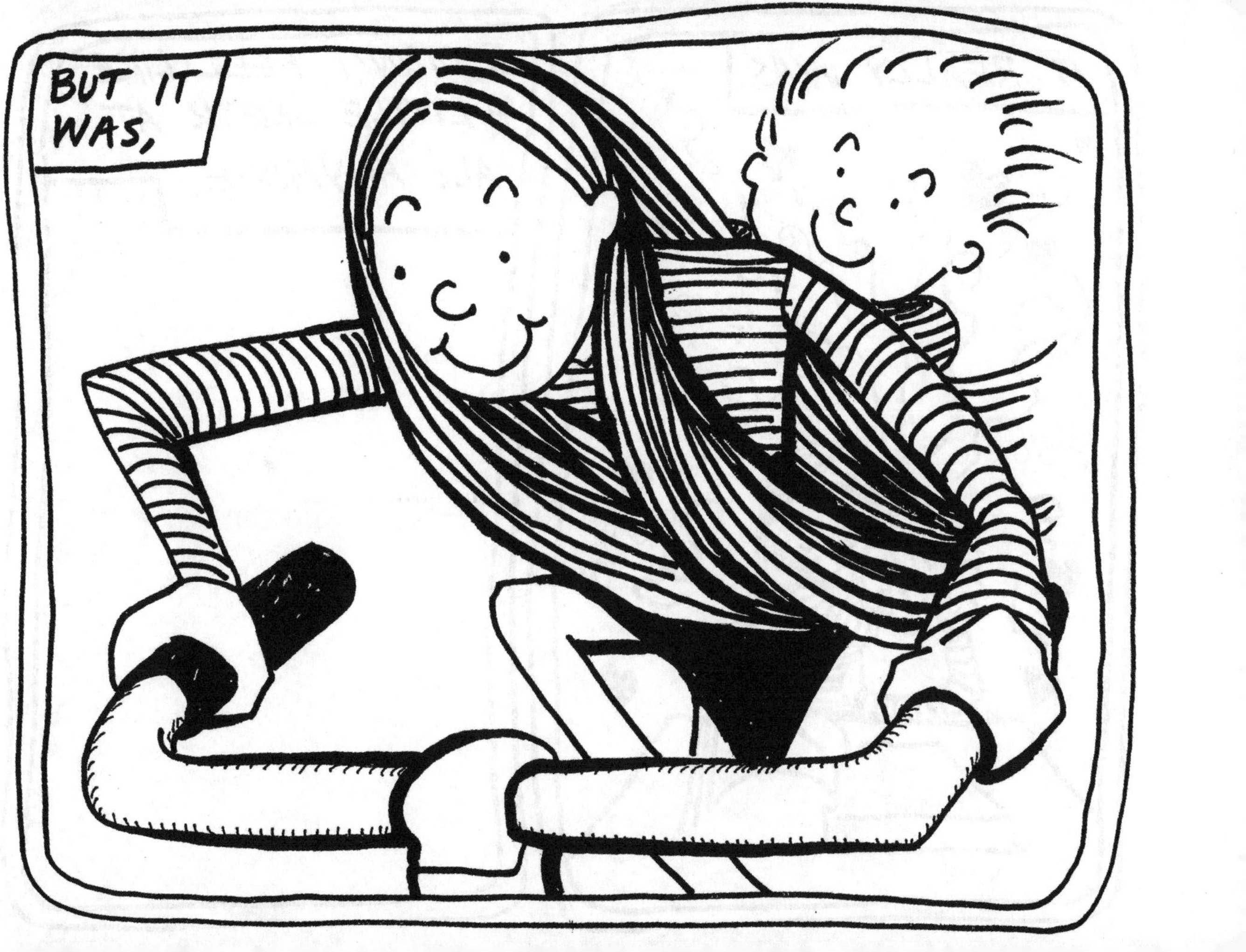
BUT IT WAS,

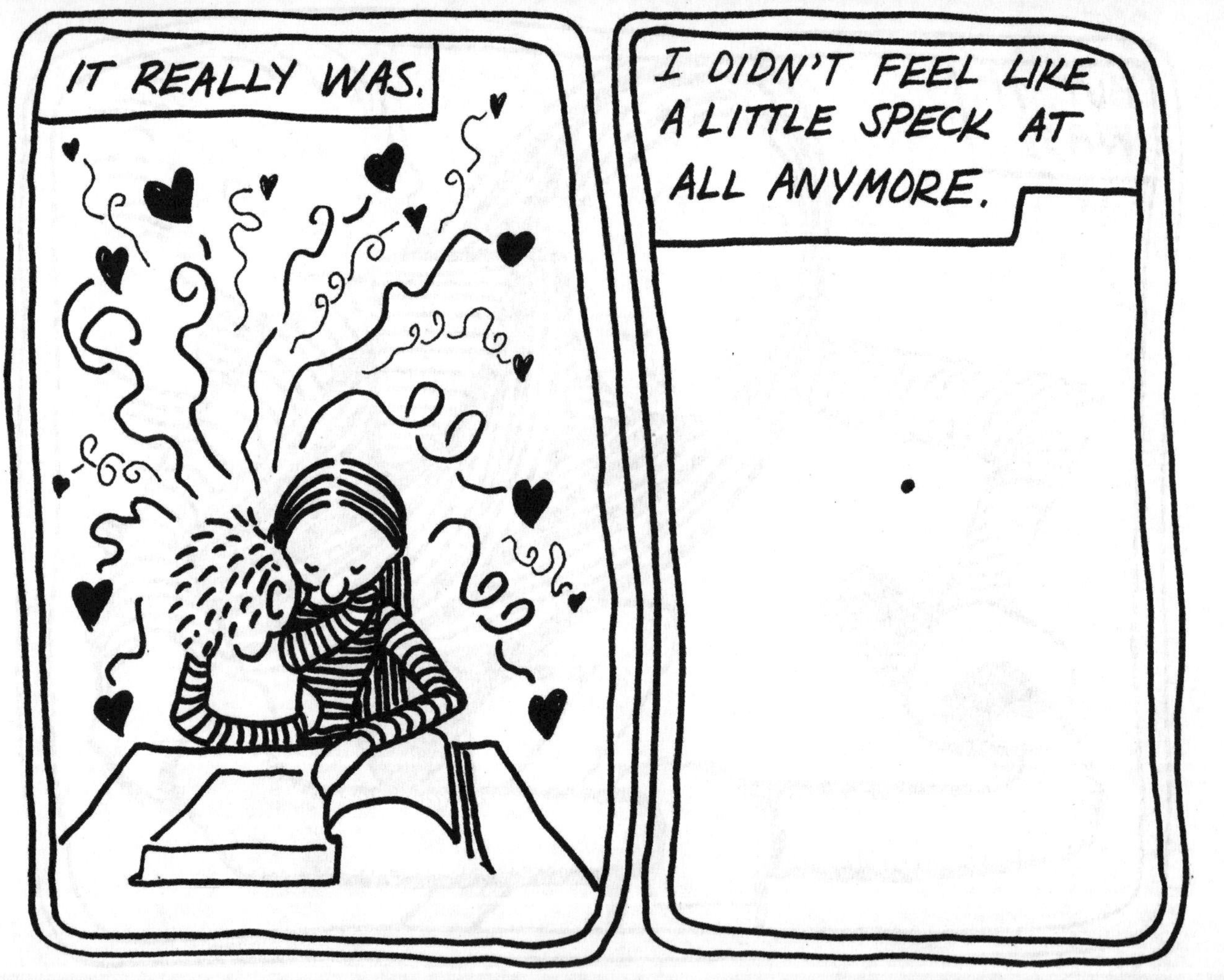
IT REALLY WAS.
I DIDN'T FEEL LIKE A LITTLE SPECK AT ALL ANYMORE.

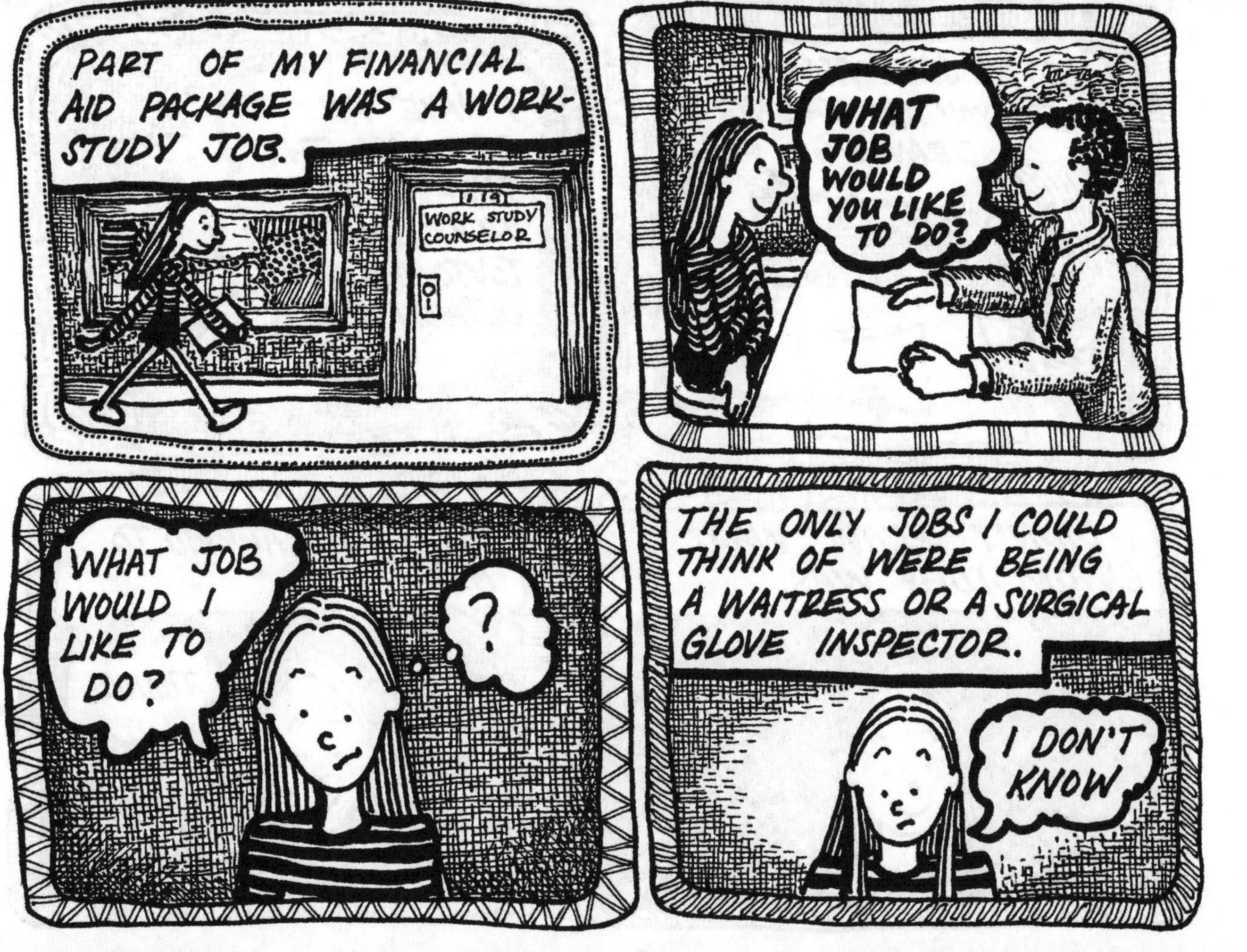
PART OF MY FINANCIAL AID PACKAGE WAS A WORK-STUDY JOB.
119
WORK STUDY COUNSELOR
WHAT JOB WOULD YOU LIKE TO DO?
WHAT JOB WOULD I LIKE TO DO?
?
THE ONLY JOBS I COULD THINK OF WERE BEING A WAITRESS OR A SURGICAL GLOVE INSPECTOR.
I DON'T KNOW

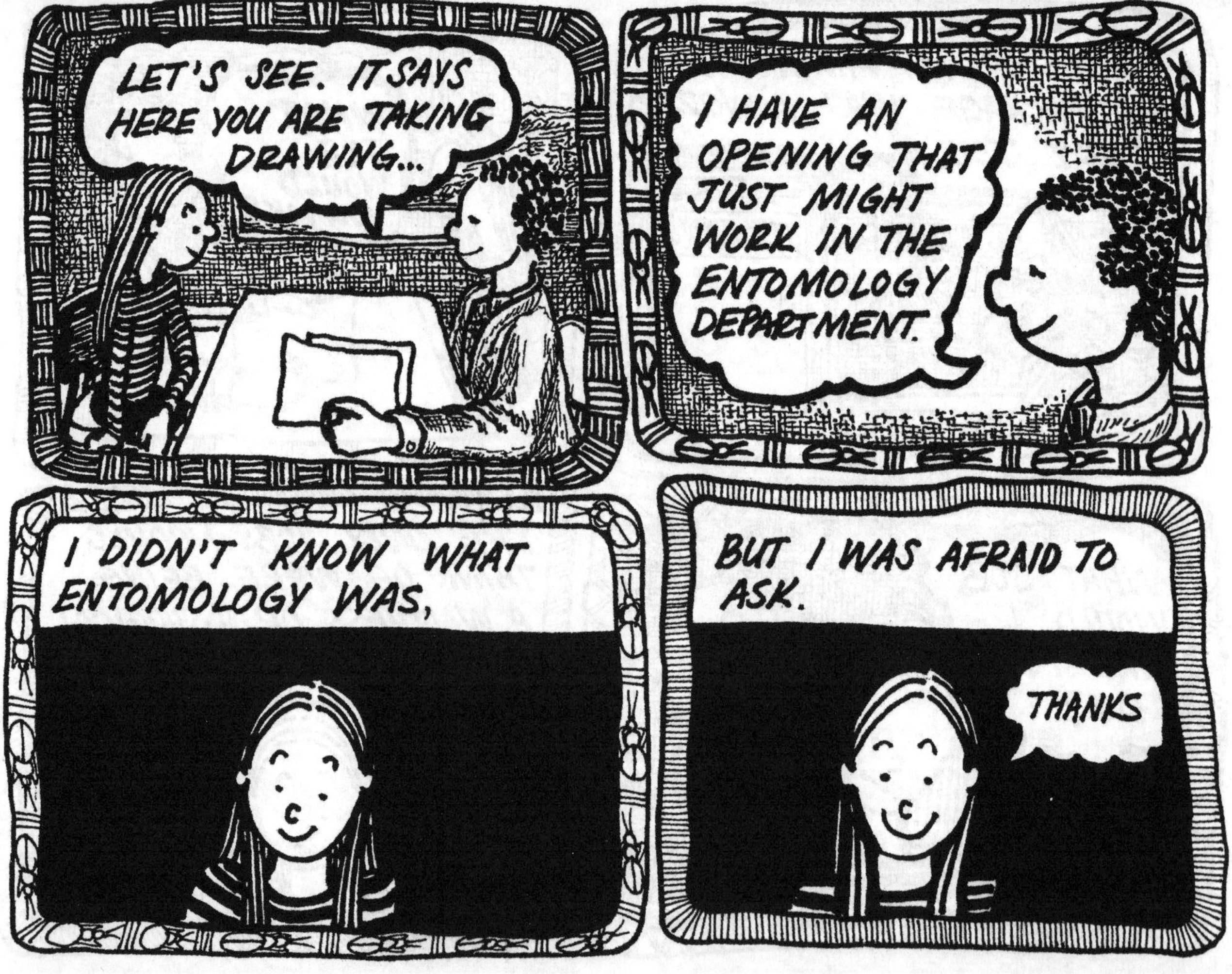

LET'S SEE. IT SAYS HERE YOU ARE TAKING DRAWING...
I HAVE AN OPENING THAT JUST MIGHT WORK IN THE ENTOMOLOGY DEPARTMENT.
I DIDN'T KNOW WHAT ENTOMOLOGY WAS,
BUT I WAS AFRAID TO ASK.
THANKS

IT TURNED OUT TO BE THE STUDY OF BUGS.

CARIBID

I WAS TO LOOK THROUGH A MICROSCOPE

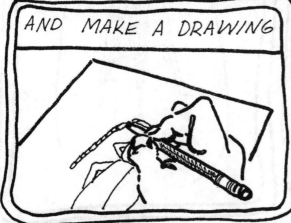

AND MAKE A DRAWING

OF A BUG.

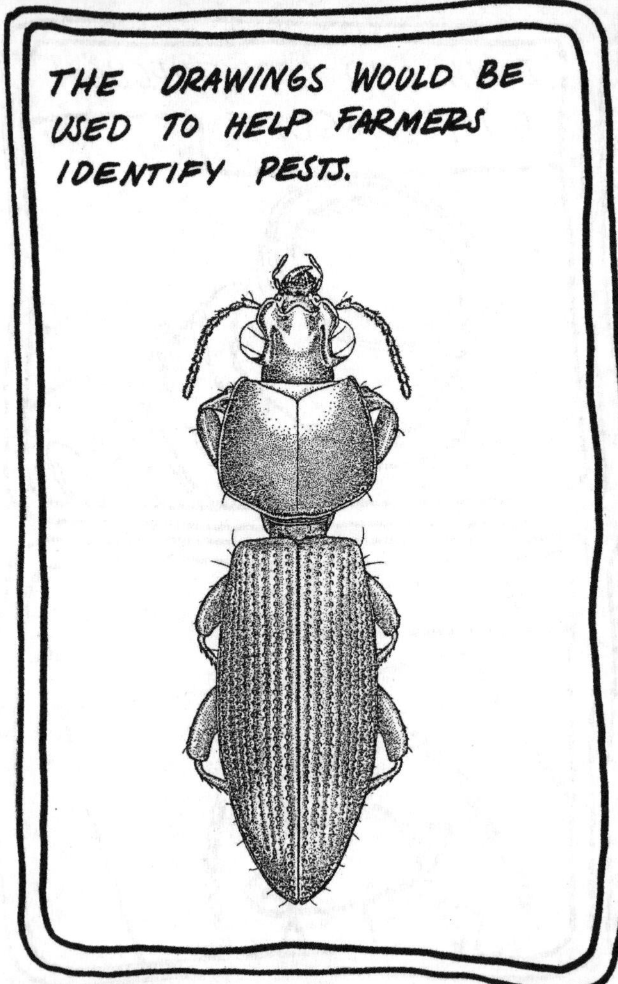
THE DRAWINGS WOULD BE USED TO HELP FARMERS IDENTIFY PESTS.

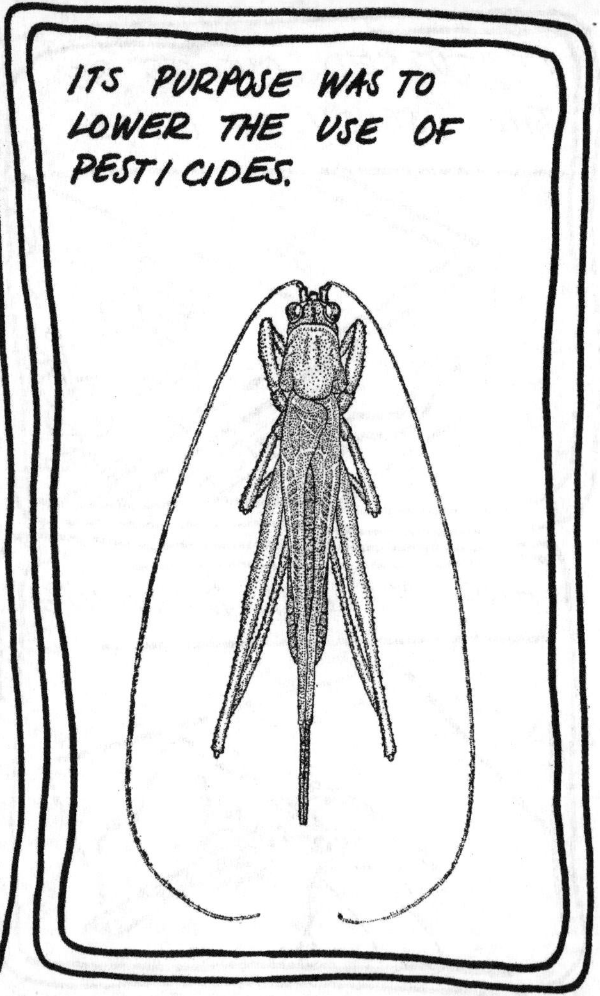
ITS PURPOSE WAS TO LOWER THE USE OF PESTICIDES.

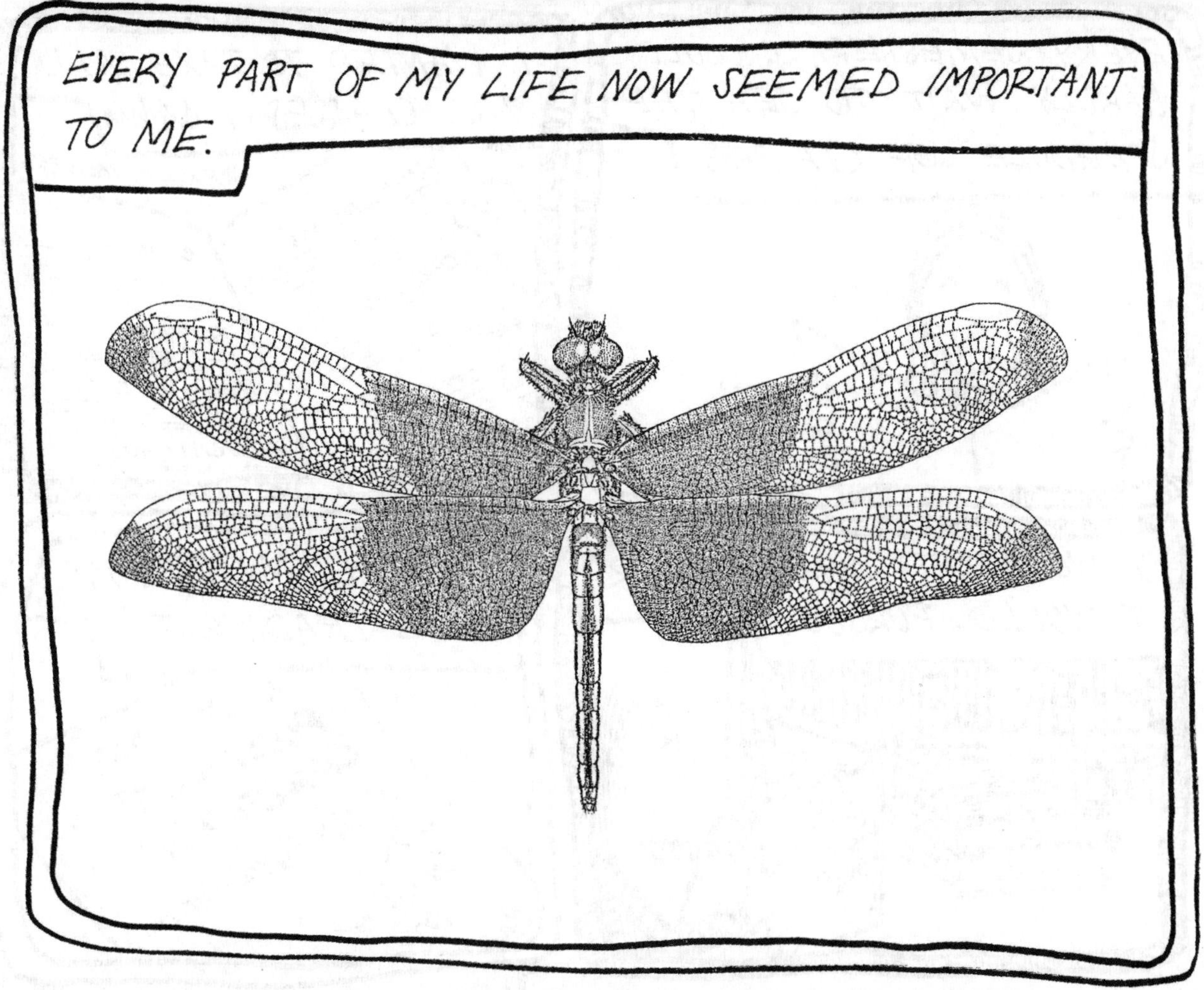
EVERY PART OF MY LIFE NOW SEEMED IMPORTANT TO ME.

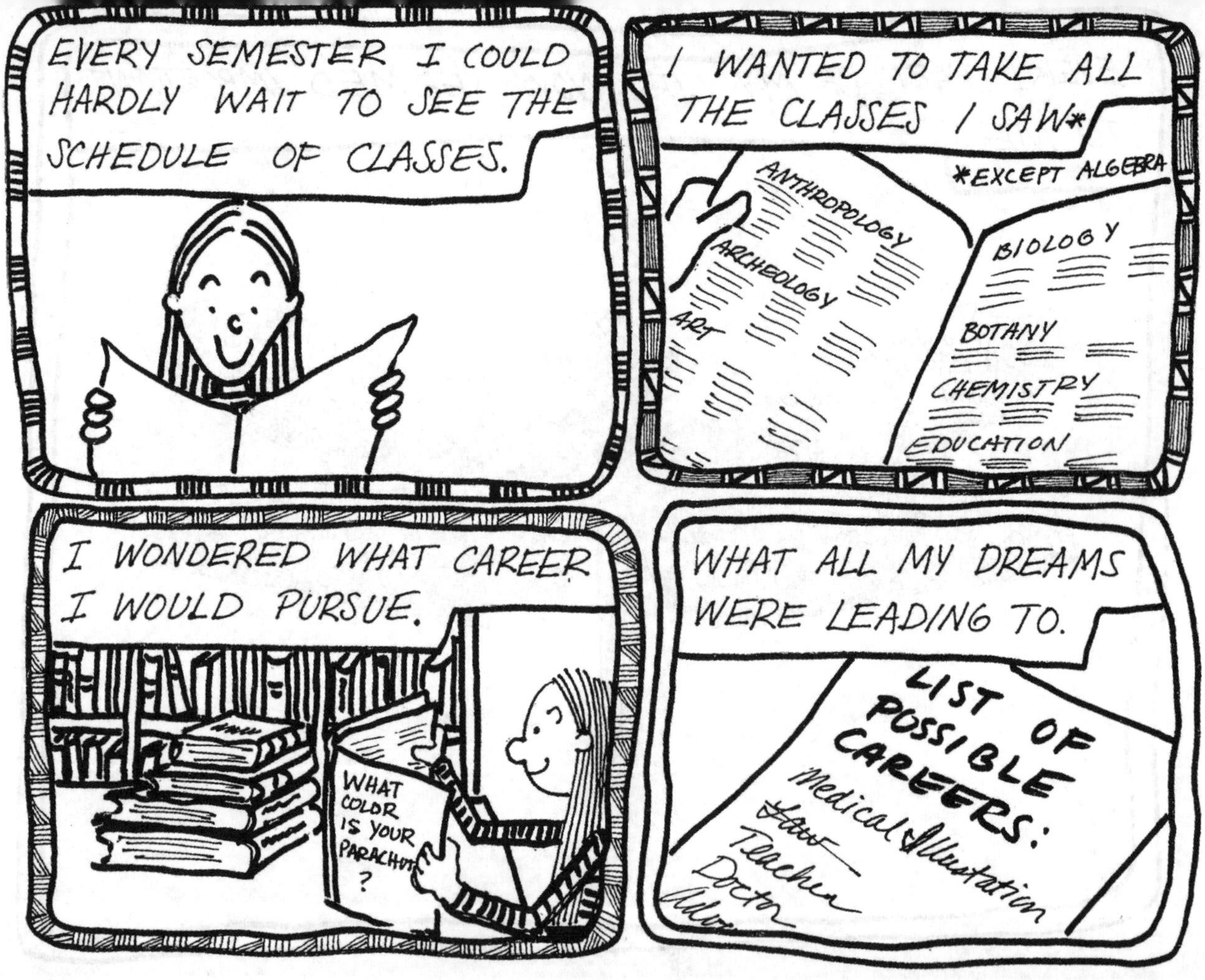
EVERY SEMESTER I COULD HARDLY WAIT TO SEE THE SCHEDULE OF CLASSES.
I WANTED TO TAKE ALL THE CLASSES I SAW*
*EXCEPT ALGEBRA
ANTHROPOLOGY
ARCHEOLOGY
ART
BIOLOGY
BOTANY
CHEMISTRY
EDUCATION
I WONDERED WHAT CAREER I WOULD PURSUE.
WHAT COLOR IS YOUR PARACHUTE ?
WHAT ALL MY DREAMS WERE LEADING TO.
LIST OF POSSIBLE CAREERS:
Medical Illustration
Law
Teacher
Doctor

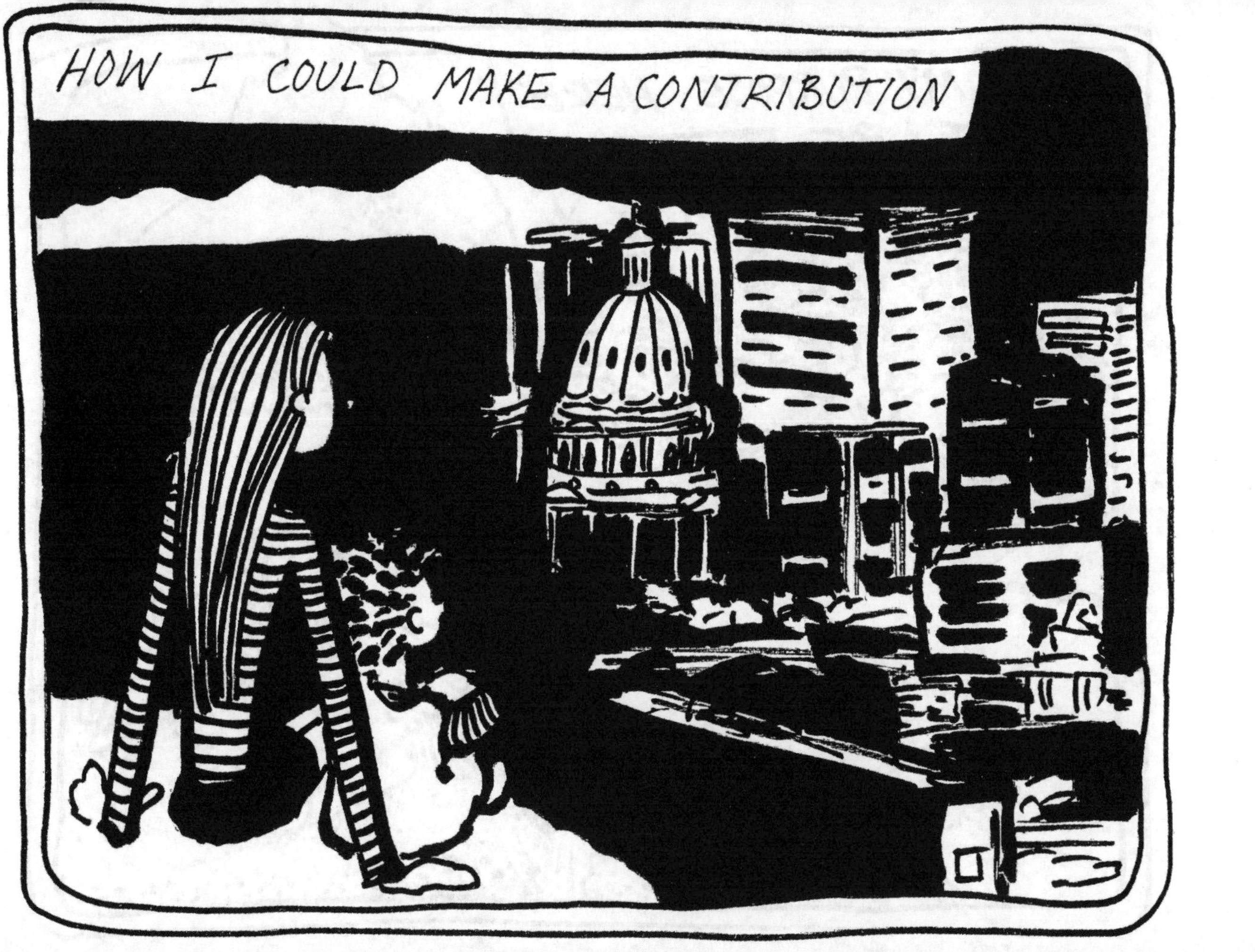
HOW I COULD MAKE A CONTRIBUTION

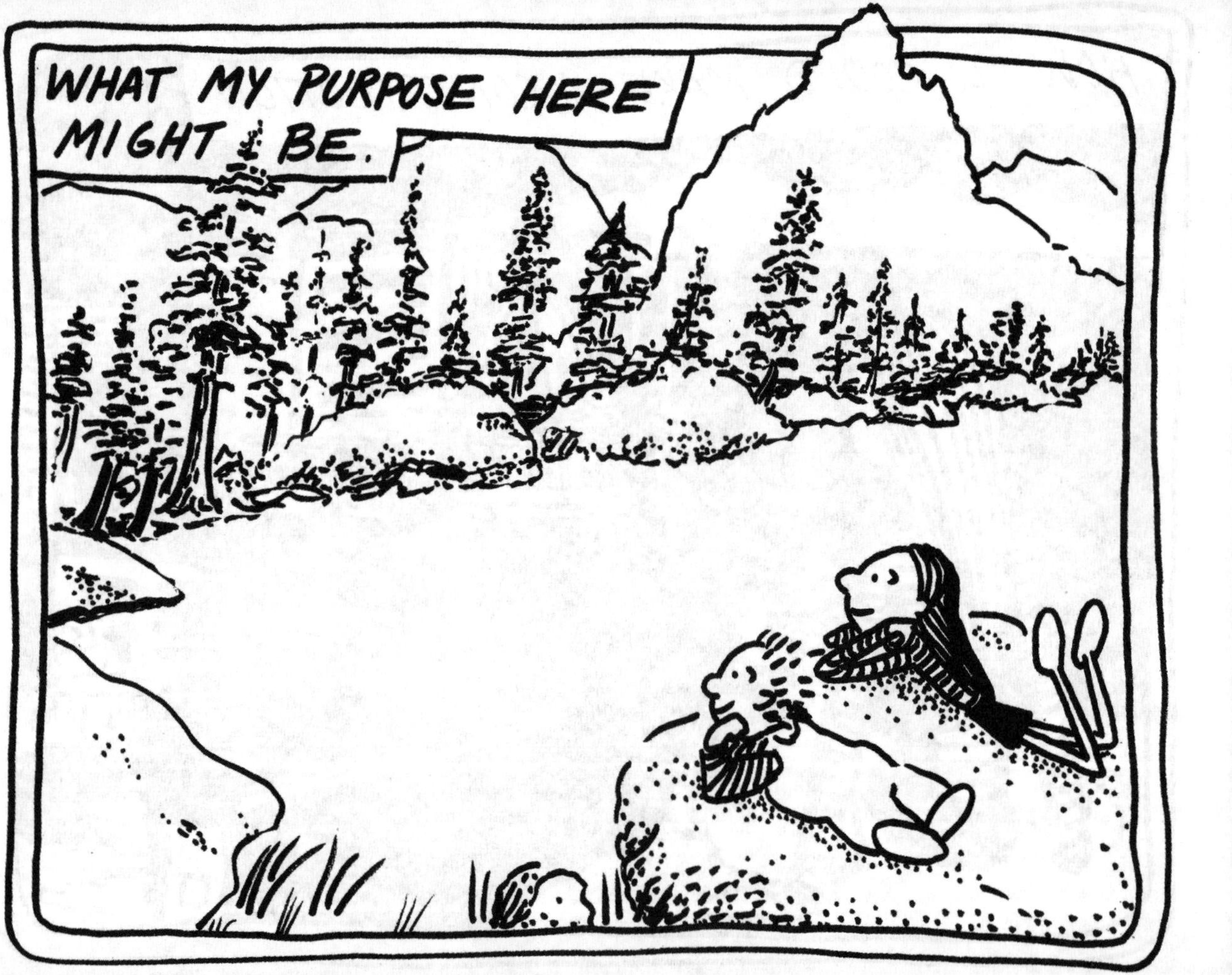
WHAT MY PURPOSE HERE MIGHT BE.

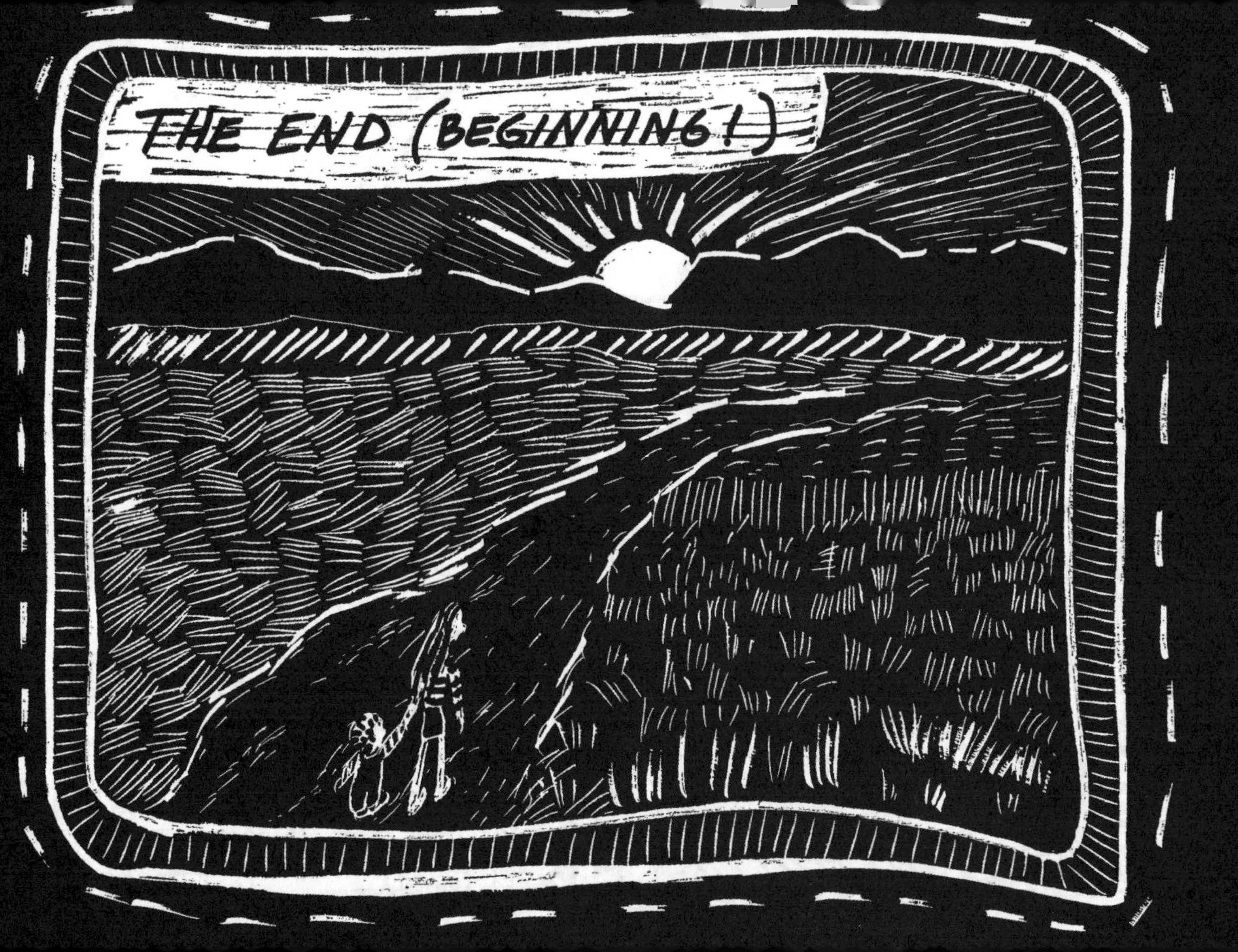
THE END (BEGINNING!)

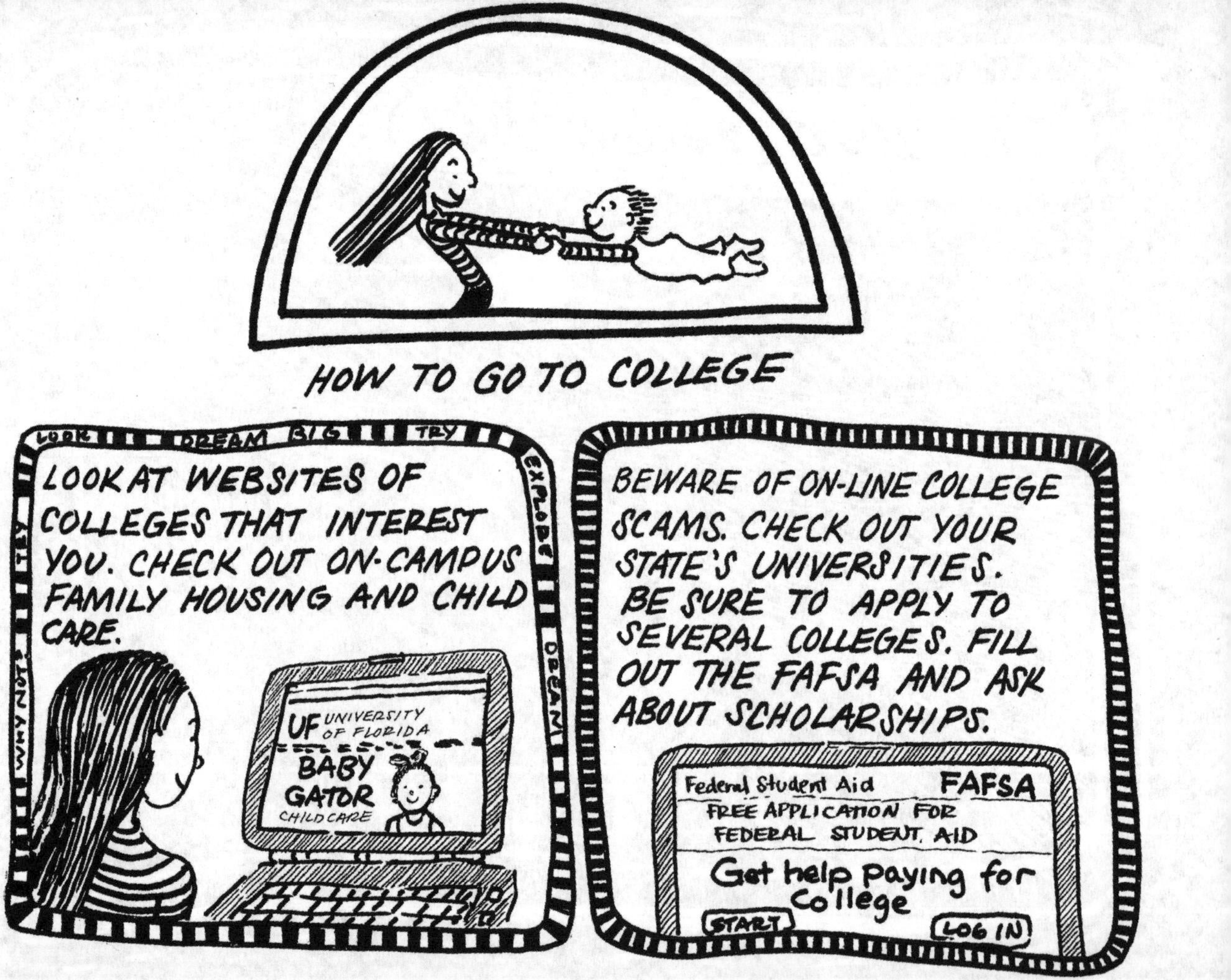
HOW TO GO TO COLLEGE
LOOK
DREAM BIG
TRY
EXPLORE
DREAM
WHY NOT?
TRY
LOOK AT WEBSITES OF COLLEGES THAT INTEREST YOU. CHECK OUT ON-CAMPUS FAMILY HOUSING AND CHILD CARE.
UF UNIVERSITY OF FLORIDA
BABY GATOR
CHILD CARE
BEWARE OF ON-LINE COLLEGE SCAMS. CHECK OUT YOUR STATE'S UNIVERSITIES. BE SURE TO APPLY TO SEVERAL COLLEGES. FILL OUT THE FAFSA AND ASK ABOUT SCHOLARSHIPS.
Federal Student Aid
FAFSA
FREE APPLICATION FOR FEDERAL STUDENT AID
Get help paying for College
START
LOG IN

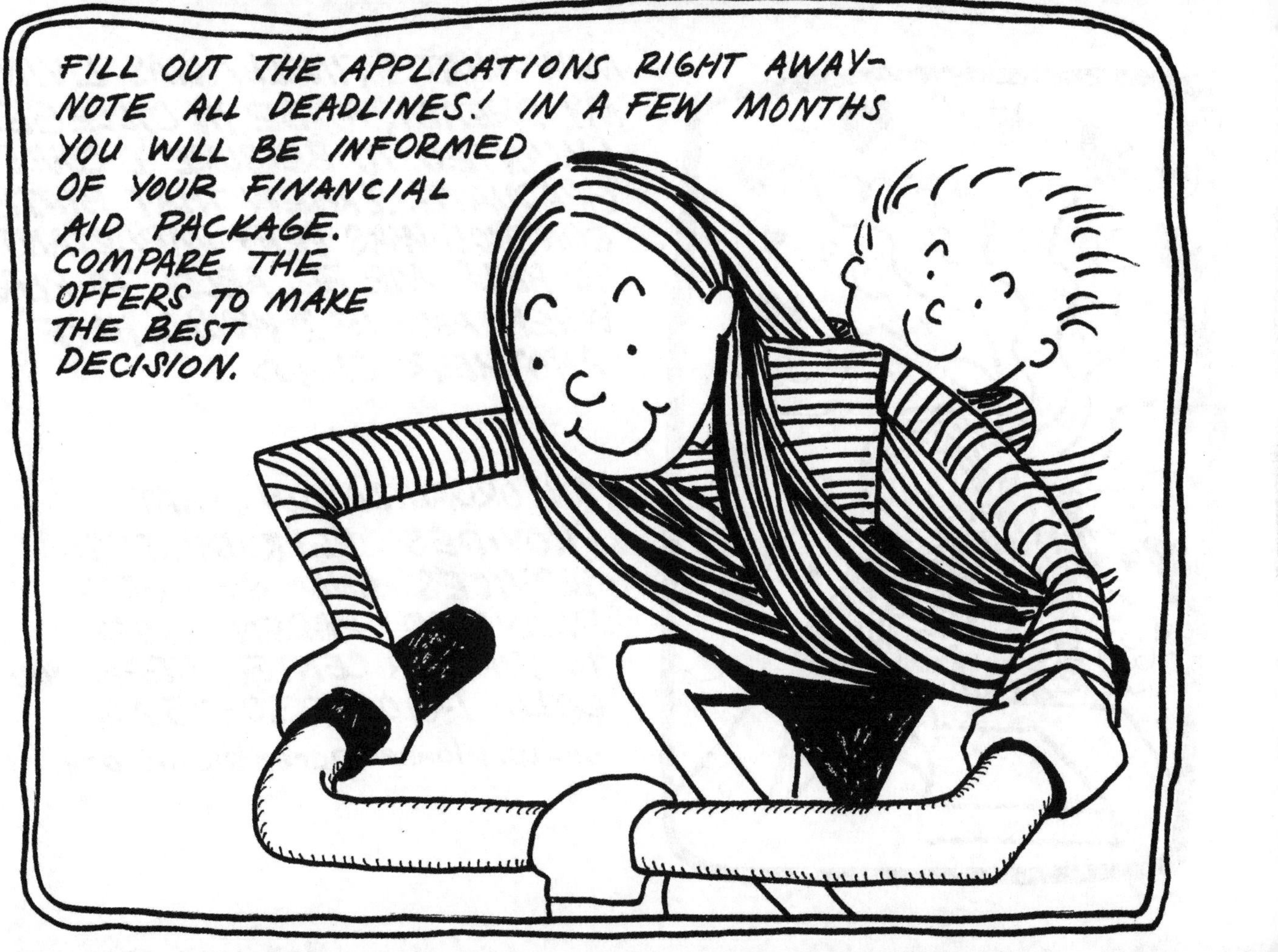
FILL OUT THE APPLICATIONS RIGHT AWAY-
NOTE ALL DEADLINES! IN A FEW MONTHS
YOU WILL BE INFORMED
OF YOUR FINANCIAL
AID PACKAGE.
COMPARE THE
OFFERS TO MAKE
THE BEST
DECISION.

NOW THAT I FINALLY WAS LIVING MY DREAM, TO BE IN COLLEGE, I WANTED TO BE SURE I COULD GRADUATE. I KNEW THAT BIRTH CONTROL WAS VERY IMPORTANT TO HELP ME BE ABLE TO PLAN WHEN AND IF I WOULD HAVE ANOTHER CHILD.

AN ORGANIZATION THAT PROVIDES REPRODUCTIVE SERVICES AND SUPPORT: PLANNED PARENTHOOD.
TO FIND A CENTER NEAR YOU.
CALL 1-800-230-7526
www.plannedparenthood.org

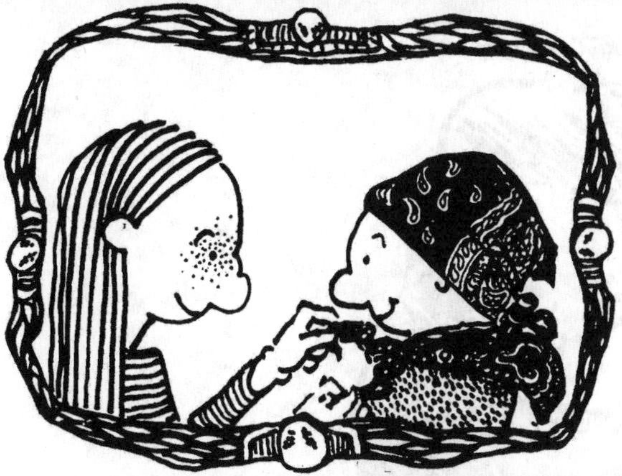

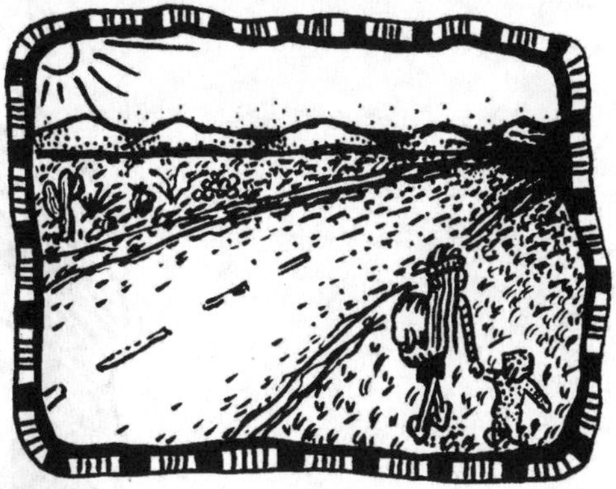

YOUNG WOMEN WITH CHILDREN NEED COMPASSION AND EMPATHY.
HELP A MOTHER TODAY!

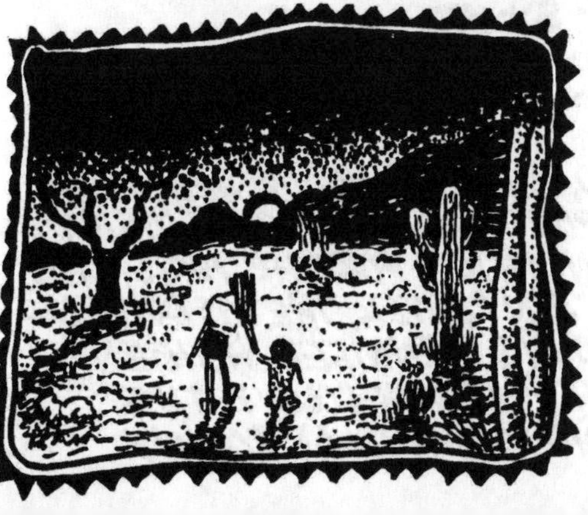

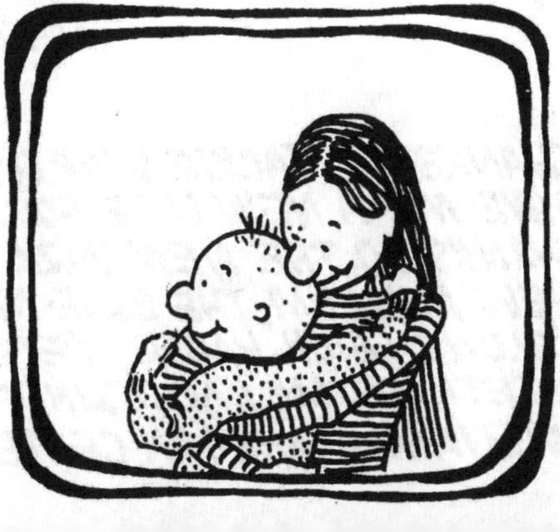

·IN APPRECIATION·

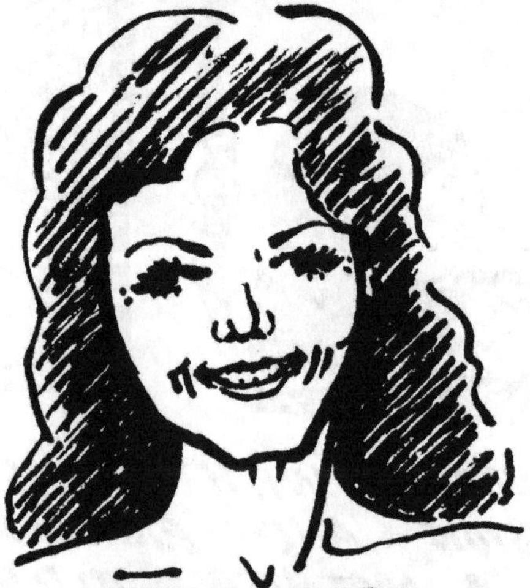

JACKIE WARD
8-18-1950 - 8-1-1997

A LIFE DEVOTED TO HELPING SINGLE MOMS.

THANKS TO JACKIE WARD, WHO, BY SHARING INFORMATION GAVE ME A NEW LIFE. FOR SUPPORT AND ENCOURAGEMENT THANKS TO THE NEW YORK FOUNDATION FOR THE ARTS, THE NEW MUSEUM, THE BLUE MOUNTAIN CENTER, THE McDOWELL COLONY, LEIGH HABER, PETER YOUNG, JENNIFER HENGEN, NEETI MADAN, DAVID ZINDEL, HEDGEBROOK COLONY, THE WILLIAM FLANAGAN CENTER AND THE MILLAY COLONY.

HITCHHIKING IS NEVER SAFE. I DIDN'T KNOW I HAD OTHER CHOICES. HERE'S SOME: NATIONAL COALITION AGAINST DOMESTIC VIOLENCE www.ncadv.org 1-800-799-7233

RAPE, ABUSE AND INCEST NATIONAL NETWORK
www.rainn.org   1-800-656-4673

AL-ANON 1-800-344-2666 ALATEEN 1-800 356·9996
www.al-anon.alateen.org

OR CALL 911

More Praise for *THE AMAZING "TRUE" STORY OF A TEENAGE SINGLE MOM*

"A wondrous, unforgettable, absolutely original book, one of the dearest books of my lifetime, transcending its form and transcendent in content. Seldom, seldom portrayed content, essential for our country's self knowledge, for here, pulsing with life and passionate truth are the experiencings, the lives of millions of our girls growing into young womanhood." **—Tillie Olsen**

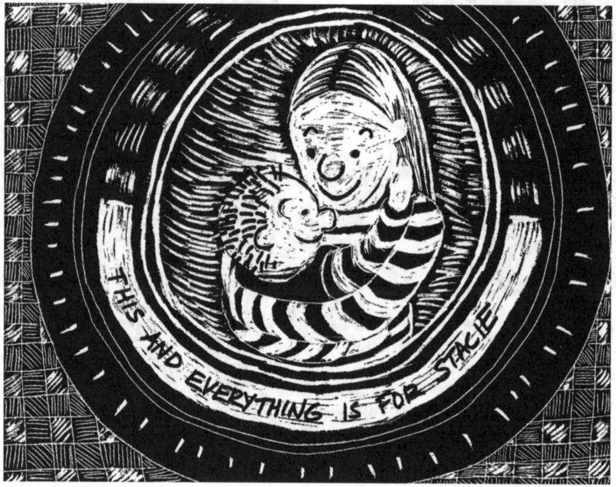
THIS AND EVERYTHING IS FOR STACIE

"Katherine Arnoldi's story is a story of real villains and heroes, no halfway-there people. It is a story of huge mother-love, not halfway-there. And all through it, the smile of a child that just melts you. **—Carolyn Chute**

"Too bad for you if you don't take this book and stick it in your heart." **—Gordon Lish**

"Katherine Arnoldi is God sent. Her pictorial memoir could become the type of tool no one can be without." **—reg E. gaines**

"This is a warm and courageous book. . . . Katherine Arnoldi's open-hearted honesty is truly amazing." **—Diane di Prima**

"A beautiful, warm, scary, and true book. . . . As deep-down sad as this comic book is, it makes you laugh. As funny as it is, it makes you wonder. As depressing as it is, it's an inspiration." **—Beverly Donofrio**

"Heartbreaking, brave, compassionate, and close to the bone, Katherine Arnoldi's story is an amazing one." **—Roz Chast**

"[Katherine Arnoldi's] book is bound to inspire other young women to do things they might have thought were impossible for them to achieve. I certainly hope it does." **—Melissa Ludtke**

"This book is a wonderful little movie you can hold in your hand. Arnoldi draws as well as she writes, and like the best memoirists, gets beyond the facts to the heart of the matter, the way things *feel*." **—Hettie Jones**